In every age man seeks to create a beautiful environment.

Building: Apartment, New York—S. M. Hexter Award "Outstanding Interior for 1958." **Interior Designer:** Virginia Whitmore Kelly, New York. **Photographer:** Alexandre Georges, New City, New York. Courtesy **House and Garden,** Copyright 1959, The Condé Nast Publications, Inc.

The Art of
INTERIOR DESIGN

A Text in the Aesthetics of Interior Design

by VICTORIA KLOSS BALL

with the help of Mary Louise Shipley

New York   THE   MACMILLAN   COMPANY

Library of Congress catalog card number: 60-5407

The Macmillan Company, New York
Brett-Macmillan Ltd., Galt, Ontario

Printed in the United States of America

To the many students of
Interior Design
who have dedicated themselves
to the hard but rewarding task
of making our surroundings
more beautiful

PREFACE

This text has placed its major focus on the design factor in interior decoration. It relates other aspects to the visual design. It likewise upholds the point of view that those who wish attractive surroundings must devote some of their own time and effort to learning to design well.

Someone has said that it requires the knowledge of the historian, the connoisseur, the merchant, the engineer, the psychologist and the artisan in order to be a good interior designer. First it requires the trained sensitivities of that person whom we call the artist. It is with him that this text is primarily concerned. All other essentials of decoration are related to his perceptions. How a building works is certainly important. We believe, however, that a structure cannot serve completely unless it is visually pleasing.

Although it is politic to seek help from those who are versed in the many matters which relate to building and furnishing, nevertheless, a total reliance on any outsider in these matters is unwise. An invitation to participate in the designing of an environment which one is purchasing is an invitation to grow in aesthetic stature through the creation of beauty. An owner has an obligation and a privilege to cooperate sensitively and intelligently in the creation of interior design.

In this text the words house and home are frequently used. This focus on one type of interior is in the interest of brevity. The reader may easily enlarge the scope of application to include other types of interiors. Illustrations frequently suggest this kind of adaptability.

V K B

Cleveland, Ohio

ACKNOWLEDGMENTS

My indebtedness is expressed to the several artists, architects and interior designers who have helped by their understanding of the need for cooperation between architect, decorator and client. Illustrations of the work of some of these friends are shown in the text.

I likewise wish to thank the many craftsmen and industries who have been of great assistance in the task of keeping our information about media up-to-date. It is difficult for the printed page to contain all of the available current data. Nevertheless it is necessary to be posted about trends. Many firms have been very generous in sharing their prescience of these.

Western Reserve University has made a significant contribution to the conception that the training of interior designers should be basically the same as the training of architects. Specifically this should include training in design and in the necessary skills. It must contain study in the basic arts and sciences which interpret life. I want to acknowledge the contributions made to this program and to my work by Dr. Helen A. Hunscher, Chairman of the Department of Home Economics, by Dr. Edmund H. Chapman, Chairman of the Division of Art and Architecture and by Mr. George E. Danforth, Chairman of the Department of Architecture.

My indebtedness to other cultural institutions in Cleveland is great. I am grateful to the Cleveland Institute of Art for design training which has always been a challenge because it was given by skilled artists who were likewise men of thought. Mr. Henry Hunt Clark was director of the Institute (then the Cleveland School of Art) when I was studying there. His sensitive presentation of the art of other cultures opened our eyes to the limitations of a provincial taste.

The Cleveland Museum of Art, because of the quality of its acquisitions and the generosity of its spirit, has been of great assistance. Mr. William M. Milliken, Director Emeritus of the Museum and Miss Dorothy G. Shepherd, Curator of Textiles and of Near Eastern Art have been very helpful. Mr. Ina T. Frary, Membership Secretary Emeritus and distinguished author of many books dealing with colonial architecture, has helped us appreciate fine old furnishings.

I wish to express my appreciation to several teachers whose efforts in my behalf far exceeded any call to duty, Miss Frances King Dolley, and the late Miss Mary E. Adams and Miss Mary E. Parker.

Dr. Donald G. Allen has given invaluable aid with the section dealing with the physiology of vision.

Miss Dorothy Nickerson, Color Technologist, United States Department of Agriculture, Mrs. Blanche R. Bellamy, Manager of the Munsell Company, and Dr. Robert W. Burnham, Research Psychologist, Eastman Kodak Company, are friends who have generously shared their color knowledge and who have given that even more precious gift, encouragement. To Mrs. Ruth E. Bowman I am similarly indebted.

My greatest debt in compiling this volume is to Dr. Thomas Munro, Curator of Education of the Cleveland Museum of Art and Professor of Art at Western Reserve University. The conception of aesthetics which forms the framework of this book is my interpretation of his teaching of aesthetics. Not wishing to make him responsible wherever I have failed in comprehension, I nevertheless wish to acknowledge my obligation to his teaching. It gives me pleasure to say that I have been a student in his classes long enough to pay tribute to his fine creative mind and to his exceptional modesty. He has been very generous in allowing others to use the results of his thinking. While recognizing differences in the arts he has carefully avoided thinking of these differences in terms of a hierarchy of values. This attitude has done much to dispel an occasionally deep rooted prejudice against the so-called practical arts, among which interior design might be classed.

For invaluable and unending help with the editing of this text I am indebted to Miss Mary Louise Shipley, Assistant Professor of Interior Design at Michigan State University. Mrs. Lola Jolly Fried has contributed the most careful editorial assistance. Mrs. Edward Schroeder has likewise given assistance with the manuscript.

V K B

Cleveland, Ohio

CONTENTS

Preface vii

Acknowledgments viii

I. THE DESIGNER'S PROBLEM 1

II. DESIGN ORGANIZATION 11

III. COORDINATION OF INTERIOR DESIGN WITH STRUCTURE 23

IV. FUNCTIONAL PLANNING OF INTERIORS 39

V. SPACE AND SHAPE IN INTERIORS 77

VI. UNDERSTANDING COLOR 93

VII. USING COLOR IN INTERIORS 127

VIII. LIGHT AS AN AESTHETIC FACTOR IN INTERIOR DESIGN 149

IX. TEXTURE AND THE MEDIA OF INTERIOR DESIGN 167

X. TOTAL DESIGN AND CONCRETE DESIGN PROBLEMS 219

XI. DESIGN AND EXPRESSION 249

XII. DESIGN AND PERIOD STYLES—HISTORIC EXPRESSION 255

XIII. DESIGN AND MODERN STYLE—CONTEMPORARY EXPRESSION 271

XIV. THE TOTAL ART FORM—A PLAN FOR ACCOMPLISHMENT 311

Appendix 323

Reading References 323

Outstanding Historic Houses in Eastern U. S. Before 1850 Which May be Visited 330

Museums Noted for Outstanding Collections of Decorative Arts 330

Current Directory of Firms Mentioned in Chapter XIII and a Few Other Representative Ones 331

Index 333

Why should you think that beauty which is the most precious thing in the world lies like a stone on the beach for the careless passer-by to pick up idly?

Beauty is something wonderful and strange that the artist fashions out of the chaos of the world in the torment of his soul. And when he has made it, it is not given to all to know it. To recognise it you must repeat the adventure of the artist. It is a melody that he sings to you and to hear it again in your heart you want knowledge and sensitiveness and imagination.

SOMERSET MAUGHAM *

Chapter I

THE DESIGNER'S PROBLEM

A. BEAUTY, THE PRINCIPAL GOAL OF INTERIOR DESIGN

We are willing to spend time, effort and money on interior design because we wish beautiful surroundings. The love of beauty is fundamental. The search for the means of its gratification is the goal of our present study.

The first procedure in any job analysis is to reach an understanding of the problems involved. As beauty is our object we must give it some thought. The word "beauty," which means so much to all, is a difficult word to define. It is easier to describe how we feel when we call something beautiful. We respond to a beautiful object with an intense, enjoyable, and enduring interest. Such concern is a worthy value in a world which would otherwise be distasteful and boring.

This tendency to define beauty in terms of feelings suggests that beauty is an experience, a special kind of interactivity between ourselves and our environment. In order to understand the interdependence of the object appreciated and

* From **Moon and Sixpence** by W. Somerset Maugham. Copyright 1919 by W. Somerset Maugham. Reprinted by permission of Doubleday & Co., Inc.

Residence of: Miss E. Blanche Harvey, Cleveland Heights, Ohio.
Photographer: Dr. Elizabeth T. Endicott.

the person appreciating, it may be helpful to study a sequence which psychologists use to illustrate all human experience. The formula is this:

W (world or environment) → S (stimulus) → O (our organism with its
sense receptors, brain and muscles)
→ R (response) → W (world)

Let us say that a bell rings. This occurs because someone in the world pushed the bell. This creates the stimulus which our ears receive. An impulse is sent along the nervous system to our brain. The brain may interpret the sound as our doorbell. In which case the brain might initiate a physical response transmitted through the muscles. This response could be that of going to the door. Or the brain may interpret the sound as

that of a neighbor's bell. In which case the response might be an attitude of disappointment because we are not to have the pleasure of receiving callers.

In the experience which we call beauty, the W (world) may or may not be physically present as the source of S (stimulus). In a totally imaginative experience of beauty the world is remote. We summon beautiful thoughts and images from a rich storehouse in our minds. In the experience of beauty the R (response) factor does not always result in overt action. When it does, such action is only an indirect result of the experience. The response can begin and end in the mind. For this reason, many writers describe beauty as a contemplative response.

The conceptual nature of our reaction to beauty

Figure 1. This is good art in the author's opinion because:

1. In this interior the emphasis is placed first on functional organization.

2. This kitchen speaks of an interest of its owner who supervises the culinary arts with great distinction.

3. Regularity of arrangement and a harmony of copper tones likewise make a pleasing design.

does not mean that the aesthetic experience [1] is passive. The simplest response to beauty is more than a mere sensation. It involves mental activity, the nature of which is dependent upon the particular experience. Because beauty is a contemplative response at the same time that it is an active experience, it ranks high in any scale of

[1] The phrase *aesthetic experience* is frequently used as a synonym for *response to beauty*. The difference lies in the fact that the reaction to beauty is always pleasant whereas the aesthetic experience may seem to be disagreeable. *Vide,* Thomas Munro, *The Arts and Their Interrelations* (New York: The Liberal Arts Press, 1949), p. 102.

This difference becomes of less importance if we believe that the aesthetic experience may be agreeable no matter how distasteful the cause of the experience is. This apparent anomaly occurs in the beauty of tragedy.

In interior design it is better to restrict beauty to aesthetic experience from pleasant sources.

human good.[2] Enjoyment through beauty does no intrinsic harm. It neither destroys the beautiful object nor interferes with the pleasure or interest of other persons.

The response to beauty is frequently called irrational or emotional.[3] This is true in the sense that it is often difficult to understand our reasons for considering something beautiful. It is equally difficult at times to persuade someone else to see beauty where we do. This intuitive reaction to beauty is good. Beauty flashes upon our consciousness with a singleness and surety which enables us to forget the *why* in enjoyment of the *is*.

[2] Ralph Barton Perry, *Realms of Value* (Cambridge, Mass.: Harvard University Press, 1954), p. 344.

[3] *Emotion:* strong, generalized feeling (*Webster's New World Dictionary*).

Rationalization requires close attention, an attitude of objectivity, and an analytical method applied for a comparatively long time in order to arrive at any logical conclusion. Unfortunately the quality of ingenuous pleasure is lost in the process—a fact which we are inclined to resent. For most losses there are compensating gains. It is sometimes necessary to tear apart in order to learn how to create.

It is important for an interior designer to create for the enjoyment of others as well as for himself. Therefore he must comprehend that the experience of beauty is not simple even though its appreciation may not require the use of the higher brain faculties. Actually we seldom grow emotional from simple causes but rather from those which are complex and vaguely understood. An analysis of the complex nature of beauty will help us to design environments which measure up to our own ideals and which likewise please others.

Beauty, even though it is quickly sensed, is a response which is derived from a number of more basic or elementary responses. Beauty is thus a developed response. Reactions are basic or primary when they are the simplest answer to a stimulus. Giving attention to a stimulus is thus basic. This is the set for all that follows. In some way a beautiful thing must first attract our notice. Having looked at a color, we may say that it makes us feel gay. Or we may call it by its particular name. These are secondary responses because they depend upon the initial focusing upon the color. If we evaluate the color as being harmonious with its surroundings we are reacting in a more complicated way. If we say that the color is beautiful we are evaluating the color as worthy in a response which depends upon the many simpler previous responses. But can we be certain that someone else will call the color beautiful? Not unless we know more about how that person will react to that color in more basic ways.

The idea that beauty is caused only by sensuous stimulation is another fallacy which our analysis will destroy. The experience of beauty, although it may not require the conscious use of the higher brain centers, can arise from the stimulation of any of the areas of the brain. These range from the parts concerned with simple sensory material to those which are taxed with more meaningful material. A child may enjoy the redness of a ball. An adult's feeling that his national flag is beautiful may rest on many meaningful associations. This too is good. It gives the instrument of beauty many strings. Which will play the richer tune? Who can say? It is a pity nevertheless if the expanding capabilities should make us deaf to a broken first string. This initial strand is sensuous experience which is fundamental and universal to all comprehension on this earth.

Our analysis of beauty in an attempt to learn why the same object may not be beautiful to everyone, returns us to the O factor, the human organism factor. In physical makeup and in respect to accumulated experience no two persons are ever exactly alike. At any particular moment the physical, mental and emotional status of two individuals who are looking at the same object may be quite different. We ourselves change from time to time. Therefore the experience of beauty is a dynamic rather than a static phenomenon. This is one reason for our pleasure in its search.

B. THE RELATION OF BEAUTY AND ART

Beauty can be found everywhere. We often see it in nature and we frequently meet it in the works of man. Whenever we say that something is artistic we usually imply that man has made something which is beautiful. The process involved in this accomplishment is one of organization, which means selection and arrangement of materials to create a new form. In the most comprehensive sense in which we use the word, this is art. Art is the organization of energies to gain

Figure 2. This is good art in the author's opinion because:

1. In this interior the emphasis is placed first on expressive organization.

2. It functions well as a small nonsectarian chapel in a hospital.

3. Its colors—gold, yellow, and brown—its beautiful cross, and the light filtering through the abstract pattern of the stained glass window and white sheer dacron curtains—these contribute to make a radiant design which carries a message.

Building: Fairview Park Hospital, Fairview Park, Ohio. **Interior Designer:** Leon Gordon Miller, Cleveland, Ohio. **Artist:** Leroy Flint, stained glass window, Akron, Ohio. **Photographer:** Rebman Photo Service, Cleveland, Ohio.

a result.[4] Ordinarily when we speak of art our meaning is more restricted. We are thinking of something which was made to be beautiful.[5] Art, as we shall use the term, is the organization of means to gain the kind of response which we call beauty.

C. THE RELATION BETWEEN ART AND SCIENCE

This book deals with the art of interior design. While so doing it frequently makes some use of science. Science observes, measures and tabulates phenomena. From this data it deduces laws of cause and effect. It considers that truth has been reached when, through reproducing causes, it can predict effects.

Actually this is not very different from what the artist is doing. The difference between the artist and the scientist is in a sense one of degree—the degree to which the personal ability of the artist is essential to the success of the end product. When man learns the exact way to organize his means to gain his ends, when reproduction of the end product can be accomplished by rule, then we have science rather than art.

Just as the creative scientist frequently steers his course by conjecture and is spiritual kin to the creative artist, so, too, the wise artist makes

[4] This is the sense in which Dewey uses the term. John Dewey, *Art As Experience* (New York: Minton, Balch and Company, 1934), p. 176.

[5] "Art is skill in providing stimuli to satisfactory aesthetic experience," Munro, *The Arts and Their Interrelations*, p. 108.

Figure 3. This is good art in the author's opinion because:

1. In this garden the primary emphasis is on visual design. The interplay of curved shapes with supporting straight verticals—the muted yellow to blue-greens against the iron red of the arches—the textures of foliage and water against harder man-made materials—these create an enhanced visual experience. Sound and motion contribute their quota.

2. Function is obviously served or there would be no verdure.

3. Expression is that of a cool oasis.

Garden Designer: Lawrence Halprin. **Courtesy: House and Garden,** Copyright 1958, The Conde Nast Publications, Inc.

all possible use of the precision material of science. In the complex field of art there is much that will remain indeterminate. Beyond the recipes there is the need for the particular artist to bring his ability to bear upon a specific problem.

D. THREE PURPOSES FOR CREATION

When we make something we usually have a purpose in mind. In reviewing human endeavor we find that its purposes might be threefold.[6] The earliest purpose for creation was probably the intention to make something of practical use. Man fashioned a spearhead and with it killed for his food. He moulded clay and built storage places for his grain. He carved a wheel and harnessed water. He built stools, beds, and houses and made his living more comfortable and safe. Using the term art in its broadest sense of useful skill,[7] these are functional art forms because the primary purpose which motivated their creation was utilitarian.

In addition to its practical use an artifact may bring us a message. One of the three reasons for creating art is to say something. *Communication, suggestion, expression, interpretation, explanation, exposition* are all words used to denote various ways of revealing the hidden aspects of things. We shall use the term *expression* to denote all of these. The art involved is that of organizing details which are known in such a way that they will illuminate the unknown. Thus expressive art implies a sensitivity on the part of the artist not only to one type of phenomenon but to at least two types. It involves a recognition of likenesses between things which may be totally unlike in kind. For instance we say that a chemist explains the chemical nature of a substance when he writes a formula. He has here shown certain causal relations between the atoms by means of symbols. By the same token we say that an Oriental artist can express the infinite by a few deft brush strokes.

When likenesses of this sort are well established in a culture they become symbols. Language is the great symbolic art. Any symbolic art is highly

[6] Munro, *The Arts and Their Interrelations*, p. 364.
[7] *Ibid.*, p. 62.

significant and useful because it simplifies our complex existence. It indicates parallels and hence the possibility of unity out of variety, order from chaos.

The third purpose for creation is for the enhancement or intensifying of perceptual enjoyment. This is without any immediate thought for either use or meaning. This reason for art we shall call design.[8]

E. THE COMPLETE AESTHETIC FORM

The three purposes just outlined enter in varying degrees into the creation of all art. Beauty lies in our response to art and to nature. Insofar as we comprehend and appreciate the fulfillment of these purposes both in man's world and in universal creation, aesthetic form will be seen as compounded of its functional, expressive, and design aspects.

Several years ago a woman was asking for advice concerning her decorating problem. She and her husband had saved funds to refurnish their home. Conflict entered when she wanted to put only Louis XV period furniture in the living room and he would not give up his comfortable old Morris armchair. This chair, she felt, ruined the effect. So it did—judged from a design point of view. Moreover the chair was incongruous in a setting expressive of an eighteenth century culture. But without the Morris chair, or a comfortable substitute, the room could not have functioned for the husband. All three points of view are important in considering interior design as an art form.

The primary purpose of this text is to set down directives for a well designed interior. If this designing is to seem beautiful to persons of mature sensibilities it must fly in echelon, flanked by a regard for the purposes of the interior spaces and for the necessity to express these purposes in terms of human values.

F. SKILL

Art requires skill and taste, two faculties which are not the same but which are frequently con-

joined. Skill is proficiency in accomplishment. The difference between skill and taste is largely one of difference of focus. Skill is the executor where taste is the director. Manual skill requires good sense organs and muscular coordination. It necessitates a mentality which is able to learn the necessary manipulation and a singleness of purpose which is willing to work toward that end.

Probably no interior designer could be master of all the manual skills required for the successful execution of his plans. But he should know standards of proficiency. He must learn that complex skill of accomplishment through the instrumentality of others.

G. A PRELIMINARY CONSIDERATION OF TASTE

Taste means a knowledge of and preference for the finest quality in any art.[9] When taste operates in the art of living it is the faculty of being able to make wise choices in many fields of human experience and to relate these selections to our daily lives.

Such taste can be acquired. No one is born with it. Nevertheless one of the earmarks of its possession is the naturalness with which it is worn. Although the timid person who is fearful of following his own preferences has not gained taste, neither has the opinionated person who prescribes for his less enlightened friends from a quickly read docket.

Taste is worn naturally when it comes from inner convictions. It is like a finely tailored cloak which can be disregarded because it fits so well. Wearer and garment seem fused and certain it is that each contributes assurance to the other.

This kind of confidence results from the nature of the beliefs which good taste demands. The person of taste must have acquired personal integrity of the kind which acknowledges other values lying deeper than surface appearance. Taste also recognizes that appearance is one important way of making these values manifest.

In its gratification by expression taste has something of the inner compulsion of the evangelist. It likewise has a soupçon of the good actor in its

---

[8] When *design* is used in the sense of *a plan* or *to plan*, we shall try to substitute these words.

[9] See Chapter XI for further consideration of this subject.

makeup, a little of that skill in presentation which makes the offering seem attractive. A dull taste may be less desirable than a poor one because it cannot project its hidden meaning.

Through breadth of understanding taste possesses that true sophistication which not only sees excellence in the familiar, but likewise in the new it recognizes old friends in new raiment. Such quick perception elevates taste above the quagmire of the hackneyed.

Taste is at once simple and difficult to acquire. It is so simple that it involves nothing more than the willingness and ability to observe and to think about what has been observed. Simplicity of this sort is always deceptive. As has been aptly said, simplicity is never simple. It is difficult because its reflections are not only about things but likewise about relations between things. The preparation for this can never be narrow, quick, or effortless.

The student who cannot recognize the fact that taste in creating attractive surroundings is dependent upon many apparently irrelevant factors, such as the kind of books that are read, the music that is listened to, the friends that are chosen, the kind of character that is evolved—such a student can never master the difficult side to designing and so his lesson will forever be half-learned.

Now there is nothing different in principle here from what is done in the furnishing of a room, when the householder sees to it that tables, chairs, rugs, lamps, color of walls, and spacing of the pictures on them are so selected and arranged that they do not clash but form an ensemble. Otherwise there is confusion—confusion that is, in perception.

Vision cannot then complete itself. It is broken up into a succession of disconnected acts, now seeing this, now that, and no mere succession in a series. When masses are balanced, colors harmonized, and lines and planes meet and intersect fittingly, perception will be serial in order to grasp the whole, and each sequential act builds up and reinforces what went before. Even at first glance there is the sense of qualitative unity. There is form.

JOHN DEWEY *

Chapter II

DESIGN ORGANIZATION

A. THE MATERIALS OF ART

If our goal is the creation of beautiful interiors through the agency of a good design, what plan for accomplishment can we adopt? At this point we grip the how rather than the why of our problem. From here we must begin to learn our trade.

In the first place, what are our building blocks? There is no limit to the material from which art can be made. Art consists of the reorganizing of the materials of this world. Therefore it is made from the things which we think of as real, such as wood, stone, plaster, paint, textiles. These materials together with the tools and processes used in fabrication are frequently called the medium (pl. media) of art.

Art is likewise made from the psychological materials of experience, such as sensations, strivings (conations), frustrations, emotions, and rationalizations. The organization of these also requires the use of tools and processes.

* From **Art As Experience** by John Dewey. Copyright 1934 by G. P. Putnam's Sons, and reprinted by permission of the publisher

Different arts specialize in the use of certain kinds of material. Music uses the sensation of sound; literature may deal with strivings and emotions. Interior design primarily uses the sensation of sight as its means. A student of interior design needs good eyes and a concern for appearances as equipment for his work.

Although the visual sensation is most important to the interior designer, other senses are significant. Through the tactile sense we gain pleasure from touching such things as china and fine wood. Through the kinaesthetic sense (the sense of muscular tension) we enjoy actual or imaginary movement through places. It is by means of this sense that interior design becomes a time-space art.

The remaining senses could make an indirect contribution to a beautiful interior. Oriental civilizations make use of incense and perfume. To the Occidental mind this seems effeminate. Nevertheless probably the most instantly recalled remembrances of our childhood are of such ephemeral things as the spicy canning odors on an early fall day or of the cedar wood odors in an old hide-away attic.

The sense of sound can also contribute to the total beauty of an interior. The best of musical art is within our reach if we merely turn the radio dial with discretion. Lesser sound effects may likewise play their part. Years ago many houses contained those little hanging glass ornaments which tinkled away in delightful fashion on invitation from a breeze. The electric stove has lost the sensuous appeal of the crackling wood fire. Where is our imagination? Can't we enrich our modern buildings with pleasing sounds? The cheerful melodies of the door chimes, the intoning of the clock, the bong of the brass dinner gong, the rustle of silk draperies touched in passing—these may be the essence of a home that our children will remember. Whatever it is, make the sounds of a building pleasant for they will be remembered after visual images have failed.

B. MATERIALS OF THE VISUAL SENSATION

Though other sensations may be used in our enjoyment of beautiful interiors, nevertheless it will be the visual sensation which will contribute

most. In designing an interior we must think of the walls and the floors and the furnishings in terms of their visual properties. First we see shapes. These are recognized through certain variations in tone (color) or other variations in tone which we call visual texture. Therefore shapes and their modifications through color are the ingredients of the visual world. For purposes of analysis we often speak of shape, color, and visual texture as the three visual components.[1]

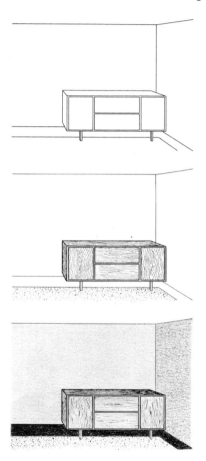

Figure 4. These are the three visual components. First we see shape, then texture, then color.

Line work: for this figure, and elsewhere in this book where no credit is given, the draftsman was Algirdas Liutkus, Cleveland, Ohio.

[1] The student may find it more convenient to use names with which he is familiar for these qualities. Thus they might be called ingredients or elements. We have adopted one term for the sake of consistency. This applies to all of the definitive terms used. The word *component* is used in Thomas Munro, *The Arts and Their Interrelations,* p. 359.

For instance we may say that a Chippendale chair has a shape composed of certain lines and masses (types of shape). It has a similar line but a different color and texture from a Queen Anne chair. If we wish to describe these two chairs more objectively we need more accurate quality terms. These basic quality terms in respect to which one example of a component may differ from another example of the same component may be called attributes.[2] Hue is an attribute of color. We can compare the mahogany and the walnut chairs in terms of their hues. If we give each hue a specific name, such as red or brown, we pinpoint one of their color traits. Red is a color trait. A square is a shape trait. Traits are concrete designations of components characterized in terms of component attributes.

C. THE TESTS OF A GOOD VISUAL DESIGN

What are the tests of a good visual design? These should be held before us during the entire creative process. These tests are incorporated in our definition of design—organization to enhance perceptual experience. Therefore there should be an experience, a oneness, a *unity* of effect. This should be an enhanced or magnified experience, an *intensity* of effect. The effect is perceptual, therefore it engages the conscious faculties of the mind. It must attract and hold the interest, must have some vital energizing power, *vitality* of effect. In short it must seem beautiful, give intense, enjoyable, and enduring interest.

D. BEGINNING OF A DESIGN

How does one begin to create a good visual design? How choose compatible visual traits, colors that seem harmonious with shapes, textures that are on friendly terms with both? Will these visual qualities be at cross-purposes with the significance of the form? *Unity*, how is it made from the many? This is enough of a problem, surely, without worrying at the outset about enjoyment and interest.

Creation involves organization, the choice and arrangement of details for a particular end.

[2] *Ibid.*

Choice or selection comes first. Why are certain qualities to be chosen and others rejected? Each visual trait is chosen because it promotes a specific effect. Therefore begin with the essence of things wished for, the ultimate effect.

One of the most practical ways to begin an interior design is to compile a list of words which would characterize the atmosphere or particular kind of effect which is desired for the interior space. These words should not be so general as to be found in the initial definition of beauty because they are to denote a particular kind of beauty. Perhaps we wish a quiet, restful, restrained character in an interior, perhaps an elegant one or a quaint one. We may be in semantic deep water if we try to define these words. However to our own satisfaction we recognize the quality which they describe.

We may finish with two compilations, one list of active conditions and another of more passive ones. Some words may seem to bridge both sets as "dramatic" and "cool" may be joined by "formal." The artist must choose the docket which is most important to him. The opposing one will then only be allowed to qualify and impose certain limitations on the first. The bridge words may provide linkages.

When a most important classification has been chosen, the designer then translates it into terms of a few component traits to which, in his opinion, the list words are related. These traits are the embryo of a design. The design begins to be unified through selection of one dominant effect and its translation into visual traits.

How are component traits related to words? Visual traits are capable of transmitting two kinds of messages, one of which is mute and the other vocal. The first type of message is so intrinsic to the sensation itself that it cannot readily be translated into any other type of experience. Perhaps the closest approximation to an oral interpretation is in physical terms such as hot, heavy, strong—but these alone will not answer. It is this essential communication to which the artist is particularly responsive and which inordinately excites his interest. The visual artist, because he is an artist, reacts to this message in kind. It is a dynamo which impels him to activity, to creation.

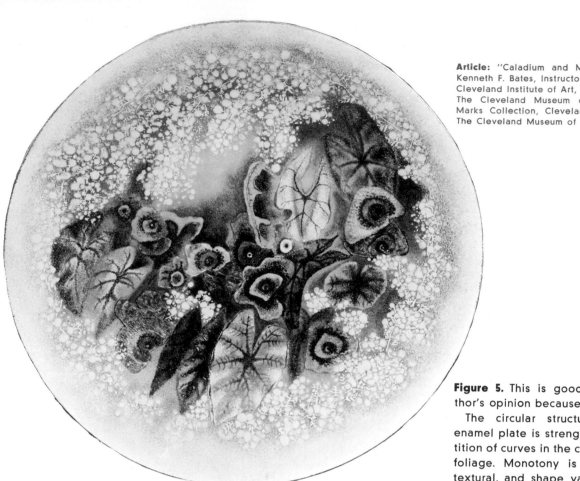

Article: "Caladium and Mimosa," enamel. **Artist:** Kenneth F. Bates, Instructor, Design and Enameling, Cleveland Institute of Art, Cleveland, Ohio. **Owner:** The Cleveland Museum of Art, Mrs. Stanley J. Marks Collection, Cleveland, Ohio. **Photographer:** The Cleveland Museum of Art, Cleveland, Ohio.

Figure 5. This is good design in the author's opinion because:

The circular structural shape of the enamel plate is strengthened by the repetition of curves in the caladium and mimosa foliage. Monotony is avoided by tonal, textural, and shape variations.

The other kinds of communication which sensations convey, those which carry over into the realm of expression of ideas, may be important to the artist but they are always secondary. These expressive statements can range from more or less vague feelings and emotions to particularized ideas. Likewise observers report the reception of similar messages from traits of different components, i.e., from a pink color and a curved line. Is there any common meeting ground for these communications, any funnel through which they all must pass? A list such as was suggested of commonly used descriptive terms would constitute such a flume.

It is not important for the artist to be able to name visual traits. Names are merely a great aid to standardization and specification. It is extremely important for the artist to train his eye to make nice distinctions of visual qualities. This is the beginning of sensitivity and hence of good art. With such sensitivity the nuances between an interior which is timid and one which is reserved, one which is pretentious and one which is distinguished, emerge.

E. FURTHER ORGANIZATION OF A DESIGN

1. General Consideration

Even a novice at interior design knows that sturdy shapes, friendly yellows and informal textures produce an aura of cheerful comfort in a room. Helpful clients frequently crystallize their thoughts to this extent before going to a decorator. Much remains to be done before these suggestions emerge as a well designed interior.

We might compare the procedure with that of baking a cake. The ingredients at this stage have been chosen largely because of a preconceived notion of their appropriateness. They must be combined so as to produce a new product with no unassimilated flour or lumps of sugar—a new unity. They must be combined so that the new product will taste better than the individual ingredients. The qualities of the ingredients are altered and enhanced because they are in the cake. The purpose of organization is to progress, step by step, so as not to destroy but rather to build up the effects of the original traits. This is a matter of choice of additional traits and it is a matter of placement. These two considerations cannot be entirely separated. Principles which govern selection are likewise relevant to arrangement. Nevertheless we shall treat consecutively these two aspects of design.

2. Enhancement of Visual Qualities

The qualities of the visual ingredients are altered because they are in the design. The company which a brick fireplace keeps in association with walls, floors, and furnishings, will make it seem redder or greyer, rougher or smoother, larger or smaller and ultimately, more or less important.

This modification of visual qualities occurs in accordance with relatively definite laws which can often be demonstrated if the evidence is kept very simple. It is obvious that there are only two possible ways of handling a basic visual quality in context. One is to repeat it and another is to

vary it. A third manipulation might be called contrast. Contrast is merely extreme variation.

Repetition, variation, and contrast in correct proportions can accentuate forces. Repetition, two of some quality rather than one, usually makes a stronger statement. If a designer begins with the texture of mahogany he frequently repeats this same wood in a room. Two pieces will probably attract more attention than one and will augment the impact of this kind of wood. If a designer uses only straight lines and a repeated color, the room will cease to be interesting and we will not look at it. Monotonous repetition of traits will destroy rather than heighten an original effect.

Instead of using exact repetition the designer frequently varies the traits which he has chosen for his design and presents the same idea in slightly altered form. In using variation he must be extremely careful. Differences are certain to tear down rather than to build up unless they are very carefully ordered. There are only two times

Figure 6. This is good design in the author's opinion because:

The straight outlines of the enamel plaque are repeated and supported in the shapes enclosed. Variety is complex through skillful manipulation of changes in size and direction as well as in tones and textures. Masterful use of contrast is seen in the employment of curves in this "Argument in Limoges Market Place."

when visual differences support one another. The first of these is when their qualities are brought into that kind of sequential order where the eye is carried from a lesser amount to a greater amount of the quality. By getting qualities into such a progressive sequence the variations build upon one another and the effect of the whole is greater than that of the parts. The truth of this statement will recur again and again throughout any study of design. It reappears in many texts under different names, such as progressive rhythm, dynamic symmetry, cumulative propulsion.[3]

The second way to regiment differences so as to heighten an effect is through skillful use of contrast. Any contrasting material should possess some similarity to the matter to which it is opposed or design will seem chaotic. However if

[3] For further discussion of rhythm see p. 18.

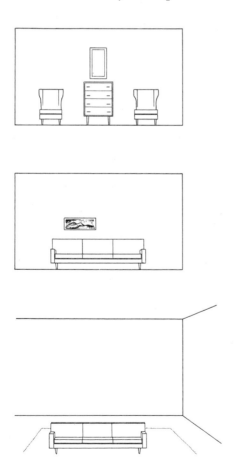

Figure 7. The artist controls our vision. We are compelled to look up and down, left and right, back and forth.

Figure 8. This Hiroshige print illustrates well one essential of good design—vitality. Starting or returning to the chickadee as the center of interest, how many tonal and spatial routes direct the eye through the picture?

Artist: Hiroshige (1797–1858), Japanese.

it is to strengthen through its dissimilarity a detail should have more traits which are unlike its opponent than those which are corresponding.

At this point in our thinking all of the visual qualities in a design must be organized so as to assume relative importance. Only through group action and the dominance of some, can the enhanced unity of all be accomplished. The flour in the cake must be quantitatively more than the soda or the result will be a sorry one. Some call this the principle of dominance or relative emphasis. The estimation of quantitative relations is a matter of proportion or relative measure. Proportion is the quantitative basis underlying all art.

Not only can qualities be changed by environment, the total environmental complex can be made to seem unchanged if the same proportional relations are maintained. Thus the sensation of constancy can be established in a fluctuating world.[4] One may plan for a large house and find himself living in a small one. By adjusting relative sizes, colors, and textures the illusion of spaciousness can be secured.

3. Visual Qualities and Their Spatial Alignment

Because visual art is fundamentally spatial, the positioning of details in a design is important. The artist thinks of the placement of objects as a problem in the alignment of visual forces. It is not enough for him to regulate the qualita-

[4] The so-called law of constancy. David Katz discusses some of the implications of this in *The World of Color* (London: Kegan Paul, Trench, Trubner and Co., Ltd., 1935), Part III.

tive aspects of his design so as to secure desirable proportional emphases; he must likewise control vision so that the viewer is compelled to look where and when the design intends.

Qualities are now transformed into visual forces. The visual force of a trait is its power to attract the eye. The visual force of any object is the sum of the forces of its constituent traits.

As the designer puts the building blocks into their final position he must think not only of securing unity and intensity which he has in a measure accomplished through the enhancement of one qualitative effect; he must seek for vitality, the ability to endure as timeless art. The features which distinguish life must be found in the design. Life is characterized by certain patterns of

Figure 9. This grouping illustrates well one characteristic of good design—a rhythmic spatial unity. The visual field may be so organized as to present unities within the total design. One way to create compact completeness is by using a triangular shape organization, as here with the heirloom nineteenth century furniture and the family portrait which provides an interesting resting point for the eye.

Residence of: Miss Frances King Dolley, Cleveland, Ohio. **Artist:** Fannie E. Duvall. **Photographer:** G. Colburn Ball, Cleveland, Ohio.

activity or change, and by an equally important condition of rest or equilibrium. Stability in change is the distinction of living things.

a. CHANGE

The evolving pattern of change in design begins with the activity set up by opposing traits.[5] Oppositions creating excitement and tensions are first introduced when varying and contrasting traits are selected. They are further carried out as the eye equates visual forces and so organizes the visual field into background and foreground, up and down, left and right.

Change is movement. This must be directed if it is to avoid chaos. This directive is assigned to a principle called rhythm. The first duty of rhythm is to cause ordered movement which may be of many kinds.

Rhythm in the temporal arts is similar to, but not quite like, rhythm in the spatial arts. There is a repetitive tempo to music within which some

variation occurs. Metric activity in both kinds of arts occurs because of alternation between accent and background. Direction is not important to music because sounds move with the elapse of time. The repetitive meter when used in the visual arts cannot direct eye movement; it can only cause metric activity.

In so doing it has some utility. It is a counterpart of the natural pulsations of the universe and should be used in the manner in which it serves in nature, as a background upon which to project more directed rhythms. If such repetitive rhythm becomes too insistent, as when our head thumps in illness, it becomes annoying and can block out more vital patterns of activity.

In the spatial arts regulated movement must be induced by directing the eye along a path of lesser to greater forces. This is most naturally done by repeating an underlying relationship between the units which is similar to the underlying ratio of all growth.[6] Because a geometric

---

[5] Actual movement of details, such as candle flames and reflections, also introduces change.

[6] Dewey's *Ordered variation in change.* John Dewey, *Art As Experience* (New York: Minton, Balch and Company, 1934), p. 154.

Figure 10. This grouping illustrates well one characteristic of good design—interesting equilibrium. Several identical objects are placed on either side of the vertical axis. Articles with equal attention force but different character are likewise paired for balance. Horizontal divisions are distributed, with some repetition and some variation in spacing, creating rhythmic paths.

Residence of: Mr. William C. Grauer, "Grassmere," East Claridon, Ohio, Associate Professor of Art, Western Reserve University, Cleveland, Ohio. **Photographer:** G. Colburn Ball, Cleveland, Ohio.

Figure 11. The architecture and furnishings of this early eighteenth century home indicate the fact that the interests of the household were centered within the building. A social gathering for a cup of tea might be found near a fire. The furniture, which is largely of the style called Queen Anne, was made in Philadelphia. The Oriental carpet is a central Persian Ispahan.

demonstration of this would relate the phenomenon to the spatial component, it is discussed in Chapter V (Shape). Such a relation between parts is sometimes called a dynamic or progressive rhythm. It unifies a design by binding details into sequences. It enhances trait qualities thereby. It moves the eye in planned directions.

Because details in a design such as a chair or a picture owe their visual force to the sum of their traits, the same detail may participate in several alignments. Thus a greyed red chair may be in a color path which will carry the eye to a picture which has bright red areas. The same chair may have a shape which will function in some shape sequence. Or it might function in a textural sequence. These sequences can move the eye in quite different directions. The eye thus could have a choice of several routes out from the chair.

Such multiplicity of choice is a characteristic of life's experience and thus is a necessity in creating vitality. The details of a design are constantly realigning themselves. It is interesting to discover new activity of this sort and continuing perceptual enjoyment is gained thereby. This principle of interlocking or integrating a detail into several themes is likewise a great help towards unifying a design.

b. REST

Rest is as important to a design as it is to life. Visual rest results from the equalizing of forces and balancing of tensions. The equilibrium of a room like that of the human body is not entirely bilateral. We wish to feel anchorage to the ground. In similar manner we react favorably to ground pull or stability in the lower section

Figure 12. One of the joys of good contemporary planning is the fact that it never isolates man from nature. A building is a shelter but not a dungeon. It provides a view of the sky, the horizon is extended and man can lift up his eyes.

Residence of: Mr. and Mrs. Robert A. Little, Pepper Pike Village, Ohio. **Architect:** Robert A. Little and Associates, Architects, Cleveland, Ohio. **Photographer:** Lionel Freedman, New York.

of a room. This is one reason that rhythms which knit groupings of furnishings into triangular shapes, broadest at the base, seem so very satisfactory.

In physical science balance is obtained by equal forces exerting equal thrusts because of their placement equidistant from a pivot or center of balance. Unequal forces must be adjusted in relation to the center of balance so that equilibrium is obtained. This is the basic principle of the level and of the seesaw.

When equal forces exert pressure at equal distances from a center, the resulting equilibrium has often been called bisymmetrical, formal, or obvious balance. Symmetry is used in the sense of analogy or likeness of measures. It is comparatively easy to gain bisymmetry in interior design. All that is necessary is to have enough money to buy two of every article and then to place one of each kind equidistant from the center, watching as well to effect a downward pull on the whole.

More than this is needed to create interesting bisymmetry. It is necessary to have the internal structure of the arrangement rhythmic in just the same way that the internal structure of the entire room must be both moving and stabilized. Two objects can be interestingly balanced on either side of a central object. The relation of each object to the central object constitutes a measure or meter which is balanced because of repetition in reverse position. Examine this meter closely. Check on the horizontal and vertical spacing as well as on the color and texture qualities which effect this balance. The introduction of a dynamic internal rhythm will bring interest.

When unequal forces attract equal attention because of their placement, the resulting equilibrium has been called asymmetrical, informal, or occult balance. This kind of balance may be illustrated by the human form in action: the center of balance is still a vertical line descending earthward between the two legs, but the body is not equally disposed on either side of this line. The muscles in such a body position are more tensed than when the body is at rest and an equilibrium which results from equalizing tensions results. Asymmetry causes a more alive situation than bisymmetry.

Asymmetry is really a rhythmic meter organically balanced around a visual axis. Such an axis is an imaginary line or cross around which all compositions should be balanced.

Sometimes it seems desirable to have both bisymmetry and asymmetry in the same arrangement. In this case it is best to plan first for the formal balance and because it is so stately and restful it might be given the greater prominence. The composition can then be enlivened with informal arrangements.

c. INTEGRATION OF CHANGE AND REST

Relative centers of interest are important in the alignment of forces. Dominance suggests that various locations in a room should be accorded first, second, or third prominence. What is to be background, what foreground? In the foreground what locations are of greatest importance? Centers of interest or focal points in a room are the spots where the greatest forces of attraction converge. They are the locations where the dominant effect has been given most emphatic statement. They are the climaxes to which the eye is moved.

If all of the details in a room moved in the same direction and supported the same detail as climax, the room would seem unbalanced. Likewise the room would lack interest because there would be no tensions. The artist should integrate the various thematic forces so that they often cooperate in building some climaxes and often oppose one another in creating different climaxes.

Climaxes at centers of interest must ultimately be balanced. Asymmetrical balance is frequently used for this. A principal climax may be opposed by two secondary ones. A center of interest containing much visual activity may be opposed by a large area of little activity. Sometimes an interior may burst its bonds and look outside for a stabilizing factor. A Georgian building looks inward. A contemporary one usually looks outward.

F. MANY TYPES OF DESIGN ORGANIZATION

Good design may be of many different types. One basis of classification of design types is with respect to their definiteness or indefiniteness. In a definite design the organization is more clearly seen. This can be accomplished by devices which are basically dependent upon the idea of limitation, regularity, and clean-cut separations. The number of component traits chosen must be limited. Their thematic development should be accomplished largely by repetition rather than variation. They may be clarified by means of isolation and by sharp contrast. Their placement may be clearly defined on either side of a central axis. This kind of definite design we frequently call a formal design. A design characterized by expansiveness, irregularity, and merging of divisions would be an informal design. There are many degrees of both types. With such freedom of choice we should be able to create for every taste.

G. DIFFICULTY OF ATTAINING GOOD DESIGN

A good design is not easily attained. It is easy to obtain unity when an object is so simple as to be indivisible. It is easy to intensify an effect by repeating it. It is possible to interest the attention by something lively and unique. It is natural to please through the agreeable sensations.

As the design organization becomes more complicated trouble frequently begins. Methods which were effective at undeveloped levels often grow to be at loggerheads. Unity can be secured at the expense of intensity, perceptual interest, and pleasure. Any one of the conditions of a good design can be exploited at the sacrifice of others. A good design is a remarkable accomplishment involving the organization of many factors into a new and lovely thing.

H. OUTLINE

1. Goal
   a. Design for one enhanced perceptual effect
   b. Test words: unity, intensity, vitality

2. Selection of principal visual qualities to gain effect (dominant and subordinate effects for relative emphasis)
   a. Ingredients
      Visual components: shape, color, texture
      Attribute: basic characteristic of a component

Trait: specific example of a component attribute
   b. Choice of initial traits because of their expressive quality

3. Further organization
   a. Enhancement of visual qualities through skillful proportional use of repetition, variation, contrast
   b. Visual qualities and their spatial alignment
      Traits as visual forces
      Evolving pattern of activity
         opposing forces (tension)
         directed movement, grouping and growth (rhythm)
      Overall stability (balance)
         bisymmetry
         asymmetry
      Integration of movement with stability.
         Positions to be regarded:
            visual axis (center of balance)
            center of interest (climax of attention)

4. Types of design
   a. Definite and indefinite
   b. Inward- and outward-looking

Thus modern architecture, having assimilated the structural and biological sciences over the last century, has now absorbed even the science of psychology.

BRUNO ZEVI *

Chapter III

COORDINATION OF INTERIOR DESIGN WITH STRUCTURE

A. IMPORTANCE OF STRUCTURE

The structure of a building might seem to be too technical a matter to concern the interior designer. Nothing could be farther from the truth. In a visual way structure is the skeleton to which all else must be related. In a very practical way it affects planning possibilities. Every interior designer should have a competent understanding of how buildings are put together. He should also be sensitive enough to understand the relationships which fabrication imposes on design.

B. MODERN CONSTRUCTION

What is modern building? This is a branch of technology which is so extensive and so constantly developing that it would be presumptious for a layman to attempt to cover it. Some construction is theoretically but not economically possible. For economical building, materials, trained men, and tools must be readily available.

* From "Italian Architecture Today" by Bruno Zevi. From **The Atlantic Monthly,** December, 1958, and reprinted by permission of **The Atlantic Monthly.**

Figure 13. One feature of this elegant building is its lift slab construction. The architect states that the advantages of this type of structure are economy of costs and freedom of shape design. Almost any number of floor slabs may be poured over a first concrete slab, thereby saving on scaffolding costs. Generally speaking, curved shapes are possible without excessive cost—the wire reinforcing inside the slab being adjusted so as to correspond to the stresses.

Building: Medusa Portland Cement Company, Cleveland, Ohio. **Architect:** Ernst Payer, A.I.A., Cleveland, Ohio. **Sculptor:** William M. McVey, Instructor in Sculpture, The Cleveland Institute of Art, Cleveland, Ohio. **Photographer:** Hube Henry, Hedrich-Blessing, Chicago, Illinois.

Everyone can understand the practical logic of structure. Its purpose is primarily to enclose space. In order to do this it must be capable of standing erect and of supporting its own weight. In addition it must carry a superimposed load. It must withstand natural stresses such as winds and snow loads. It must resist chemical enemies such as fire and corrosion, physical such as soil erosion, and animal such as termites. What are some of the ways of building which are designed to do this?

1. Structural Type: Masonry of Small Units

Solid masonry built from small building blocks of stone, brick, concrete block, or hollow tile is one of the oldest important types of construction. Solid masonry walls are one type of so-called load-bearing walls because they are designed strong enough to carry the weight of any superimposed structure. We seldom see complete buildings of stone or brick today although a large fireplace wall or end walls of these materials are often used.

One of the advantages of masonry lies in its easy maintenance. It needs no protective coating against the weather. Solid masonry, however, does require some engineering planning to consider problems of moisture removal.

Every kind of construction presents technical problems which competent architects and builders can solve. The novice who wants to build his own home should study the properties of his materials thoroughly before he begins so that he may cope with the performance of his structure.

2. Structural Type: Solid Structure of Concrete, Ferro-concrete and Steel

The advantages of concrete and of steel as structural materials have been proven. Used separately or in combination (ferro-concrete) where concrete provides the compression strength (ability to bear a superimposed load without collapsing) and steel provides the tensile strength (ability to carry a load without bending), they are the principal means of modern large-scale building. Concrete is fireproof, plastic, isotropic (of steady and similar properties in all directions), and comparatively cheap. Steel is isotropic and of great and calculable strength. Its disadvantages are its high rate of heat conductivity in all but paper thin layers and its cost of fabrication in small amounts.

These materials will undoubtedly be used more extensively in houses of the future. Concrete and ferro-concrete are now used for floors and roofs. The concrete may be poured on the ground and then the slab can be lifted to position. Prefabricated ferro-concrete joists are available. Steel is coming into general use not only as a basic wall material, frequently covered with enamel, but for strong framing members. In the future thin concrete curved roofs on steel supports and suspension houses held up by central steel supports [1] may be more frequently seen.

3. Structural Type: Wood Framing

The supporting framework of many buildings is made of wood attached to a base of concrete. When there is a basement [2] this foundation is the basement wall which is widened at the bottom into a footing which spreads the load. Cinders and drainage tiles are placed outside the foundation walls to keep them watertight. Waterproofing of joints and of outer surfaces is essential. Sills are placed on top of the foundation walls. Their purpose is to hold the wood framing to the foundation.

The wood joists are the horizontal members which support the floors. Larger horizontal members are called beams. Sometimes the wood supporting members are supplemented by steel or ferro-concrete ones where it is necessary for a floor to bear a heavy load or to span a long distance. Wood joists for residences vary from $2'' \times 6''$ to $3'' \times 14''$. Joists are usually spaced sixteen inches apart. They are said to be 16" o.c. (on center).

Studs or upright framing members are likewise placed 16" o.c. Sixteen inches is one of the common modules [3] or units of measure for wood framing. Studs are of $2'' \times 4''$ lumber placed so that the broad side is at right angles to the wall. The studs are multiplied at the corners and at openings and are frequently interbraced for greater strength. It is therefore economical of lumber to plan a house so that there will be relatively few openings.

Additional rigidity is given to wood-framed walls by an outer covering of a stiff compositional boarding or by diagonal wood strips. Waterproofing is added to the exterior of this.

In early American and European timber structure the vertical supports were large wood posts into which huge horizontal beams were tenoned. This supporting framework was very strong and its individual members could be widely spaced. Many contemporary structures are utilizing this same principle, known as post and beam construction. The posts are not as large nor as widely spaced as they were in the earlier type of construction. Frequently they utilize a four or six foot module. This type of skeletal support may likewise be made of steel.

In traditional post and beam construction in Europe, the supporting framework was left exposed and the wall spaces between the posts were filled with some form of branches (wattle)

---

[1] Such as Buckminster Fuller's "Dymaxion House."

[2] Cubic footage cost of building a basement must be compared with cubic footage plus land cost on the first floor. Therefore where land values are high and additional space is needed, it may be more economically sound to place service features in the basement. It is more pleasurable, however, to have them located on the first floor.

[3] A module was originally the unit of measure of one half the base of a column. This unit was used to establish the proportions of the rest of a building.

and clay or cement (daub). These plaster walls were in no sense load-bearing walls. This same construction principle is carried out in the contemporary post and beam structure. The space between the supporting members is filled with thin walls of composition board, enameled metal, or glass, sometimes known as screen or curtain walls. The supporting members are frequently left exposed and the comprehension of the work which these members are doing becomes part of the aesthetic enjoyment derived from viewing the building.

The traditional roof in Northern European countries is the gabled roof. The rafters are the sloping, supporting, structural members of such a roof. They are generally reinforced by wood trusses or tie beams.

Wood structure is justifiably popular in America. Timber is plentiful and relatively inexpen-

sive. Wood is a warm, friendly material. American builders are accustomed to the techniques required in wood positioning and wood is easily handled. Although wood requires protection from sun drying, moisture seepage, and from termites, it is durable. It is a good thermal insulator because of its porosity. It is lively enough to withstand vibrations. It is a strong material.

The chief disadvantages of wood construction are that it is inflammable and that wood does not have the same properties in all directions. It will shrink more in one direction (with the grain) than in another. Uneven shrinkage of woods leads to warping, splitting, and to the cracking of materials which are bonded to it. Through manipulation into plywood and into impregnated [4] wood, wood is entering the category of precision engi-

[4] Impregnated with a plastic which gives it greater hardness and strength.

Models on pages 26–27 by: Students of the Department of Architecture, Division of Art and Architecture, Western Reserve University, Cleveland, Ohio.

Figure 14.

(Above) Wood frame construction on a masonry base. Reflective white gravel built-up roof.

(Right) Wood frame construction (balloon frame—studs the entire house height). Low pitched hip roof.

Figure 15. Post and beam structure permits wide bays which may contain large windows. It is enjoyable to perceive the visible supports and to appreciate their function.

neering materials. Its architectural use will therefore probably be extended in the future.

The outer sheathing of framed houses may be of one or several materials. Perhaps the most common sheathing is of wood clapboards which overlap one another to form a watertight finish. Such clapboarding was used on the provincial New England house to afford greater protection from the inclement winters than was possible from the exposed timber and plaster construction.

Many contemporary houses are finished with vertical or horizontally placed wood siding which is joined without an overlap. As this siding is frequently made from fir, cedar, or redwood, it requires little or no additional finish because the natural oils in the wood are its preservatives. Most other woods require the protection given by paint.

Stucco may be used as an exterior finish on any well braced wood frame. The metal lath which supports the stucco is fastened to the bracing of the frame. This type of finish is frequently found on houses in many sections of the South where the gaily painted stucco walls lend a note of lightness to the scene.

Brick is always a popular though relatively expensive facing veneer. Facing bricks are bonded to the rigid wood sheathing with metal ties.

Other surfacing materials less frequently seen are metal, plastics, and ferro-enamels.

4. Roof Structure

Roofs are the lids to buildings. They must either bear or drain off water and snow. Gutters and downspouts are part of some roof equipment.

Roofs may be curved or straight in silhouette, and slanting or flat in direction. Curved roofs are descendants of the arch, the vault, and the dome. They originated in lands where small building units such as stone and brick were available. The curved form is seen today as an economical, functional, and graceful shape which can be made out of some of the more plastic materials.

Straight line roofs have various contours and pitches. Every break in the contour necessitates carefully applied flashings to make it watertight. The final finish material of all roofs is dependent upon their pitch. Steep roofs must be covered with small overlapping pieces. Wood or asphalt shingles are customary. Slate, metal shingles, and tile can be placed safely on roofs which are not too steep.

As the roof pitch becomes low, small unit shingles are not practical because of the tendency of water to back up under them. Asbestos and metal rolled roofing is frequently used in this situation. These finishes are seldom used when the roof pitch is high enough to be seen. They may be used on nearly flat roofs if great strength is not required. Canvas rolled roofing is frequently seen on small decks.

Figure 16. The nature of the exposed interior structure is of importance to the interior designer. In this house the steel framework, glass, plaster, wood, and cork tile possess family resemblances of rigidity, hardness, and gloss. Certain characteristics of the furnishings echo the building, while the wool pile of the rugs, the broken light through the curtains offer needed depth and light modification.

Residence of: Mr. and Mrs. Ben Rose, Highland Park, Illinois. **Designer:** A. James Speyer. **Architect:** George E. Danforth, A.I.A., Cleveland, Ohio. **Photographer:** Tom Yee, New York. **Courtesy: Record Houses of 1956,** F. W. Dodge Corporation, New York.

When the roof is flat and the span is large, the basic structural support is made of such materials as wood, concrete, or metal. Upon this base a built-up roof is placed for watertightness. This is generally a lamination of tar and roofing felt topped with gravel or marble chips. Such roofs can stand up against the snows of northern winters. They can carry off excess water.

5. Plumbing

Any habitation today which is not equipped with a hot and cold water supply under pressure is considered to be substandard. The necessary piping for this and for the heating system is called the plumbing. In addition to the plumbing the organic structure must carry the electrical wiring.

All of these pipes and wires travel between the studs in a wood frame and between or within the walls in other types of structure. Extra space allowance must frequently be made for them. It is economical to plan so that they can be located as compactly as possible.

In the laying of all of this duct network the building is protected by building codes and sanitary ordinances which specify sizes, construction, and types of fitting.

All of this organic structure should be planned before building. Otherwise it is like a human operation, the skeleton and the skin may have to be cut into for alterations. Our grandparents may have bought more enclosed space for their dollar.

But their buildings consisted of bones and covering within which there was no organic flow.

6. Interior Floors, Walls, Ceilings

The structure of interior partitions is important to the interior designer. Wood, stone, or concrete are basic floorings. Wood is customarily nailed to a subflooring which in turn rests on the joists. Wood or stone (slate) may be a finish material laid over concrete. Concrete or ferro-concrete flooring is poured into forms and may be integral with its support. In one story construction it rests on a properly drained and insulated bed.

Post, beam, and rafter are frequently left exposed. Any rigid material may form the walls between the supports. Plaster applied to metal lath is a usual interior finish. Wood fiber or gypsum boards are frequently used in place of plaster. This is commonly known as drywall construction. Solid or veneer masonry may be used for some interior walls.

Additional surfacing materials may be added to introduce economy of upkeep, comfort in use, and desired appearance. These fall into the following categories:

Aggregates—such as chipped marble and concrete.

Tiles in relative thicknesses—such as ceramic, cork, plastic, rubber, acoustical.

Wallpapers, wall-fabrics, and wood veneers.

Linoleum and carpets.

7. Openings

The doors and windows of a building are its principal routes of communication with the outside world. Necessary and desirable, they are also weak links in a structure because they are breaks in its continuity. If they are not fitted tightly the heated interior air can escape. If their surrounding area is not well braced it may sag. It costs money in time and materials to cut holes in a wall and then to fill them satisfactorily.

Therefore we arrive at the idea that it would be wise structural planning to have as few openings as possible and to have them extend between already existing supports. This is not always feasible. Planning factors may dictate other solutions. This line of reasoning does suggest that one large window or several large windows designed to fit into the building module are better than several small windows which break a wall.

Windows and doors which fit into large openings are now available in stock sizes. Contemporary structure does not use interior doors except where privacy (bedrooms and baths) or protection from dirt (storage and closets) makes them necessary. The building is designed so that spaces are isolated visually when required and so that sound barriers are considered.

Doors and window frames are made of wood, steel, or light weight alloys. Wood doors are of solid or of hollow core construction. Windows and glass doors are designed to facilitate cleaning. Panes are large. Casement (vertical opening) and awning (horizontal opening) windows are designed on a moving pivot arm so as to open and turn without destroying a screen arrangement.

Sectional divisions of large windows provide for directed ventilation. The jalousie window, where the panes of glass are not set into a sash, accomplishes the visual effect of a solid expanse of glass and affords the maximum ventilation. The hopper opening which pivots from its base provides ventilation with the minimum of draft. Louvred doors permit the passage of air.

Screens and storm sash are necessarily considered with some windows. On most window types this extra equipment fits on the exterior of the window and hinges to the exterior trim. On many newer types it fits on the interior. Windows equipped with screens which roll away when not needed are time, energy, and space savers. When such windows are likewise double-glazed the problem of interchanging parts is solved.

Doors and windows which permit the widest openings and which do not occupy valuable space when open are frequently desirable and sometimes necessary. For this purpose they are designed to slide horizontally on themselves or to slide into a wall panel. Folding doors can be collapsed into small space. Garages utilize the overhead sliding door. More use of this might be made within a building. Revolving doors permit airtight closure while in use. Swinging doors permit opening from either side.

8. Stairs

Stairs should be designed to function well. A flight of steps is composed of treads which are frequently 10 inches wide and risers which are about 7½ inches high. This provides a safe comfortable incline of about 36° from the horizontal. A stringer or finishing strip is usually provided along the side. Minimum head room should be at least 6'–8". For safety there should be a balustrade and the individual balusters should not be too widely spaced. A common stair width is three feet.

Spiral stairways are economical of floor space. Care should be taken to insure that the individual wedge shaped treads are not too narrow. Narrow wedge sections are dangerous. Modern architects frequently use the open stair which consists of a tread and no solid riser. Each tread in such a flight should extend far enough under the tread above to insure safety from tripping.

Stairs are usually supported by a wall. Some stairs are free standing and are supported by their own rigidity or by suspended or attached supports. Ramps are occasionally used in place of stairs. They should be inclined less steeply than a stairway.

9. Chimney and Fireplace

All buildings which have fuel-burning heating equipment require chimneys. An open fireplace may be considered a luxury in our centrally heated house but what is the price of emotional warmth? The chimney for one reason or another is probably due for a long stay.

A fire requires oxygen from a fresh supply of air. It requires some avenue for harmful gases to escape. These two requirements are met by the chimney flue. This is a tile pipe which extends from a small chamber above the fire to the outdoors. This small chamber is known as the smoke chamber. It is isolated from the main fire by a smoke shelf designed to prevent gusts of wind from coming down the chimney and causing smoke to back up into the room. Below the smoke shelf is a damper which can be opened and closed to cause or to shut off an upward draft of air. There must be a separate flue for every fireplace or fuel-burning furnace. Who has not seen pictures of the many tile flues, known as chimney pots, which project like sentinels above the chimneys of English Tudor houses? These flues must be higher than any surrounding roof so that no swirling air currents will enter.

Figure 17. Contemporary architects frequently use the open stair. They feel that it conveys an impression of lightness and of space. It has the practical advantage of being easy to clean.

(Opposite page) **Residence of:** Mr. and Mrs. Bruce M. Walker, Spokane, Washington. **Architect:** Walker, McGough and Trogdon, Architects, A.I.A., Spokane, Washington. **Photographer:** Morley Baer, Berkeley, California.

(Left) **Building:** Medusa Portland Cement Company, Cleveland, Ohio. **Architect:** Ernst Payer, A.I.A., Cleveland, Ohio. **Photographer:** Hube Henry, Hedrich-Blessing, Chicago, Illinois.

Chimneys could be vulnerable spots in the fire armor of a construction. In order to reduce fire hazards chimneys are completely separated from the rest of the structure. No part of the building walls holds up a chimney and it supports no part of the building load. The chimney rests on its own spread footing. The space between the framing and the chimney is filled with fireproof insulating material. Chimneys made of prefabricated sections are now available.

Crickets are just one of the living things which love a hearth. The hearth is the essential part of an open fireplace. It consists of a front hearth which is in reality the area of a fireproof floor material surrounding the essential hearth. When the back hearth on which the fire is laid, is elevated, there may be no need for a front hearth. The firehearth should be provided with an open-

ing through which the ashes can be pushed down to the ashpit whence they are collected. The inner hearth is surmounted by a fire chamber. This has slanting sides and sloping top for heat reflection. Some hearths are of open construction and have no sides or back. The damper is at the front top of the fire chamber. Medium-sized fire chambers are about 36 inches wide by 30 inches high and 18 inches deep.

10. Jointing

Every joint in a structure, like every opening, is a potential weakness. A chain can be no stronger than its links.

The system of jointing should fulfill certain requirements. It should be uncomplicated, inexpensive, strong, and weathertight. Wood struc-

Figure 18. Love of a glowing fire is deeply rooted. Embers on the hearth add to the emotional warmth of homes of all periods.

Residence of: Mr. and Mrs. Robert A. Little, Pepper Pike Village, Ohio. **Architect:** Robert A. Little and Associates, Architects, Cleveland, Ohio. **Photographer:** Lionel Freedman, New York.

tures are customarily nailed together. Wood dowels are found in place of iron nails in some early American homes. Major structural parts were often mortised and tenoned together.

In keeping with the experimentation in new building materials, the building industry is investigating jointing. Some builders are finding that modifications of the older methods of fitting parts into parts are good. The use of synthetic adhesives for plywood construction suggests possibilities for the future. A continuous structure without joints would be ideal. Steel structures with welded joints indicate a step in this direction. Monolithic concrete is in this respect excellent. Watch for developments. Advancement may come in this direction.

C. ART FORM AS RELATED TO STRUCTURE

Structure is important because it is basic to architectural form. Contemporary structure provides the artist with a wider aesthetic potential for today's needs. An inferior designer may find in this nothing but an opportunity to make more mistakes.

Our interest in the great strides which have recently been made in structural technology may blind us to the fact that structure is the servant rather than the master of art. The initial creator of an architectural form should ask the same questions about structure which everyone who enters the planning sequence later must ask.

Is the type of structure functionally justifiable? Is it the simplest solution to the problem of use? Should a system suited to spanning great spaces be chosen for smaller ones? To what degree should performance of structure be evident? Is this to be shown through exposure of supporting elements, through cloaking the skeleton in a manner which is harmonious with its performance, through choice and handling of materials in a manner consistent with structural function? For instance, is it desirable to have posts and beams revealed? Why and how should framed walls be covered? Is a brick wall, a wall or a hodgepodge of masonry units?

Is the structure compatible with the character of the building? Some mature and therefore open-minded thought should be given to structures for churches, civic and industrial buildings, homes.

Then the intrinsic design of the structure should be considered. Problems involving shape, color, and texture must be well handled at this stage or the problems which come later can only be solved by camouflage.

D. REFINEMENTS UPON BASIC STRUCTURE

The contemporary builder wishes to plan for every addition to basic structure which will contribute to comfort and physical well-being. He studies lighting,[5] air and sound conditioning,

[5] Windows in relation to solar heating are likewise discussed in Chapter VIII.

sanitation and safety control. Directly or indirectly these refinements affect the design of the building and its furnishing.

1. Air Conditioning

The objective of air conditioning is the maintenance of fresh, clean air which is free from objectionable odors and possesses desirable humidity and temperature. There are two methods of accomplishing this. The first is to plan the building so that it will further this end. The second is to use mechanical equipment for the purpose. They should be considered in this order.

The building should be well insulated. Insulation is for the purpose of preventing the passage of heat. A building should be weathertight and insulation should be provided for outside walls and for those adjacent to unheated areas. Insulating materials depend upon any of three different ways of preventing heat loss. The insulating

material itself may be a poor conductor. Wood and glass fiber are of this nature. The material may be in finely divided state and the minute air pockets separating the particles will prevent heat transfer. Or the material may be reflective and turn back heat as a paper-thin layer of metal foil does. Reflective materials likewise act as vapor barriers to prevent moisture condensation within the walls or seepage from the ground.

Double-glazed windows are insulated because of the small air pocket between the panes. This air space has been dehydrated and sealed. After sunset it is well to provide additional insulation against the loss of heat to the outdoors by traverse draperies. These may be of a material, such as wool, which has insulating properties. Some materials have heat reflective backing.

Once we are certain that heat cannot escape, then we begin to think about heating during cold weather. Natural heat sources should be used whenever possible. This is where solar heating is

Figure 19. This house of ten foot modular steel structure clearly expressed has used this measure to create a quiet, spacious rhythm in its interior.

Residence of: Mr. and Mrs. Ben Rose, Highland Park, Illinois. **Designer:** A. James Speyer. **Architect:** George E. Danforth, A.I.A., Cleveland, Ohio. **Photographer:** Tom Yee, New York. **Courtesy: Record Houses of 1956,** F. W. Dodge Corporation, New York.

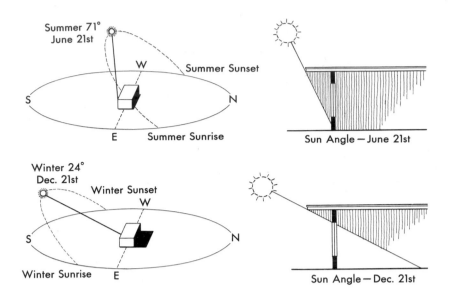

Summer 71°
June 21st

W   Summer Sunset

S   N

E   Summer Sunrise

Sun Angle—June 21st

Winter 24°
Dec. 21st   Winter Sunset
                         W

S   N

Winter Sunrise   E

Sun Angle—Dec. 21st

Figure 20. The angle made by the direct rays of the sun in relation to a building differs with the seasons. The structure should be planned to utilize solar heat in the winter and to shut it out in the summer. This diagram illustrates a situation in the northern hemisphere.

important because the sun is the great source of free heat. It heats by radiation. Radiant energy in the band known as infrared carries the most intense heat. These heat waves easily travel through double-glazed windows. Not all radiant energy waves carry such intense heat. The rays of low heat intensity which may be present in the heated air in a room may not be sufficiently strong to escape outwards through these very same windows. Hence large double-glazed windows, if properly oriented to catch all of the infrared rays of the sun, become a great channel for trapping heat.

How can a structure be planned to secure the benefits of solar radiation? Large windows should face the sun. In the northern hemisphere such windows should face south. Inasmuch as the sun rides high in summer [6] and low in winter, the eaves outside these large windows can be designed to permit the sun to sweep a room in winter and to miss it in the summer. When a building is only one room wide it is possible to receive the benefit of this low winter sun across the width of all the rooms in the house. Eaves can be designed which are made of individual lattices which will be as effective in regulating the flow of radiant energy as a solid eave would

[6] About 60° above the horizon in the summer and 30° above the horizon in the winter in Latitude 40° N.

be. A heavy concrete floor is an aid to solar heating because it acts as a reservoir to store heat.

As a corollary to the do's of solar heating there are also a few don'ts in the picture. North windows and those which face northeast or northwest are useless for solar heating. Therefore it is not wise to open up these areas to large expanses of glass. Moreover in the summer the rising and setting sun hangs low in the east and west for a long period of the day. Windows in these orientations will let in much unwanted heat and cannot be sufficiently protected by eaves or awnings.

Solar heating can only be used as a partial heating system. It must be supplemented in most climates by mechanical heating equipment. Such equipment may be classified according to the source of heat, i.e., the fuel which it uses. This may be coal, oil, gas, electricity, solar radiation, or even, in some newly experimental work, the inner temperature of the earth itself. Each heat source will necessitate its own mechanical equipment which should be carefully installed and maintained. All furnaces today come in comparatively neat packages and can be operated with a minimum of labor. The type of fuel chosen does not therefore greatly influence the structure in plan, or design.

Systems for transmitting heat do have some relation to plans. For instance, hot air and hot water heating systems are very economical, but are most effective in a compact building with a basement. Both systems may be used in larger areas if the heat is forced through the pipes. Heat conveyed by steam is used in many large installations.

One of the newer types of heat transmitting systems (the principle, however, was used by the Romans) is known as a panel heating system. In this system large portions of the room surface are heated to relatively low temperatures rather than small portions of the room being heated to relatively high temperatures. This heat is usually transmitted by hot water or steam which flows through coils in the floor, ceiling, or baseboard. By heating large areas in an insulated space the heat radiates from hot surfaces to cooler ones until an equilibrium is established. All objects and persons in the space share this even temperature.

Panel heating has many obvious advantages. In the first place no heating apparatus is visible. Also there is no dirt which is thrown up on the wall in the path of rising air currents. When the floor is a heated panel it becomes a warmer, safer place for children to play. Room temperatures are evenly distributed and there should be no drafts. Although this system is expensive to install, especially in old buildings, it is well suited to the house without a basement. The saving incurred by not digging a basement may offset the installation costs of the panel heating. It is very economical to operate.

Summer cooling is likewise the task of climate control. The building itself can help this project. Good insulation is as important to summer cooling as it is to winter heating because it prevents heat passage. Old masonry and adobe houses are deliciously cool in summer.

Planting provides evaporative cooling. Trees shading the south side of a house should be deciduous so that they will not screen the winter solar heat. Southern terraces should be of medium lightness in tone. A light terrace will reflect heat whereas a dark one will absorb and hold too much heat. Light toned roofing is advisable in order to reflect heat. Solar windows should have properly designed overhangs. Screens which have small reflective metal openings are of value in turning back the sun's rays.

The use of convection currents through ventilation is a desirable way to cool air. A building should be opened toward the prevailing cool breezes and there should be an opposite and somewhat higher opening for the escape of warm air.

Forced mechanical ventilation is frequently included in a ventilating system. Fans are the usual method of accomplishing this. They may be blow fans which stir up the existing air or exhaust fans which pull the hot air out of a space. Exhaust fans are customarily used in kitchens and baths. Many homes are equipped with exhaust fans at ceiling level. These pull the air from a ventilator placed near ground level up into an attic or upper air chamber. Air chambers close to the roof should always be equipped with louvred ventilators which are located at opposite ends of the space. Such openings not only serve to create a wash of moving air through the space and thus prevent pockets of warm air; they likewise carry off the moisture which accumulates with trapped warm air. Breathing vents are useful to prevent moisture damage in insulated walls.

When temperatures soar above ninety, the climate control afforded by the building should be supplemented by mechanical cooling. This machinery operates on the same principle as refrigerated food storage units. The cost of mechanical air cooling is moderate when the building is properly planned and when the system is used only in severe heat.

Fresh air intakes are necessary and cleansing the incoming air is good. Air may be introduced through a fine mesh filter or through a water spray. Electrostatic cleansers are often used in industry.

It is important to give air the proper moisture content. Air may take on moisture from passage over a spray. Cooking vapors, baths, and washing add moisture to the atmosphere of a small house. The problem is more liable to be that of dehumidifying the indoor air. All moisture producing apparatus, such as driers, should be vented. The suggestions under ventilation apply also to this problem. Chemicals of an absorbent nature can be used in attic and basement spaces. Cooling the air and removing the moisture at the place where it is cooled is a part of summer air

Residence: in Shaker Heights, Ohio. **Architect:** Ernst Payer, A.I.A., Cleveland, Ohio. **Photographer:** C. W. Ackerman, Cleveland, Ohio.

Residence of: Mr. and Mrs. James Kelso, Ken Woodlands, California. **Architect:** Wurster, Bernardi and Emmons, Architects, San Francisco, California. **Interior Designer:** Maurice Sands, San Francisco, California. **Photographer:** Roger Sturtevant, San Francisco, California. **Courtesy:** **Record Houses of 1956,** F. W. Dodge Corporation, New York.

Residence of: The architect, Moreland Hills, Ohio. **Architect:** Ernst Payer, A.I.A., Cleveland, Ohio. **Photographer:** C. W. Ackerman, Cleveland, Ohio.

conditioning and a principle of some mechanical dehumidifiers.

Climate control today affords more than just winter heat. Its equitable environment makes possible the use of many fragile materials which were heretofore prohibitive in upkeep. Likewise it should aid our comfort and health.

2. Sound Conditioning

Small quarters, open planning, thin walls, and much use of glass has made it necessary to pay especial attention to sound conditioning.

Sounds are caused by longitudinal wave-like vibrations of an elastic material medium such as the air. Because it is difficult to illustrate longitudinal impulses, sounds are usually illustrated as though they were transverse waves like those of the sea. The wave is set up by the vibration of a taut, thin, nonporous material such as that of our vocal chords. Materials which are similar to the original broadcasting material transmit sound easily. Flexible but inelastic, thick, porous materials absorb sound. Rigid, thick, nonporous materials reflect the waves.

Undesirable sound is called noise. Noise is sound which is too intense, out-of-place, or of poor quality. These three conditions are closely interconnected. The sound of the neighbor's

Figure 21. Planning for audio-visual equipment is important.

In top installation, the 170-pound television set sits on a plywood platform fastened to a turntable which in turn rests on a drawer. The drawer slides on double extension guides with nylon rollers. Under the center of the turntable on the underside of the drawer is a pivoted carriage which has two grooved steel wheels which run on the top edge of a 1/4 inch thick swinging bracket of boiler plate. This, fastened to the side of the reinforced walnut cabinet, actually carries the weight of the set.

Center installation shows a view of a family room with the television equipment adjacent to the fireplace, thus making possible one center of interest.

In bottom installation, 2 loud speakers are placed 16 feet center to center, above a curved light cove. A 20 inch diameter speaker is set into the top of the storage wall to the left of the portrait, directing sound at a 30° angle against the low ceiling and toward the living room. The volume of all of the speakers is individually controlled from the hi-fi set housed in the cabinet which stands against the storage wall. The cabinet also contains a record player.

radio, no matter how good the music, is out-of-place when it intrudes into our bedroom. The sound of our own children playing may be desirable even though intense.

Despite the relative nature of the psychological reactions to sound, we know that sound which is too intense can inflict bodily damage, fray the nerves, and create emotional disturbances. Too little sound can be depressing. A guide for gauging the ideal tolerance level for homes is a level where an average whisper can be heard four feet away.[7]

The sound level in and around a building can be controlled by construction and isolation. It is suggested that two hundred feet should separate a dwelling from a very busy street. Foliage is a very effective baffle against noise. The building itself should be on a firm structure. Machinery should be selected which operates quietly. Noisy apparatus may be mounted on shock absorptive blocks. The building should be planned so that quiet areas are well insulated from those where noise originates.

In addition to exerting some control upon the intensity of sound, a structure should facilitate the creation of good quality sounds. This is done by providing conditions which will accurately render the intensity, pitch, and timbre of the waves. Intensity correlates with the amplitude of a wave or displacement from a median position. Pitch corresponds to the frequency[8] of a vibration and timbre is modification by the smaller waves known as overtones which a long wave carries in its train.

These qualities of sound can be impaired by the way in which sound is reflected from the surfaces of a room. Sound waves bounce off surfaces like a rubber ball. Each time they bounce back some of the impetus is absorbed. Finally the vibrations are completely stilled. The time required for this to happen is called the time of

[7] Two sources have been referred to for data used in this section: American Public Health Association, Committee on the Hygiene of Housing, *Construction and Equipment of the Home, Control of Noise* (Chicago: Public Administration Service, 1951), pp. 33–48. Ramsey and Sleeper, *Architectural Graphic Standards* (4th ed., New York: John Wiley & Sons, Inc., 1948), pp. 301–302.

[8] It is more customary to refer to sound in terms of frequency and light in terms of wavelength.

reverberation. Its length has a great effect upon the quality of the sound. If it is too long the sound seems muffled. If it is too short the sound seems harsh. The placement and amount of sound absorptive material in relation to reflective material in a room in relation to the size of a room regulates this. Soft draperies, pile carpets, porous ceilings, cloak closets which are full of soft garments—all of these things are useful in absorbing sound.

The quality of sound is impaired if the reflected sound waves coincide in certain rhythms with the incident waves. To prevent this the walls of rooms which are intended for musical uses are frequently not parallel. Sound may be directed towards a live wall (sound reflective) and sent back to a dead wall (sound absorptive). Flexible treatment, such as is afforded by soft traverse draperies, may be required when audiences vary in size.

The ways we live are different from the ways people lived in other times, and this perforce alters the premise from which the architects begin designing, and thus affects the ultimate solution.

KATHERINE MORROW FORD
and THOMAS H. CREIGHTON *

Chapter IV

FUNCTIONAL PLANNING OF INTERIORS

A. FITNESS TO PURPOSE

A design can express many things. As a building exists for a use, its design should herald that use. This is second only to designing the building for performance.

It requires a disciplined mind to appreciate both of these qualities. The observer must analyze purposes, means of solution, and sensuous expression. Fitness, suitability, and appropriateness are not universally recognized. The designer must add visual artistry without destroying the practical and meaningful values. To a mature taste beauty and function are married and they speak happily to each other.

B. SPACE AND ITS USES

It is not within the possibilities of this text to analyze the functions of all buildings. A dwelling house is one of the most important and complex

* From **The American House Today** by Katherine Morrow Ford and Thomas H. Creighton. Copyright 1951, Reinhold Publishing Corporation, and reprinted by permission of the publisher.

buildings in any civilization. We will concentrate our attention on it and anticipate that some of our conclusions will have more general application.

A house is made to provide the best possible environment for living, usually for group or family living.[1] The physical well-being of the occupants must be considered first because life is dependent upon it. Primarily a house must provide space in which to exist. The American Public Health Association[2] suggests 400 square feet of house space as desirable for one person, 750 square feet for two, 1,000 square feet for three, 1,150 square feet for four, and 1,400 square feet for five.

What must this space provide? First it must provide shelter from predatory animals or human beings and from inimical weather and climate. It must provide safety from unnecessary physical hazards. This is the negative side of its function. We expect more than this from a house. We expect positive provisions for light, sanitation, and climate control. We may go further in planning our environment. We may plan for optimal sound conditions. In the disposition of spaces we can provide for making the work of the house easy. This work sometimes goes under the prosaic title of housekeeping. It is usually more than that—it is family-keeping. The family is the social unit that is charged with the responsibilities of nurturing the young and of caring for the old. It likewise has the responsibility of helping the interdependent sexes. This is all included in the work of family-keeping. The space of the house must provide for this work.

A house must provide the means for man's spiritual as well as his physical life. The two are strangely interdependent. When the husband returns home tired from a day's work he should feel that it is good to be home. The next day should find him revitalized for his activities. Life should seem to have more worth to all members of the household. This re-creation is compounded of food, sleep, and spiritual inspiration. The house is an artifact which should be judged with respect to its ability to provide an environmental background for this.

The mind looks inward and outward for incentive. Many is first an introvert. Every man must learn to develop his inward strength. Each must do this in his own way. One finds help in books, another in music, another in creative activities. A house should provide opportunity for each inhabitant to pursue his invigorating interest. If this were supplied there would be fewer men postponing retirement because there is nothing at home for them to do and fewer women wanting to get away from home because it is so full of drudgery.

Man is also an extrovert. A house must provide for some of his social activities. The house is a social artifact which can help its household to gain from and give to the rich treasures of friendship.

C. THE CHANGING CHARACTER OF THE HOUSEHOLD

Houses are planned for people. The American household has decreased in size remarkably during the last one hundred and fifty years. Likewise the number of children per household has become fewer.[3] Although this trend may have been altered since the last census, there is every indication of demand for houses to accommodate the single person, the couple, and two- and three-child family.

Not only has the average family grown smaller through the years but any one individual family household changes in character during its years. It is small at the beginning and increases in size with the years. It frequently cares not only for children but ultimately for an older generation. Finally there usually comes a time when the household is again small and the house which had been bulging at the seams becomes sparsely occupied.

---

[1] The *family* is defined by the U.S. Bureau of Census as a group of two or more persons living together and related by blood, marriage, or adoption. A *household* is defined as the entire group of persons who occupy a separate living quarter.

[2] American Public Health Association, Committee on the Hygiene of Housing, *Planning the Home for Occupancy* (Chicago: Public Administration Service, 1950), p. 36.

[3] American Public Health Association, Committee on the Hygiene of Housing, *op. cit.*, p. 4.

D. PLANNING THE HOUSE

Structure has provided the means of securing a house. The plan dictates the way in which it functions in our lives. Structure is concerned with the material mass. Plan is concerned with spaces and their interrelations. The plan arranges the interior so that it will serve the purposes, both physical and psychological, for which it was created.

1. Cost

Structure dictates the practical potentialities of house building and hence of planning. It is, however, the economy of the mid-twentieth century which regulates both structure and planning. The cost of buying and maintaining habital space is the limiting factor. Most households want to live as well as they can afford. They are ingenious in getting the best living out of all kinds of situations. A family that is in the middle class bracket today can live as nicely as one similarly situated in the past. But the present family will occupy smaller space. Enclosed space today costs a great deal to buy and to maintain. Therefore this generation must plan its house differently.

One way of computing house costs is to figure the square footage of the enclosed space and then to telephone the local Home Builders Association,[4] builder, or architect and ask for an estimate of square footage costs. Naturally this figure is an average. It will differ with the section of the country and will certainly differ in relation to the elaborateness of the building. The current average in the North Central states is between sixteen and eighteen dollars per square foot with unheated garage costs averaging from one-third to one-half this amount. This estimate does not include the cost of the lot which as a suggested rule should not exceed twenty percent of the house cost.

The shape of the house will bear a relation to its cost. In general a rambling dwelling will cost more than a compact one because it has more

---

[4] An affiliation of firms engaged in the house building industry. The purpose of the association is to seek ways of building better houses and to effect economy in their building. There are over two hundred such associations throughout the country.

square feet of wall and roof per cubic feet of interior. However, this cost may be offset by the gain made by not digging a basement. The one story house is particularly suited to panel floor heating. Nevertheless basic shapes like the square, the rectangle, the L or H shape are most economical. Excessive deviation from a simple shape plan should be avoided for functional, economic, and design reasons.

2. The Complete Space Picture

The complete planning for a house should include thought for the community in which it is located and thought for the site upon which it is placed. The community through its definite zoning laws and through its suggested character becomes one of the dictators of the form of the dwelling. It is important for every intelligent person to consider a community from all of its aspects before becoming a householder in it. It is likewise important that, once he has joined a community, he should cooperate in seeing that its planning is intelligent, wisely permissive rather than unwisely restrictive, and that its standards are maintained.

The house site is important. What values are obtained from personal ownership of land? It provides private outdoor space and the isolation of a building. Land expenditure can also be justified because it improves the appearance of the house and of the community. It is a very generous custom to reserve some of our property to give pleasure to persons beyond our household. Except for this public beautification area a lot is purchased for private needs. In modern planning the house and lot are the subject of coordinated designing.

3. The Effect of Space Limitations on Planning

A house today must conserve space in every possible way. Outdoor and indoor space should be wisely used. No space should be wasted.

What is waste space? The parlor of our great grandparents which was opened only on formal occasions, we label waste space. A careful study of the society of their day will show us how useful this reserved space was in their lives. Space is only wasted if it serves no physical or psychological function.

The modern planner eliminates unusable space. Space which is unused because it is uncomfortable becomes expensive waste space. The modern planner attempts to eliminate rooms which are too hot for use in summer or too cold in winter. He objects to unfinished space unless it is serviceable for storage.

The modern builder considers the structural economy of space as essential. Post and beam construction, the use of the cantilever principle, the use of thin plywood walls—these are a few of the structural expedients used to conserve interior space. Built-in furniture is planned in the interest of space conservation.

The planner likewise thinks in terms of mechanical economy of space. He will plan for the most compact machinery units which are available.

Flexible and multiple use of space is part of the program. Flexible partitions, multipurpose furniture, flexible furniture arrangements, the provision for ample storage—these help in making space available for several uses. A small space is in general more useful if it is not cut up into too small rooms.

Space saving is closely related to energy saving. There is a correlation between the size of enclosed space, the function for which it is intended, and the energy required to maintain it so that it can function. A neat adjustment of these factors must be considered. Service, whether human or mechanical, costs money. A big house certainly requires energy to service but a small house is not always easy to maintain. It is the planner's job to adjust the procurable space to the family's needs so that service cost is kept low. This is saving space through work conditioning.

4. Planning Considerations: Planning for Personalities

The initial approach to house planning should be personality planning. Each of us has a unique contribution to make to life. In order to develop his resources each person makes individual requests of a house. The first step in planning is to assemble these requests.

At this stage neglect the obvious things that we expect a house to do and concentrate upon the dreams of what we wish it to do. A mother may want a view from the kitchen window and forget to ask for a laundry. Father may ask for a workshop and forget to ask for a place to eat. Perhaps all of these desires cannot be fulfilled. A reasonable psychological substitute should be obtained if a house is to be a home.

This kind of personality planning gives us at first a somewhat chaotic picture. It might look something like this.

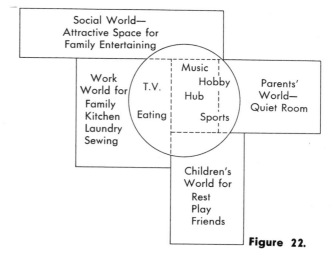

Figure 22.

5. Planning Considerations: Planning for Functions

Having thought about the house as the place where the household enjoys being, we turn to consider the various functions of the building in terms of the activities which it must accommodate. These break down into two categories: the major activities which the household needs and wishes for its physical and spiritual recreation, and the service activities which are not ends in themselves but which exist for the purpose of expediting major activities. Many activities fall at times into both categories. For instance, gardening may augment the food supplies of the household and it may likewise be an enjoyable end in itself.

The list of activities may look like this although there will be different emphases in different households. The following list is merely suggestive and will not be complete for all households.

A. Major Activities
1. Private family
   a. Physical
      (1) sleeping and dressing
      (2) personal cleanliness and sanitation
      (3) care of infants, sick and infirm
      (4) eating
   b. Spiritual
      (1) reading
      (2) writing
      (3) hobby interests: sewing, woodworking, painting, gardening, etc.
2. Social, both physical and spiritual
   a. Dining
   b. Recreation: music, television, conversation, provision for house guests, etc.

B. Service Activities
1. Communication within and to the house
   a. public deliveries
   b. social entering
   c. family entering
   d. movement between various areas of house
   e. audio communication to and within house
2. Storage
3. Housework
   a. food preparation and service
   b. laundry
   c. housecleaning
   d. operation of utilities: heat, water, etc.
   e. care of grounds
   f. car servicing
   g. productive industry: sewing etc.

This kind of analysis gives us a first intimation of the orientation of the various areas. We will probably assign the space which is most pleasantly located to the major activities and the choicest parcel will be allocated to the social activities because these are shared by the greatest number of people. Service areas are planned to be attractive but they are not usually given the best in view, breeze, or sun.

Planning for function will proceed from this point to decisions about the best size of the space required for each activity and the choice and arrangement of the essential equipment.

6. Planning Considerations: Planning for Coordination

The planning for the various functional activities in a household dictates more than the pleasantness of their locations and the suitability of the allotted space and of the equipment to use. One aspect of such planning is so important that it should be given a great deal of attention: this is the interrelation between the various functional areas of a house. A house is filled with people doing things. It is an alive organism. Space and time must be coordinated with these human movements.

The first step in planning for good correlation is to plan so that no space need function at the expense of any other space. For instance, a bedroom is sometimes used as a powder room for callers. A living room is frequently used for a social conversation group. If the bedroom is placed on the diagonal corner from the entrance to the living room then the social grouping is interfered with by the guest who must go from the entrance to the bedroom in order to lay off wraps. This is poor planning for coordination.

Good planning for coordination will consider flexibility in the use of space and equipment quite critically. An analysis of activities will be made to see if any of them make similar space and equipment demands. If they do not make the same time demands, then they may be coordinated in use. A dining space adjacent to a living area may make it possible to collapse dining furniture and to use the entire space at times for entertainment.

Coordination planning likewise implies an analysis of the movements of persons in a household as they go about their daily activities. If any one person's activities must be in various locations, those locations should be so placed as to expedite the activity. If a maid must be involved in preparing meals and in answering the door, the stove and the door should not be too far apart.

Lastly, good coordination planning means that the functioning spaces in a house are so interrelated that the engineer, or manager, or coordinator can control the household activities easily.[5]

In a house where the mother does most of the work the planning for good coordination may result in some such organization as the following figure. The plan may be quite unorthodox.

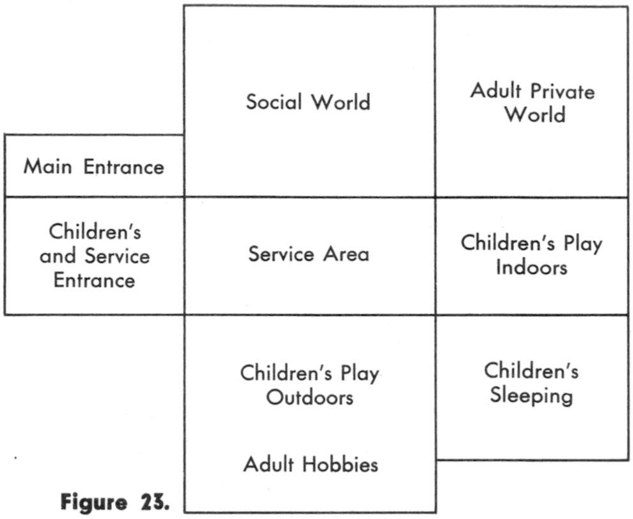

	Social World	Adult Private World
Main Entrance		
Children's and Service Entrance	Service Area	Children's Play Indoors
	Children's Play Outdoors	Children's Sleeping
	Adult Hobbies	

Figure 23.

7. Planning Considerations: Planning for Design

After planning a house from all possible functional angles, then the designer must correlate his functional design with his visual design. A consideration of this will be the purpose of the next five chapters. Certain factors which are particularly tied up with the plan should be mentioned here.

In the first place the plan of any building should dictate a shape that is related harmoniously to the landscape. A high formal house on a low rambling hillside would seem out of place.

A building is a work of time-space art and should be ordered in these sets of dimensions. It should have its routing clearly expressed. Paths, corridors, and stairs should beckon. When they lead to several areas they should relate them in the order of their functional importance.

A good piece of time-space art will evolve its visual pleasures in time. The complete interior space will not be revealed at once. By means of the plan, the builder should help us to have an inter-

[5] This is discussed further under Housework, p. 51.

esting visual trip through space. It is possible to have such an experience in well planned formal as well as informal houses. When a house is very limited in size it is, of course, almost impossible to plan for such a visual excursion. When the architecture must be very restricted then the furnishings may be planned with special care to provide a time-space experience.

A visually well designed house will always present a pleasingly designed space to view no matter where a person stands. It is unfortunate, for instance, if a front door is faced closely by a wall unless there is a glimpse of an interesting space beyond.

House planning, we then see, is space designing. A good house plan should have such simplicity and logic that it will result in well designed spaces, suited to use. Through this coalition a plan is capable of expressing certain qualities. It can inaugurate an expression of formality or informality, graciousness, hospitality, and withal a degree of aloofness.

E. FINAL DETAIL PLANNING

The best planning solutions are the simplest. This simplicity is only attained after giving certain attention to the interrelation of functions in a manner that is economically, practically, psychologically, and visually satisfactory. Inasmuch as solutions have always differed with time, place, and cultural circumstances, the considerations presented under final detail planning must be related to these variables.

1. The Service Areas

The planner should make sure that all work areas have a fundamentally sound layout. This means that service areas should be planned to perform their particular service with the greatest possible economy of human energy.

a. COMMUNICATION ROUTES

Communication routes are the passageways through which movements into and within a building occur. Efficient circulation routes are direct and economical of space and they should not cut across any other functioning area. They should not appear cramped.

Figure 24. A gracious home has solved the problem of associating children's activities and the amenities of family and social life by coordination around a central service area.

Photographer (living room): Lionel Freedman, New York.

Residence of: Mr. and Mrs. Charles Hickox, Pepper Pike Village, Ohio. **Architect:** Robert A. Little and Associates, Architects, Cleveland, Ohio. **Courtesy: House & Garden,** Copyright 1955, The Condé Nast Publications, Inc. **Photographer** (service areas): Andre Kertesz, New York.

The first communication area is the public, social entrance to the house. This should be the most accessible approach. It should be easier for the guest to reach this door than to reach any other door. Many of our friends arrive in cars. Therefore a social entrance should be placed adjacent to an adequate parking area. Many houses have attractive entrance courts which combine parking facilities, covered walk, and main doorway. The social entrance opens upon the main artery of the house. The social entrance should be readily accessible from the kitchen and may have telephone connections with other parts of the building.

A service entrance should be clearly indicated. It should be easily accessible from the street or drive but should not command as desirable a location as the social entrance. The path to the service entrance should not cut across any outdoor living area. The service entrance should lead directly to the main service areas of the house such as the kitchen, laundry, basement, and drying yard.

A household with automatic washer and dryer, automatic heat, incinerator, and similar apparatus is fast becoming a self-contained unit. For mail and parcel delivery the main social entrance is most frequently used. Therefore a service entrance is deprived of some of its former functions and is frequently combined today with what is called a family entrance. This entrance connects the house to the garage. It is generally off the entrance court but is beyond the main entrance. This family entrance may lead into a passage from which routes lead to the service space, cloak rooms, and eventually to the principal corridor. In country houses this family entrance may be closely connected to wash rooms and to storage space for muddy clothes. Near the sea it is often adjacent to dressing and shower rooms for bathers.

The principal entrance will of course open into the main thoroughfare of the house. When this thoroughfare cannot be separate from the living areas, then it is very important to see that the passage way does not cut across space which is reserved for conversational groups. Any corridor space should preferably cut directly across the short side of the living space.

Social routing is first to a reception area, a cloak room, the major social areas, the various dining areas (with heed for outdoor dining), and the minor social areas such as the hobby rooms. Some provision should be made for shielding the complete living quarters and dining areas from the immediate view of one entering the doorway. This protects the living space from any inclement weather and protects the occupants from intrusion by the caller who comes on some momentary errand. It is usually best to have the kitchen areas at least partially concealed from the view of anyone in the principal corridor.

The routes leading to the private areas of a household can be quite separate from the social corridors, if the private areas are never used by a guest. This complete isolation, however, is seldom practical. Some isolation is always advisable and should be planned for. In some contemporary plans the bedrooms open onto a larger space which is frequently called a family room or "shirt sleeve" living room. Again caution that two antithetical functions cannot occupy the same space at the same time is in order. A corridor is not so much useless space. It functions for movement. If a family room is strewn with children's toys and the family's effects, for instance, it becomes a hazardous area to use as a hall.

SIZES OF CIRCULATION AREAS

	Minimum	Average
Width Hall	3′ (2 persons)	4′
Entrance Hall	4′–6″ × 4′–6″	5′ × 7′

Communication areas should not be encumbered with equipment. A shelf or small table for the temporary placement of packages and mail is a help, however. A waterproof flooring near the door with facilities for handling rainy weather togs is good. A stool, chair, or bench may prove useful.

b. STORAGE

1) Types

A house without adequate provision for storage is not really useful. It is no more efficient than the nomad's tent in providing for the needs of

Figure 25. A well considered plan where the two control centers, the kitchen and storage-hobby shop, are not too far apart. Play yard, family room, and children's bedrooms can be supervised. Laundry is placed close to bedrooms.

Residence of: Mr. Ralph Sherman, Boise, Idaho. **Architect:** Grider and La Marche, Architects, A.I.A., Boise, Idaho. **Builder:** Ralph Sherman. **Decoration:** Sherm Perry. **Courtesy: Living for Young Home-makers,** Copyright, January, 1959, **Photographer:** Dearborn-Massar, New York.

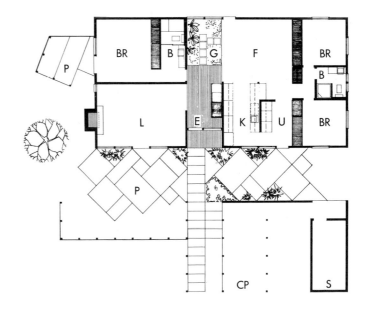

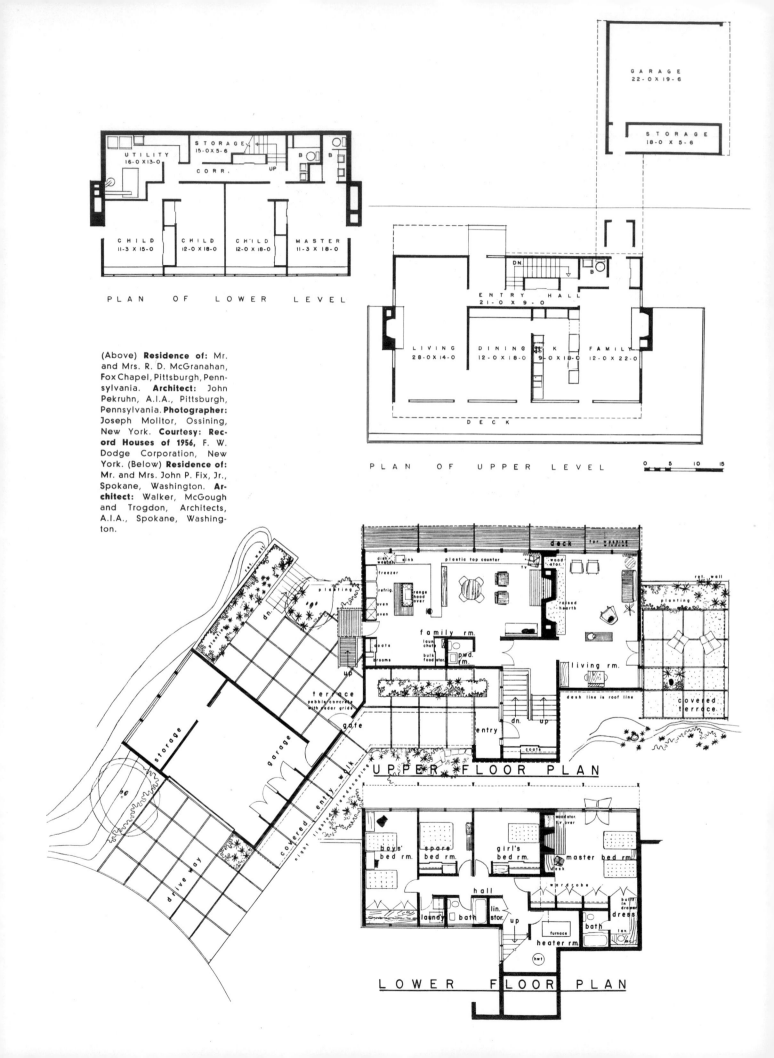

UTILITY
16-0 X 13-0

STORAGE
15-0 X 5-6

CORR.

UP

CHILD
11-3 X 15-0

CHILD
12-0 X 18-0

CHILD
12-0 X 18-0

MASTER
11-3 X 18-0

PLAN OF LOWER LEVEL

GARAGE
22-0 X 19-6

STORAGE
18-0 X 5-6

DN.

ENTRY HALL
21-0 X 9-0

LIVING
28-0 X 14-0

DINING
12-0 X 18-0

K
9-0 X 18-0

FAMILY
12-0 X 22-0

DECK

PLAN OF UPPER LEVEL

0 5 10 15

(Above) **Residence of:** Mr. and Mrs. R. D. McGranahan, Fox Chapel, Pittsburgh, Pennsylvania. **Architect:** John Pekruhn, A.I.A., Pittsburgh, Pennsylvania. **Photographer:** Joseph Molitor, Ossining, New York. **Courtesy: Record Houses of 1956**, F. W. Dodge Corporation, New York. (Below) **Residence of:** Mr. and Mrs. John P. Fix, Jr., Spokane, Washington. **Architect:** Walker, McGough and Trogdon, Architects, A.I.A., Spokane, Washington.

UPPER FLOOR PLAN

LOWER FLOOR PLAN

our twentieth century household. Civilization began when it became possible to keep the treasures of the past and to store for the future. Both storage of supplies and storage of sources of knowledge facilitated the advancement of learning.

The modern dwelling needs storage space for many types of articles. In the first place it needs storage which frees space for different kinds of use. Card tables and chairs may be brought out for a card party at the same time that collapsible furniture is put away to make room for the tables. A list of the occasional use furnishings which a household may wish to store should be made.

Every household stores some supplies and movable equipment which are used to service its present possessions. Mops and the vacuum cleaner, for example, are such servicing equipment.

Some storage is planned merely in the interest of providing the best kind of care for a family's soilable possessions. Silverware is placed in chests which are compartmentalized and lined with a tarnishproof felt. Storage care of this sort must be provided for.

Some storage is planned to help a household provide for its future. Almost all seasonal equipment may be so considered. In addition a household gives thought to other foreseeable needs. The old-time vegetable cellar may be gone but the large-sized freezer is with us.

All of the types of articles so far considered for

Figure 26.

(Above) This house is well planned for family living and for more formal entertaining. The kitchen is not only the control point for the children's activities, it likewise is so placed as to permit expansion of operations into the family area when used by a catering staff. The laundry is placed on the bedroom level to reduce transportation. Views of this house appear in Figures 48, 82, and 84b.

(Below) This residence built on a rocky hillside was designed for a family with four young children. The major living areas open to a handsome view over the city. The children's play corner is adjacent to the kitchen and service door. The laundry is near the bedrooms.

storage have supplied some physical need in the lives of the household. There is also call for storage of articles which fulfill an emotional need. Our modern civilization is apt to deplore the preservation of belongings for sentimental reasons. We have adopted this attitude from the necessity for space saving and because the nineteenth century seems to have overindulged in romantic preservation of keepsakes. The value of this kind of article to a household bears no relation to its intrinsic worth. Such mementos may vary from a child's broken toy to the rosepoint lace on grandmother's wedding gown. To criticize the storage of such articles within the household vaults is to criticize all attempts to revive the past and to establish continuity with it. Inasmuch as the animals alone are forced to live only in the present we would be foolish to limit ourselves to the immediacy of a similar existence. A proportional relation between past, present, and future is more desirable. Rightly used the modern counterpart of the attic may give our children the key to rich experience.

We store many articles in the household which help us to have a more varied and satisfying personal life. The household tokens to which we have just referred may serve this end in a purely associational way. Other objects are useful in more practical ways. This motley grouping of articles for family interests should have storage space.

Some articles of locomotive equipment help the household to take flight in a physical as well as a mental manner. These, too, must be stored.

It will be clearly seen that a listing such as the above indicates the various functions of storage in a household, but such a list must include articles in groups which are certainly not mutually exclusive. It is extremely difficult to classify storage needs. This does not mean that the equivalent of the old-time attic which could embrace all kinds of articles is the best solution to our storage requirements. Storage requirements are specialized.

2) Conditions

Various storage needs can be satisfied with space at different cost levels. Structural costs may be low. Walls can be nonload-bearing. Air con-

ditioning requirements of various storage spaces and their costs may differ. Storage space for summer furniture needs no heat. Storage for outer wraps in use does. Humidity control is essential for many articles.

The location of the storage space is important. It should be near the place where the article is to be used. When articles are to be used in several places it may be advisable to duplicate storage facilities. This might be true for storage of children's toys and cleaning supplies.

The frequency of use of the stored articles will be a certain clue to the location of their storage space. Things which are used only occasionally can certainly be placed farthest from the usual household activities. Articles for quick emergency use should be most accessible. Concealed locations are important for some valuables.

Within the allocated space, storage should be planned so that the article is readily accessible and the space is easily cleaned. Storage which is too high or too low for easy reach should be avoided for all but infrequently used articles. Storage which is too deep is likewise inefficient. It should not be necessary to remove one set of articles in order to reach another set.

Planned storage gives thought to the size of the article to be stored. It is uneconomical to plan a full room height closet and a five foot high garment pole in order to hang jackets, shirtwaists, skirts, and trousers. There are a number of references which give tables of standard sizes of everything from washcloths to phonograph records to trays.[6] In storage which is really designed

[6] Francis de N. Schroeder, *Anatomy for Interior Designers* (2nd ed.; New York: Whitney Pubs., 1951),

(A) **Building:** A vacation house. **Architect:** Robert A. Little and Associates, Architects, Cleveland, Ohio. **Photographer:** C. W. Ackerman, Cleveland, Ohio.

(B, C) **Building:** An apartment in Spokane, Washington. **Architect:** Walker, McGough and Trogdon, Architects, A.I.A., Spokane, Washington. **Photographer:** Morley Baer, Berkeley, California.

(D, E) **Residence of:** Dr. Constance M. McCullough, Berkeley, California. **Designer:** Paul Hamilton. **Artist:** "One Hundred Birds," Pien Wen Chin, Chinese Kakemono screen, Ming Dynasty. **Photographer:** Chris Kjobech, Oakland Tribune, Oakland, California.

(F) **Residence of:** Mr. and Mrs. C. K. Reynolds, Jr., Hudson, Ohio. **Photographer:** William A. Wynne, courtesy **Cleveland Plain Dealer**, Cleveland, Ohio.

well one should tailor the spaces to fit the stored
articles.

AVERAGE SIZES OF COMMON STORAGE AREAS

Space	Length	Depth	Height
Closet in bedroom	3'–0" per person	2'–6"	6' to 8'
Bookshelves and magazine shelves		9" to 12"	10" to 12" average shelf

c. HOUSEWORK

A home is an important workshop where several persons must carry on an industry which con-
sumes a lot of time.[7] Women and men are asking
for easier housekeeping because they realize that
better planning and better equipment can make
it possible.

In the usual household the woman does most
of the inside work and the man does most of the
outside work. The controlling locations for their
respective tasks should be near the kitchen and
garage-tool house respectively. Inasmuch as their
work sometimes overlaps and because a husband-
wife team usually enjoys working together (there
isn't much time to play together!), these control
centers in a servantless household should not be
too far apart.

Charles G. Ramsey and Harold R. Sleeper, *Architectural
Graphic Standards* (4th ed.; New York: John Wiley &
Sons, 1951).

[7] Nearly 40 hours a week in a home without children
with an increase of nearly 50% with the advent of the
first child. Frederick Gutheim, *Houses for Family Living* (New York: The Woman's Foundation, Inc., 1948),
p. 15.

Figure 27. The manner of food preparation
and dining may differ. Meals are nevethe-
less occasions for ceremony.

(A) Kitchen-dining arrangement in a vacation house in the Central United States.

(B, C) A partial separation of kitchen-
dining facilities is favored by many in the
Northwest. Some of the cooking is done
right in the dining room.

(D, E) A living room-dining area arrangement as seen in a California home.

(F) For many the separate dining room is
the answer.

Figure 28. Only those who have lived through it appreciate the amount of work which even today's mechanized housekeeping entails. A home is an important workshop. Space for equipment, and those involved in the activity should be carefully considered. The solution will differ with each household.

Residence of: Mr. and Mrs. Bruce M. Walker, Spokane, Washington. **Architect:** Walker, McGough and Trogdon, Architects, A.I.A., Spokane, Washington. **Photographer:** Morley Baer, Berkeley, California.

The housewife should be able to walk easily from the kitchen to the dining areas (indoor and out), the children's play areas and washrooms, the entrance doors, the laundry, and the sewing room. From the man's headquarters there should be easy access to the yard, the children's play areas, the heating apparatus, the incinerator, and to the family entrance with its nearby clean-up room.

Both of these work centers should be pleasant. The kitchen should have windows looking toward an attractive view. Many women are requesting a view to the living room from the kitchen. A hearth fire either in the living room or in the kitchen is a heartening sight on a chilly day. The television set may be a modern substitute. The man's headquarters should be equally attractive. Too frequently the man has divided his at-home time between the furnace room in the cellar and a dark garage in the rear of the lot. Bringing the basement workrooms and utility rooms upstairs and placing them adjacent to a space well designed for car service has been a forward step in planning.

In the woman's world the laundry was the erstwhile basement activity. Soiled clothes were sent from the second floor to the cellar, were brought up a flight of stairs to the drying yard from whence they might go downstairs again for ironing before they retraced their steps to the wardrobes in the various bedrooms. Mechanical dryers can eliminate the back yard trip and good planning can do away with many of the remaining steps. There is no reason today that a laundry need be in a basement. It should be near the kitchen (preferably not in it) so that the housewife can supervise operations in both centers. It should not be far from bedrooms, baths, and dining areas where soiled clothes come from and to which clean clothes must be returned.

It is obvious that in the planning of the work areas of a household the important question is: who does the work? Because of a revolution in our social structure the householder and housewife usually do their own work and this work must be done while caring for children. That is the reason that such planning coups as the combination of the various work areas with family living areas make sense. A house should work easily and play graciously. Each family must decide for itself whether it wishes to serve its meals and have some of its social life in an open kitchen, in a dining-living area or in a separate dining room. Some households operate with day help; some require assistants at all times. To the degree that a house is serviced by persons outside the family an isolation of the work area is desirable. If the household manager (the mother) must supervise the kitchen and laundry rather than work in it constantly, then a managerial space near the kitchen and adjacent to the playrooms may be needed. Where the housewife may do the cooking but have a laundress, a laundry in the basement is not amiss.

The amount of space which is required for these various work centers varies with the kind and amount of equipment used. The purchase of energy saving equipment is no luxury in our present day economy. It is just good common sense. Therefore houses which are built for sale in the general market are planned with work areas large enough to accommodate the necessary mechanical equipment.

AVERAGE SIZES OF WORK AREAS AND EQUIPMENT

Kitchen 9'-0" × 12'-0"

	Length	Depth	Height
Range — 4 burner with counter space	36" to 40"	25" to 30"	40" to 49"
Sink and dishwasher unit	48"	25" to 30"	36"
Refrigerator (10 cu. ft.)	34"	30"	65"

(Heat-producing equipment such as refrigerators should have clearance on all sides. This ranges from a minimum of 1" to a maximum of about 6" where surrounding walls are high.)

	Length	Depth	Height
Countershelf with cabinets above and below	96"	24" to 30"	36"
One counter with knee space below for sitting			30"
The smallest kitchenette	48"	25"	87"
Freezer (15 cu. ft.)	72"	38"	30"

Laundry 10'-0" × 10'-0"

	Length	Depth	Height
Automatic washer	2'-4"	2'-4"	3'-0"
Automatic dryer	2'-7"	2'-4"	3'-0"
Rotary ironer	2'-6"	1'-9"	2'-6"
Standard portable board	5'-0"	1'-4"	2'-6"
Sorting shelves	4'-6"	1'-6"	

Equipment may need 6" clearance from wall if plumbing cannot be located in wall.

Utility Room 4'-0" × 6'-0" Minimum

The utility room is the modern counterpart of the furnace room. It usually houses the air conditioning units, the hot water heater and may contain the garbage and rubbish disposal unit. The tendency in the manufacturing of these types of equipment is to design for maximum efficiency in minimum space.

TOOL ROOM AND GARAGE

	Length	Depth or Breadth
Size of average car	19'–7''	6'–10''
Size of average garage	21'–0''	12'– 0''
Size of average 2 car garage	21'–0''	18'– 0''
For large cars dimensions should be increased	2'–0''	1'– 0''
Garage door	9'–0''	
Workbench, 3' high		3'– 0''

In arranging equipment in a service center, production line technique should be observed. This means that the material should move in the direction of its processing with as little criss-crossing as possible and with no interference by traffic going to and from other areas.

In the food preparation center the equipment is best placed in a shape which approximates the letter U. Variations of this shape into one or two straight lines or into an elbow L may be necessary because of the architecture.[8] At least 2'–6'' empty floor space in a U shape, and 4' to 5' in a shape in which the space between counters is also used for passage should be allowed. This arrangement creates what is known as a work triangle between the refrigerator, sink, and stove. It gives enough space between the centers so that the worker can reach them easily but will not grow dizzy from making too many turns in a restricted area.

In sequence from the outside door the first unit is a storage center containing the refrigerator, closets for canned goods, and a work top for receiving and sorting supplies. Adjacent is a food preparation center, with cabinets for the utensils and staples required in food preparation. The sink follows because water is so essential to all food work.

The sink becomes the nucleus of the kitchen cleaning center. In elaborate plans a second sink is located in the area devoted to the storage of tableware (the butler's pantry). The washing of the cooking utensils is done at the one adjacent to the food preparation center. This sink is fre-

[8] The island kitchen where the major work units are concentrated in the center of the space, is used by many planners. This may free window walls and living areas. Production line sequence of equipment is as important here as in any other planning type.

quently located below a window for air and view. In many small houses this sink is used for such water as is needed for house cleaning. In some houses an extra sink and faucet is placed in the cleaning supplies storage space.

The cooking center is next in order. This should include the range and space for storage of the utensils used at the range. Lastly there should be a serving center because many foods go directly from the range to the serving dish. In some contemporary plans the different units of the range are dissociated, the grills are sunk in the counter top and the oven may be separately located in a wall unit. When the counter top is used as a pass-through shelf to the dining space, the cooking grills should not be located where they will conflict with the passage. The oven should not be located where it would be difficult to lift pans onto a serving counter space.

Many kitchen areas include a small informal spot for eating. These are variously known as breakfast rooms, lunch or snack bars, or dinettes. The best location for this space is between the cooking center and the dining room. It functions more pleasantly if it is on an outside wall. Located near the dining room it is a useful baffle for kitchen noise and sights. It can be well used as a space for setting out extra utensils and special courses such as a salad or dessert course for dinner. Storage of dining equipment may be in this place. One end of this space may be used for a pass-through shelf.

As dining in the modern house may be in several different areas, such as in an indoor and outdoor dining room and perhaps in a playroom, the kitchen work areas must be planned so that they will be conveniently located to all of these spots. Some juggling and even some compromise may be required in order to effect this.

Laundry equipment should be placed in the following order. First comes the receiving center, with its chute and hampers and sorting shelves. Next is the washing center which, in addition to the washer, may contain a hot plate for the heating of starch or special preparations. The drying center is adjacent to the washing center. This contains the dryer or wringer and drying lines. Last in order is the ironing and storage center. This may require a sprinkling counter, ironing equipment, racks for hanging some ironed articles, and shelf space for laying other articles. Sewing equipment for repair work is located here. This kind of production line technique in the placement of kitchen and laundry equipment should be followed in planning other work areas in a house.

2. The Major Activity Areas

a. SLEEPING AND DRESSING

The area primarily devoted to sleeping and dressing frequently must serve many functions. The bathroom, a private sitting room and a work area are usually part of this private apartment within the general confines of the house. With careful planning, provision can be made for these activities within quite limited space.

The sleeping quarters are best located on the quiet side of the house away from the street and from the service areas. Many people prefer an elevation above the ground floor for these areas. Early risers like an eastern orientation, late risers may prefer other locations.

The several sleeping areas are usually grouped together. Sometimes a room reserved for guests is isolated from the family sleeping rooms. This gives the guest a feeling of greater privacy. As the guest room may be flexible in its uses, a position near the main living quarters allows it to be used for general functions when not occupied by a house guest.

In the complex of bedrooms the relation of parents' to children's rooms must be carefully considered. When the children are very young the parents' room must be close to the child's. As children grow older greater isolation is desirable. This flexible sort of arrangement can sometimes be accomplished by the addition of doors to what were previously open passageways. A parents' room should be placed nearer than the child's room to the main circulation artery. Thus the parent is aware of the child's whereabouts and is in a position to be his guardian.

In considering the planning of the principal bedroom there are divided opinions arising from divergent reasoning. If the dressing area is considered to be a very private sanctum then it should be least accessible. When, however, it serves as a guest's powder room, it is then placed closest to the main hall. It is adjacent to the bath.

Certainly the sleeping compartment should be the most remote of the entire bedroom grouping. Unless complete air conditioning is supplied, it is advisedly placed where it will benefit from cross ventilation. On the other hand a space too near the windows often results in too much glare for sleeping. Moreover the window area is frequently reserved for a seating arrangement because of the light and view. The problem of regulating both light and ventilation without air conditioning is one which is difficult to solve, especially in warm climates. With complete air conditioning the expedient of planning sleeping cubicles grouped in the center of the house and soundproofed and lightproofed for the best sleeping conditions has been sensibly suggested.

As the household continues over the years there is inevitably the time when the sick and the infirm must be cared for. For this purpose a separate room near a bath and near help but out of the main line of traffic is ideal.

AVERAGE SIZES OF BEDROOMS

Small bunk room for child	8′–0″ × 8′–0″
Single bedroom	8′–0″ × 10′–0″
	9′–0″ × 12′–0″ to
	11′–0″ × 13′–0″
Double bedroom	10′–0″ minimum width
	12′–0″ × 14′–0″

The American Public Health Association recommends 74 square feet of bedroom area for one person and 148 square feet for two.[9]

The beds are the major articles of furnishing in a bedroom. It is convenient to have some sort of small table adjacent to the bed. Many modern bed headboards include provision for this table space in addition to accommodations for books, light and perhaps a radio. A bed with such a headboard requires extra length space. A low so-called slipper chair is frequently placed in a bedroom for convenience in dressing. A chest for clothes storage and a dressing table and bench

[9] American Public Health Association, Committee on the Hygiene of Housing, *op. cit.*, p. 36.

are usually included. Extras such as comfortable chairs and desk and chair may be added. A full-length mirror is desirable. A low folding rack for use for luggage should certainly be available. Some of this equipment may be built into the house and need not be provided as separate pieces.

Children's bedrooms should be equipped with furniture which is suited to children. As childhood is a rather temporary thing, such furniture should either be inexpensively produced or it should be flexible enough in use and permanent enough in structure to survive the growing and changing years. Closets with rod grooves at different heights, temporary wall finishes such as tackboard or blackboard, double bunk beds which can collapse into single beds, movable partitions which will isolate the bed sections from the larger play sections now and which will subdivide the space into separate rooms later, temporary storage shelves built at child height—these are all helps.

In the arrangement of bedroom furniture the position of the sleeping accommodations has already been considered.[10] The bed itself should be placed away from the wall for ease in servicing. The remaining furniture will be placed so as to perform its function. For example, mirrors should be placed where the light will fall on the face of the person in front of them, easy chairs should command views and light.

In small houses bedroom areas may need to be flexible in their uses. They frequently substitute for general living areas and for specific hobby areas. Equipment is on the market which aids this duality.

Although flexibility and attendant multiple use of bedroom space may at times be necessary, it should not be forgotten that the bedroom is the most private of man's castles. When the private areas of the home are made too public the mind is robbed of an inner retreat. A child's private sitting room often becomes his private study. It is noteworthy that the American Public Health Association recommends a separate bedroom from birth for each child. Two children of the same sex should not share a bedroom if there is an excessive age difference. Children of opposite

sex should have separate rooms if either is over six years old.[11] In other words there is every reason for giving a child the kind of surroundings for his private life which will help him to adapt to the standards which are customary in our society.

In contemporary planning a bedroom area is frequently integrated with its own private yard. The private porch or balcony is reappearing as an adaptation of this idea.

b. BATHS

Perhaps no feature of our houses has undergone more change during the short period of its existence than the bath with plumbing.

The most noticeable recent change has been in the increase in the number of separate baths provided in a house. The equivalent of two bathrooms is now found in many houses of 1000 square footage. An increasing number of houses in the $15,000 range now have two and one-half (wash basin, toilet) baths. When extra fixtures are added a double wash basin usually comes first, then a toilet and lastly a shower or tub. The priva-room, a combination bath and dressing room for each person is a probability in the near future.

The greatest expense in building baths is in the plumbing. Therefore baths should be grouped around central plumbing whenever possible. This has led to the compartment bath. A compartment bath should be carefully planned if it is to function well.

The functional relation of the bath areas to other areas of the house varies with the household. The first requirement is that the principal bathrooms should be near the bedrooms. It is becoming rather common to find two baths with entrances into the master bedroom. One is completely isolated from other rooms. The other may adjoin a children's room or even a guest room and should be accessible from the hall.

A bath area which is intended for use by the sportsman, the gardener, and the children during the day should be located near the service or family entrance to the house. This bath is also useful to the helpers of a family.

[10] See p. 55.

[11] American Public Health Association, Committee on the Hygiene of Housing, *op. cit.*, p. 40.

If there is only one first floor lavatory it should be placed so that it is accessible to the rear yard, the kitchen, and the living rooms. A position off a back corridor may be the solution. A bath should not be placed so that it is exposed to view from the main living areas or corridors. Nevertheless its position should be apparent.

AVERAGE SIZES OF BATHROOMS

Two fixture lavatories
  (wash basin, toilet)

$4'-0'' \times 4'-6''$ or $2'-6'' \times 5'-8''$

Powder rooms (wash basin,
  toilet, dressing table)

$4'-2'' \times 5'-6''$ or $4'-0'' \times 6'-5''$

Three fixture bathroom
  (wash basin, toilet, tub)

$5'-6'' \times 7'-1''$ or $5'-0'' \times 7'-8''$

Three fixture bathroom
  (wash basin, toilet, square tub)

$6'-5'' \times 6'-5''$ or $4'-0'' \times 8'-5''$

Three fixture bathroom
  (wash basin, toilet, shower)

$5'-4'' \times 5'-6''$ or $4'-0'' \times 7'-1''$

Four fixture bathroom
  (wash basin, toilet, tub, shower)

$6'-2'' \times 7'-6''$ or $5'-4'' \times 8'-0''$

SIZES OF BATHROOM FIXTURES

Shower	$3'-0'' \times 3'-0''$
Tub, rectangular	$5'-0'' \times 2'-7''$
Tub, square	$4'-0'' \times 4'-0''$
Wash basin	$2'-0'' \times 1'-8''$
Toilet	$2'-0'' \times 2'-6''$

c. PRIVATE RECREATION AREAS

The pendulum always swings back. The modern house planner is thinking in terms of two recreation areas. They may not be the erstwhile parlor and living room or even the living room and sun room combinations, but the separation of functions and of spaces exists.

The less formal of these twin areas will be planned around the family's leisure pursuits. For small children this is play suited to their age level. For the older years the recreation interests are as varied as personalities. Although the accent today is on creativity which is usually of an active kind, this may easily be overemphasized. The relaxed pace of James Whitcomb Riley's little boy who played aimlessly with summer at "noon time and June time down along the river" has been found to be psychologically sound. Therefore spaces intended for recreation need not be filled with specific equipment.

The location, size, and equipment of leisure areas will be as varied as the household's spare time pursuits. However, a general family recreation area may well be the one from which the more particularized areas stem. If a household does not center around children and if its unscheduled activities are on the quiet side, a family area is usually planned adjacent to the master bedroom suite. A library or study is frequently flanked by a more public living room on one side and is accessible to a bedroom on the other. Where children and more active enterprises are in the picture, the family areas (in a servantless house) are usually integrated with the service areas. Such an area may be adjacent to the children's bedrooms and be within easy access to the kitchen.

Quite specialized equipment may frequently necessitate the reservation of some space in addition to this general household room. Photographers and gardeners, for instance, preempt space which cannot be easily varied in use.

Outdoor space should be planned so that some of it can be used for family leisure interests. Children's leisure is all the time. Therefore a part of the lot should be devoted to their play. Pave some of the space for their wheeled toys. If their sandboxes and swings are covered and raised above such pavement they will be more useful after rains. Built up seats around such an area may open for storage of some of the children's outdoor tools and provide places off the ground for them to sit.

The area reserved for the general family recreation may serve in many different ways throughout the years. It may be a children's play space and parents' hobby space during the early years of family life. It may become a comfortable relaxation room for the parents of older children. There comes a time when older children want to entertain in the more formal living room and garden.

d. FOOD SERVICE AND EATING

Food service and eating are major activities in every household and some specialized space must be reserved for them. However, the eating habits of the American household are more diversified than they used to be, so it seems uneconomical to use too high a percentage of a small house's space for just one kind of more formal dining. Some of our meals are quick. These may be eaten near the food preparation centers. Some are more leisurely. These should occur where the atmosphere is less bustling. Summer meals, winter meals, morning and midnight repasts—each occasion brings its own conditions.

The location for dining should always be cheerful and should be given one of the best orientations in the house. This is frequently a southeast or southwest corner. The area should be semiprivate. Outdoor dining areas should be shielded from the street and neighboring lots. They should be sheltered from excessive sun and wind. A mesh screened enclosure is desirable protection from insects.

The main dining area is frequently adjacent to the more formal living area. In a small house this permits a visual increase in living room space. It also makes it possible to extend a dining table into the living room when necessary or to use the dining space for extra seating. Many planners prefer to separate the dining space from the living space by some sort of barrier, visual or physical. Often this is no more than a barrier caused by distance as when dining rooms are placed across a corridor or up a small flight of stairs or across a breezeway. This seems to lend a certain air of anticipation to "going to dine."

Certainly all dining areas must be conveniently located with respect to food service areas. Opinion is divided upon the advisability of concealing the view of the kitchen from the dining area.

All of the more social food service areas should be reached from the main living room without crossing the service areas of the house. It is not convenient to take guests through a kitchen to an outdoor eating area. Likewise the dining areas should be on the same level as the kitchen areas for ease in serving.

The size of dining areas should be calculated to avoid an overcrowded feeling on the one hand and a lonely feeling on the other.

AVERAGE SIZES OF DINING ROOMS

	Width	Depth
Dining table and space for 4 seated persons	10'–0" × 10'–0"	
Dining table and space for 6–8 seated persons	10'–0" × 12'–0"	
Dining alcove with built-in seats for 4	4'–0" × 5'–0"	
Dining alcove with chairs for 4	6'–6" × 5'–0"	
Passage space between edge of dining table and a wall or large piece of furniture	3'–6"	
Allowance for seating	2'–0" × 1'–6"	
Dining table for 2	2'–0" × 2'–6"	
Dining table for 4	3'–0" × 3'–0"	
Dining table for 6	3'–6" × 5'–0"	
	3'–0" × 6'–0"	
Dining table for 8	3'–6" × 7'–0"	
	3'–6" × 8'–0"	

In addition to a table and seats, a complete dining assemblage includes some sort of service shelf that can be used for extra utensils and for buffet equipment. Near or in the dining room there should be space for storage of dining paraphernalia. Much of this equipment is built-in today.

The dining table is customarily placed in the center of the room. Sometimes a table is placed along a window wall or at right angles to it. This kind of arrangement is less formal and makes the room seem larger. The service shelf should be near the kitchen. Frequently a space for quick meals is located between the kitchen and the more formal dining area. It then can supplement a service shelf.

Sometimes a dining room is used as a TV room. This requires a different arrangement of both tables and chairs so that no one will have his back to the screen. Small tables or long narrow tables with seats along the walls seem to be one answer.

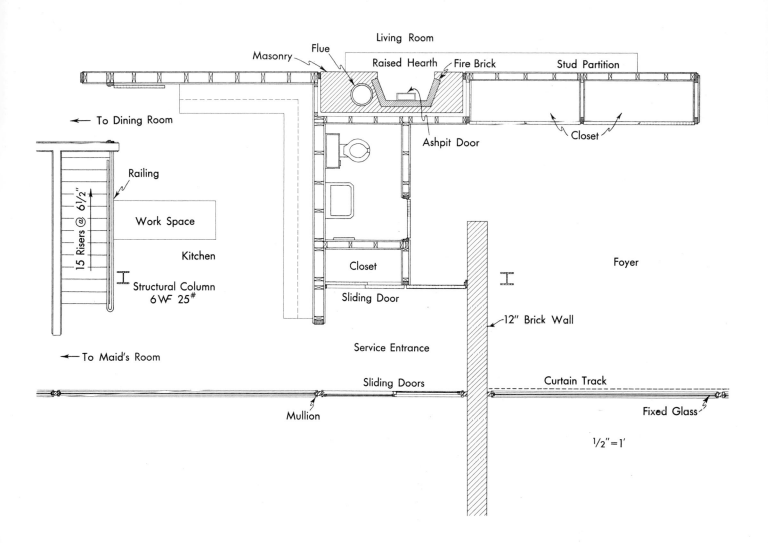

Figure 29. Architectural symbols as used on a floor plan.

e. SOCIAL AREAS FOR USE OTHER THAN DINING

The social life of most households is diversified. Some households have many guests, others have few. The social life of some households is largely at home. For others the church, the theater, or the club is the important social center. Some households can plan for a social life suited to one age group. Most must plan for the social needs of several ages. For one reason or another conditions and needs differ among households. Some conditions, however, seem constant and these give qualities of universality to the solutions.

The locations of the social areas should take advantage of the best physical situations in the house. Their relation to the main social corridor has been discussed.[12] Whether or not it is desirable to locate social areas completely away from the street is an individual problem. For shut-ins and for many others, a completely sheltered social area is not desirable. The opposite kind of situation where the living area is completely on view to the passer-by is not wished by most people. It has always been a good idea to locate social areas in several different places in a home if possible. This creates variety and allows group separation.

The main social area or living room will be the core space to which all other living spaces relate. This area is far from being the seldom used parlor of the last century. Nevertheless it must be planned so that it is easy to keep it attractive at all times. This factor is so very important to the women of the household that, left to themselves, they may overemphasize appearance and forget functional qualities. This stems from a family pride which is focused on its most obvious emblem, and therefore it is basically a good thing rather than a bad thing.

The house must be planned to preserve the reception tidiness of the main living space at the same time that it is usable for general living. In the first place it should be kept as free of traffic lanes as possible. Secondly, there should be sufficient and convenient storage space for outdoor wraps so that the living room chairs will not need to function as temporary depositories. There

[12] See p. 46.

should be adequate places for laying down magazines or papers or smoking paraphernalia without knocking over ornaments or disarranging the room.

Outdoor living areas are a distinct advantage. They substitute for and enlarge the indoor areas. The principal outdoor area is often adjacent to the living room. It is no longer the "front porch" but it may be a breezeway connecting the house with the garage. It may be an interior court or patio, a balcony or a roof. Many modern planners prefer this area to be detached from the house as an open or enclosed terrace. It should be oriented so as to receive the amount of sun and breeze and provide the amount of privacy which the family desires.

The sizes of living areas are dictated by furniture groupings. A minimum size is about 13'–0" × 13'–0". An average area is about 13'–0" × 17'–0". This is 221 square feet which is the size suggested by the American Public Health Association for a living area for three persons.[13] A medium size area is approximately 17'–0" × 23'–0" which approximates the suggestion of 383 square feet for six persons.

The selection of furniture for a living area will depend upon the uses which the area must serve. Seating furniture for the family and several guests is a basic requirement. Built-in window seats and ledges can provide seats for groups. The younger crowd prefers stools and floor cushions. Adequate lighting equipment is like-

[13] *Op. cit.*, Table 26, p. 29.

Figure 30–31. The lower figure shows the plan of this residence. This night view indicates clearly the open plan and the accompanying sense of spaciousness which owes much to the height of the living area.

All furniture and equipment, both stationary and movable, which the purpose of the space calls for, should be drawn on the building plan. In that way all of the circulation details can be studied. The lighting plans can also be projected. This diagram shows a large residence with an excellent circulation plan.

Residence of: The architect, Moreland Hills, Ohio.
Architect: Ernst Payer, A.I.A., Cleveland, Ohio.
Photographer: C. W. Ackerman, Cleveland, Ohio.

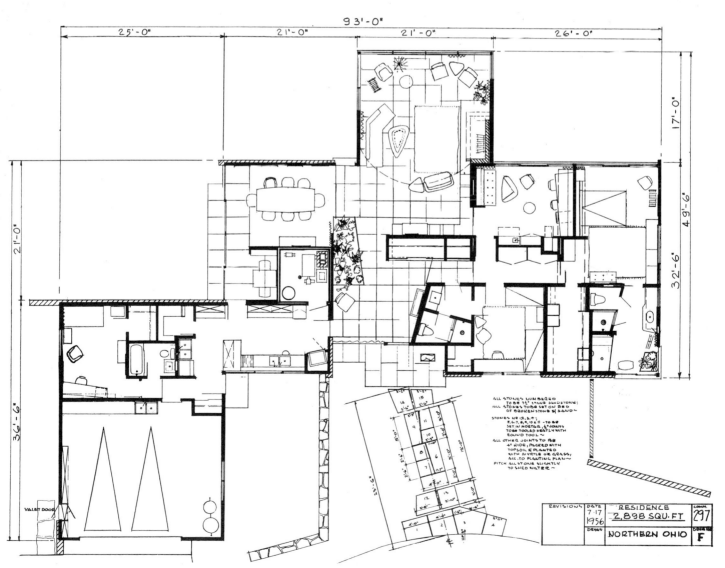

93'-0"

25'-0"   21'-0"   21'-0"   26'-0"

17'-0"

21'-0"   49'-6"

32'-6"

36'-6"

VALET DOOR

ALL STONES NUMBERED
TO BE 7½" THICK SANDSTONE;
ALL STONES TO BE SET ON BED
OF BROKEN STONE & SAND ~

STONES Nº 1,2,3,4,
5,6,7,8,9,10,11 - TO BE
SET IN MORTAR, ½" JOINTS
TODD TOOLED NEATLY WITH
ROUND TOOL ~

ALL OTHER JOINTS TO BE
4" WIDE, PACKED WITH
TOPSOIL & PLANTED
WITH MYRTLE OR GRASS;
ACC. TO PLANTING PLAN ~
PITCH ALL STONE SLIGHTLY
TO SHED WATER ~

| REVISIONS | DATE 7-17 1956 | RESIDENCE 2,898 SQU.FT | COMM. 297 |
| | DRAWN | NORTHERN OHIO | DWG. NO. F |

wise necessary to the general functioning of a social area. Low tables for accessories complete the list of basic furniture requirements.

The placement of seating furniture in the social areas is dictated by the size of the space as well as by the immediate use. When conversation is intended, the chairs should occupy no more than a conversational unit space. This is about thirteen to fifteen feet square. The unit should be held together by a compact arrangement and by the use of decorative equipment such as carpet or wall treatment which makes it cohesive. If possible such a conversational unit should have a central focal point, such as a hearth, or window, or table. Contemporary living rooms are frequently planned so that a conversational group can congregate around the hearth and the view at the same time.

Too rigid or straight line planning of seating furniture is seldom satisfactory. Therefore built-in seats are improved in functional efficiency when they can be supplemented by chairs which are arranged so as to break the rigidity of row seating.

When a social area is large it frequently houses several seating groups. Sometimes these groups are isolated; many times they must be integrated. This latter can be best accomplished if some of the furnishings are selected to be pivotal. A person seated on a chair which is adjacent to a secondary group should be able to face in either direction. There may be occasions when this pivotal piece should be moved into either grouping. The so-called pull-up chair answers this requirement. Benches, chairs without arms, and stools make better pivotal pieces than do large stationary pieces of furniture. Objects which are large in size or which have high backs and arms are apt to act as barricades. Thus they isolate rather than unite groupings. Occasionally such isolation is required and a chair which has been carefully selected with this in mind becomes just as much a room divider as would a larger piece of furniture. A seat backed by a table or desk is very effective for this purpose.

The seating groups in the social areas are not always arranged solely to further conversation. Households desire various kinds of social relaxation. Therefore provision must frequently be made for music centers, reading centers, television centers, and game centers. In each case the necessary equipment should be provided. It should be arranged so as to function well and the arrangement should provide for flexibility of use when necessary.

The placement of large musical instruments in a home should be considered from several points of view. First should come attention to obtaining good quality sound. This was considered under sound conditioning.[14] Likewise such instruments should be placed where air conditions are favorable to the instrument. They should not be placed too close to an outside wall unless it is well insulated. Neither should they be close to a radiator. Instruments placed in southern window exposures must be carefully protected from radiant heat.

[14] See p. 37.

Figure 32. This minimum size house of 1000 square feet was winner of the National Association of Home Builders and Architectural Forum award, House Design Competition, 1951. It is unusual to find such good planning for the needs of a family of four or five in such limited space.

Architect: Bruce Walker, A.I.A., Spokane, Washington.

If the instrument requires a player, then the conditions must be physically and psychologically good for his performance. Adequate light is essential. Some pianists do not like a position with their backs to the audience. Many like the instrument to separate them from the rest of the room.

A special word might be said about the placement of the television center inasmuch as it is the newest type of equipment to be accommodated. It is frequently placed near some center of focal interest such as the fireplace. Then the seating can be arranged so as to turn towards both interesting points. If chairs are arranged to flank a fireplace then the television may be placed at the opposite end of the room in order to obtain the necessary focal distance from the screen. This distance should be in feet approximately equivalent to the diameter of the television tube in inches. The image is best seen at eye level or 4'-0" from the floor for a seated viewer.

Many times the television screen is in a compartment of the fireplace wall which can swing out for greater visibility and then swing back into a closed compartment of the wall when not in use. In planning for this remember that the depth necessary for the tube encasement varies from 1'-0" to about 2'-10". Often such other equipment for modern entertaining as the movie screen and the record player are mounted in the same manner.

Many households prefer to place this sort of equipment in a more secluded room such as a family entertainment room nearby. Often a television set is mounted on a turntable chassis so that it may be pivoted to either room. As has been mentioned, some households have made television viewing an accompaniment to dining and have altered their entire dining area to accommodate the set. A view through from the kitchen and dinette is frequently demanded by the small fry (to say nothing of the oldsters) who must see their favorite program from this

source. Personal solutions such as bedroom placement are also used. A movable set which can be wheeled onto the porch seems to be the only solution for some devotees.

3. Needs in Particular Households

This finishes our discussion of the plan as a functional basis for designing. We have only considered those problems which many households have in common. There will be special problems of expansion and contraction and diversification. Each household is individual and must be considered as an unique case.

F. MAKING AND READING A FLOOR PLAN

One should know how to read and how to make a good floor plan. Plans are the symbolic language of the designer. They tell us the exact position of everything in space. Horizontal floor plans are drawings of the way a room would look if a big slicing knife were to cut it horizontally near the floor.

Architects and draftsmen make their drawings to scale. On the drawing they usually indicate this scale, for instance, as 1 inch equals 1 foot ($1'' = 1'0''$). This means that an inch on the draftsman's paper represents one foot on the actual object. Here the word *scale* is used in a most definite sense referring to two objects which are exactly measured and compared in size. The word *scale* can likewise refer to an indefinite relation of measure between two details, as when we refer to the relative scale of a chair to a room.

An adequate type of floor plan for us to use for all subsequent purposes may be made in the following manner. Take all inside measurements of a room at floor or window level. Reducing these measures to a scale which is suitable to our purpose, draw the cross section of the room. Walls project outside these measures and for this type of drawing are filled in with a heavy black line. Load-bearing walls can be made eight inches thick to scale and screen walls the actual thickness of the material.

Windows are indicated by very fine lines. A sash window may be symbolized by four lines, two for the outer and inner edges of the sill and

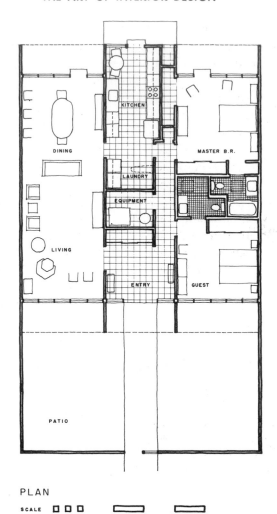

PLAN

SCALE

Figure 33. This average size residence (1,492 square feet with 500 square feet patio) was built on a city lot in New Orleans. It provides unusual privacy and integrates well with its surroundings. An interior view of this house appears in Figure 144.

Residence of: Mr. and Mrs. John T. Upton, New Orleans, Louisiana. **Architect:** Curtis and Davis, A.I.A., and Associated Architects and Engineers, New Orleans, Louisiana. **Photographer:** Frank Lotz Miller, New Orleans, Louisiana.

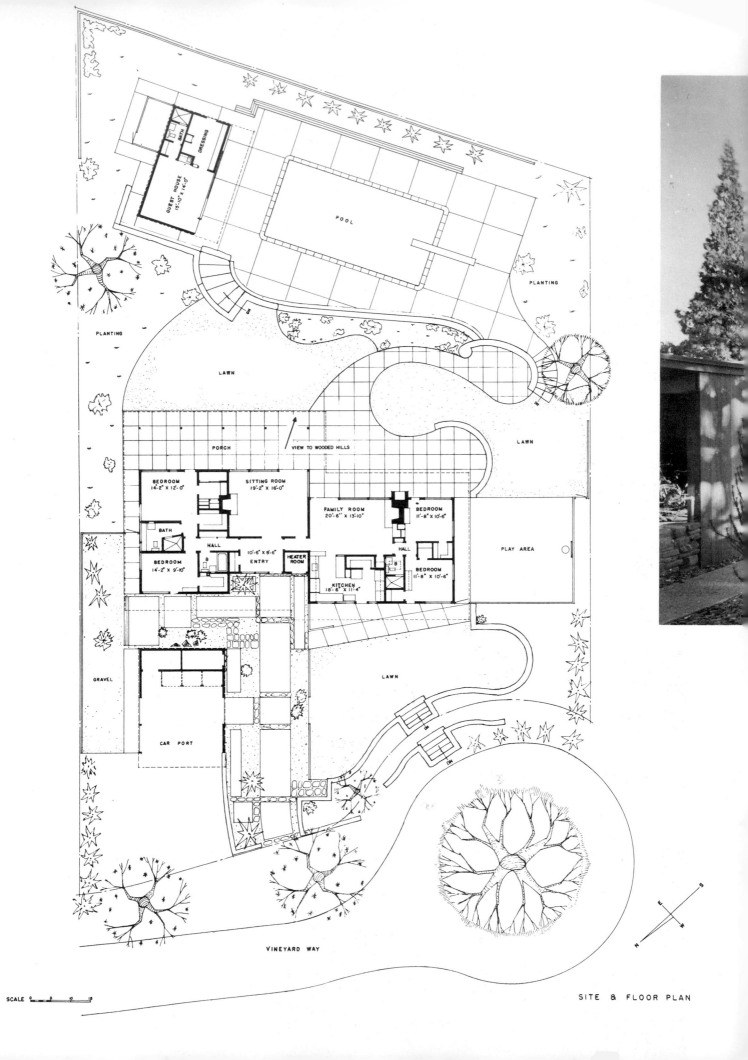

GUEST HOUSE
15'-10" X 14'-0"

BATH

DRESSING

POOL

PLANTING

PLANTING

PLANTING

LAWN

PORCH

VIEW TO WOODED HILLS

LAWN

BEDROOM
14'-2" X 12'-0"

SITTING ROOM
19'-2" X 16'-0"

FAMILY ROOM
20'-6" X 13'-10"

BEDROOM
11'-8" X 10'-6"

PLAY AREA

BATH

HALL

HALL

BEDROOM
14'-2" X 9'-10"

HEATER
ROOM

10'-6" X 8'-6"
ENTRY

KITCHEN
18'-6" X 11'-4"

BEDROOM
11'-8" X 10'-6"

GRAVEL

LAWN

CAR PORT

VINEYARD WAY

SCALE

SITE & FLOOR PLAN

CAR PORT   ENTRY   LIVING ROOM

SCALE   0   5   10   15

SECTION LOOKING NORTHEAST

Figure 34. This well considered plan of a larger residence (about 2100 square feet) was built in California for a family with three children. The owner's desire for the separation of the boy's sleeping quarters from those of the parents and daughter suggested the divided facilities. Another view of this house appears in Figure 21 (center).

Residence of: Mr. and Mrs. James Kelso, Kent Woodlands, California. **Architect:** Wurster, Bernardi and Emmons, Architects, San Francisco, California. **Landscape Architect:** Duncan S. Munro, San Francisco, California. **Photographer:** Roger Sturtevant, San Francisco, California. **Courtesy: Record Houses of 1956,** F. W. Dodge Corporation, New York.

two for the double sash. Other types of windows are drawn with several thin lines according to the type and spacing of the sash. Openings are usually represented by a fine broken line drawn through their center perpendicular to their plane. Door openings and casement window openings should have their swing indicated by an arc and straight line. The straight line should be drawn on an angle from the wall where the door is hinged and the arc drawn from this to the other side of the opening. Fireplaces and built-in features should be indicated in cross section. It is wise to include electrical outlets on a complete floor plan, together with line and dot signs for their switches.[15] A line of dashes indicates a construction above the plan level such as a lowered or furred ceiling.

Most architectural plans have their dimensions indicated on the plan. The figures used for the dimensions are of uniform size throughout. If the room size alone is given, the dimensions are

[15] See Chap. VIII for symbols.

usually written just below the room name. If the plan is carried out in greater detail and measurements for doors and windows are also given, then the dimensions are grouped and are indicated on lines which terminate with arrows abutting on definite extension lines. These light extension lines are extensions of the lines between which the measures are taken. Any system of lettering and figures may be used but the letters and figures should be consistent throughout. Lettering may be of different sizes to indicate the relative

Figure 35. Many apartments provide satisfactory environment for contemporary living. The penthouse shown in these photographs is a large one (approximately 2000 square feet). Other views of this residence appear opposite, and in Figure 27 B and C.

Building: An apartment building and interior, Spokane, Washington. **Architect:** Walker, McGough and Trogdon, Architects, A.I.A., Spokane, Washington. **Photographer:** Morley Baer, Berkeley, California.

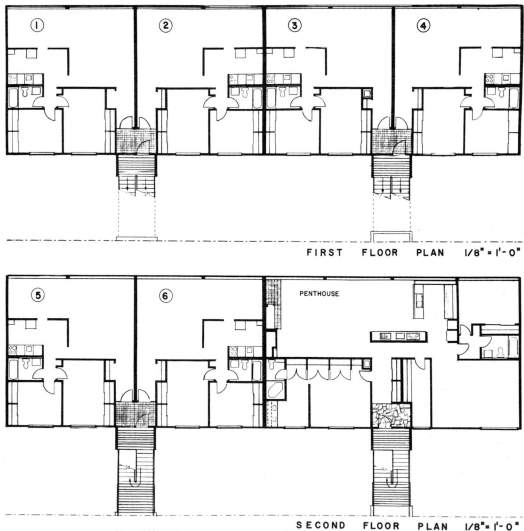

FIRST FLOOR PLAN 1/8" = 1'-0"

PENTHOUSE

SECOND FLOOR PLAN 1/8" = 1'-0"

FURNITURE TEMPLATES

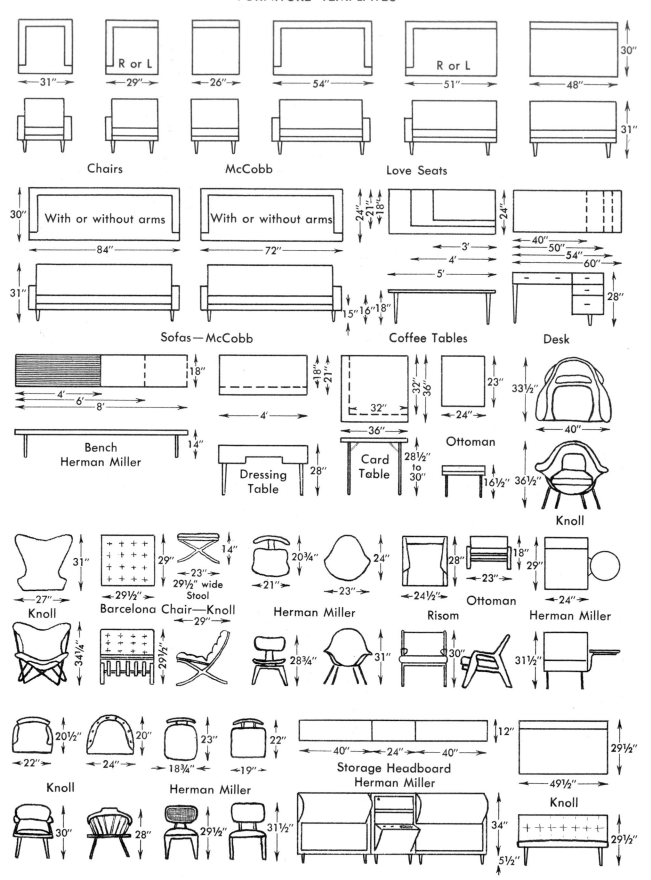

Chairs   McCobb   Love Seats

With or without arms — 84″   With or without arms — 72″   Coffee Tables   Desk

Sofas—McCobb   Coffee Tables   Desk

Bench Herman Miller   Dressing Table   Card Table   Ottoman   Knoll

Knoll   Barcelona Chair—Knoll   Stool   Herman Miller   Risom   Ottoman   Herman Miller

Knoll   Herman Miller   Storage Headboard Herman Miller   Knoll

Line Drawings, dimensions adapted from: Herman Miller Furniture Company, Knoll Associates, Inc., Paul McCobb, Jens Risom Design, Inc., **Architectural Graphic Standards,** 5th edition, by Charles G. Ramsey A.I.A., and Harold R. Sleeper, F.A.I.A. **Courtesy:** Reprinted by permission from John Wiley & Sons, Inc., New York, 1954.

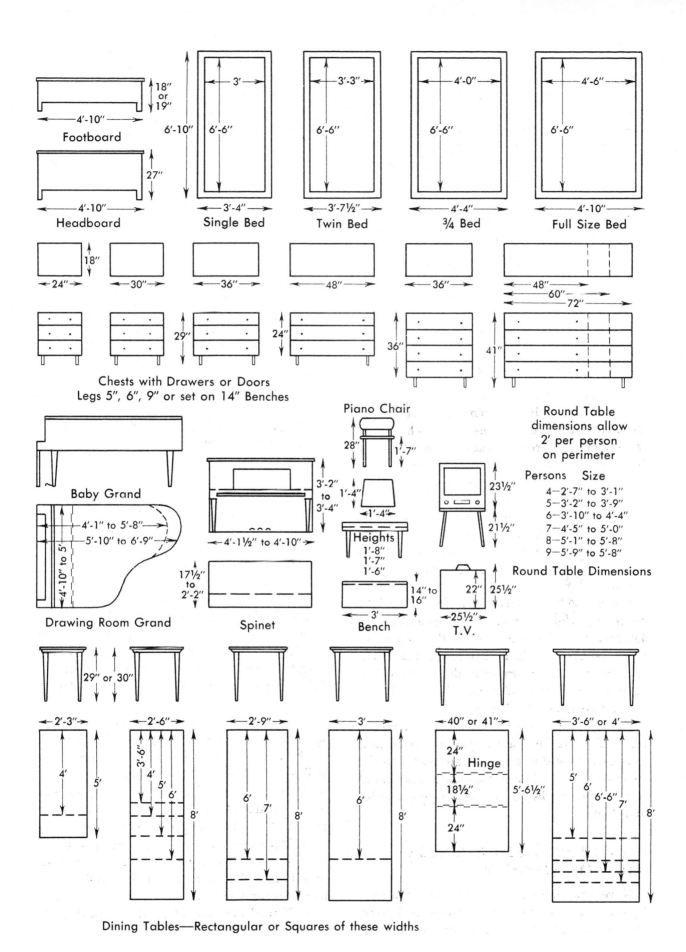

Figure 36–37. Plan and elevation templates of contemporary furniture.

importance of the various sections of the house plan.

Furniture to be placed in the plan may be measured and indicated in the same way. It is well to cut out small-scale patterns, called templates, of the various pieces of furniture to be used. Thus they can be shifted around on the floor plan until the most satisfactory arrangement is discovered.

G. PLANS OF SPECIFIC HOUSES

The house plans on pages 62–71 represent some well-considered house sizes, together with contemporary furniture templates.

H. DRAWING WALL ELEVATIONS

A plan represents only the floor of a room. The four walls can be drawn in similar manner. These drawings are called room elevations. The ceiling is seldom illustrated. Elevation drawings show how each wall of a room would appear if all the light rays coming from the wall to our eyes were parallel. Thus we would see only the front face of all objects which are parallel to the wall. No depth is represented just as no height was represented on the floor plan. This sort of drawing is known in technical language as a type of orthographic projection.

If any object is not placed parallel to a wall its rendering in elevation is slightly irregular. The location of the four corners of the object are transferred from the floor plan to the base of the wall. From these points verticals are erected to represent the four sides and horizontals are drawn to represent the heights.

Elevation templates of furniture, corresponding to plan templates, are helpful in making such drawings. Elevation drawings are useful to the designer because they give accurate measures of heights and widths just as the plan gives width and depth.

I. A GRID TO REPRESENT A ROOM IN THREE DIMENSIONS

If we want to obtain a greater illusion of reality than is secured through elevations and plans, one kind of such drawing is a perspective draw-

ing. A perspective view of a room is one which presents the room as it actually appears to the eye. There are many methods of making a perspective drawing. One of the simplest and most practical ways to do it is described below. This method will give a basic perspective grid for a particular room. Over this we can place tracing paper and suggest many alternate arrangements for the room.

Grid for Drawing Three Walls of a Room

1. Draw a floor plan of the room to scale.
2. Decide which three walls of the room you wish to represent. Call them wall A, B, C in order.
3. Draw a cross or an arrow on the floor plan to indicate your position. This is usually about one to one and one-half times the width of B and is measured from wall B. It is likewise a foot or so nearer wall A than wall C. It is placed off-center because that makes a more interesting drawing. This is known as *station point* or *SP*.
4. To whatever scale desired (frequently $\frac{1}{2}'' = 1'$ is used on $15'' \times 20''$ illustration board, or $\frac{1}{4}'' = 1'$ is used on smaller cardboards) draw wall B in vertical projection. Mark it off in $1'$ squares. This is known as the *true height wall* or *THW*. It is placed near the center of the cardboard. The height of most rooms is $8'$ or $9'$.
5. Draw a *horizon line* or *HL*, five feet above the floor line on *THW*. The *HL* represents the height of your eyes in viewing this wall. If the *HL* is higher you will see more of the tops of objects.
6. On *HL* place a dot in a position corresponding to your position from the side walls on the floor plan. (The same number of feet from wall A as *SP* was from it on the floor plan.) This is called *central vanishing point* or *CVP*, because it is the place where all lines which are parallel to walls A and C will appear to converge.
7. Place one end of a ruler successively on corners of *THW* and the other on *CVP*. Extend lines from *THW* to represent floor and ceiling lines of walls A and C.
8. Extend base line of *THW* and mark at $1'$ intervals.

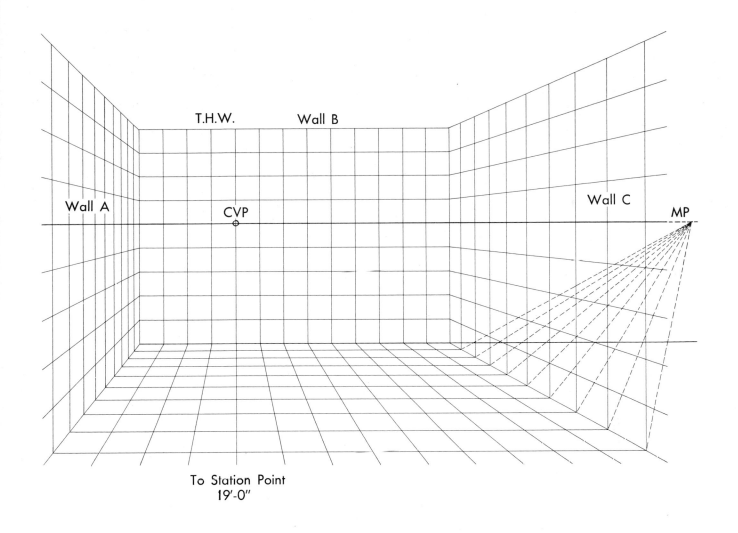

Wall A   T.H.W.   Wall B   Wall C

CVP   MP

To Station Point
19'-0"

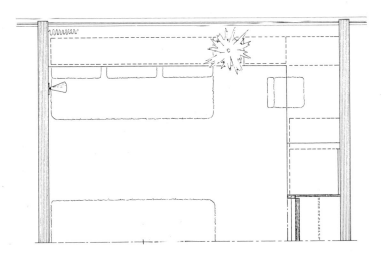

Figure 38. A one point perspective grid planned as an aid to drawing a room.

73

Figure 39. One point perspective drawn from plan of Figure 38 with the aid of perspective grid.

9. Measure on the horizon line from the *CVP*, the distance the *SP* was taken from wall B. (See Point 3.) This marks the *measuring point* or *MP*.

10. Place one end of the ruler on *MP* and the other on the 1′ marks on the base extension of *THW*. Put dots where the ruler successively crosses the floor line of wall *C*.

11. From these dots draw horizontal lines to intersect the floor line of wall *A*. These lines mark off the feet of the floor plan as they recede into distance.

12. Draw vertical lines on walls A and C from the ends of each of these floor lines. These lines mark off the feet on the walls.

13. Place one end of the ruler on *CVP* and the other end on the foot markings of height and breadth of *THW*. This will finish the grid by marking off the walls A and C and the floor into sections representing foot squares as they look in perspective.[16]

[16] A similar two-point perspective grid may be made by placing the right and left vanishing points 30′ and the

J. DRAWING FROM THE GRID

The drawing of furniture in a room from a grid may be done in the following manner.

1. Draw the furniture on the room plan. Know the heights of all pieces or draw them in elevation.

2. Place a piece of tracing paper over the perspective grid.

3. Draw in the walls and floor of the room only.

4. Consider the furniture which is parallel to the walls of the room first.

   a. Draw the base of this furniture on the perspective grid according to its position on the floor plan. Each division on the perspective grid corresponds to one square foot on the floor plan.

right and left measuring points 14′ from the corner of a room on a horizon line. This corner of the room is used as a true height wall. All lines parallel to the right wall vanish in the *LVP* and all lines parallel to the left wall vanish in the *RVP*.

b. Extend vertical lines from the base of the furniture to represent the sides of the furniture.

c. Measure the height of the furniture on the side walls following this procedure. Draw a horizontal line through any corner on the base of the piece to the side wall. Measure the height on the side wall from the point where this base extension crosses the side wall. Project the height back to the furniture by drawing a horizontal extension line from this height point to the corresponding side line of the furniture.

d. All lines which are parallel to the *THW* on the plan are drawn on the perspective parallel to the *THW* horizontal lines.

e. All lines which are parallel to the side walls on the plan are drawn on the perspective through the *CVP*.

5. Consider the furniture which is not parallel to the walls of the room next.

a. Draw the base of this furniture on the perspective grid according to its position on the floor plan.

b. Extend vertical lines from the base of the furniture to represent the sides of the furniture.

c. Measure the height of each vertical through each corner on the base of the piece to the side wall. Measure the height on the side wall from the point where this base extension crosses the side wall. Project the height back to its corner vertical by drawing a horizontal extension line from the wall height back to the corresponding side line of the furniture. Connect the height points for the top of the piece of furniture.

K. FUNCTIONAL CONSIDERATIONS IN FURNISHINGS

Every article of furnishing should be analyzed from a functional point of view. This requires a knowledge of materials and fabrication [17] and of design in relation to use.[18] The favorite byword of modernists about furniture is that it is functional. And yet there is much about some modern furnishing which is not functional—beds too low for making, pitchers with spouts too narrow for cleaning, arm chairs with no brace for a lateral thrust, chairs with a maze of underpinning to dust.

In order to approve an article for use we must think of very practical things. Does its structure and form, in addition to being well designed for its prime use, meet the following tests:

1. Is it durable? Will it stand up under the kind of use it will be given?
   Under this heading would come such tests as the sunfast tests of drapery fabrics, the abrasion tests of floor fabrics, the hardness tests of furniture woods.
2. Is it easily serviced? Will it be expensive to maintain?
   Under this heading would be such questions as: is it easily soiled, easily cleaned, easily moved?

The complete house and its furnishings should be considered from the practical point of view of safety factors. An analysis of these has not been undertaken in this text. But it is an important study. Foresight may prevent regrets.

[17] See Chap. IX for furnishings.
[18] See Chap. XIII for contemporary furniture.

Taking possession of space is the first gesture of living things, of men and of animals, of plants and of clouds, a fundamental manifestation of equilibrium and of duration. The occupation of space is the first proof of existence. . . .

LE CORBUSIER *

Chapter V

SPACE AND SHAPE IN INTERIORS

A. THE MEANING AND IMPORTANCE OF PROPORTION

Most art students expect to dislike mathematics. This represents one of the most unfortunate failures in our educational system. For modern mathematics has much to offer art. It shows the connections which exist between abstract relations and visual configurations in space. The only danger to the artist which lurks in a study of the science of measures is the risk that he may become so intrigued as to turn mathematician.

The basic numerical aspect of the wedding of space and number is called a ratio. In mathematics a ratio is the quotient of one quantity divided by another of the same kind. It is the same thing as a fraction in arithmetic. The simplest spatial demonstration of such a relation would be two lines, one of which might be five times as long as the other. The ratio would be 1 to 5 or $\frac{1}{5}$.

* From **New World of Space** by Le Corbusier. Copyright 1948, Harcourt, Brace and Company, Inc. and reprinted by permission of the publisher.

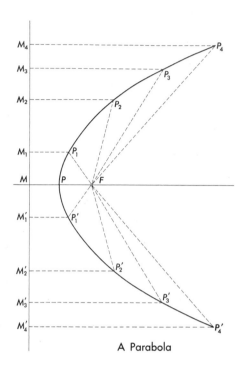

A Parabola

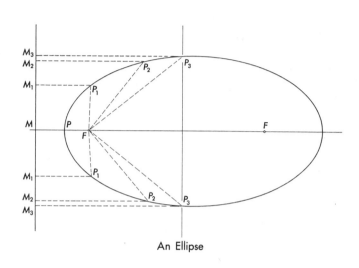

An Ellipse

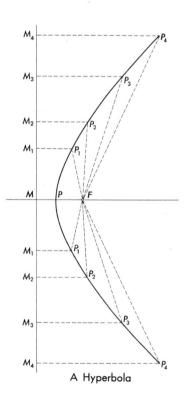

A Hyperbola

Figure 40. Notice the order brought about by the constant ratios.

Mathematics says that four things are in proportion when the ratios between them are equal. Thus the sequence 2 is to 4 as 8 is to 16 is in proportion, each pair of numbers possessing a ratio of ½. This particular proportion is likewise called an *extreme-mean* or *xm* proportion because in any sequence of four numbers the two end numbers when multiplied together give the same result as when the two intermediate numbers are multiplied. General language is not so definite and calls two quantities proportionate when they possess some regular ratio linkage. All things in life that change or grow in an orderly fashion are governed by ratios and proportions. It is this metric recurrence which produces rhythms in the physical world and in good design.

B. THE PROBLEM OF WHAT CONSTITUTES PLEASING PROPORTIONS

It would certainly be convenient if we could point to one or several sets of proportions and say that they were most liked. However it is not possible to do so. As a matter of fact experiments have shown that there is very little consensus of opinion on this matter.[1] About all that can be said is that persons who have similar tastes seem to prefer the same kind of proportional relations. Apparently everyone is pleased to sense some clear quantitative analogies. Among persons who might be said to have a developed aesthetic taste there is a preference for related measures which are subtle in addition to being understandable.

One ratio which exists between the sizes of two things and which can be expressed in numbers is called in many art text books static symmetry.[2] An illustration of such a ratio would be a picture frame which was twice as high as it was broad, or which had four units in height and three in width. Nature uses such proportions in crystalline growth.

Static ratios help to unify a design by introducing a common unit of measure. They likewise intensify a design when this measure is repeated

in proportion. When such a proportion is in sequence (i.e., where the internal numbers of an *xm* ratio are the same number, e.g., 1:2::2:4::4:8) then there is an interlocking or integrating of the series by an identical number link. Proportions of this last sort do impel the mind's eye onward by the very rhythm of the sequence. However, such a sequence soon grows too large or too small for our mental agility and we tend to drop it before going far. The internal cohesive force of any single proportion is probably greater, for this reason, than its rhythmic propulsion onwards.

There are degrees of subtlety in numerical proportions dependent upon their initial ratios. In general this initial relation is obvious and so there is a sort of naïveté introduced into a pattern through its use. Folk art frequently employs recognizable ratios which are in part responsible for its ingenuous appeal. The mechanical nature of numerical divisions has something in common with the mechanization of our machine world. Early modern art frequently used the equilateral figures of geometry and it may have been for this reason.

We have been describing the simple case where a numerical ratio of measures exists between two things, in this case two shapes. Such a ratio can likewise exist between two positions in space or two points on a line. The ratio must of course be made with reference to some external point or points. In mathematics a line whose path can be traced by an equation (equality of relations) which can be applied to every point on it is a curve. When a series of positions bear an equal size relation to a controlling position (called the center) a circle or a sphere results.

A *parabola* is a curve any point of which maintains its distance from a fixed point equal to its perpendicular distance from a given line. Notice the order brought about by the constant ratio.

$$\frac{PF}{MP} = \frac{1}{1} = \frac{P^1F^1}{M^1P^1} = \frac{P^2F^2}{M^2P^2} \quad \text{etc.}$$

An *ellipse* is a curve any point of which maintains the ratio of its distance from a fixed point and a given line constant and less than one.

$$\frac{PF}{MP} \quad \text{might be} \quad \frac{4}{5} = \frac{P^1F^1}{M^1P^1} = \frac{P^2F^2}{M^2F^2} \quad \text{etc.}$$

[1] Albert R. Chandler, *Beauty and Human Nature* (New York: Appleton-Century-Crofts, Inc., 1934), Chap. 3.

[2] Jay Hambidge, *Dynamic Symmetry, the Greek Vase* (New Haven, Conn.: Yale University Press, 1920), p. 138.

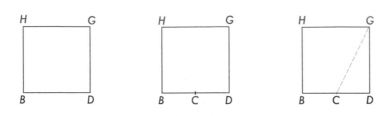

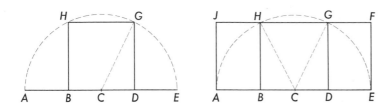

Figure 41. Drawing Extreme-Mean (xm) rectangles from a square.

An *hyperbola* is a curve any point of which maintains the ratio of its distance from a fixed point and a given line constant and greater than one.

$$\frac{PF}{MP} \text{ might be } \frac{3}{2} = \frac{P^1F^1}{M^1P^1} = \frac{P^2F^2}{M^2F^2} \text{ etc.}$$

These are only a few of the many curves which can be plotted by reference to some regimented relations or ratios. The graphs made by engineers frequently are beautiful tracts because ratios of resistance to stresses must be systematically ordered and an equality of force must result. Curves become more complex as their points move in three dimensions. There are cycloid, catenary, and spiral curves. It is not an accident that a suspension bridge [3] or a thin convex concrete slab roof assumes the shape which is seen. It is the order inherent in its construction which creates the beauty of a mathematical curve. It likewise indicates the vitality which is seen in such a curve because the points of the line maintain a constant ratio but a continuously changing measure in relation to the reference points.

The symmetry that we have been examining is that based on whole number ratios. An even more intriguing set of proportions is not arithmetical in nature. It is completely geometric and can only be approximated in numbers.[4] This system has been frequently called dynamic symmetry.[5] We are told that dynamic symmetry was a designing tool which was perfected by the Greeks. If it was not their invention it certainly was the conception of some clever geometrician.

Builders previous to the Greeks learned to construct a right angled corner by a practical expe-

[4] If you wish the answer to this paradox we suggest a further exploration into the enticing reasoning of modern mathematics and a study of so-called irrational numbers. In the figures of dynamic symmetry, unity (the square) when divided by the geometric space which has been added to it, results in an irrational number.

[5] Hambidge, *op. cit.*

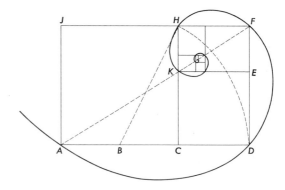

Figure 42. Drawing a spiral from the Extreme-Mean rectangle (Rectangle of the Whirling Square).

[3] D. B. Steinman, *The Builders of the Bridge* (New York: Harcourt, Brace and Company, Inc., 1950), p. 179.

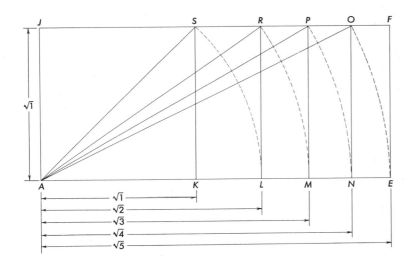

Figure 43. Drawing the Root Rectangles from a square or from a Root 5 rectangle.

dient known as cording. A rope was divided by knots into twelve equal divisions. This rope was so laid on the ground that four knots made one side, three knots the other side and the five remaining knots thus formed the hypotenuse of a right angled triangle. Further extensions of this technique could be used to coordinate a whole building. Design resulted and architecture had begun.

It is useful to study a few of the geometric tools which came from a study of right angled triangles. Let us begin with a square, here lettered BDGH. The base of this square is bisected at C. Drawing a diagonal of half the square from C to G, it may be used as a radius to draw the semicircle AEGH. The top and base lines of the square are then extended and are terminated by perpendicular lines at AEFJ. In this process the rectangles ADGJ and BEFH are formed. Each of these is called an *xm* rectangle because the ratio of its short side to its long side equals that of its long side to the sum of its short plus its long side. The large rectangle AEFJ is called a root 5 rectangle because the ratio between its two sides is that of one to the square root of five.

A more detailed construction of the *xm* rectangle is shown in the illustration opposite. BH, the diagonal of half of the square ACHJ is used as the radius of a circle which cuts the base line at D. The rectangle ADFJ made by erecting a perpendicular to AC at D and by prolonging it to meet the extension of JH at F, is an *xm* rec-

tangle. Moreover the rectangle CDFH is an *xm* rectangle. If the square CDEK is taken from this rectangle, the rectangle KEFH is an *xm* rectangle. An *xm* rectangle will remain every time an end square is removed. As the path of these squares turns about the so-called eye of the rectangle (the intersection of the diagonal AF with the diagonal HD of the reciprocal or same proportioned rectangle CDFH), we can see why the *xm* rectangle has sometimes been called the rectangle of the whirling square. From the illustration it can likewise be seen how this rectangle can be used to design a constant angle spiral such as is found in shell life. This rectangle contains a continuous *xm* proportion in which the short division of a side is to the long division as the latter is to the whole side. These *xm* ratios likewise hold for the corresponding areas.

The quality of onward propulsion found in all continuously progressive *xm* proportions is thus demonstrated spatially in the rectangle of the whirling square. We are not surprised to be told that the law of phyllotaxis or that law which governs plant growth progresses in this proportion.

The *xm* rectangle possesses the fault of all extreme mean ratios of growing or diminishing too fast. And rather than follow the example set years later by Alice in Wonderland of drinking or eating an antidote, the ingenious classical designers discovered another set of rectangles which were more suited to their needs.

They began with the root 5 rectangle and made a series of rectangles in each of which the relation between the short side to the long side is as one is to the square root of the number which gives the rectangle its name. Only in occasional cases such as the root 4 rectangle is this ratio a numerical one. In the root rectangles the members of the series are not interlocked by an identical ratio but by geometrically related factors. Each successive rectangle is related to the one of a lower root number through the identity of the diagonal of the smaller rectangle with the longer side of the larger rectangle. As all of the root rectangles evolve from a basic square a very effective growth propulsion due to the interrelations is felt.

In the next illustration it can be seen how a handy designer's tool can be made from the root rectangles.[6] The accompanying illustration shows such a tool, called a proportional triangle, made from the root rectangles. Here the triangle is made from the diagonal AF of a root 5 rectangle AEFJ. The triangle is AFJ. The diagonals of the corresponding root 4, 3, 2, and 1 rectangles mark off root proportions on the line JF. If it is de-

---

[6] In a similar way a triangle could be made from an *xm* rectangle which would divide a line into *xm* ratios. A study of mathematics will reveal quite a number of such applied devices which will help the student to get ordered relations into a design.

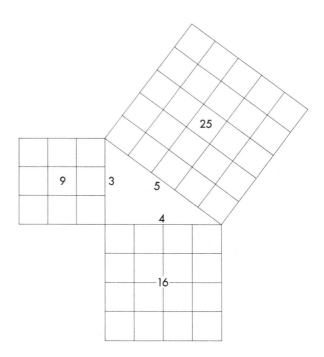

Figure 45. Illustration explaining the reason for the term "Root Rectangles."

sired that any other line should be divided into these proportions it is only necessary to insert the line to be so divided into the triangle so that it lies parallel to JF and is cut by the diagonals.

In these several pages we have considered a few of the fascinating relations which order shapes and their behavior in space. These thoughts provide an initial glimpse of the truth that there is no beauty without some kind of order. Mathematics is capable of demonstrating this order because it is a method of reasoning from cause to effect about those things which can be measured, counted, and related.[7]

Most compound sensations and their resulting affections are at present beyond measure. Mathematical proportions can be used by the artist as training for sensitivity to such complexity.

---

[7] D. Miller, *Popular Mathematics* (New York: Coward-McCann, Inc., 1942); J. R. Newman, ed., *The World of Mathematics* (New York: Simon and Schuster, Inc., 1956).

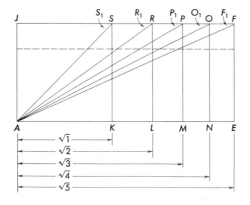

Figure 44. A designer's tool—the proportional triangle.

They may be used to teach the causes of order, to train the eye to see and the hand to draw spatial orders, and they may be used to check established order. Artists usually attain satisfactory shape delineation because of intuitive coordination of hand, eye, and brain. Centuries of gauging the rate of change in natural forms has given man this power. The artist needs to remember that the laws governing all natural phenomena likewise govern art. Ratios and proportions can unify and intensify by repetition and ordered variation, integrate by interlocking and make the design dynamic by establishing rhythms. The artist must accomplish similar results.

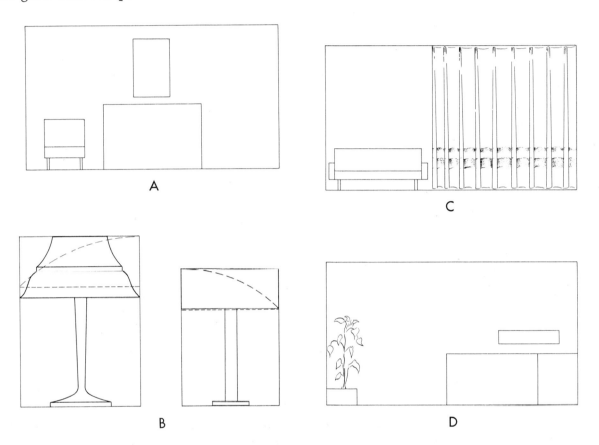

Figure 46. Mathematical proportions can be used by the artist as training for sensitivity.

A. A root 3 rectangular picture in relation to a root 2 rectangular fireplace creates pleasing variation in proportion. The wall is a root 3.

B. Lamps frequently utilize the root 2 rectangle as the basis for their structural shape.

C. An entire wall with root 3 proportions is broken at the root 1 forming a square. Within the square the upper part of the drapery is a root 2. The bands are designed to progress upwards from a base square at the root 2, 3, and 4 division lines.

D. A wall with root 3 proportions has a fireplace or wall cabinet in a root 7. The break in this creates a root 3 horizontal and a root 2 vertical. The plant base is a root 3 horizontal and the entire plant is designed in a root 7 vertical. The ends of the long narrow picture come at the root 1 and the root 4 diagonals of the fireplace rectangle.

C. THE MEANING AND IMPORTANCE OF SHAPES AND SPACE

Shape and the space which is associated with it becomes the first component to be considered in interior design. It might be well to remind ourselves that the word *shape* originated in the Anglo-Saxon *sceap*—a creation. It would be impossible to create art if it were not for shapes which are definite measurable objects which exist in space. Visual design involves spatial relations qualified by colors and textures.

There are different names for different types of shapes. A dot is the first kind of shape, a simple location in space. When a dot projects itself along a path it becomes a line. As someone has facetiously said, a line which bites its tail is an area, or an enclosed two-dimensional space.

Every area in reality has three dimensions because even the thickness of the paper upon which it may be drawn has a certain depth. If then we regard only the exterior of anything which has length and breadth we are speaking of its surface. A surface is explained in geometry as a magnitude which has length and breadth only. When a surface is without any elevations or depressions we speak of it as a plane surface or a plane. A volume is a three-dimensional shape. Volume is occupied space as measured by cubic (three-dimensional) units. Volume can then be subdivided into mass which is the solid matter of the volume and space which is defined in the dictionary as that which is characterized by dimension only.

D. ATTRIBUTES OF SHAPE

Shapes and spaces have aesthetic qualities which are derived from the combination of their attribute traits. A shape attribute is a basic way in which one shape can differ from another. How might the space in one room differ from that of another? One room could have large dimensions and the other small dimensions. The two rooms might have the same proportions but they would differ in positive size. A thick line is different in size from a thin line of the same length. Size is the first attribute of shape.

Shapes can differ from one another in direction. Direction is always estimated with relation to the horizontal which is parallel to the apparent horizon. Thus vertical is at right angles to horizontal and oblique is at acute angles to the horizontal. Obviously there are many different kinds of oblique directions. Direction is the second attribute of shape.

The character of any particular detail is a composite of all the attribute traits which it possesses. By its very definition we see a shape as one object or configuration. We must therefore describe its character in terms of the attribute traits which it possesses plus any change which has occurred in these traits within its boundaries. Thus the character of a shape is the sum of its size, of its direction, and of any change in its direction in relation to its size.

Direction   Size   Change in
                                       a Measure

Figure 47. Illustration of shape attributes showing how one shape can differ from another in direction, size, and change of size and direction in a measure.

It would be possible but very labored to describe all shapes scientifically in terms of their sizes, directions, and changes of direction. We frequently do this in general terms expressive of the shape character when we describe shapes as jagged, sinuous, angular, bulbous, or graceful. These are not scientific words but when thoughtfully used they make valuable contributions to the language of art.

E. CHOICE OF DOMINANT SHAPE TRAITS

The first step in planning a room design is to choose dominant shape traits. This involves preliminary thinking about the architectural shape character, about many practical things such as the physical strength of certain kinds of shape and then about the expressive message which shapes can convey.

What is the room shape? Is it large or small? Does it open to larger space or is it enclosed?

Figure 48. The dominant straight lines of the architecture and furniture, which are emphasized in the picture, create an atmosphere of sturdy livability appropriate to this family room.

Residence of: Mr. and Mrs. R. D. McGranahan, Fox Chapel, Pittsburgh, Pennsylvania. **Architect:** John Pekruhn, A.I.A., Pittsburgh, Pennsylvania. **Photographer:** Joseph Molitor, Ossining, New York. **Courtesy: Record Houses of 1956,** F. W. Dodge Corporation, New York.

Does it have horizontal emphasis or vertical emphasis? The room is a shape with which all furnishing shapes must come to terms.

What are some practical considerations relative to shapes? Modern techniques have reduced the size of furniture without impairing its strength and comfort. We are accustomed to thinking of the strength of wood as lying parallel to the straight grain. Contemporary bent metal and plywood provide strength with curvature. Furniture legs joined with wedges are stronger for being diagonal in direction. Low horizontality in furniture may not be suited to the human anatomy.

Our choice of dominant shape traits is largely dictated by their expressive power. Size is relative to the size of the surroundings and only in relation to these is it significant in conveying an expressive message. In many cases relatively large size creates an impression of greater solidity and small size an impression of instability.

Directions derive their expressive quality from the imaginary projection of the human body in directional positions. The horizontal suggests the greatest stability as well as the greatest movement along earthbound space. Direction is modified toward greater activity in the diagonal and to a lesser extent in the vertical. Seldom is the diagonal suitable as the dominant directional emphasis in a room. Greater mental activity and therefore increased dynamics is suggested when the shape changes its direction frequently and when the degree of change is great. Thus the feelings aroused by a particular kind of shape are modified by its direction and change of direction within a measure.

Although an object may be defined by its size and direction, what we notice is its outline. A room can be analyzed in character by observation of the outline of furnishings, the linear patterns on walls and floor, and the imaginary lines which exist between objects because of their relative positions. A line is a most economical means of expression. It says so much in such a little space.

The following chart may illustrate some of the messages which a straight line suggests. They range from intimations of simple physical and emotional states to suggestions of a complex character quality. It is easily seen that our final decision as to whether we like or dislike straight lines in a room comes as a result of much that we read into them.

Many shapes have curved outlines. It is more difficult to appraise their statements because there are so many varieties of curves. As compared to the suggestions made by straight lines, all curves veer in the direction of flexibility, weakness, indirection, informality, frivolity, and grace.

A line is one of the simplest types of shape. Each type of shape is a configuration which grows more complex as interrelations between length, width or breadth (the horizontal front measurement), height (the vertical measurement), depth (the front to back measurement) and division to division are involved. How can one choose artistic or well designed shapes? An artistic shape will have the same type of order regulating the interrelations of its parts which all good design possesses.

Figure 49. The dominant curved lines seen in this interior create a cheerful, even gay, homelike quality.

Residence of: Mr and Mrs. Wallace G. Nesbit, "Smultron Backen," northern Ohio. **Designers and builders:** Mr. and Mrs. Wallace G. Nesbit. **Artist:** Rolf Anderson. **Photographer:** G. Colburn Ball, Cleveland, Ohio.

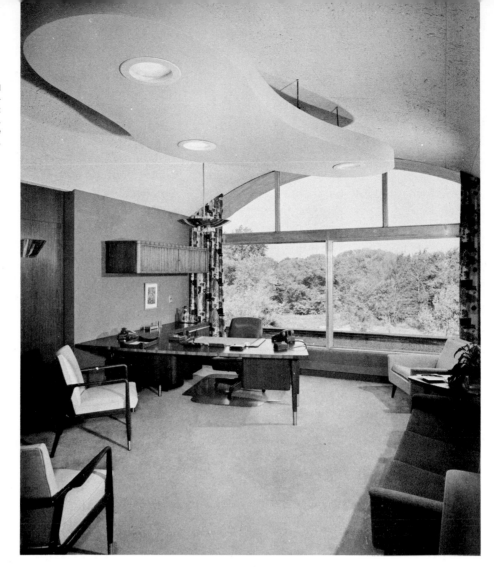

Building: Medusa Portland Cement Company, Cleveland, Ohio. **Architect:** Ernst Payer, A.I.A., Cleveland, Ohio. **Photographer:** Hube Henry, Hedrich-Blessing, Chicago, Illinois.

Figure 50. In the design of this office interior the geometric curve of the window and ceiling and the regular lines of the furniture are skilfully combined with the organic shape of the dropped canopy ceiling.

STRAIGHT LINE

Feeling in Terms of			Modified in Terms of		
			Vertical	Horizontal	Diagonal
Physical Response	Rigidity Strength	Stiffness	Less Stable	Most Stable	Least Stable
Simple Emotional Response	Directness Positiveness	Forcefulness	Spirited	Calm	Energetic
Complex Intellectual Response Projection of Character Meaning	Formality	Dignity	Austere Spiritual	Earthy	Youthful

Thus a line is said to be rhythmic when it changes its width or direction according to an ordered proportion. It might be called graceful when the order of its change is continuous and not abrupt. In two dimensional areas the relation of length to breadth should possess a pleasing ratio. When an object is seen in three dimensions then the problem of design becomes more involved. Sometimes in considering a three dimensional object such as a vase or piece of sculpture it is helpful to run one's hands over the surface trying to feel the rhythmic relation of mass to mass. This act will help us to appreciate the great artistry which exists in the most apparently simple forms. Interesting simplicity is great art.

Shapes bounded by curved lines may be described as geometric (mathematical) and regular, or organic, free form, and irregular. Geometric curves are arcs of simple mathematical shapes such as circles, ellipses, hyperbolas, and parabolas. These curves, changing their direction in a consistent manner, cause effects which are similar to those of a straight line.

Organic and free form curves are less regularly ordered. They are the artist's creation. In addition to having a good irregular curved outline, a free form area or volume should be so designed that there is variety as well as repetition in its opposing sides. Its longitudinal and its transverse visual axis should not be at right angles to each other. Thus any opposite contours do not run parallel for any extensive distance. They should be similar to the curves of a vertebrate in action where the stretched muscles of the forward members bear a relation to but do not parallel the untensed muscles. To give a homely example, when a snake moves, the edges of its body are parallel. When a tiger moves there is an interesting variation of the masses from haunches to thorax to head. Organic curves hold the interest for a comparatively long time. They can frequently be used as relief for the precise character of straight lines and regular curves.

Having chosen a well designed basic or structural shape, we consider standards for judgment of its embellishment. Decoration may be desirable. It may make an object personal, unique, or more interesting. It may soften the structural contours. It may be beautiful of itself. Occa-

sionally we discover an object of such ornamental character that it can act like costume jewelry to adorn a plain background. The decorative design of such an object must be of a very high order of artistic excellence if it is permitted center stage.

The modern designer accepts certain disciplines in regard to his decorative design. First he believes that the structural design is of prime importance and that it must be good. Decorative design should not detract from structural design but should strengthen it in every way. Good decoration, like good structure, should evolve from the medium and the function. In short, it should not be easy to differentiate between basic structural design and added decoration. The two should be a unit in purpose, expression and design.

F. SHAPES AS VISUAL FORCES

After selecting the dominant shapes for our space we must study shape forces.

The intrinsic force of a shape is first, large size. A large object or any grouping of smaller objects seen as a large object will attract our attention. As one use of forces is to regulate emphases, there are times when the design of a room will be improved by making some of its accents larger. It may tax our ingenuity to accomplish this. A too small picture may be hung on a larger cloth backdrop. A stencil border placed on the wall surrounding a small picture may serve the same purpose.

The diagonal direction is the greatest attention getter. Its oblique position, because it suggests instability, movement, and change, commands more attention than the more stable vertical and horizontal positions. Sometimes a drapery which is tied back into a moderate diagonal loop may create just the needed emphasis at a window.

Shapes which change their direction frequently and abruptly attract much attention. Pattern activity attracts the eye. From this point of view a straight line lacks attraction because it lacks variety. Because a straight line is relatively unobtrusive it is especially useful in a small room. By the same line of reasoning curves should be used with caution in small areas.

Article (top): "Running Tiger," Terra-cotta bas relief. From a tomb near Sian Fu, Shensi, Chinese, Han Dynasty. **Owner:** The Cleveland Museum of Art, Charles W. Harkness Collection, Cleveland, Ohio. **Photographer:** The Cleveland Museum of Art, Cleveland, Ohio.

Article (center): Pottery, painted. "Bull," Chinese, T'ang Dynasty or earlier, and Horse, Chinese, Northern Wei Dynasty. **Owner:** The Cleveland Museum of Art, The J. H. Wade Collection, Cleveland, Ohio. **Photographer:** The Cleveland Museum of Art, Cleveland, Ohio.

Article (bottom): "Animal Form," ceramic by Charles Lakofsky, American, Cleveland School. **Owner:** The Cleveland Museum of Art, Mary Spedding Milliken Memorial Collection, Gift of William Mathewson Milliken, Cleveland, Ohio. **Photographer:** The Cleveland Museum of Art, Cleveland, Ohio.

Figure 51. Artists of every age have understood the rhythms of organic forms, especially those of the vertebrates in action.

A shape may gain force from its neighbors. Exact repetition will augment its importance. Two identical lamps or a pair of chairs may be of greater value for this purpose than one. This idea cannot be carried too far or visual monotony cancels its effectiveness.

Differences in shapes will make for greater strength when they are aligned into rhythmic or contrasting patterns. A rhythmic arrangement of a group of furnishings enables us to see it as a single group. The group is larger and more important than its pieces. A busy object surrounded by blank space attracts attention through contrast. A round shape, such as a mirror, will be very forceful in a room which is filled with straight lines.

G. SPECIAL SPATIAL EFFECTS FROM SHAPE INTERACTIONS

When we look at a room we visually organize it spatially. It becomes foreground and background, up and down, left and right. Shapes in relation to one another help effect these arrangements. More forceful shapes and groups of shapes come forward and others recede. Shapes which appear quite inactive as visual forces and which we are apt to regard as plain background are frequently of great importance to a design. When background space of this sort is artistically related to shapes which attract our attention, it can be at once interesting, stimulating to the imagination, and restful. If the size of vacant space is rightly chosen it can serve as a path for the eye to travel from one detail to another. The amount of such space relative to the amount of foreground active shape which is to be used in a room must be decided. A designer may vary this ratio and produce various aesthetic effects each of which can be artistically done.

One type of special space effect is known as a space illusion. Optical illusions are caused by visual laws in accordance with which effects differ from those expected from the stimulus. Shape interrelations are especially able to create illusions of altered spatial proportions.

The following suggestions indicate a procedure to follow in seeking any illusion in interior design. First state the problem positively. For instance, if a room were thirteen feet wide and twenty-seven feet long it would be poorly proportioned. The problem is to elongate the short wall or to shorten the long wall. Let us first consider the latter problem.

At first a physical answer is suggested. If feasible cut the space by erecting a false cross wall or eradicate the long opaque wall by opening it wide to windows. If these solutions are undesirable, try the next line of attack. This is to place more forceful objects on the short axis and thus to distract attention. Unless such objects elongated the short wall, this remedy, however, might only divert the trouble.

If neither a physical solution nor a mental sidestepping of the problem seems desirable then we must resort to optical illusion. This involves some treatment of the offending wall so that it will not appear so long. That means marshaling visual shape forces in such a way as to keep the eye from traveling towards the end of the wall. Our eyes must be made to travel toward the ceiling or to the center of the wall. The shapes placed on or against this wall can be given vertical emphasis. Thus the eye travels upward and the wall seems less long.

Or the more commanding shape forces could be concentrated near the center of this long wall. This may be done in one of several different ways. A large shape or a grouping of smaller shapes can be placed there. Or the shape rhythms can be so arranged that the eye is carried to this central axis. For instance, a vertical picture might be placed over a central mantel. Two low pieces of furniture and two well placed pictures might flank the mantel. This entire grouping would make a triangular rhythmic closure which would attract the attention from the corners of the room. A contrasting shape, such as a round mirror, placed over the mantel would accentuate this effect.

When the possibilities of shortening the long wall are exhausted one then turns to the equally challenging possibilities of lengthening the thirteen foot wall. Broad low shapes placed against this wall might accomplish this result. Furniture placed parallel to the thirteen foot wall and near the center of the twenty-seven foot wall would serve the double purpose of extending

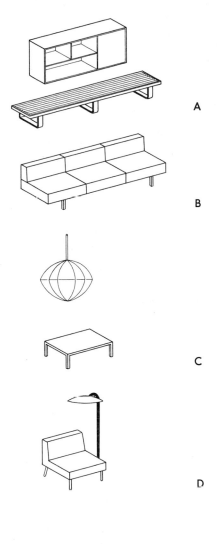

Figure 52. Suggestions for a living room starter set. Keep it simple—Keep it functional—Keep it spatial.

A. A platform bench to use as a seat with cushions, as a base for shelves and drawer units, or to set the television upon.

B. A daybed with bolsters which serves as a sofa or doubles as a bed. Excellent for temporary apartment use and later as furniture for guest room.

C. Low square table which is functional for corner groupings, between chairs, or as an individual piece of furniture. The ceiling light for good general illumination used in sofa and table grouping.

D. Two straight line chairs with back of comfortable height. An inconspicuous reading lamp.

E. A plain modern grass woven rug which can be used later in a recreation room.

F. A screen, wall hanging, interesting piece of sculpture, or driftwood which may relate to the personality of the owner.

the direction of the former and of breaking up the latter.

One of the frequent necessities in furnishing today's house is that of creating the illusion of more space. The problem is given considerable attention in Chapter XIII. A brief outline of the role which shapes play in the contemporary solution is:

1. Use an open plan. Avoid breaking the available space with partitions, furnishings, pattern, and opposing lines.
2. Design rhythms to carry the eye to space. Manipulate spaces, planes, and furnishings to this end.

H. PLANNING SHAPES IN A LIVING AREA

At this point we turn to specific living areas with furniture arrangement as planned in Chapter IV. Being satisfied that the furniture arrangements are functional, our next thought must be for the visual shape design.

It is good policy from every viewpoint to buy relatively few pieces of furniture in the beginning. If the initial house is small it is wise to keep the lines quiet and to keep the emphasis on space. One multiple seat or sofa, two chairs or stools, several lamps, a table and a bench (perhaps for portable television) are suggested. An additional chest, desk, or musical instrument may be required in larger spaces. Some floor covering and some wall piece may be needed. These should not be purchased until some preliminary drawing has been done.

Our work from now on is a process of plan and replan, check and recheck. Better have some lightweight tracing paper handy. It is cheaper to correct mistakes by tracing in a new plan over the old one than it is to correct them in the actual materials. If at any stage in the drawing we are dissatisfied with results, we can rearrange the furnishing, secure some new addition, or consider the possibility of altering the effect through color or texture. The best course will be the one which does least harm to the already established values.

We planned our furnishings to function for our physical needs. How does this placement plan coordinate with the visual design of the living space? The area we are furnishing has visual axes around which it is designed. Are the room axes disposed at right angles to each other? Is the room bisymmetrically or asymmetrically balanced around its axes? What are the architectural climaxes and centers of interest? What is the room rhythm? Our furniture placement should strengthen the architectural design if it is good and make it better if it is poor.

With our furniture placed upon the plan so as to create a satisfactory functional and visual relation to the room, we are ready to purchase. We should have decided upon the shape traits which we wish to make dominant in order to establish the effects desired. We should likewise decide whether we wish to intensify our effects largely by use of repetitive, similar or contrasting shape traits. In our purchases the dominant and subdominant shape themes are thus begun and are given their proportional emphasis.

Now draw elevations of the four walls of the living area showing the furniture only. Perspec-

tives may be drawn if preferred.[8] Elevations may be brought up to surround the floor plan so as to make a more realistic depiction of a room.

At this stage check critically on the furniture groupings. Is there too much of one kind of size, direction or line quality in one part of the room? Do the individual groupings hold together as two and three dimensional designs? If not then draw in a proposed remedy. It might consist of an arrangement of branches in a vase, a picture on a wall, an area rug, or a screen. Its actual embodiment should do the necessary visual task and it should not destroy the functional operation of the grouping.

After the isolated furniture groupings appear satisfactory then the next problem is to secure the necessary design integration between groups. This is done by introducing some rhythmic relations. Perhaps a picture may be chosen, the shape and placement of which helps group unity but the internal lines of which carry the eye to the next group. A repetitive or progressive rhythm of wall shapes from one group to the next may be the solution. The placement of a picture in relation to the blank space beyond may direct the eye onward.

At this point (actually all of these considerations are probably occurring at once) note whether your predetermined centers of interest have been established. Has the eye been carried to them in the order desired?

For additional interest, some details should permit the eye to lead off in several by-paths. Have any of these been provided by the choice of shapes and their arrangements? The possibility for such interest is increased as color and texture are added.

Finally comes the appraisal of room balance. There should be a balance of shape qualities and of shape forces on either side of the room axes. Its nature, bisymmetrical or asymmetrical, should usually correspond to the room design. Within the prevailing balance some minor arrangements of the opposite type of balance may prove interesting.

At this stage we may leave the shape design and begin to consider the application of color.

[8] See Chap. IV for directions.

In ink-sketches the brush is captain and the ink is lieutenant, but in coloured painting colours are the master and the brush is the servant.

SEI-ICHI TAKI * as quoted by Laurence Binyon

Chapter VI

UNDERSTANDING COLOR

A. IMPORTANCE OF COLOR AND ITS STUDY

Color is the second component to be studied. It is difficult to describe color except by saying that it is one aspect of everything we see. It is red and orange and yellow and all the hues of the rainbow. It is likewise black and white and grey which we seldom see in nature. Even the white paint on a house or the new white of the snow borrows a yellow or blue from the sky or a green from the trees.

If we half-close our eyes and if we possess good long eyelashes, we suddenly find that we have left the rainbow world and have entered a black, white and grey one. This is a world in which we become especially aware of shapes because it is the position of the light and dark on a shape which helps us to locate and identify it. We glean much of our understanding of what we call the real world from our visual knowledge of shapes. A black and white knowledge of the earth is all that we need in order to get around.

* From **Flight of the Dragon** by Laurence Binyon. The Wisdom of the East Series, copyright 1911, 1943, by John Murray Ltd. Reprinted by permission of the publisher.

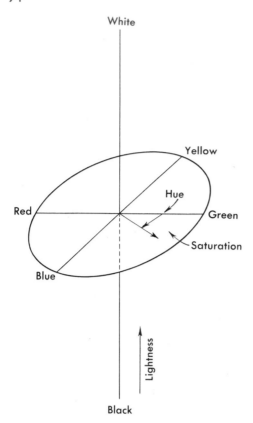

Figure 53. Organization of color perception in space.

The color of the rainbow in the firmament is an extra gift of the gods. When we use this gift well we are playing on an instrument which can turn our prosaic lives into poetry.

Many persons work well with color who are untutored in its use. Color is such a complex subject that a scientific comprehension of it cannot be a substitute for an emotional sensitivity to it. It should be an aid to such sensitivity.

It is especially important for the decorator to possess that certainty in his color work which scientific knowledge helps to provide. Color perceptions are more ephemeral than space perceptions. Variations in the color stimulus, in the eyes and nervous system and in the physical and mental state will affect the colors seen. Only with knowledge of all of the attendant factors can the artist control what he wants us to see. In an interior there is no escape from the pervading colors. Emotional responses even to small areas of color can be explosive. The decorator must be able to avoid color mistakes which would be magnified, costly, and dangerous.

Color knowledge comes from many sources. The physicist tells us that color comes from light which he has studied as a form of energy. The psychologist is interested in the entire process of perceiving color. He is helped by the physiologist who studies the eye and the brain. The aesthetician is concerned with our liking for colors. The chemist tells us how to control color through pigments and dyes. The lighting engineer helps us to produce it through light. As artists, we wish to use color as an aid towards creating a good interior design. We must not lose sight of our purpose as we study each branch of color science.

Fortunately there is a group of colorists in this country which recognizes the importance of preserving the total concept of color. This organization is called the Inter-Society Color Council. Its membership consists of a number of professional societies of national scope, each having a particular interest in color. In the meetings of the ISCC, color is discussed from all points of view.[1] The appreciation of color which results is like a diamond whose many facets give it added brilliance.

B. THE PSYCHOLOGICAL ATTRIBUTES OF COLOR

It is difficult to think about color without using some color names. Color concepts have been given many designations, each set related to a specific type of use. The most essential terms to the artist are those which qualify our basic color responses. These descriptive words are called the basic psychological color attributes.

The first of these is hue. If we see several pieces of colored cloth the first thing we are apt to notice about them is whether they resemble one another in hue. Hue is that attribute of certain colors which enables us to be aware of them as different from black, white, and grey. Colors such as red, orange, and yellow, which have hue, are

[1] The author is a member of the ISCC sub-committee 20 which is working on the problem, "Basic Elements of Color Education." Dr. Robert W. Burnham is the chairman of this committee. Although this chapter essentially antedates the establishment of the committee, every effort has been made to keep pace with the problem and the committee's work. The provisional manuscript of the committee compiled by R. W. Burnham, R. M. Hanes, and C. J. Bartleson, should be credited wherever its contents have crept almost unavoidably into the present work.

known as chromatic colors. We call black, white, and grey the achromatic colors, meaning the colors which do not have hue.

If we look again at our pieces of colored cloth we shall notice that some of them are what we call light and some are what we call dark. We can notice differences in this quality more quickly among the achromatic colors than among the chromatic colors. In naming this lightness-darkness attribute of colors we adopt the shorter name and speak of the lightness of the color. It is defined as that attribute of color by reference to which it can be classed as equivalent to a member of the achromatic series from black to white. Thus we describe a color as being about as dark as a certain grey or as being almost as light as white.

If we look once more at our textiles we may notice that there is a third kind of difference

between them. We might say that one is more colorful than another. To this kind of difference the name saturation has been given. This descriptive term suggests that the cloth is highly saturated with the hue. Saturation is that attribute of any color which determines its degree of difference from a grey of the same lightness. Thus we discriminate between two red samples which are equally light, by saying that one of them is more nearly grey, or is less saturated than the other.[2] Saturation refers to the strength of the color.

C. THE COLOR STIMULUS—LIGHT

1. The Character of Radiant Energy

Variations in the color stimulus will affect the hue, lightness, and saturation of the color we see. In general we see colors only when our eyes are stimulated by light. Light is a part of the great field of energy which activates our universe. This energy is sometimes called electromagnetic energy because similar energy can be produced by the relating of magnetic and electric force. It is often called radiant energy because it can radiate from a source like the sun.

Scientists have found that this energy may travel in the form of waves or in a wave-like motion. These waves travel through space at a uniform rate of speed which is known as their velocity. As these waves differ a very great deal from one another in wavelength (the distance from the crest of one wave to the crest of another), they likewise must differ in corresponding frequency (the number of waves which pass a given location in a length of time). It can be seen that the wavelength (symbol λ) varies inversely with the frequency (symbol f). Therefore either one of these quantities may be used to describe a particular kind or quality of wave. In color work reference is usually to the wavelength.

Radiant energy waves may likewise differ from one another in the amount of energy which they contain. The power of a light wave is related to its amplitude. The amplitude of a wave is its

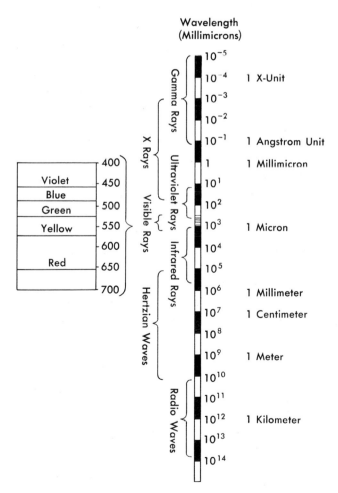

Figure 54. Light is a part of the electromagnetic energy band.

[2] All color terms, unless otherwise stated, are taken from the list compiled by Sidney M. Newhall and Josephine G. Brennan. *The ISCC Comparative List of Color Terms* (Washington, D.C.: The Inter-Society Color Council, 1949).

height or depth as measured from its position of equilibrium. Like the waves of the sea, those which rise to the highest peaks and which have the deepest troughs have much more vigor than the shallow little ripples.

We are made aware of energy when we observe the results of its performance. Thus we recognize the energy of a man when he lifts a weight, or of a horse when he pulls a load. We are conscious of the energy of a radio when it makes a sound, of an X-ray machine when we see the photographic X-ray of our bones. It is this same kind of energy which passes through the complicated machinery of our eyes and is observed as light.

Light is similar in form of energy to the energy of the radio, radar, infrared heat rays, ultraviolet medicinal rays, X-rays, radioactive rays, cosmic rays, and indeed to electricity (power transmission) itself. A *ray* is a word for a limited section of such energy.

2. Wavelength of Light

The wavelengths of radio waves [3] are very long as compared to the wavelengths of X-rays which are very short. Light rays are likewise very short waves. The eye is a delicate receiving instrument which is receptive to a very limited band of radiant energy which is seen as light.

The wavelength of this narrow band of rays is measured by units which are billionths of a meter [4] long. Because Greek was the language commonly understood by learned men of former centuries, many of our scientific terms are known by the Greek name which was assigned to them. Often just a Greek letter might be given to a term. This could be the first letter of its Greek name. One millionth of many substances was given the prefix *micros,* the Greek word for a very small part. Thus a millionth of a meter has been called a micron. It is called by its first letter, the Greek letter *M*, pronounced *mu* and written in script μ. Latin was likewise a scientific language. The Latin word for thousand was *mille*. It is used as a prefix *milli* meaning one thou-

sandth of a part and abbreviated *m*. One thousandth of one millionth of a meter equals one billionth of a meter and is called a milli-micron and is symbolized mμ.[5] Thus do we mix our ancient languages and our modern concepts. The narrow band of energy to which the eye is tuned has wavelengths of approximately 380 to 760 mμ.

In everyday language when we speak of color we are apt to mean chromatic color. We mean red, green, or blue rather than white. Chromatic color is the sensation which we experience when we look at a fractional narrow band of the total span of light. For instance, a band of wavelengths measuring from 380 mμ to 450 mμ will be seen as violet light, from 450 mμ to 490 mμ as blue, from 490 mμ to 560 mμ as green, from 560 mμ to 590 mμ as yellow, from 590 mμ to 630 mμ as orange and from 630 mμ to 760 mμ as red.[6]

How is light broken up into these smaller bands? We learned that light traveling through space has a constant speed or velocity. When this light strikes an obstacle in its path it may be slightly retarded. The shortest wavelengths are slowed down most and the longest wavelengths least. As a waveband of light is delayed it is bent proportionately off its straight course. Thus the shortest or violet-hued lights emerge from such an obstacle in a most oblique direction. The long or red-hued lights emerge with the least deviation from the normal and the other bands are relatively situated between these extremes.

The name given to the bending of light rays when they travel through a medium of greater density than a vacuum is refraction. It is commonly demonstrated by means of a glass prism which is a piece of clear glass having triangular ends and nonparallel sides. Inasmuch as glass is denser than air and is transparent, the white light will be refracted and will emerge in narrow bands each having a different hue. This we see in the rainbow where the drops of moisture in the air have acted as myriad prisms to refract

---

[3] Radio waves are usually referred to by their frequencies rather than by their wavelengths.

[4] A meter is an international standard of length. It is equivalent to 39.37 inches.

[5] Sometimes the wavelengths of light are designated in *angstrom units* for which the abbreviation is *A.* An angstrom unit is $\frac{1}{10}$ of mμ. It was named in honor of the Swedish astronomer and physicist, Anders Jens Angstrom (1814–1874).

[6] Optical Society of America, Committee on Colorimetry, *The Science of Color* (New York: Thomas Y. Crowell Co., 1953), p. 41.

the sun's rays. The process of breaking up a total band of light into its component rays is known as dispersion.[7] The band of colored light which results from dispersion is called the visible spectrum. The hues as seen in the spectrum are the spectral hues.

Every hue in a continuous spectrum merges imperceptibly into its neighboring hue. The average eye can differentiate about one hundred and twenty-five different spectral hues.[8] However, for the sake of convenience, the spectrum is frequently and arbitrarily divided into the six broad visual regions previously mentioned.

3. Additive Color Mixture

Not only is it possible to break achromatic light into chromatic bands but these bands can be recombined into achromatic light. This process of adding lights together and obtaining a light which is an integration of all their characteristics is frequently called additive color mixture.

The results of additive color mixture are absolutely certain and are readily predictable. In the first place the amounts of the component lights add up as simply as a sum in arithmetic. Thus if we add together several dim lights we obtain a much brighter light. When talking about light as so much illumination we customarily speak of its brightness rather than of its lightness. The two words refer to different visual aspects of the same thing, namely the amount of light.

The combination of the hue and saturation of a light is known as its chromaticness. If several lights are added together the chromaticness of the resulting light is likewise predictable. Now, however, the process is not quite like adding together two things which have the same sensation quality, i.e., two brightnesses. We are combining two lights which may have different qualities of chromaticness. Perhaps one light is a strong blue light and the other is a weak yellow light. Blue and yellow seem to be quite different in quality although their saturations may be visualized as magnitudes or quantities.

[7] Diffraction, interference films and polarization are other means which can be used to isolate fixed portions of the spectrum. These may be studied in any text dealing with the physics of light.

[8] Ralph M. Evans, *An Introduction to Color* (New York: John Wiley & Sons, Inc., 1948), p. 120.

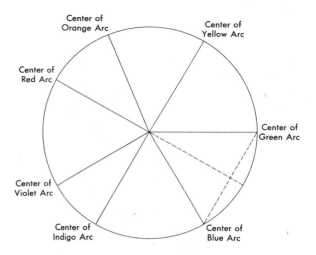

Figure 55. Interactions of colored light after the manner of diagraming by Sir Isaac Newton.

The process at this point more nearly resembles a combination of tones of several different instruments in an orchestra. The amount of sound which the instruments make in unison is equal to the sum of the amounts of sound which the individual instruments make solo but the kind of sound which they all make in unison is a new kind of sound which is a composite of the pitch and timbre of the individual instruments.

In general we can say that any two lights when added together will have the hue of a light which is halfway between them on the spectrum. A red and a yellow light will make an orange light. Thus two chromatic lights could be found, each of which would be a combination of the lights of one-half of the spectrum. These two lights then would combine to make the entire spectrum, or achromatic light. Two such paired lights, which when added together make achromatic light, are called complementary lights. It has been found that for every monochromatic light[9] (one hue light) with the exception of the green band, for which there is not complementary spectrum light, there is a complementary light.

[9] Light energy of a single wavelength is more accurately called homogeneous light as opposed to that composed of several or all visible wavelengths or heterogeneous light.

We may wish to predict the saturation which will result when several lights are combined. The more homogeneous a light is, the more saturated it will appear. The more heterogeneous, the more achromatic it will appear. All thinkers frequently use diagrams as a concise method of illustrating ideas and relationships. In a familiar color diagram the spectrum band is represented as a circle.[10] This is the way that Sir Isaac Newton (1642–1727) illustrated it. It was he who first demonstrated that white light was composed of chromatic light. The circle diagram is useful and generally reliable in helping us to determine the saturation of a combination of lights.

If we take the spectrum band and join its short wavelength or violet end to its long wavelength or red end it becomes apparent that the spectrum does not contain colored lights of the hue which we call purple. This hue, however, can be formed by the addition of red and violet light. When this synthesized purple light is added to green light, white light results. Here is the missing complementary range for the green light band.

If a purple band is included between the red and the violet bands, our circle diagram of chromatic light is complete. The circle should be arranged so that complementary lights are opposite to each other and thus lie on a straight line extending through the center. At the center will be found the achromatic light which results from a mixture of the complementary lights. Such a circle diagram might be known as a chromatic light circle because it illustrates the interactions between chromatic lights in relation to their appearance of chromaticness.

On this chromatic light circle the hue resulting from the addition of equal amounts of two lights can be visualized by connecting the two with a straight line. At the midpoint of this connecting line place a point. Project a radius of the circle through this point. The new hue is located where this radius meets the circumference. Where two complementary lights are mixed in equal amounts the point falls on the center and an achromatic

[10] A circle diagram is not the most accurate way to illustrate color relations but it is a useful one. We shall discuss other diagrams later.

light results. If two lights are not complementary it will be seen that their summation light will be pulled towards the center (achromatic light) by an amount which is commensurate to their distance apart on the circle. If two lights are combined in unequal amounts the resultant light will be of a chromaticness which is proportionate to their relative amounts but which is dictated by the general principles outlined above.

The procedure just outlined will likewise indicate the saturation of two combined lights of less than spectrum saturation. The new saturation will fall on the line connecting the diagram positions of the lights. For prediction on several lights, work from the extremes to their adjacent lights and proceed until the number has been reduced to two.

Inasmuch as lights always combine qualitatively to form an intermediate light, it is possible to match the chromaticness of any light by the proper selection of several carefully chosen chromatic lights. Three chromatic lights have been found to be the smallest number which would accomplish this satisfactorily. These three chromatic lights are so spaced that if combined in equal amounts they will form achromatic light. In other words they are about equidistant from one another on the spectrum. The three lights which are usually chosen for this purpose are of red, green and violet-blue hues. They are conveniently located at the extremes and in the center of the visible spectrum. They are sometimes called the primary lights. Here the word primary means coming first in a process. They are the basic lights which are used in larger or smaller amounts to match any other light in color.

4. Light Sources

Much of the light around us is not composed of equal amounts of energy at every visible wavelength. Indeed such an ideal spectrum, known as an equal energy spectrum, is theoretical.

The largest direct source of light for our world is the sun. Sunlight is an incandescent light. Incandescence is caused by the transforming of one kind of energy into another, in the process

Figure 56. Light energy from indirect or non-selfluminous objects.

A. Directional or specular reflection from a smooth surface.

B. The total light which impinges on a surface is accounted for in one of three ways—**R**eflection, **A**bsorption, **T**ransmission. (The so-called R-A-T formula.)

C. Diffusion of light may result from nondirectional reflection from a relatively rough surface, from internal reflection and refraction, and from a resulting transmission.

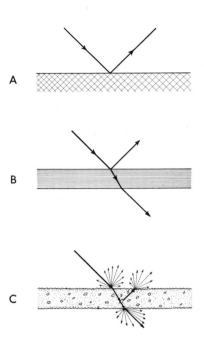

of which light and heat are given off. The light from a filament light bulb and from burning gas is incandescent.

A direct light source may emit light energy without heat. This is called luminescence. One kind of luminescence is due to the secondary action of very short wave radiations (ultraviolet light) acting upon fluorescent or phosphorescent materials causing them to emit rays in the visible range. Fluorescent light tubes are a potential light source of this variety.

Small particles of matter, about the size of the dust particles in the air, are able to deflect light. This is known as scattering. As the shortest light waves are most readily scattered we see many of them in the zenith.[11] The bluish light which results is known as skylight. A mixture of direct sunlight and skylight is known as white light or daylight. It is described as the kind of illumination experienced at noon outdoors on a slightly clouded day. It is seen as achromatic or hueless and is the norm to which other lights are compared. Colored materials seen under this white light are said to have genuine color.[12] When colors are seen under other circumstances their color is referred to as apparent color. Their

[11] Called Rayleigh's law of scattering. Optical Society of America, *op. cit.*, p. 182.

[12] David Katz, *The World of Color* (London: Kegan Paul, Trench, Trubner & Co., Ltd., 1953), p. 82.

genuine color is the norm to which we may relate their apparent color.

5. Light Modification by Matter

Material in the path of light can affect it in three ways. Some of the light may be bounced off as sunlight ricochets off the moon and so illuminates our night. This is reflected light. Some of it may seep through. This is transmitted light. Light energy can likewise be absorbed by an object. It is then invisible. The total light energy which strikes a substance must be accounted for in these three ways.

The ratio of incident light to reflected, transmitted and absorbed light upon any object is constant. This causes us to think of the color of the object as unchangeable and to think of that color as being part of the object. This fact has led psychologists to say that we see colors in context in certain phenomenal ways which are known as the modes of color appearance. We visualize colors of opaque surfaces in the surface mode of appearance and colors of transparent volumes in the volume mode. Both of these are subdivisions of the object mode where color appears to belong to an object located in space. Other modes are the illuminant, the illumination and the aperture or film (color as seen in an optical instrument) mode. There are many attributes of these modes. Glossiness would be an attribute of the surface mode. These phenomenal qualifications of color are explainable and thus can be reproduced in actuality and in imitative effect.[13]

Reflection of light occurs at the boundary between any two substances when the difference between their indices of refraction [14] is high. Light enters a material when this difference is less. Light passes through when the difference approaches zero.

Boundary reflection is quantitative rather than qualitative. It is nonselective reflection. That means that the returned light has the same spectral character as the incident light.

Light which enters a material is usually selectively absorbed and reflected. That means that the material absorbs more of some wavelengths than it does of others. The reflected wavelengths account for the hue of the substance.

Light which passes through an object may likewise be selectively absorbed and transmitted. The transmitted wavelengths account for the hue of the substance. As most materials are in reality compound substances, all three of these types of occurrences may happen.

6. Diffuse and Directional Light

Light is reflected so that its angle of incidence with the surface is equal to its angle of reflection. When the surface is smooth this boundary reflection is said to be directional light, or light reflected in a definite direction or pattern. It is likewise known as mirror or specular reflection. It accounts for the glossiness of a surface. Transparency of a material is the result which occurs

when transmitted light leaves a substance in a regular directional manner.

Nondirectional light is called diffuse light. It may result from the nondirectional reflection from a relatively rough surface or from internal refraction, reflection and transmission of light from inner particles which are relatively large. Diffuse light produces a matte surface in an opaque material and a translucent light from a transmitting material. Many substances reflect and transmit some directional and some diffuse light.

7. Colorants

a. THEIR GENERAL CHARACTER

A colorant is any substance which is used to produce the color of an object. The chief colorants are the pigments and the dyes. Pigments are colorants which are insoluble in their liquid media whereas dyes are soluble. Lakes are soluble dyes precipitated upon an inert insoluble base. Toners are concentrated dye salts. When mixed with a carrier the colorants become the paints, lacquers, varnishes, dyes, and inks of commerce. But we must not forget that many natural colors such as the green of the grass, the grey of slate, the brown of the earth, owe their hues to natural colorants which they contain. Colorants extracted from natural sources were the only ones available until the eighteenth century.

Paints and similar products are highly compounded commodities and their characteristics are to a large extent due to the ingredients other than the pigments, dyes, or lakes which they contain. Nevertheless it is these colorants to which their pronounced color is due. Therefore it is helpful to the decorator to know the performance potential of many colorants.

Pigments and lakes ground in oil are suggested for this analysis because they are closely related to the decorator's work. For an initial step, small tubes of oil pigments may be used. A mixture of two parts turpentine and one part linseed oil can serve as diluent and film former. Four-ply Bristol board or canvas paper will make a support. Squares painted full strength will indicate the

[13] Suggestions and illustrations for painters of pictures are offered by F. Birren, *Monument to Color* (New York: McFarlane Warde McFarlane, 1937).

[14] The index of refraction of a substance corresponds to the rate in which the velocity of light is slowed down by the substance relative to the velocity of light in outer space.

mass tone, diluted with 50 or 75 per cent white will show the tint tone and tinting strength. In addition it is helpful to know the general composition, relative permanency, and covering power of the pigments. The paint manufacturer must likewise know many other facts, such as their resistance to chemicals, their bleeding into diluents and their combining power with oil.

Colorants are first divided into two large classes, the inorganic and the organic. These are distinguished primarily by the absence or presence of carbon in the molecular structure.[15] The inorganic compounds in general are salts of the minerals to which they owe their color.

A second major colorant division is that by which the synthetics are distinguished from the natural pigments. The former term is restricted to its customary usage as referring to colorants made from basic raw materials (largely carbon, oxygen, hydrogen, and nitrogen) as obtained from intermediate crude products (largely benzene, naphthalene, anthracene, toluene, and xylene) of the coal tar industry, and built into structures for color. The visual and practical qualities of the synthetics have given them precedence in the commercial field. Only a few are obtainable as artists' pigments.

The following list contains many important colorants:

A. Inorganic
1. Native earths: such as ochre, sienna, umber (in raw or burnt state) permanent ochre opaque; the others somewhat less so—tinting strength not great—frequently used to dull other colorants while supplying a warm tone—useful for antique glazing.[16]
2. Minerals: such as aluminum, copper, gold, zinc—difficult to keep in solution—uses specialized.
3. Mineral compounds:
a. Alumina hydrate (or aluminum hydroxide)—an inert base for lakes.

[15] Some carbon compounds are customarily classed as inorganic, however.

[16] A good glazing medium is as follows. It may be used as the vehicle for incorporating thin glazes of transparent colorants over an opaque coating. Mix: 1½ oz. damar varnish, 1 oz. stand oil, 5 oz. turpentine, and ¼ t. cobalt linoleate (drier).

b. Cadmium compounds: usually as a sulphur salt—hues red to yellow—permanent—opaque—great saturation and tinting strength——largely used in artists' pigments.
c. Chromium compounds: such as lead chromate—hues similar to cadmium compounds but less saturated—not sufficiently permanent for artists' use—economically used for exterior and interior house paints.
Chrome orange used as a metal primer.
Chrome oxide green: relatively permanent—opaque.
Chrome green: Prussian blue plus chrome yellow—not permanent.
Hydrated chromium oxide: better known as viridian—saturated green—permanent—transparent.
d. Cobalt compounds: such as cobalt aluminate—blue hue with slightly greenish undertone—relatively permanent—nearly transparent—cobalt greens and violets are available, some of the latter are poisonous and must be used with care.
e. Iron compounds: such as iron oxide—hue of dull red, yellow—in natural state known as Indian or Venetian red—synthetics known as Mars colors—permanent—opaque.
Prussian blue (or ferric ferrocyanide): not absolutely permanent—transparent—high tinting strength.
f. Lead compounds:
Red lead: various lead salts—not permanent—opaque—used industrially as a priming coat for steel and as a drying agent.
Flake white: basic lead carbonate (organic)—high quality corroded, so-called Dutch process lead, much used for exterior and interior painting—poisonous if taken internally.
g. Lithopone composed of zinc sulphide and barium sulphate (blanc fixe): extensive use for white interior house paint because of good performance and low cost.

h. Titanium dioxide: a permanent white of great opacity.

i. Ultramarine: original was ground lapis lazuli—now a form of colloidal sulphur-blue—best are permanent—semi-transparent.

j. Vermilion (or mercuric sulphide): red—being replaced largely by the cadmium colors.

k. Zinc oxide (Chinese white): a permanent opaque white.

B. Organic

1. Vegetable: such as indigo, madder—seldom used except in craft work.

2. Animal: such as cochineal, lac, Tyrian purple—seldom used—bone black and ivory black (a high grade bone black) are intense blacks which mix well with water.

3. Carbon black: often used as a generic name for all blacks made from carbon—specifically made from natural gas—mixes well with water—permanent—opaque.
Lamp black—pure carbon—permanent—slightly bluish in color.
Ivory black—impure carbon—generally a high grade bone black—brownish undertones.

4. Synthetics:
The principal synthetic lakes which are available as artists' colorants are:

a. Alizarin: produced from anthracene—blue-red hue—permanent—transparent.

b. Phthalocyanine green and blue—saturated tones—high tinting strength—deep copper mass tone overcome by preparation with a percentage of inerts—permanent—transparent.

b. PAINTS AND PROTECTIVE COATINGS

The manufactured colorants provide the coloring matter for all objects which are artificially colored. When such coloring is placed on the surface of an object (as opposed to being integrally incorporated as with a dye) it must be further manufactured into a paint or similar product.

These commodities are produced by a vast industry dealing in protective and decorative coatings. A protective coating may be quite specialized in its purpose. Those which the decorator uses are designed to protect a surface from harmful atmospheric, bacteriological and chemical action. They likewise are intended to improve its appearance and modify its light reflection.

The manufacture of paints and of those protective coatings which are used for their visual appeal as well as for their practical utility, has developed into a large scale industry during the last century. Earlier developments in this field were slowly attained through the empirical methods of the artist. Crayons made from natural earths have been found which were the instruments used in the early cave paintings. Other media, variously known as tempera or gouache, added a binder of casein, egg, glue, or gum to opaque earth colors, with water as a diluent. There is little excess binder in these coatings and the film dries by coagulation to a matte porous finish. Therefore these paints have little protective value and their color can be washed away.

This fault was remedied in two early forms of mural painting which are being revived today. The first of these is fresco painting in which pigments which are ground only in water and which are inert to lime, are placed upon a newly laid plaster wall. The pigments set with the plaster and so are as permanent as it is.

Encaustic painting is likewise an early decorative technique. It is pigmentation applied in hot wax which sets as a hard film when cool. Waxes possess great protective value because they are practically impermeable to atmospheric moisture. Therefore thin coatings of wax alone are frequently used for finishes. Their disadvantage is that they are not impervious to dirt.

The film forming property of a protective coating is very important. Such a film must be hard enough to be protective and have other desirable physical qualities such as adherence, durability, ease of application, and quick setting. It is counted upon to provide the appearance quality of gloss. Various film forming ingredients excel in various ways; therefore combinations are often used.

When resins and drying oils were added to paint composition the protective function of paints may be said to have begun. These substances come second to the waxes in resisting atmospheric changes. The oils belong chemically to the same category as the animal waxes, e.g., beeswax. The drying oils are a number of vegetable oils such as linseed and tung (Chinese nut) oil which dry by oxidation to a hard solid film. In oil paints the pigments are not only ground in oil as a binder, additional oil serves as the film forming material. A dried oil film has the pigment particles permanently encased in its glossy surface.

Resins are substances which can be dissolved in suitable solvents and which harden to a glossy film either by oxidation or by evaporation of the solvent. Natural resins are the saps of certain trees or the deposits of insects which feed upon this sap. Synthetic resins have practically revolutionized the protective coating industry within the last thirty years. They have made possible durable films which dry quickly and adhere to all kinds of surfaces.

Some resins are solvent in drying oils. A homogeneous solution containing such resins and oils is the traditional recipe for a varnish. The word *varnish* sometimes is loosely used as a generic name for all clear resinous finishes. Many of today's oil paints and varnishes contain synthetic resins which impart desired qualities of gloss, hardness, and quick drying. The paint or varnish vehicle must then contain suitable solvents for these resins. Such paints are frequently known as enamels.

Spirit varnishes contain resins which must be dissolved in mineral spirits such as alcohol. Film hardening is the result of the evaporation of the solvent. *Shellac* is a spirit varnish made from a resin which is the deposit left by an insect which lives on the sap of a resinous Indian tree. Its solvent is alcohol. *Lacquer* is made from a synthetic nitrocellulose resin dissolved in a suitable solvent.

Instead of being dissolved in a solvent, some synthetic resins of high molecular structure can be dispersed in a medium in the same manner that pigment particles are. This produces a coating which has many advantages of application.

A recent development in a dispersed resin paint is a latex paint. A latex is a colloidal dispersion of a high molecular resin in water. This latex can then be combined with pigment and oil to make a paint. This paint unites the advantage of drying to an oil and resin film with the ease of application of a water base paint.

In addition to pigment and added film forming ingredients with binders and solvents (known collectively as the vehicle), paints may contain diluents, fillers, driers, and other ingredients added to provide practical qualities. Turpentine is a diluent for oil base paints, alcohol for shellac, special diluents for lacquers and water for latex and all water base paints.

Coatings may be classified according to their functional uses. Reliable paint companies have produced these products which are carefully balanced to do what they are supposed to do.

1. *Primer and sealer:* designed to prepare and seal a porous surface such as plaster so that it will hold up to finish coats. Some sealers are especially designed to seal against bleeding by stains.
2. *Surfacer* (which may also be a primer): designed to provide a smooth surface for finish coats.
3. *Enamel undercoater:* designed for use with one coat enamels to take the place of primers and surfacers.
4. *Finish coat:*
   a. Flat and egg shell: no gloss.
   b. Gloss paint: paints which come in a variety of sheens and are called by a variety of names.
5. *Floor paint:* designed for hard usage and to counteract the harmful effect of moisture on some resins.
6. *Spar varnish:* designed for use on surfaces exposed to moisture.
7. *Paint for metal surfaces.*
8. *Stain:*
   a. Wiping stain: pigmented linseed oil in diluent—designed for use on nonporous wood or to create special effects on porous wood. The pigment percentage is low compared to that used in paint. A preservative such as creosote is usually a component of shingle stain.

b. Water or penetrating stain: dyes immersed in water—designed for use on porous wood—should be followed by diluted clear coat of shellac or lacquer—sand paper when dry to reduce raised grain.

c. N.G.R. (nongrain-raising): dyes dissolved in alcohol.

9. *Wood filler:* designed to fill pores in open grain wood.

10. *Plastic wood:* designed to fill larger holes in wood.

Luminescent paints are composed of pigments plus radioactive substances (those which emit ultraviolet rays). These rays convert some of the light energy which is normally absorbed by the pigment to the wavelengths which are normally reflected by it. Thus these pigments reflect more energy of a specific wavelength than is present in the impinging light. Colorants can be made to fluoresce in the dark by being similarly activated by a special ultraviolet or so-called black light.[17]

c. SUBTRACTIVE OR COLORANT MIXTURE

Colorant mixtures are not as predictable as light mixtures. Many factors, not always recognized by the artist, enter into the problem. In the first place the exact physical composition of the reflected light is a factor. Likewise such characteristics as the relative size of the particles

[17] For an account of luminiscent coatings see J. R. DeVore, "Luminiscent Coatings," in Edward G. Bobalek and William Von Fisher, *Organic Protective Coatings* (New York: Reinhold Publishing Corp., 1953), pp. 99–101.

in the coloring media, their relative opacity and their chemical activity and permanence will be important. General rules, therefore, can serve only as a guide.

What may be expected to happen in colorant mixture? It is important to notice that the resultant color is duller than any of the separate colorants which are in the mixture. This is due to two causes. The first is the fact that no colorant can be manufactured so that it is quite physically unadulterated. In multiplying the colorants we multiply the impurities which usually are achromatic. Secondly no colorant is spectrally pure. A yellow colorant may likewise reflect some green and red rays. A pure red colorant may reflect red rays plus a small amount of yellow and blue. A mixture of the yellow and red colorants reflects red, yellow, and small amounts of green and blue rays. The green rays tend to dull the red and the blue to dull the yellow, resulting in an orange which is duller than either the red or the yellow. Thus if a painter wishes very saturated colors he should use them as free from admixture as possible.

With this proviso the first thing the painter should do in mixing colorants is to try to obtain the hue he wishes. With the colorants arranged in the well-known rainbow sequence this should not be difficult to do because the mixture of any two colorants usually results in the intermediate color. Blue and yellow, for instance, should make green. Here we obtain our definition for colorant primaries. A colorant primary is primary because it cannot readily be obtained from the admixture of any other two colorants and from three primaries any other hue can be made. At least these colorants will give the painter the maximum

Figure 57. Colorant (subtractive) and light (additive) color mixture: designations apply approximately to Munsell colors. Colorants are always absorbent to light. Primary lights will add to white light if they are not modified by a colorant.

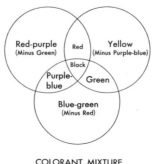

COLORANT MIXTURE

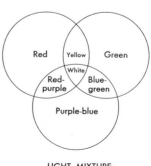

LIGHT MIXTURE
(Unmodified by Colorants)

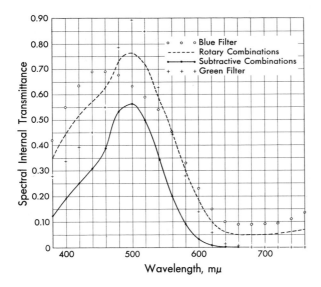

Figure 58. Spectrophotometric diagram showing how a green and blue filter subtract from the total light energy (as seen in resulting solid line) when the light is transmitted through them and how the mixture is additive when the light from them is mixed by rotary mixture (seen in the dotted line).

Graph adapted from: D. B. Judd, **Color in Business, Science and Industry,** New York, 1952, p. 63. **Courtesy:** Reprinted by permission from John Wiley and Sons, Inc., New York.

range of colors on mixture. The usual colorant primaries are yellow, blue and red. When the colorant primaries are defined as those colorants which will absorb the primary lights, then the primary yellow is a pure lemon yellow, the blue is really a bluish-green and the red is close to the color we know as magenta.

When a painter mixes pigments he soon finds that the yellow and blue combinations will make the greens; the yellow and red combinations will make the oranges and the red and blue combinations will make the violets. If then he mixes the red with the combination of the yellow and blue (the green) he secures a darkish grey. Theoretically he would secure a black but impurities in the pigments make the obtaining of a good black unlikely. In other words a combination of all three of the primary colorants is capable of absorbing all of the light rays. Every colorant that is added to another colorant subtracts more of the total rays, and when these colorants are capable of supplementing one another so as to subtract all the rays of visible light then the sensation of black results. Black as a color sensation exists whenever the amount of light reflection is exceedingly small as compared to that of the surroundings.

One can understand why the mixture of colorants is known as subtractive color mixture. It is because colorants selectively subtract (or absorb) light. This is the negative side to

their positive reflection of light. Any two colorants which when mixed in the proper amounts subtract all of the visible light rays are said to be complementary colorants. Inasmuch as a saturated colorant absorbs the light ray which is complementary to the one it reflects, it will be noted that the three primary pigments absorb the three primary lights. This fact is utilized in color photography where the filters which screen out colored light are the three primary colorant hues.

Any arrangement of colors in a circle is a purely arbitrary arrangement and therefore should be dictated by some use. A color circle which is arranged so that complementary colorants can be visualized quickly because they are opposite one another, might be called a painter's color wheel. Such an arrangement has been made to facilitate the work of the painter in mixing colors.

Once we understand the principle of subtractive color mixture we know how to lower the saturation of a color to any desired degree. This is done by proportional mixture with its complementary colorant. Or a color may be mixed with proportional parts of black and white or of their admixture, a neutral grey, in order to lessen its saturation.

As paints dry they often seem to change in

saturation. This is of course due to changes which take place in the indices of refraction of the vehicle during the drying process. In general water color paints become less saturated and oil paints more saturated during the drying process.

After the desired hue and saturation are obtained in a colorant mixture, the last problem is to create an acceptable lightness. For opaque paints this requires the addition of an achromatic extender of the proper degree of reflectance. Transparent colorants can be diluted but will only be lightened if the material which supports them is light in color.

Extension of colorant mixtures in this manner presents special difficulties. When white pigment is added or when concentrations are changed, the hue is frequently altered too. The reds are apt to slide counterclockwise towards violet and the greens clockwise to blue. Moreover when light colors ground in oil are used for tinting they frequently contribute the yellowish cast of the oil. A black colorant may be a dark tone of a chromatic hue. When extended or diluted this basic color becomes apparent. Lightening or darkening colorants is known as tinting and shading respectively. In this process a reduction of saturation will occur because of subtractive mixture and lessened concentration. Compensation must be made by the painter for all of these changes.

Likewise the painter should realize that achromatic boundary reflection will weaken the apparent saturation and lighten the tone of chromatic color by adding white light. The extent of such boundary reflection also allows less internal selective reflection. This dulling is particularly noticeable when a gloss paint is illuminated by a large source of diffuse light.

D. THE VISUAL PROCESS

1. The Eye Receptors

The eye and the neural system connecting it with the brain are the receiving station for all color waves. The optic mechanism translates radiant energy into visual images in a predictable manner. Therefore an understanding of this visual process will often be helpful in forecasting color effects.

The human eye has two distinct functions. One is to transmit the sensation of light. The other is to transmit the perception of form or shape as seen through a configuration of light. The transmission of light by the eye can be further subdivided into the transmission of chro-

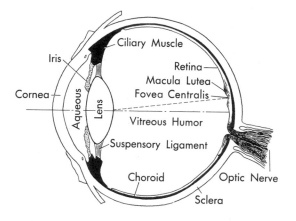

Figure 59. Diagram of the human eye.

matic light and the transmission of achromatic light. It is possible to see light without seeing either chromatic color or form, although the reverse is not true. These several kinds of visual sensations require specialized mechanisms in the eye. Thus it is not idle talk to separate form and color or to separate chromatic from achromatic color.

The visual process registers images because the eye contains various refractive media which focus light rays on the innermost lining of the eyeball, the retina. The optical system of the eye includes the cornea or transparent tissue forming the outer coating of the front of the eyeball, the aqueous humor or watery fluid between the cornea and lens, the crystalline lens and the vitreous humor or jelly-like substance that fills the eyeball between the lens and the retina. The lens is the principal refractive instrument of the eye. Whereas it is most wonderful in its ability to adjust to a variety of distances and of illuminations, it is not a good focusing instrument for chromatic light. Strong contrasts of long and short wavelengths cannot be focused on the retina at the same time.

The lens and other refractive media of the eye are like the lens of the camera. Their purpose is to focus light rays on the retina. The retina is the real light-receiving apparatus. It is like the film of the camera which is sensitive to the light which is collected upon it. The retina consists of ten layers. It is the second layer, lying adjacent to the outermost lining layer, which contains two kinds of cells whose importance as receiving stations for light impulses has long been known. These photoreceptors or light-receiving mechanisms of the eye are minute cells, some shaped like ninepins and called cones and some shaped like elongated cones and called rods.

There are about thirty million rods and nine million cones in the eye but they are not evenly dispersed over the retina. Near the periphery of the retina there are only rods. The cones are sparsely scattered in the next retinal zone and become more numerous towards the center of the eyeball. The rods become less numerous as the cones increase. Near the center of the posterior of the eyeball is the region called the fovea centralis. The fovea is the area in which vision is most acute. In this area only cones are found. The fovea is located in the center of an area about one millimeter in diameter which contains a yellow pigment. This is the macula lutea. The function of this so-called yellow spot (macula lutea) of the eye seems to be similar to that of a highly selective yellow filter which would absorb some of the shortest wavelengths. This absorption makes the achromatism of the eye less serious because it helps to equalize the plane of absorption of short and long wavelengths.

When the retina of the eye is extracted in dim or in red light it appears to be a magenta color. This color quickly fades upon exposure to bright light. It is due to a purplish coloring matter called rhodopsin, or visual purple, which is found in the rods. Rhodopsin is insensitive to red light but is particularly sensitive to blue. In dim illumination, red light can only be distinguished when the eye is about on a level with its source. For this reason red was used for lights on the ground and on shipboard at night during the wartime blackouts because it was not visible to aircraft. Blue light, on the other hand, is the most visible at night when all light takes on a bluish hue.

2. The Nervous System

Nasalward and near the fovea there is a hole in the sclera (the membrane covering all of the eyeball except the area covered by the cornea) through which the optic nerve passes. The optic nerve is really a bundle of nerve fibers which are actually a continuation of the retina. These fibers of the optic nerve continue to a spot known as the optic chiasma. From the chiasma a crossing of certain fibers is made so that almost all of the fibers of the right sides of both eyes proceed to make connections with fibers leading to the right side of the brain and almost all of the fibers of the left side of both eyes make connections with fibers leading to the left side of the brain.[18] Just beyond the chiasma there exist two deep bends in the optic nerve fibers before they reach the rear occipital lobe of the brain. These are known as the lateral geniculates. Here the optic nerve fibers connect with the fibers leading to the brain. Their impulses are carried to the occipital lobes of the cortex or back portion of the brain where the response of seeing color is finally made.

The difference in the disposition of rods and cones on the retina indicates a difference in function between the two. It is believed, on the evidence of their greater receptivity to images seen in dim light, that the rods are only capable of transmitting impulses from achromatic color and that they function at low illumination. The cones are believed to transmit chromatic color sensations and to function at higher illumination levels. The fact that chromatic color sensing is unequally distributed over the retina and that its distribution bears a relation to the distribution of the cones has aided this theory. By means of an apparatus called a perimeter it is possible to determine the zones or lateral distances from the eye at which various color sensations are perceived. The extremities of the visual field are

[18] The fibers near the center of both eyes go to both sides of the brain.

sensitive only to achromatic sensations; except for this margin the entire field is susceptible to blue and yellow and only the fovea to red and green.

3. Color Blindness or Anomalous Color Vision

The selective sensitivity of the visual field to chromatic color is linked conjecturally with color blindness, the chief types of which are:

A. Monochromatism or achromatopsia: complete inability to experience chromatic sensation.
B. Dichromatism: chromatic sensations consisting of only two hues.
  1. Common forms:
    a. Protanopia: red and bluish green seen as grey—no light seen at extreme long wavelength end of spectrum.
    b. Deuteranopia: bluish red and green seen as grey.
  2. Rare forms:
    a. Tritanopia: purplish blue and greenish yellow seen as grey—there is a possible weakness in seeing light at extreme short wavelength end of spectrum.
    b. Tetartanopia: the spectrum appears red at the long and at the short wavelength end of the spectrum but green in the middle.
C. Anomalous trichromatism: all hues are frequently recognizable but there are occasionally confusion colors.

Normal color vision requires three primary chromatic lights in order to make a match for any color; dichromatism requires two and monochromatism one. Monochromatism generally occurs when there is complete destruction of the fovea with attendant loss of cone function.

4. Tests for Color Vision

There are numerous tests for color vision. Three of those which are of general application are:
  1. The American Optical Society Test (AO Test) purchased through the Instrument Division, American Optical Society, Buffalo 15, N.Y. A series of charts composed of figure and background which can be distinguished by a person with normal color vision but which are confused by the person with abnormal color vision.
  2. The Farnsworth-Munsell 100 Hue Test purchased through the Munsell Color Company, 2441 North Calvert St., Baltimore 18, Md. Designed to test discrimination in seeing color differences by arranging colors in series.
  3. The Inter-Society Color Council Color Aptitude Test purchased through the Federation of Paint and Varnish Production Clubs, 121 S. Broad Street, Philadelphia 7, Pa. Designed to test color aptitude, which is the ability to make nice distinctions in color whether acquired as a result of color training or inherent because of good color vision.

5. Theories of Color Vision

How does the eye see color? The answer to that question we do not have. Although we know something about the mechanism that enables us to see color we can only conjecture about its method of functioning. The facts of additive color mixture have forced the opinion that in the visual process there must be three spectrally selective substances each sensitive to certain bands of radiant energy. Little evidence of the presence of these substances has been found but the visual process works as though they were present.

One of the earliest theories to suggest the presence of these substances which are tuned to different chromatic rays has been called the Young-Helmholtz theory. This is in honor of the investigators Thomas Young, 1773–1829, a British physicist, and Hermann von Helmholtz, 1821–1894, a German physicist who developed Young's studies. The theory supposes three separate substances in the cones, each capable through photochemical reaction of receiving and transmitting one kind of color impulse to the brain. The red, green and blue lights, some form of which are usual to color mixture experimentation, are the colors which the Young-Helmholtz theory supposes to be basic eye stimulants. This theory explains the facts of color mixture satisfactorily.

There are several theories of color vision which attempt to account for the fact that black and white, yellow and blue, red and green are primary color sensations. A psychological primary sensation is one which is unique in the sense that it does not seem to be mixed with any other color sensation.

The Hering theory (Ewald Hering, 1834–1918, German physiologist), one of the best known of these theories, assumes six fundamental color sensations. These are coupled, the black with the white, the yellow with the blue, the red with the green. There is imagined in the retina three distinct photosensitive substances each capable of anabolic (constructive) and katabolic (destructive) reactions under the influence of radiant energy. The anabolism of each of these photochemical substances creates the first of each of these paired sensations; the katabolism creates the second. This theory accords well with zoned retinal sensitivity and with some of the facts of color blindness.[19]

E. COLOR AS A PERCEPTUAL EXPERIENCE

1. The Complexity of Color Experience

Color perception is a very complex phenomenon. Many conditions of the light energy, of the visual mechanism and of the complicated functioning of the brain, affect the color we see. Changes frequently occur in perceived color which are not accounted for by the straightforward analysis of the spectral character of the light energy. These have been the object of considerable psychological study, and a great deal is known about them. Therefore many of these phenomenal occurrences can be predicted. Although there is nothing that relates to color per-

ception which is unimportant, there are some of these predictable changes in color which are of major concern to the decorator.

2. Visual Adaptation

One of the principal reasons for both change and constancy in color, as in all perception, is the attempt on the part of the visual mechanism to adapt itself to changing conditions in the stimulus and to fatigue. This is known as visual adaptation.

a. CHANGING LEVEL OF ILLUMINATION

When the stimulus is changing constantly, short range adaptation is attempted by the eye. This is not always successful. Images and colors merge rather than stay separate when a time interval is too short. A continuous television picture, which is in reality a number of individual pictures, illustrates this.

When the stimulus change is more gradual a careful observer notices other kinds of perceptual modifications. Progressive changes in the illumination level will affect both the saturation and the hue of colors.

Every hue reaches its greatest saturation at a certain intensity of illumination. As light falls below or rises above that level, the saturation for that hue recedes.[20]

As luminance rises the hues which contain yellow seem to shift more toward yellow and those containing blue shift toward blue.[21] This we note as a characteristic change in nature's colors on a bright day.

It is recorded that the psychological primary hues do not change in appearance as the level of luminance is changed. They are therefore called the invariant hues.

Under color measurement [22] we note that hues differ in their ability to produce the awareness of brightness. This potential changes with the level of light. Quite low levels of illumination are known as scotopic levels as opposed to daylight or photopic levels. If luminance recedes

[19] But it does not explain all of the important facts of color blindness. The recent Hurvich-Jameson quantification of the Hering theory seems to have eliminated the faults of the latter and to have provided a more accurate means of predicting color responses.

[20] The Purdy effect. Evans, *op. cit.*, p. 129.
[21] The Bezold-Brücke effect. Committee on Colorimetry of the Optical Society of America, *The Science of Color*, p. 106.
[22] P. 120.

slowly and to a low level the short wavelength hues gain over the longer wavelength hues in their ability to appear bright.[23] A yellowish-green evokes a peak perception of brightness at high illumination, a greener hue seems brighter at lower levels.

b. SATURATION OF ILLUMINATION

Not only the level of illumination but likewise its saturation will change the apparent hue of an object. In a highly homogeneous light, the light portions of the scene will be strongly tinted with the hue of the light. This is particularly true for light objects seen against dark backgrounds. Middle tones retain their genuine hue. Dark tones, especially when seen against light backgrounds, will be strongly colored with the hue which is complementary to the color of the illuminant.[24]

c. DURATION OF LIGHT ENERGY

The fatigue of the visual mechanism is given as the reason for another visual phenomenon known as the after-image. The response called *after-image* is the result of the factor of attention modified by time and environment. When a subject has focused (attention factor) on one color for a certain length of time (time factor) and then looks away quickly to a white surface (environment factor) he will see a color projected

[23] The Purkinje effect. Committee on Colorimetry of the Optical Society of America, *op. cit.*, p. 105.
[24] The Helson-Judd effect. Evans, *op. cit.*, p. 183.

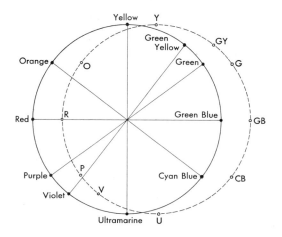

Figure 60. Rood's diagram illustrating the contrast effect of one color on another.

upon that white surface which is the visual complement [25] of the color upon which he has previously concentrated.

In real situations, few colors stand in isolation on a white ground. Therefore, we seldom experience successive after-images. In a group of colors, however, adjacent colors will affect the appearance of one another as if the complementary after-image were projected. Colors do affect neighboring colors by seeming to project their complements upon one another.

M. E. Chevreul (1786–1889) first described the action of this kind of eye adaptation on colors.[26] He was master dyer of the Gobelin tapestry works near Paris. Clients came to him to choose colored yarns which were to be used in weaving tapestries. When the tapestries were completed these customers frequently complained that Chevreul had substituted other colors. He was puzzled by this until he deduced that the colors looked different in the finished tapestry from the way they did when seen in isolation. They had been altered somehow by being placed next to other colors. But how altered? Was there any way of predicting how one color would alter another color?

Chevreul's answer was the formulation of the so-called law of color contrast. It is a general fact that visual differences always seem to create greater differences. In color work the direction which the greater differences take is always away from the genuine colors either in hue, lightness-darkness, saturation, or in all three color attributes.

We are not often conscious of this apparent alteration of one color by a neighboring color. However, the effect can be very clearly demonstrated in controlled experiments. (A controlled experiment is one in which all of the conditions are kept constant except one variable which is the item being tested.)

The nineteenth century colorist Rood diagrammatically illustrated the way in which colors

[25] Sometimes called psychological complement. It is similar to but not necessarily the same hue as the light complement. See complementary, *The ISCC Comparative List of Color Terms.*
[26] M. E. Chevreul, *The Principles of Harmony and Contrast of Colors*, trans. Charles Martel (3rd ed.; London: George Bell & Sons, 1890). Chaps. I, II.

work on one another.[27] Imagine any two color circles of equal size and corresponding hue placements, the one circle falling slightly to the right of the other. On the circles here illustrated we will observe first the effect of red upon an orange. On the solid circle at the left locate the two colors. Then glance at the position of the orange on the dotted circle at the right. The center of the first circle illustrates neutrality and as a color moves nearer to this center it becomes less saturated. Notice that the position of the orange of the dotted circle has moved nearer to the yellow of the first circle and that it has likewise moved nearer to the center. This illustrates the fact that when red and orange are seen together, the orange becomes more yellow and less saturated. The red would likewise be affected by an orange and would become more blue and less saturated. Here for the purpose of controlled experimentation we are keeping the red constant. This effect of contrast can be stated as a general law thus: *when two colors lie in the same hemisphere of a color circle (i.e., are similar in hue) they will push each other farther apart in hue and will weaken each other in saturation.*

Now observe the effect of a red on a green-yellow by observing the position of the green-yellow on the dotted wheel. The green-yellow has moved towards green. Thus the first portion of the general law holds true and the two hues are seen to be pushed farther apart on the color wheel. The green yellow, however, is seen to be farther away from the center of the original wheel. This signifies that it appears to be more saturated when it is placed next to a red. The second part of the general law will read: *when two colors lie in different hemispheres (i.e., are quite different in hue) they will push each other farther apart in hue and strengthen each other in saturation.*

Notice again that the only color which red cannot displace from its hue position on the circle is its visual complement or in other words the color which is projected as an after-image when focusing on red. The only way that red can alter this opposite color is to strengthen its ap-

parent saturation. The third part of the general law would thus read: *when two colors are visual opposites they will not change each other in hue and will strengthen each other in saturation.*

The reason and the logic behind this phenomenon and Rood's diagram is not difficult to find if we return again to the fact of after-images. Look again at the Rood chart. The after-image of red would be a green blue. This green blue projected onto orange would dull it slightly and it would likewise make it slightly more yellow. Carry this logic right through and we see that the law of color contrasts is an example of the occurrence of after-images except that the after-image falls upon another chromatic color and thus affects it.

d. SIZE OF THE OBJECT COLOR AREA

Do two colors seen together always affect each other in this way? No, unfortunately for ease of prophesying, they do not. The actual sizes of the colored areas have a great deal to do with the way in which we see them. If the colors are arranged in very narrow stripes or in small amounts the light from the color will overlap and be mixed in the eye. Thus by additive mixture, similar hues will strengthen one another and dissimilar hues will mix to grey and will destroy one another. This principle was fully exploited by the impressionist painters when they used small amounts of pure color juxtaposed. Chevreul's statements about the effects of adjacent color must be qualified to say that they are valid only when comparatively large amounts of each color are used.

There is yet another way in which the amount of the adjacent colors becomes the decisive factor in forecasting effects. If the areas of the two colors are quite disproportionate, the larger area is apt to reflect some of its color quality onto the smaller area. Watch a photographer place a white screen in such a position that it will catch and reflect white light onto the sitter's face. If the screen were chromatic the light reflected onto the face would be tinted with this hue.

The so-called color spreading or color assimilation effect is similar in consequences to reflection. Assimilation is the tendency of neighboring colors to look more alike. According to this effect

---

[27] Ogden N. Rood, *Student's Textbook of Color* (New York: Appleton-Century-Crofts, Inc., 1908), p. 248.

Designer (Figures 61 and 62): Designed and made available through the courtesy of Miss Dorothy Nickerson, Standardization Section, Cotton Branch, Agricultural Marketing Service, United States Department of Agriculture.

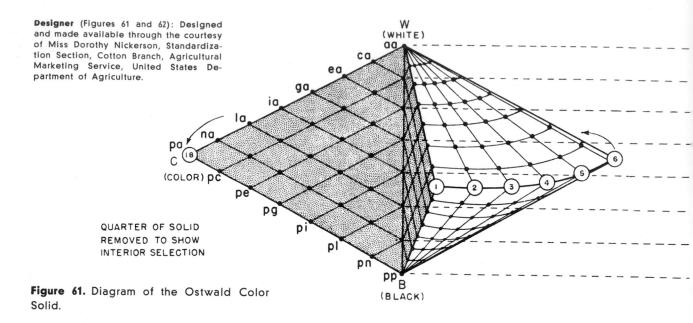

QUARTER OF SOLID
REMOVED TO SHOW
INTERIOR SELECTION

Figure 61. Diagram of the Ostwald Color Solid.

small amounts of color adjacent to another color are made similar to it. This is especially true when one color is interlaced with the other. It is as though the latter spread out onto the former or the former assimilated some of the character of the latter. Actually this effect may be connected with the additive effect of light. In the assimilation effect, however, the individual colors remain distinct and the result is not quite that of an intermediate color. As color assimilation is just the reverse of color contrast, it is clear that the artist must know how to adjust his areas in order to produce the result desired.

It should likewise be noted that object hues bear a direct relation to size because of the disposition of the rods and the cones on the retina. For instance, objects which are very small (with respect to the whole scene) will either look red or green or achromatic. There is a larger span of size at which yellows and blues become distinguishable as well as reds and greens.

3. The Effect of the Response Mechanism

A viewer's mental set at the time of observation of a color will likewise affect the color seen.

The eye is truly blind to what the mind cannot see. For example, what has been customarily associated with a color will influence the color seen. The painter may make flesh tones green but one must concentrate on their color to see them that way.

4. Lessons for the Designer

The various illusions of which we have been speaking are all so interesting when demonstrated that one sometimes wonders, the law of color constancy notwithstanding, whether it is ever possible to see a genuine color. Likewise one wonders if it is possible to predict which illusion will occur under various everyday conditions. In other words, how important to the decorator is a knowledge of or regard for these illusions?

The problem is not unlike that which a painter meets in painting the shadows of objects. Some inexperienced artists paint shadows as though they were achromatic. Shadows are usually chromatic but they are not always a darker tone of the genuine color of the object. In some cases conjoined shadows, known as shades, on the section of the object which is not directly illumi-

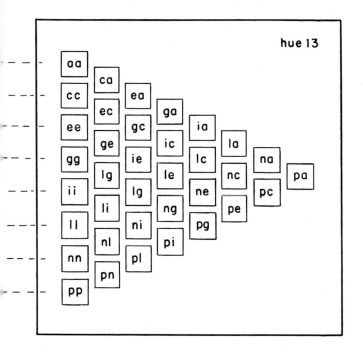

hue 13

ference should be tolerated. Any difference will be accentuated by contrast and may distort a planned relationship very much. If there is to be a difference in colors, order that difference by rhythm or great contrast so that it will work for rather than against the color scheme.

Remember that the life of a color literally depends upon contrast. This may be introduced in a color seen from a room, or it may be accomplished through dulling all of the colors with their complements or it may be acquired by adding just a spot of contrasting color or of white.

Dark rooms will appear brighter in light greens or green-yellows.

We must realize, at this stage, that color is really more meaningful when interpreted as a conscious response. What we have to learn, through close observation leading to knowledge, is how to adjust all parts of the stimulus in order to obtain a desired response.

F. THE ORGANIZATION OF COLORS

1. Nature and Importance of a Color System

Most of us enjoy listening to a good jazz improvisation. At the same time there are few who would be willing to give up the great written symphonies or operas for transient unrecorded music. Registered music is made possible because of the standardized arrangement of instrumental tones and of musical notation.

Colors too have been recently placed in systematic order. This makes color work easier because color interrelations are seen. If this order is carried out in any comprehensive way it amounts to a color system.

A *color system* is an ordered but arbitrary and limited sampling of color. All colors, like all sounds, would merge into one another in a natural kind of arrangement if all the intervals were represented. When it becomes expedient to limit the color selection then the basis for choice must necessarily be an arbitrary one. That does not mean that the basis for selection should be a capricious or a useless one. Every good color system should be designed to serve some particular kind of function.

nated, should appear slightly more blue and duller and darker than the genuine object color. The brighter the apparent illumination the more certain is this effect. In the case of cast shadows and in a light which is apparently chromatic a cast shadow may appear complementary to the color of the form. Again an adjacent surface may reflect its color onto the form. Do these various possibilities throw the painter into a hopeless state of confusion? Quite the contrary is the case because he recognizes them as the cause of the ever-changing kaleidoscope of the natural world. The fluctuations of colors are what make the visual scene interesting.

In a similar way the play of colored light over objects in a room is a source of visual pleasure. There are some words of precaution, however, which should be given. These relate to the relatively constant changes which appear to occur in colors because of their areas and locations.

In adjacent areas the sizes of the colors should be noted. An anticipated effect can be turned topsy-turvy if the areas are miscalculated. It is very important to plan adjacent large areas of color carefully and to estimate the effects of reflection and contrast. If two colors in such areas are planned to be used as a match, then no dif-

2. Tests of a Good Color System

What are the tests of a good color system? First the color order should be dictated by a particular kind of use. Then there should be sufficient color samples chosen to make the system really serviceable. Likewise these samples must be standardized and permanent. It is helpful if their measurements can be transferred to other kinds of systems. Finally, it is most important that the system should be demonstrable in some manner which will make it convenient to employ.

It should be clear at the very beginning that a color system is no more a recipe for color harmony (good color relationships) than an ordered piano keyboard is a recipe for musical composition. A good musical composition is a selection from the symmetry of the keyboard. But it is a varied and interesting selection. Given the keyboard and an understanding of its relations, the musician is helped in creating harmony. So much and no more can be claimed for color systems in relation to color harmony.

3. Color Mixture Systems

A color mixture system is dictated by mixtures of colored lights. Additive mixtures of colored lights are used in lighting, in halftone screen printing and in all color processes which obtain color effects by juxtaposing small areas of color. An easy way to visualize the effects of color mixture (as additive light) is by rotating sector disks. A disk is so constructed that its sectors can be adjusted in size. When the disk is spun rapidly the light reflected from the various sectors merges so that a single color sensation results. The percentages of the colored disk areas then become an automatic measure of the light and indicate its place in the color order system. The color obtained by disk mixture can be duplicated

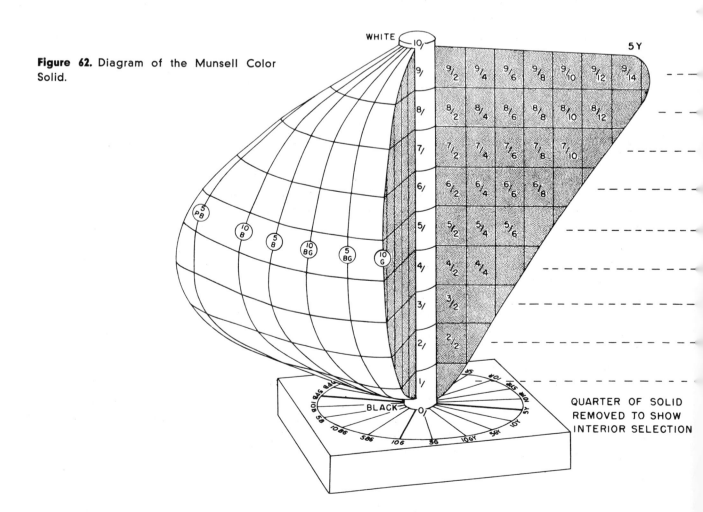

Figure 62. Diagram of the Munsell Color Solid.

QUARTER OF SOLID REMOVED TO SHOW INTERIOR SELECTION

in colored material standards for convenient reference use.

Certainly one of the best examples of a color mixture system is the Ostwald color system. The German physical chemist and psychologist Wilhelm Ostwald (1853–1932) worked on the problem of systematizing colors during and following World War I when an enforced absence from his daily routine gave him more free time to devote to a study which had long been of interest. His concern in perfecting a color system was associated with his thought for demonstrating color harmony. However, both the Ostwald color system and Ostwald's theories on color harmony have independent merit.

In a color mixture system the colors of the primary lights or primary colored disks are important because they determine the range of colors. Ostwald used a near black and a near white for two of his disk sectors. The third sector was a hue which was as near as possible to a chromatic light of one hundred per cent purity. Any color can be matched by a suitable mixture of monochromatic light plus white light in the same manner that it can be matched by three primary lights. Therefore the Ostwald disc sectors provided a complete color gamut.

The first consideration in conceiving a color system is the arrangement of a black to white achromatic scale. This becomes the central pole of any three dimensional arrangement of color space. The present charts of the Ostwald system show eight steps on the neutral scale. From white to black they are assigned letters of the alphabet, a, c, e, g, i, l, n, p. Alternate letters and k are omitted. Recent modifications have added a step b between a and c. The per cent of white and black added between steps is by constant ratio in an attempt to have the steps appear visually equidistant.[28] All actual percentages are available.[29]

In the Ostwald system the pure colors are arranged clockwise from yellow through red, purple, blue, and green, on what would correspond to the equator of two cones placed with their largest areas adjacent. The original Ostwald hues were twenty-four in number. They are designated by numbers one to twenty-four. Recent charts have added six more hues which are located so as not to interfere with the placement or numbering of the original hues. The order on this hue circuit is dictated by the fact that complementary light wavelengths are opposite each other. Complementary hues are thus twelve numerals apart.

The next kind of order on the Ostwald system involves the relating of the achromatic colors to the pure hues. If we think of a section of the Ostwald double cone solid as being sliced down through any pure hue we have a triangle with white at the top, black at the bottom and full color at the apex. All of the internal colors on

---

MUNSELL BOOK OF COLOR

Yellow

(Y)   [5.0 Y]   (25.0)

VALUE	/0	/2	/4	/6	/8	/10	/12	/14
9/	N9/	Y9/2	Y9/4	Y9/6	Y9/8	Y9/10	Y9/12	Y9/14
8/	N8/	Y8/2	Y8/4	Y8/6	Y8/8	Y8/10	Y8/12	
7/	N7/	Y7/2	Y7/4	Y7/6	Y7/8	Y7/10		
6/	N6/	Y6/2	Y6/4	Y6/6	Y6/8			
5/	N5/	Y5/2	Y5/4	Y5/6				
4/	N4/	Y4/2	Y4/4					
3/	N3/	Y3/2						
2/	N2/	Y2/2						
1/	N1/							

→→ CHROMA →

---

[28] This is an application of the Weber-Fechner law which holds approximately over the central intensities. "The eye tends to indicate a constant change when the stimulus is changed in a constant ratio." Evans, op. cit., p. 103.

[29] E. Jacobson, W. Granville and C. E. Foss, Color Harmony Manual (3rd ed.; Chicago: Container Corp. of America, 1948), p. 39.

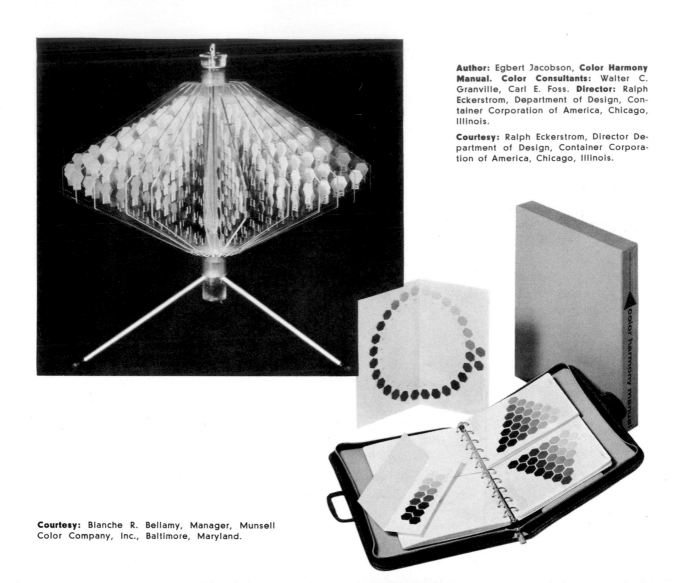

Author: Egbert Jacobson, **Color Harmony Manual. Color Consultants:** Walter C. Granville, Carl E. Foss. **Director:** Ralph Eckerstrom, Department of Design, Container Corporation of America, Chicago, Illinois.

Courtesy: Ralph Eckerstrom, Director Department of Design, Container Corporation of America, Chicago, Illinois.

Courtesy: Blanche R. Bellamy, Manager, Munsell Color Company, Inc., Baltimore, Maryland.

this triangle were planned to have a constant dominant wavelength.

The sampling of these triangles was then arranged as follows. The triangle is divided into bands which trace obliquely by eight steps to the neutral scale. Thus the complete triangle is divided into twenty-eight sectors. The color in every one of these is composed of the per cent white found by tracing it obliquely downward to the grey scale, and of the per cent black found by tracing it obliquely upwards to the grey scale. The percentage remaining is that of the full color content.

In naming the colors on the Ostwald system the number which designates the hue comes first. This is followed by the letter designating the white content. Thus all colors with *a* immediately following the hue number have equal white content with achromatic *a*; all hues with *c* following the hue number have equal white content with grey *c*. The second letter following the hue number indicates the black content in a similar manner. Thus a number plus two letters will always give the percentage by disk mixture of full color, white and black in an Ostwald color. Ostwald called his equator colors his full color series; he called full color plus white, his bright clear series and his full color plus black dark clear series. Colors with both black and white content were named the shadow series. Colors with equal white content were isotints and those with equal black content were isotones.

Disk mixture data would not be of any great value to the colorist if the results were not reproduced in some permanent way onto some easily

Figure 63.

(Top) Model of Ostwald Color Solid.

(Center) The Color Harmony Manual, The Container Corporation of America.

(Bottom) Background: Munsell Book of Color, Library Edition; Munsell Color Tree; Munsell Book of Color, Library Edition. Center: Munsell Book of Color, Pocket Edition; Hand Spinners with Munsell disks; Munsell Book of Color, Opposite Hues Edition. Foreground: Farnsworth-Munsell 100 Hue Test; Munsell Value Scales for Judging Reflectance; Munsell Student Charts.

handled samples. Ostwald himself made the original set of such samples. The most recent and best developed set of Ostwald charts is now published by the Container Corporation of America.[30] Both Ostwald and the color scientists who have produced this latest edition of Ostwald standards have found it necessary to make a few modifications from the ideal specifications due to the limitations of the materials in which the chips were produced. There have likewise been a few changes introduced for the purpose of making several of the color intervals seem more visually equidistant. Essentially, however, these latest and very excellent charts of the Ostwald color mixture system are of the utmost value to anyone interested in ordering color especially in additive mixture.

4. Colorant Mixture Systems

The second type of color system is one in which the sampling of color space is made by adjusting ratios of colorants in a prescribed manner. Although a basic knowledge of the laws of colorant mixture is indispensable to anyone who would make minor adjustments in colorant tones, it is more economical in large quantity work to refer to a colorant mixture system in order to visualize the results of the major mixtures. Most of the large paint companies have compiled recipes for the admixture of their paints and have charts to illustrate the results. When these recipes provide a wide selection of colors and when they are systematically developed they make what amounts to a colorant mixture system.

The Plochere color system represents a mixture gamut of ten base paints which when intermixed and added to white will result in 1,248 samples of wall paint. These may be procured on 3″ × 5″ cards in a file box.[31]

One of the more extensive colorant gamut systems on the market today is the Nu-Hue Color Coordinator System.[32] This represents a mixture

[30] There is a supplement to the Jacobson, Granville and Foss *Color Harmony Manual:* H. D. Taylor, L. Knoche and W. C. Granville, *The Color Names Dictionary* (Chicago: Container Corp. of America, 1950).

[31] *Plochere Color System*, 1820 Hyperion Ave., Los Angeles, Cal. (1948).

[32] *Nu-Hue Color System*, Martin-Senour Co., 2520 Senour Ave., Chicago, Ill. (1946).

gamut of ten strong chromatic colors and six greyed chromatic colors. Neighboring colorants are combined in equal part combination to form the seventy-one colors of the basic chart. For use these colors are then combined with an extender base. Choices from these basic chart colors are let-down with white in varying ratios to form the colors (tints) on the six additional charts. On all the charts there are 497 colors which can be obtained by easy formula and many more can be obtained in an extension of this principle. A second Martin-Senour colorant system is the Custom color system which is illustrated by the Nu-Hue Custom Color Directory and Plexiglas® charts.

5. Visual Color Order Systems

The third and last type of color system is that in which the sampling is based on uniform visual steps. The step between any color and its neighbor should appear to be the same as the step between the next two colors extending in the same direction on that system. A color system which is arranged on the basis of visual order is basic for the artist and the Munsell color system is in the opinion of many colorists the most adequate system yet devised for describing color as it is actually seen.[33]

The Munsell color system was the work of the Boston art teacher and artist, Albert Munsell. During the years 1900 to 1912 he became impressed with the need for some systematic arrangement of color to help him in his teaching and he devoted the major part of his time and attention to the task of perfecting such a system. Since his death his work has been continued by the Munsell Color Company, Inc.[34]

The Munsell system is illustrated on a three-dimensional solid where lightness-darkness (Munsell *value*) is the vertical axis, saturation

(Munsell *chroma*) is the horizontal axis and the hues progress clockwise around the central pole. Thus the directions on the Munsell solid illustrate the psychological sensation attributes of color.

The neutral central pole of the Munsell solid is divided into nine (theoretically ten) steps of value. The purpose which dictated their spacing was that they should appear visually equidistant. These values are numbered from 1 (near black) to 10, (near white).

The five principal Munsell hues are called red, yellow, green, blue, and purple. To these were added five intermediate hues which combined the names of the original hues in counterclockwise order and were called yellow-red, green-yellow, blue-green, purple-blue, and red-purple. For further discrimination numerals are now used before the hue name. Each of these ten principal and intermediate hues is designated by the number 5. This number is understood even when it is not expressed. The numerals 1 to 4 refer to gradations which become progressively more like the designated hue and the numerals from 6 to 10 refer to variations of the hue which become progressively more like the hue found clockwise. Thus 100 hue steps of the Munsell hue circuit are arranged with the purpose of having them visually equidistant. Likewise opposite hues are those which the eye projects as visual complements.

The Munsell chroma scale extends from zero at the neutral pole out to fourteen or more steps for some of the most vivid color chips. Hues come to their fullest visual saturation at different lightnesses (Munsell value) level. This is seen in the spectrum where yellow is lighter than blue. The normal lightness level of a hue as seen in the spectrum is called its spectral level. The Munsell color solid places each hue in its most saturated chroma at its spectral value level. Thus the chroma steps of yellow extend farthest from the neutral pole at value eight, whereas red extends farthest from the neutral pole at value four.

Munsell chroma steps project varying distances from the neutral pole for different hues. In depicting saturation Munsell first began with

---

® Registered trade-name.

[33] Dorothy Nickerson, "Color and Its Description," *Bulletin of the American Ceramic Society*, 27, No. 2 (February 15, 1948), 47–55.

[34] The Munsell Color Company, Inc. (under the direction of the Munsell Foundation), 2441 North Calvert St., Baltimore 18, Md.

a physical circumstance.[35] He too began with disk mixture. Complementary hues in the strongest colorant saturation were revolved in equal sector amounts. He found that the resulting sensation was not a neutral grey but a very warm or reddish grey. This meant that the strongest colorants of the warm hues were more forceful than those of the cool hues. Working with red he reduced it in saturation until the red sector would neutralize blue-green. This saturation was assumed as chroma 5 or five steps of chroma from the neutral axis. Visual chroma steps were then adjusted with reference to this chroma. Therefore the number of chroma steps assigned to each hue is dependent upon the strength of the available standardized pigments in that hue. As colorants exhibiting stronger visual saturations are developed the chroma steps can be projected farther without disturbing the internal arrangement.

In some of the Munsell charts now available[36] the chroma steps are illustrated only in the even numbers. This reduces the cost and size of the charts. A Munsell designation of a color is given as number and hue name, followed by value and chroma designation, e.g., 5R 4/14 which designates a very strong red.

6. Other Systematic Color Arrangements

There are other systematic arrangements of color samples which should be known to the decorator. There are several color dictionaries or atlases. These present a systematic array of colors as made with printing inks. Usually their organization is a cross between a color mixture and a colorant mixture system. Inks are actually mixed in order to obtain some of the basic hues and then screen printing (additive mixture) with hues plus black plus the white of the paper provides the color gamut. Much information concerning the various names of colors and their pigment affiliations is frequently given. The Maerz and Paul *Dictionary of Color*[37] is a standard work of this kind. Conversion tables of many of its colors to Munsell and Ostwald designations have been made. The Villalobos *Colour Atlas* should be mentioned for Spanish as well as English nomenclature.[38]

For colors in fabrics the charts of the Color Association of the United States are standard.[39] In addition to showing the basic fabric colors as they appear on different textile textures, these charts give the current fashion names for the colors. Popular color names are important to merchandising. Just think of the verbal suggestion in "jungle-green." Although conversion tables of these colors with the basic color systems are made, we feel certain that "misty dawn" will sell more stockings than R 6/2. The British Colour Council has published a *Dictionary of Colours for Interior Decoration*. In it the colors are shown on pile carpet samples as well as in samples in gloss and matte finishes.[40]

One more color name system should be known to the colorist. It is the Inter-Society Color Council—National Bureau of Standards or ISCC-NBS method of designating colors.[41] These color charts have blocked off 267 areas of color which have been defined in terms of Munsell notation and to which names have been assigned which are those most used by colorists and laymen. The arrangement of colors combines features of the Ostwald and the Munsell systems.

[35] It was the original belief of Munsell that one system would be found to illustrate all types of color relationships. This belief had to be abandoned and the present Munsell system has been developed along the lines of visual order for which it was uniquely suited.

[36] For example, the Munsell student charts.

[37] A. Maerz and M. R. Paul, *A Dictionary of Color* (2nd ed.; New York: McGraw-Hill Book Co., Inc., 1950).

[38] D. Villalobos and J. Villalobos, *Colour Atlas*, 1947. Available in U.S.A. from Stechert-Hafner, New York.

[39] The Color Assn. of the United States, Inc. (formerly, Textile Color Card Assn.), 200 Madison Ave., New York 16, N.Y. This association has enlarged the scope of its activities to include investigation of color trends in all merchandise.

[40] The British Colour Council, *Dictionary of Colours for Interior Decoration* (London: The British Colour Council, 1949).

[41] This includes a cross reference of color names from all of the prominent systems as well as names used for specific colors by many government agencies. U.S. Dept. of Commerce, National Bureau of Standards, *ISCC-NBS Method of Designating Colors and a Dictionary of Color Names*, Circular 553 (Washington, D.C., U.S. Dept. of Commerce, 1955).

G. THE MEASUREMENT AND SPECIFICATION OF COLOR

1. The Measurement of Radiant Energy

Science depends upon quantitative measurement and upon the possibility of interrelating similar metrical systems. The watt is one yardstick of radiant energy which measures work capacity. The initial wattage of electromagnetic energy is taken on an instrument known as a spectroradiometer. These calculations are the fundamental spectral energy measures.

2. Measurement of Relative (Light) Energy

Comparative rather than ultimate analysis is used in most color work. Comparison is relative to the reflectance or transmittance of a nearly perfect reflector or transmitter. As the wattage of these latter is predetermined, the wattage of the tested color can be determined if necessary. For most analyses this is not done.

This comparative analysis is made on a spectrophotometer. The separated rays of a standard light are alternately directed to the standard substance [42] and to the trial substance. A photoelectric cell can register the relative energies reflected or transmitted by each. The result is known as the spectral reflectance or transmittance of the unknown color.

3. Graphs

A scientist wishes to convey his ideas in as unambiguous, precise, and concise a manner as possible. That is his reason for using exact definitions, symbols, and equations. He likewise uses graphs which are diagrammatic pictures explaining interrelations. A graph showing the spectral distribution of light reflected from a typical green paint is illustrated thus—

On the base line (called the axis of abscissas) are located the component wavelengths. Parallel

[42] Magnesium oxide is an ideal reflector and distilled water a transmitter.

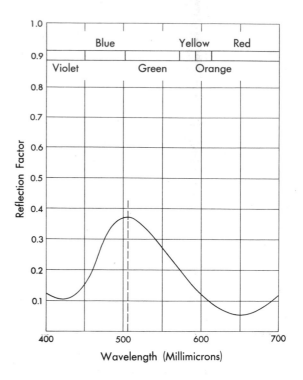

Figure 64. Graph of light energy reflected from a typical green paint under a standard light source.

Graph adapted from: A. C. Hardy, **Handbook of Colorimetry,** Copyright 1936. Reprinted by permission of The Massachusetts Institute of Technology, The Technology Press, Cambridge, Mass.

to the verticals (called the axis of ordinates) is located the relative amount of radiant energy reflected at each wavelength. The path made by the many points of separate measurement is known as the locus of the measurement.

The physicist can solve many color conundrums through a study of these charts. When the physical measures for each modifier of light are known, the physical measures for the resulting color can be predicted.

4. The Importance of the Visual Mechanism—Psychophysics

It is not possible to visualize the appearance of the color at this stage. The eye is an additional factor in the total stimulus. The eye is the camera whose potentialities limit visual impressions.

One of the puzzling color phenomena is the fact that two samples may look alike under certain viewing conditions and yet have quite different spectral reflectance or transmittance curves. These color samples might appear quite dissimilar under other viewing conditions, a fact which should be carefully noted by the designer. Colors which are visual rather than physical spectral matches are known as metamers. Metamers are a clear indication that there is more to the appraisal of color than a spectrophotometric reading.

The reason for the matching of metamers, inasmuch as it is not to be found in the physical composition of the colored lights (the source of the stimulus color), must reside in the visual process. For source (light) plus receiving instrument (visual process or organism) always equals response (sensation of color). Therefore a measure of visual efficiency must be added to the physical measurement in order to give the correct picture of a color. In other words the photographer needs to know his camera as well as his subject if he wants to get a good likeness.

This visual process through the working of which a visual evaluation of color is made is described as *the eye of the normal or standard observer*. This merely means that the characteristics of a number of normal eyes with respect to their reaction to color have been noted and this has been taken as the standard way in which normal eyes work.

The eye registers brightness differently for different wavelengths. It responds from zero just below 400 mμ to a maximum at 555 mμ and retrogresses to another zero just beyond 700 mμ. This ability of the eye to evoke the sensation of light is diagrammed on a curve which is known as the relative luminosity curve of the eye.

If the eye luminosity curve is integrated with the spectral reflectance or transmittance measures which define a color, the resulting measure will be a physical estimate of the amount of light evoked by that color. If a standard light is adjusted to the same measure, a visual picture of the brightness of the color can be obtained.

In respect to the ability to produce chromatic

sensation the eye reacts differently to various wavelengths. The measures for this reaction are taken on a colorimeter, an instrument which uses varying amounts of the three primary lights to make a visual match for any color. These amounts are known as the tristimulus measures of a color. If the tristimulus values are taken for a hypothetical spectrum composed of light of equal energy at each wavelength (the equal energy spectrum), they will describe the sensitivity of the eye to an interpretation of chromatic color at each waveband. The luminosity curve measures can be omitted when the tristimulus measures are used as the latter incorporate the former.

This chromatic sensitivity of the eye has been diagrammed on graphs which are known as the tristimulus specification of the equal energy spectrum or more simply as the color curves of the eye.

If the color curves of the eye are integrated with the spectral reflectance or transmittance

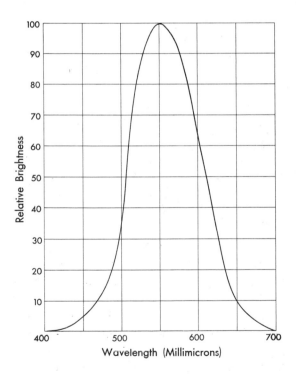

Figure 65. The relative luminosity curve of the eye.

measures of a color, the resulting measure will be a physical estimate of the amount of the three primary lights needed to match that color. Turning the dials of a colorimeter to the required amounts, the appearance of the color can be seen. The comparatively new and rapidly growing science which has devised this system of measurement whereby spectral energy or reflectance, transmittance charts can be transformed to color sensations, is known as psychophysics.

The computations involved in psychophysical measurement of color have been simplified through the use of mathematical tables for all of the factors with the exception of the spectrophotometric reading of the sample. Marvelous instruments such as the General Aniline automatic tristimulus integrator perform these calculations instantly.

5. The C.I.E. System of Psychophysical Measurement

The psychophysical measurement of an unknown sample of color can vary with viewing conditions and with the characteristics of the eye of the viewer. Therefore as many different measurements, all correct, could be obtained as there were changes in these two factors. In order to standardize at least one procedure, the International Commission on Illumination met in England in 1931 and decided to adopt certain viewing conditions and one set of reaction characteristics for the normal eye. This recommended procedure is now called the "C.I.E. Standard Observer and Coordinate System of Colorimetry." [43]

The C.I.E. specifications involved standard viewing conditions which were prescribed for the purpose of eliminating all distracting effects such as gloss or flicker. They likewise specified three standard light sources under one of which a color sample could be viewed. The particular source used must be stipulated in giving the measurement. These light sources are typical of the light under which color is usually seen. Thus

[43] In 1951 it was voted to adopt the French name of the Commission, *Commission Internationale de l'Eclairage* (C.I.E.).

light "A" is spectrally similar to the light from common tungsten filament light, "B" is similar to noon sunlight and "C" corresponds to average daylight illumination.

The C.I.E. likewise specified three primary chromatic lights to be used in the original colorimeter determinations. These are lights of 700.0 mμ (the red light), 546.1 mμ (the green light) and 435.8 mμ (the blue light). These real primary chromatic lights were only used in the initial color curve measurements taken on a colorimeter. For subsequent measurements imaginary primaries are used. Why are imaginary primaries chosen and what is their significance? It was found in these initial colorimeter measurements that the three actual primary chromatic lights would always make a match for any spectrum color in hue, but they could not

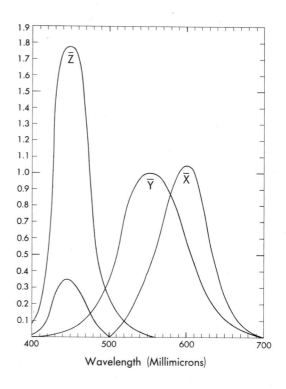

Figure 66. Standard C.I.E. Color Mixture Curves of the eye or the Tristimulus Values for the Spectrum Colors.

Graph adapted from: A. C. Hardy, **Handbook of Colorimetry,** Copyright, 1936. Reprinted by permission of The Massachusetts Institute of Technology, The Technology Press, Cambridge, Mass.

always effect a match in saturation (purity). For instance if a match were desired for some of the pure spectrum colors it could not be accomplished unless a complementary light were first added to the spectrum color to dull it. Scientists are imaginative people, too. They could easily imagine that if primary artificial light sources were more spectrally pure, the need for desaturating the spectrum light before matching it would be obviated. And if we remember that all the measurement data is essentially relative, it becomes apparent that all that is necessary in order to get a set of color mixture curves for the stronger imaginary primaries would be a mathematical adjustment of the real set to fit the imaginary conditions. Thus the C.I.E. imaginary primaries have been so adjusted that there is no need for desaturating any spectrum light in order to find tristimulus values for it.

The C.I.E. color mixture curves are further removed from the real curves in yet another way. The central curve representing the eye sensitivity to green light is the same as the luminosity curve of the eye. The original real primary lights represented this ability of the eye to rate wavelengths according to their luminosity as an integral part of each curve. This is true because in making a match for a sample color on a colorimeter, the testing eye equates the known and the unknown color in all of its characteristics, brightness as well as chromaticness. It is frequently useful to have the luminosity function of the eye rated separately from its ability to measure chromaticness. Therefore the real color mixture curves are juggled again. The luminosity curve of the eye is substituted for the green color mixture curve from which it was actually not very different inasmuch as green light evokes the greatest sensation of lightness. The mathematical operation required in making the green curve carry all of the luminosity involved a small proportional shift in the red and blue as well as in the green curves. The final color mixture curves evolved in this manner become the "Standard C.I.E. Color Mixture Curves of the Eye."

The C.I.E uses the symbols X, Y, and Z to represent the amounts of the three primary lights, red, green and blue respectively, needed to make

a metameric match for any heterogeneous color. The C.I.E. system uses the lower case letters with a bar over each, $\bar{x}$, $\bar{y}$, $\bar{z}$, as symbols for the amounts of the primaries needed to make a match for any spectrum light of one wavelength. Another way of utilizing these symbols consists in finding the ratio of each of the integers X, Y, Z to their sum. The coefficients x, y, z are thus obtained which represent the fractional part of the total light which is supplied by that particular primary light. It must be remembered in using all of these symbols that luminosity is expressed by the Y (or $\bar{y}$) evaluation. Thus the luminosity of X, Y, Z (or $\bar{x}$, $\bar{y}$, $\bar{z}$) is 0–1–0 respectively. In referring to the tristimulus coefficients x, y, z, the total luminosity Y is usually expressed separately.

The psychophysicist uses a graph on which to arrange all colors with respect to their tristimu-

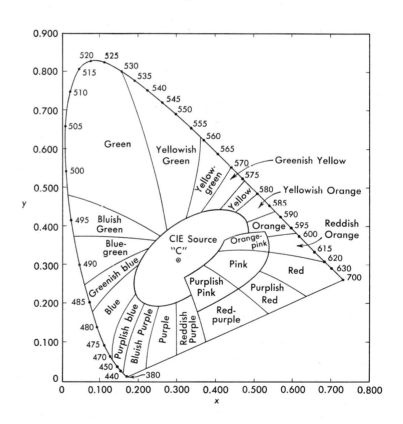

Figure 67. The C.I.E. Chromaticity Diagram.

Graph adapted from: D. B. Judd, **Color in Business, Science and Industry,** New York, 1952, p. 147. **Courtesy:** Reprinted by permission of John Wiley and Sons, Inc., New York.

COMPARATIVE LIST OF COLOR TERMS [1]

	Physics	Psychophysics	Psychology	
			Sensation	Perception
1. Source	Radiant energy	Luminous energy	Color sensation	Perception (i.e., dependent upon interpretation) Modes of Appearance (e.g., surface colors, volume colors, and film colors)
2. Measured by	Radiometer	Photometer Spectrophotometer Colorimeter	Personal Estimation	
3. Attribute of total energy	Radiant flux radiance	Luminous flux luminance	Brightness (when speaking of a primary light source) or Lightness (when speaking of a secondary colorant source)	Brightness (and specific attributes such as flicker) or Lightness (and specific attributes such as sparkle, transparency, glossiness, and luster)
4. Attributes of spectral quality	Radiant purity	Dominant wavelength and purity or Tristimulus values	Hue and Saturation	Hue and Saturation
5. Trait names	Specific designations in the language of physics	Specific designations in the language of psychophysics, i.e., either the notation of dominant wavelength and per cent purity, or *xyz* values	Bright to Dull or Light to Dark (for total energy); Red to Purple (for hue); Saturated to Grey (for saturation)	

[1] Compiled from *Comparative List of Color Terms*—published by the Inter-Society Color Council–P.O. Box 155, Benjamin Franklin Station, Washington 4, D.C.

lus values. The "C.I.E. Chromaticity Diagram" is one such graph which is most frequently used.

As there are three tristimulus values one would expect them to be located on a triangular graph. Such a graph was originally used by the famous physicist James Clerk Maxwell (1831–1879) who located a color on a triangle by charting the relative amounts of three primaries used to match it. The C.I.E. tristimulus evaluation of a color is charted on a rectangular diagram. On this diagram obviously there can be only two coordinates of a point. But if x plus y plus z equals unity, then z can always be found when x and y are known.

The point at the left hand corner of the C.I.E. diagram represents zero percentage of either red or green light. Therefore it represents one hundred per cent blue light. From this as a reference point the abscissa indicates the fractional amount of the red light used in making the color match and the ordinate represents the fractional amount of the green light. The value of Y given independently indicates the luminosity. The point representing the total red light is located at the lower right hand corner of the graph and the total green light at the upper left hand corner.

Perpendiculars erected at the appropriate spot on the abscissa or the ordinate representing the x and y values respectively would locate a position for the color to which these linear coordinates (two lines which locate a point) refer. When the tristimulus coefficients of the spectrum colors are used to locate the spectrum on this graph they take the position illustrated by the triangular-shaped locus. The purples are located on the straight base line connecting the reds and the blues. It is seen that the points representing the three imaginary primary light sources which were used to dictate this diagram lie well outside of the spectrum locus. This illustrates how these sources were imagined to be purer than any light which the eye can visualize. Likewise notice that the few colors which touch the base line, although they give practically no luminosity, may give a strong red and blue chromaticness.

The C.I.E. diagram of a color can give some information to the physicist even though no spectrophotometric measurements are available. The standard illuminant that was used for computation is always given and can be located on the chart. Inasmuch as it approaches white light it will be located near the center of the diagram because white light is composed of equal amounts of the primary lights. A straight line drawn from the illuminant point A (or B or C depending upon which standard illuminant was used) through P (the point for the color under discussion) will intersect the spectrum locus at a point S which locates the dominant wavelength (λd) of the color. All points on this line have the same dominant wavelength. By taking the ratio of the distances CP to CS a percentage is found which is the measure of the purity (excitation purity, P) of the sample color. Dominant wavelength is the psychophysical term which is roughly the counterpart of the psychological attribute hue, and purity is approximately the counterpart of saturation. These two psychophysical concepts denote chromaticity which is the counterpart of the psychological chromaticness. Luminance is the psychophysical correlate of brightness and this can be found from the Y value.

Likewise if the line on the C.I.E. diagram connecting the dominant wavelength to the illuminant source is projected to the opposite side of the locus it will cross the locus at a point indicating the complementary wavelength. For the green there is no complementary wavelength in the spectrum although the greens are the complementary wavelengths of the purples.

This color diagram will also tell us something about the effects of color mixtures. If two colors are located on the diagram, their mixture will lie on the straight line connecting the two colors. The exact location on the line will be relative to the percentages of the two mixture colors. Thus it will be seen that mixtures in the yellow-red range will be as pure as spectrum colors because the spectrum locus in that region is a straight line.[44] Mixtures of greens, however, will not be as pure as spectrum colors because the locus in this range is a convex curve. The line connecting

[44] This gives a more accurate picture of additive mixture than the customary circle diagram.

the red and violet ends of the spectrum locus is drawn straight because the purples must be made by a combination of red and blue, there being no purples in the spectrum.

It should be made quite clear that, although an experienced worker may be able to visualize a color through its position on the C.I.E. diagram, there is no color which is inherent in the diagram. Only through translating the diagram data to some sort of visual standard will its colors really be seen. Frequently a C.I.E. diagram is shown with the various colors charted on it. This is an aid to the colorist but is, of course, an addition to, rather than an integral part of the diagram.

There was a child went forth everyday,
And the first object he look'd upon, that object
he became.

. . . .

The early lilacs became part of this child,
And grass and white and red morning-glories,
and white and red clover,
and the song of the phoebe bird.

WALT WHITMAN [*]

There is a close analogy between what takes place
in the mind of a military commander when plan-
ning an action, and what happens to the artist
at the moment of conception. The former does
not renounce the use of his intelligence. He draws
from it lessons, methods and knowledge. But his
power of creation can operate only if he posses-
ses, in addition, a certain instinctive faculty
which we call inspiration . . .

CHARLES DE GAULLE [†]

Chapter VII
USING COLOR IN INTERIORS

A. IMPORTANCE OF COLOR FACTS FOR USE

The facts of color should help us to obtain color effects. A constant association with ordered color is almost certain to suggest images made from that order. A knowledge of color should indicate ways of producing these images. It should provide us with an intuitive sense about what will happen as we walk abroad in a color world everyday.

Our object is to create a well designed color grouping which will be functional and significant for an interior. In conjunction with the shapes and spaces it should produce an enhanced and vitally interesting color experience.

B. CHOICE OF COLOR TRAITS TO GAIN AN EFFECT

We will choose visual color qualities which seem to assure the results desired. Let us think

[*] From "Leaves of Grass" by Walt Whitman.
[†] From **Le Fil de l'Epée** by Charles de Gaulle (Editions Berger-Levrault). Reprinted from **The Edge of the Sword** by Charles de Gaulle, by permission of Criterion Books, Inc. Copyright © 1960 by Criterion Books, Inc.

EFFECT OF HUE

Feeling in Terms of	Red	toward	Green	toward	Blue or Purple
Physical Response (effects interpreted as affecting us bodily)	advancing hot loud glowing				retreating cool quiet
Simple Emotional Response (effects interpreted as affecting us emotionally)	exciting stimulating		restful cheerful— (especially yellow)		depressing subduing
Complex Intellectual Response (projection of character-meaning)	garish primitive vivid		youthful		regal conventional drab

THE LIGHTNESS-DARKNESS EFFECTS WILL MODIFY THOSE OF HUE

	Light	Medium	Dark
Physical Effect	light		heavy stable
Emotional Effect	cheerful gay	restful	depressing
Intellectual Response	frivolous feminine	mysterious	dignified masculine impressive somber

of hues first, realizing that hue messages are modified by lightness-darkness and by saturation. Accompanying is a chart of some hue effects. It is not meant to be exhaustive but merely suggestive. Notice how the communications in color, just like those in shape, progress from those interpreted as physical about which most of us seem to agree, through the emotional effects about which there is some cause for disagreement, to those responses which are more intellectual and which project a characterization and, hence, an evaluation upon the color. About these last messages there is even less unanimity of opinion.[1]

The saturation of a color will modify the impressions caused by the other color attributes. In the first place the physical and emotional tone of a hue will be emphasized through greater saturation. Greyed colors are emotionally balanced in tenor. Black and white being extremes of the lightness-darkness scale confer qualities which extreme lightness or extreme darkness would give. In addition to this they are such pure color sensations that they provide an impact similar to that given by a saturated color, a sort of visual electric shock. In this they are quite dissimilar to a greyed color.

C. COLORS AS VISUAL FORCES

The visual force of a color is its ability to attract our attention and thus to influence us in the manners indicated. The visual force of colors must be appreciated in the decorator's mind from the start. Color pervades everything. If it comes forward it likewise brings objects into focus. If it recedes it creates space.

The intrinsic force of a color is a composite of its hue, lightness-darkness and saturation. The hues on the warm side of the color circuit are advancing. The strong saturations are more forceful than the weak ones. Relative loss of sat-

[1] Scientific psychology was greatly interested, during the early years of this century, in the effects of colors. Some psychologists reported agreement among observers on color effects. Others reported disagreement. The experiments seem to strengthen the fact that background conditions of association and memory are very important. Only through an understanding of these conditions can a response really be predicted.

uration is one of nature's ways of making distances seem to recede. Thus greyed colors will always seem more distant than saturated ones.

Lightness is a more powerful magnet than darkness. Distant colors in nature approach a medium lightness-darkness range. Dark trees seem very dark and white snow very white when close at hand. They seem to be almost the same tone when far off. Therefore middle tones are really less forceful than either extreme.

As with all visual forces, their extent is altered in context, which is the matter for the next section.

D. COLOR EFFECTS DUE TO INTERRELATIONS

As with other visual forces, color can be manipulated in a design by means of the other colors with which it is associated. The extent of a color force can be enlarged by repetition, by placement in a rhythmic sequence or by being opposed by severe contrast. These ways of modifying a color force may often make a less important color take precedence over a more forceful one. As color is related to shapes it is obvious that the magnitude of a color force bears a direct relation to the size of the area upon which it is seen.

In working with color we encounter the problem of creating what is frequently called a color harmony. We use the phrase color harmony to mean a grouping of colors which will seem pleasant in ensemble. It is too much to expect that everyone will like all color groupings even though we think they are well ordered. Color preferences for individual colors are difficult to anticipate. For grouped colors they are even more unpredictable. The emotional and consequent evaluative responses to color are so strong and closely related that some people are prone to condemn a color scheme as poor simply because they do not like it.

Frequently distastes for certain color combinations can be analyzed. Often it is due to the fact that a particular kind of color order, a particular grouping of colors, is unusual. If such an unusual combination is well planned then we may expect that a general liking for it will grow. It is hard

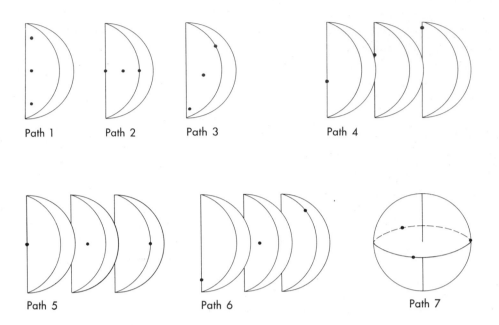

Figure 68. There are just seven regular paths through color space.

to realize that when the van Gogh color scheme of yellow and orange first became apparent it was disliked by many who now like it because they have seen it more often. Mexican color schemes combining blue-reds with yellow-reds are still too novel for many people to give them wholehearted approval.

If we are sensitive to color relationships and have achieved a grouping of colors which is pleasing to ourselves, we can be reasonably certain that it will eventually be liked by others. In every phase of design observers enjoy well-considered groupings despite their personal preferences for other particular kinds.

An harmonious color grouping will be made of colors which are related, which have something in common. What are the various ways in which we can relate a group of colors? Many great colorists have thought about this problem and our color knowledge is a heritage from many minds. Three fundamental ways of relating colors seem to be agreed upon. Colors may be related in one or all of the three following ways:

By the repetition of a color attribute trait, i.e.,

the repetition of the exact hue, or lightness, or saturation.

By an orderly arrangement of color intervals, i.e., the repetition or ordered variation of the spacing between colors as visualized on a color order system.

By the positioning of colors in a design so as to utilize optical laws which will create illusions of the above.

1. Repetition of Color Traits

This first idea is expressed most definitely in the work of Wilhelm Ostwald.[2] He said that object colors were harmonious if they contained equal amounts of pure color, white, or its absence, black. Such colors can be located on the system of Ostwald color standards.

An extension of this idea into the realm of film or light color would say that the underlying factor which could unite a group of colors through its repetition would be the percentage

[2] Wilhelm Ostwald, *Colour Science,* authorized trans. by J. Scott Taylor (London: Winsor and Newton, Ltd., 1931–33); and *Die Farbenlehre,* 2 vols. (Leipsig: Verlag Unesma G. m.b. H., 1921–1923).

of monochromatic to white light which was present.

On any colorant system the colors would have the same percentage of pure pigment, white, and black.

In the language of color in psychology a group of colors could be related by repeating the same hue, lightness, or saturation throughout. Such combinations must be located on a visual order system.

2. Orderly Arrangement of Color Intervals

Repetition, as we likewise know, may create monotony. The complete and undeviating repetition of an original color throughout a room would not result in the emphasis of this color in an interesting way. Therefore some change from the original color must be considered. This may be in hue, in lightness-darkness, or in saturation. Indeed, unless all attribute traits are duplicated in a color grouping, some must automatically be varied. Alteration may likewise be in all three attributes. In change (variation) what the mind records is the measure of the change, the interval. This was evident in the analysis of proportional relation through shapes. It is equally true in interval relations in color.

a. PATHS THROUGH THE COLOR SOLID

All color systems are based upon the idea that, in relation to some point of reference, the intervals between adjacent colors are even. Thus on any good color system we can trace paths or scales the steps of which are equidistant with respect to an ordering factor.[3] It is excellent color training to trace paths through a color solid or to arrange colors so that their intervals of change are repetitious.[4]

There are seven principal routes or progressions through a color solid. The first three of these can be found on any slice of a color sphere where the hue or dominant wavelength is kept

[3] Maitland Graves, *Color Fundamentals* (New York: McGraw-Hill Book Co., Inc., 1952), Chap. 15.

[4] Herein lies the great value of the Munsell student color charts where the colors must be arranged in systematic order by the student.

constant. On the Munsell solid we could travel vertically on a path of changing value (progression 1), horizontally on a path of changing chroma (progression 2), or diagonally on a path where both value and chroma change (progression 3).

In the next four routes the hues are varied in orderly fashion. Progression 4 is a duplication of progression 1 where saturation is constant and lightness changes in an orderly fashion along with the hues. A counterpart of progression 2 where lightness is constant and saturations change in an orderly fashion with the hues makes progression 5. A duplication of progression 3 where both lightness and saturation change in orderly fashion with the hues makes progression 6. Progression 7 is where hues change in an orderly fashion but both lightness and saturation are repetitive. Similar kinds of progressions could be located on other color systems although their repetitive and variant factors would be related to the ordering of the system.

Progression 1, where colors change from dark to light without altering their hue or saturation, is found in nature on overcast days. It is a good relationship to use when large surfaces are planned to be united as background. This might be in a carpet and wall harmony where the floor would be of darker value and the same hue and chroma (Munsell) as the walls. An illustration would be the use of a dark, greyed green carpet and lighter, greyed green walls.

Progression 2 is reserved for using examples of the same hue on two different planes of attention. A wall might be a greyed yellow and a saturated yellow could appear in a picture used as foreground area.

Progression 3 is a force in directing the eye toward a lighter color. This could be used where a window was focal and its curtain was a lighter and more saturated example of the wall hue.

Progression 4 is frequently seen in nature where hues are generally varied. This may be used in the same manner as progression 1. It introduces a little more variety and interest. A darker blue-green carpet could be combined with a slightly more yellow and lighter wall. In this kind of order saturations are not changed.

Progression 5 functions in a manner similar to path 2 but introduces greater change. It is sometimes interesting to use in a minor portion of a design as when a more saturated green is used in an enamel which is placed near a duller blue chair of the same lightness.

Progression 6 goes from the dark and dull of one hue to the light and saturated of a neighboring hue. It is one of the most exciting progressions found in nature. It invariably suggests bright sunlight and it swiftly moves the eye toward the parts of the design which are most brilliant. In a room scheme this kind of order is very forceful in directing the eye to the chief centers of interest.

The seventh path (progression 7) through color space can be visualized on a Munsell solid by sampling all the hues at some arbitrary value and chroma level, say 4/6. The colors then become so very much alike that they can be mixed at will in one attention plane of a design. A rainbow of hues can be used as one pattern in the background, in the middle ground or in the foreground if the intervals between are interesting and if their saturations and lightness-darkness are constant.

Progression 1, 4, and 7 are especially useful in coordinating eye movement on one plane of attention. In progressions 2, 3, 5, 6 transitions between planes of attention can more readily be made.

b. NATURAL ORDER OF COLORS

Reconsidering, for a moment, progressions 4, 5, and 6, we note that they are characterized by a change of hue accompanied by a change in either one or both of the other color attributes. In the natural phenomenon of the rainbow spectrum the hues become lighter as they approach yellow and darker as they approach the purples and blues. This has been called the *natural order of colors*.[5]

Yellow is opposite one of the blues or bluish purples on any standard color circle. In using the natural order in a decorative scheme first note the respective positions of the hues on a circle. Then use the color which is nearest to the blue

[5] H. Barrett Carpenter, *Colour* (New York: Chas. Scribner's Sons, 1932), pp. 25–31.

as the darkest and probably dullest color. The others are regulated in saturation and lightness-darkness according to their respective positions between blue and yellow. This applies as a somewhat reliable guide when close progressions between hues are being used. Thus a green wallpaper would be lighter than a blue carpet. When many hues are involved, problems of planes of vision and of major and minor emphases are apt to introduce considerations which would invalidate such oversimplification of precept.

As safe and usable as the natural order of colors has proved to be, a slavish following of this order at all times would be uninteresting. Even nature shows us a blue in the sky which is a lighter blue than the green in the grass or the brown in earth. It may suit our purpose for sparkle or for dramatic effect to use a topsy-turvy order in our hue-lightness-saturation relations. How about a saturated vermilion (slightly yellowish red) and a crimson pink (blue and lighter red)? The Indian maharajahs often caparison their elephants and entourage in these colors. Observe the dark yellow-reds or oranges used with light lavenders on many Persian miniatures.

c. THE KINDS OF INTERVALS

The kinds of intervals chosen in color work are very important to the securing of an effect and should go hand-in-hand with any discussion about the choice of color traits to gain an effect. Small intervals result in greater uniformity and quietness of effect. Wider intervals may create greater interest. They create a more balanced but likewise a more vigorous and exciting effect. Intervals can be measured on any color progression. Even intervals would be 1-2-3-4-5 or 1-3-5-7. Variant intervals would be 1-5-7. For contrasting intervals 1-8 might be considered.

Many texts in the past have given names to different kinds of color schemes. These names, however arbitrarily assigned, are frequently useful in color work. They afford a firm handle by which to grasp color combinations. In one frequently used group of nomenclatures we find such labels as monochromatic, analogous, triadic and complementary color schemes. These represent groupings of colors the hues of which are characterized by small interval spacing to large interval spacing respectively. Inasmuch as it is natural to think of color first in terms of its hue, we might consider these different types of hue schemes more completely.[6]

The monochromatic or one hue harmony indicates a group of colors all possessing the same hue with changes introduced through lightness-darkness and saturation. The analogous or closely related hue harmony indicates a group of colors with closely related hues. A group of colors such as the purples which have varying amounts of both red and blue in their composition are very closely related. Two colors such as yellow-red and red-purple which have only red in common are less closely bound.

Using any of these closely related hue schemes is apt to be overpowering in its one-sided emotional effect and fatiguing to the eye unless precautions are taken to introduce contrast in some subtle way.

The triadic hue harmony refers to a scheme which uses three hues about equally spaced around the color wheel. A complementary hue harmony consists of hues which are approximately opposite each other on a hue circuit. Obviously those two hues which are visual complements will provide the greatest contrast to each other, but any two hues which are so mutually exclusive will have an intense complementary effect. Another example of this kind of hue choice where colors from all parts of the wheel are sampled would be a quadratic harmony using four hues about equally far apart from one another. These schemes utilize all of the various hue sensations and so are often most satisfactory to use in a room which is much occupied. At the same time they are more restless than are hue arrangements which are of more closely related hues.

The major notes on any of these hue harmonies will be regulated by some clearly expressed order found on one of the color progressions. They are like musical chords with definite relationships between tones. Minor developments must likewise be ordered but they need not follow in the major progression.

3. Color Order Through the Positioning of Colors

The third way to order color so that harmonious relationships are felt to exist is to assign colors to such areas and such locations as would be conducive to obtaining this result. This, of course, is not easily done and it is even more difficult to set down any rule for executing it.

A simple explanation of what the artist is attempting to do may help to clarify the matter. The artist seeks to create a color grouping the members of which seem united by some perceived relation. If no qualitative ordering factor exists or if the area relations in the design are such as to destroy the perception of order, then the artist must adjust his colors and his other design components so as to create an illusion of harmony.[7] As an illustration, two colors which are of unequal saturation might be perceived as of equality if their size and positioning were regulated.

a. AMOUNTS OF COLOR

The simplest explanation of how to effect order through manipulation of color areas came from the pen of Munsell.[8] He called it the principle of balanced color. The idea of balanced color is that if all the colors in an harmonious color scheme were to be rotated on a disk in the relative amounts (proportions again!) in which they were present in the scheme, they would appear to balance to a neutral grey of about middle tone. Thus for every bit of dark area used, a proportionate amount of light area would be required. As a large amount of greyed color would be balanced by a small amount of saturated color and hues would be balanced across the wheel, an adjustment of all of these attributes in relation to areas would be necessary.

[6] M. E. Chevreul, *The Principles of Harmony and Contrasts of Colors*. Trans. Charles Martel (3rd ed.; London: George Bell and Sons, 1881). Chevreul was among the first to publish the idea that the psychological effect of a color combination is closely related to the kind of intervals used. He went into this problem thoroughly, studying not only hue intervals but also lightness-darkness intervals and saturation intervals. Most texts, however, have focused their attention principally on a discussion of hue intervals.

[7] See color as perceptual experience, Chap. VI.

[8] A. H. Munsell, *A Color Notation* (Baltimore, Md.: Munsell Color Company, Inc., 1954), pp. 31–41.

To follow this rule of balanced colors would undoubtedly produce a safe livable interior provided other requirements of color order were regarded. But the rule represents an oversimplification which would be limiting. There are many occasions in decorating when the desired color effect is not balanced in the Munsell sense but is oriented towards some particular hue, or lightness-darkness, or saturation level. Amounts of color are important provided they are adjusted to serve the artist's purpose.

b. PLACEMENT OF COLOR

In choosing colors for a harmony, not only their relative amounts but likewise their relative placement in the design must be considered. A color placed on one side of a room may appear to make an harmonious relationship and placed on the other side on an area of exactly the same size it may seem inharmonious. Such a discord may be caused by many factors such as the optical effect of adjacent colors, the effect of different lighting or the effect of a different spatial order. For recognizing all this no specific rule would be adequate.

E. RELATION BETWEEN COLOR AND SPATIAL DESIGN

The selection of colors and their placement is governed not only by the intent of the artist to create a pleasant color grouping but likewise to create one which will promote all of the spatial design purposes. He selects and arranges so that the colors will fit into his room plan. Some colors will group with others on the same level of attention. Some progressions will direct eye movement. Some repetitions will aid stability. The real color artist has the added problem of introducing color vitality into his work. This is the great challenge.

There are innumerable ways of doing all this, each of which will seem particularly right to the designer for a particular set of conditions. The following suggestion is merely a generalized example for illustration.

The background of a room may be organized in path 1, holding all of the colors together by use of the same hue and saturation. Assuming the carpet to be a dark yellow-red (brown), the upholstery of the largest pieces could tie in with this background by picking up the same saturation of the hue in lighter tone (tan). From there the rest of the furniture could progress by path 2 to a more saturated color (orange) for smaller pieces. Accents could begin with this strong note and pick up a triad of hues in path 7. This would give the eye many chances for movement in color, along the background tones, in the linkages from background to middleground, along the middleground, in the linkages from middleground to foreground and along the foreground path. If in all of these there was some additional linkage of lightness-darkness, the eye would pick up this route. If to this were added the possibilities of choice in visual channels of shapes, how vitally complex the design would become.

F. SPATIAL ILLUSIONS ACCOMPLISHED THROUGH COLOR INTERRELATIONS

The adjustment of visual forces creates effects which may be illusionary. The following are a few of the spatial illusions which may be accomplished through color.

1. To create space through color:
   Use cool hues.
   Use light tones.
   Use dull saturations.
   Keep contrasts to the minimum dictated by the necessity of relieving monotony.
   Use color rhythms to direct the eye to more expansive space.
2. Do the reverse of 1 to contract space.
3. To lower a ceiling:
   Use warm hues.
   Use dark tones.
   Use strong saturations.
4. Do the reverse of 3 to heighten a room.
5. To shorten a room:
   Duplicate any of the suggestions under 2 on the narrow wall of the room.
6. Do the reverse of 5 to lengthen a room.
7. To take away from the squareness of a room:
   Use different hues, lightness, or saturations on one or several walls.

8. To obliterate an undesirable feature:

Use colors for the surroundings which present little color contrast with the object.

Break up the object by color areas so that it can no longer be seen as a complete object.

Extend the object through the use of color to make it part of a more desirable object.

G. ACTUAL PLANNING OF COLOR IN INTERIOR DESIGN

Even though we may know in general how to make a good color design, there are many particular considerations which arise in fitting colors to special interiors.

1. Functional Considerations

Thoughts about function should come first with colors as with shapes. Actually the thought for the expression or feeling which a space is to convey is a functional consideration. A space is not right for its use until its purpose is manifest through color quality.

A simpler functional concern is for the practicality of colors from the interrelated standpoints of cleanability, availability, and cost. Some thought must be given to the fact that light colors show soil easily. Will the cleaning of the fabrics be costly in time or money? Slipcovers, the new synthetic materials which can be wiped clean, and detachable upholstery make light colors seem more feasible.

The market availability of certain colors should be considered. The large volume market is the average price market. Colors which are adaptable to many situations or which are currently in fashion will be found on the large volume market. A manufacturer cannot expect as extensive a sale for a light lavender carpet, for instance, as he might for a middle tone rose or green. Therefore, the unusual color frequently would not be a wise budget choice. There might be a season, however, when some world event or some cycle of emphasis would tell the style promoters to feature an unusual color. In this case the fact often phrased, "they are doing it this year," really becomes useful. The practical planner might well decide that it would be wise to swim with the tide rather than against it.

Cost in its relation to a practical consideration of color is certainly important. However, the right color has a value beyond price. A clever budgeter may learn ways of keeping costs low and color values high. Skill with the dye-pot, the paint brush, the needle, and the loom may help to turn the general market colors into a palette of personal color choices.

2. Consideration of the Expressive Message of the Colors

A careful analysis of the expressive message of colors should come next. Colors should advance the general room character. If a room is a private room, one may be allowed considerable free rein in creating a personalized color atmosphere. If a room is to be shared by many persons then individual color preference and the atmosphere resulting from its indulgence should be set aside. Group preference and the appropriate functional feeling should determine the room colors in this latter case. It is usually possible to create a happy union in the expression of personal, group, and functional color requirements.

It is a very good idea to allow a young son or daughter to choose the dominant color for his or her room. Such opportunity makes children color conscious. It is likewise an equally good idea to show children how their personal choices may need to be modified to fit into the color scheme of the entire house and the economic planning of the family. This teaches them that even in artistic matters the happiness of the family takes precedent over the individual and that this opportunity entails thoughtfulness for others.

3. The Visual Aspects of the Space As a Factor

The visual aspects of every space are particular and should influence the choice of colors. In the first place a building is located in a certain setting—country, city, woodland, or seaside. The colors chosen to complement the interior may be similar to these surroundings or they may be divergent from them. The color scheme of a rural house could be saturated with the warm browns and greens of the earth and the foliage.

This might be quite desirable in a contemporary house which opened wide to the scenery. On the other hand an older house with limited window space could use gay saturated colors which might seem like fresh flowers brought indoors.

The light coming through the windows is just as important as the view from the windows in helping to dictate colors for a room. The effect of a cool north light can be minimized by a warm color scheme and the effect of a warm light can be changed by a cool color scheme. On the other hand if one wishes to accentuate the light which is reflected into a room from a blue sea- or sky-scape, then cool colors should be chosen.

The size of the space is an important consideration. Colors that give the illusion of space are often essential. Sometimes a careful adjustment of colors with respect to location, orientation, and size is required. A small north room in an apartment might suggest a warm hue. This could make the walls seem to advance and the space seem unduly small. A greyed yellow-red in a light tone might be the solution. Advancing colors are out of place in front of any transparent medium which suggests a continuity with space.

Colors already in a room can be played up or down by the colors put with them. Textures of room surfaces bear a suggested relationship to certain colors and this should not be disregarded. A terra-cotta flagging at an entrance can be made quite at home if associated with deeper toned furniture woods which have a soft rubbed down finish.

Movable possessions which one must use further limit the choice of colors for a room. It is often necessary to build around these, first evaluating them in terms of color to see whether they are worthy of being awarded first place in a color harmony or whether they should be forced into a subordinate position. In a Baluchistan oriental hearth rug there are interwoven with the brown tones of its camels' hairs certain subtle rose and blue tones which cast purple lights about the room when direct light plays upon them. If these purplish tones are repeated throughout the room, with care exercised not to overbalance the subtlety of the rug scheme, a most charming result can be obtained. On the

other hand a Baluchistan rug can be very easily forced back to an all brown oblivion and in this event it will not really dictate the color harmony of the rest of the room.

It is frequently necessary to tie together a number of seemingly unrelated color objects by means of a well selected color scheme. This accounts in part for the enormous popularity of chintz or cretonne draperies. An old blue chair, rose rug, and gold framed pictures may be unified by the use of a drapery which combines all of these colors. Sometimes the unrelated colors in a room may be made to fit into a color sequence and so be given some emphasis. A faded blue chair and a less faded blue wallpaper may be united by using a slightly more saturated blue in a picture or drapery. Occasionally a belonging may not seem to fit into any desirable color harmony. Then it may be necessary to be ruthless by either painting it another color or discarding it.

4. Advisability of Making a Painting of the Color Scheme

After thinking about those preliminary considerations which might affect a color scheme, then the choices should be narrowed to a definite selection. There are two methods of arriving at an ultimate decision. The first method would consist of working out the scheme as it progressed, modifying our views as choices presented themselves. Undoubtedly a certain amount of this kind of choosing will be necessary but we would advise another method of procedure. This advisable method might be called the a priori or thinking-it-out-beforehand method. Make a drawing of the room by one of the methods described in Chapter IV. It should be made on a piece of white paper or cardboard which is heavy enough and absorptive enough to stand up under water-color paint. A piece of illustration board, 15″ × 20″, will serve excellently for several sketches.

Buy a small inexpensive box of transparent or opaque water-color paint. Remember the general rules about how to secure desired colors from pigments. With a little practice one usually finds it possible to reproduce any preconceived room color scheme. If it should prove too difficult to obtain the desired pigment color, it is possible to search for the colors either in colored papers or cloths. These could then be cut out and pasted into place on the drawing. This a priori method provides the opportunity of visualizing the resultant color scheme before making costly purchases. We often see where the effect could be improved by changing certain of the colors. It is surprising how much can be learned by this simple and inexpensive process. It will certainly be worth the effort if it saves a lot of expensive grief later. Besides, it is fun.

5. Choice of Dominant Color

After paying attention to the several factors which might predetermine color choices, we are free to choose one color from a limited number of colors which would be possible for the situation. This we may call the dominant color in our scheme.

What do we mean by dominant color? It might be easier to say what a dominant color is not. It is not necessarily the color which is most in evidence. Nor need it be the most saturated color. It is the color from which all other colors take their point of departure. It is the color by which the relationship of all other colors is gauged. It is the starting point of a color scheme, much in the same way that a keynote establishes the tonal relations in a piece of music. The effect of this color is to be enhanced through the design.

This color around which we wish to build may be of any value or chroma because we have not yet decided how much of it we want to use or where we want to place it.

Once a dominant color is chosen, keep it at hand for ready reference. As we are about to embark on a color journey we must at all times be aware of our starting point lest we become lost. There will be times when we do not know exactly where we are going. The fortuitous element in choices will make the exploration more exciting. And it may make the result better. But if we completely lose our bearings the result is doomed.

6. The Locations of Color in a Room

Every area possesses color. These locations may be grouped under seven headings: floor, walls, ceiling, windows, furniture, accessories, people. There is little one can do about the colors worn by the occupants. Families have been known to choose their pets to accentuate a color scheme! The largest color areas in a room should usually be handled so that they will remain in the background. Thus floors, walls, windows and ceilings are not generally obtrusive. Furniture and accessories then take their places respectively as middleground and foreground and can attract more attention. Other kinds of ordering are possible and under certain conditions may be more advisable. In the following paragraphs we will consider customary treatments first, and then note some exceptions.

7. Hues to Accompany the Dominant Hue

Our next decision should be concerned with the hue harmony. Do we wish the effect of a close or of a divergent hue harmony? Once this decision is made, a flip of the hand on a color wheel will disclose the other hues which might be used with the dominant.

8. The Usual Hue Placement

In locating hues in a room, many designers seem to place one hue on the floor, to place a second on the walls and to make the ceiling white or a tint of the walls. The only factor determining the choice of hue placement is the general rule that the bluer hues may be placed in the position of the darker colors, namely, on the floor. Thus if the two hues to be used were blue and green, the blue would be selected as a darker blue and would appear in the carpet. The green would be selected as a lighter green and would be placed on the walls. In the hypothetical room we are describing, the woodwork could be painted the same green as the walls or left in natural tone.

The furniture then picks up either or both of the background hues and frequently adds other hues of the preliminary plan. In this pattern

room the furniture could be green, gold, and rose. The background of the draperies would then be planned to repeat the hue of the floor, wall, or trim and the pattern of the drapery may pick up any or all of the hues already used in the room. It may even add small bits of related accent hues which might then be located in flowers, pictures, lamps, or small accessories.

The room described above illustrates one of the more frequently seen hue arrangements in the American home. However, other trends are evident and indeed seem more in keeping with the concepts of the modern house. As the contemporary house fits into a picture of indoor-outdoor living, the tendency to keep hues quiet and hence similar is noticed.

In many instances all furniture upholstery is in one hue or in several closely related hues with contrast provided through texture. Occasionally for a unique effect, the furniture will be in many different hues kept to the same saturation. Thus porch furniture could have cushions of rainbow hues. Sometimes the furniture will be planned in two accent hues which are quite independent of the room background. A beige room could have green and plum colored furniture colors.

It is not alone the furniture which may depart from the usual plan. Either floors or walls or both might use several hues. In the contemporary houses where the living quarters are one large area, a break in its spatial continuity is often made by the use of different colors. Thus the dining end of a living-dining room combination could have yellow walls and the living end could be green. In keeping with the architectural concept that the spaces are connected, one wall

Figure 69. Various lightness-darkness arrangements.

A. A usual lightness-darkness arrangement.

B. Dark furniture against light walls.

C. Dark ceiling.

D. Walls, ceiling, floor, the same lightness-darkness.

E. Dark walls.

F. Light floor.

Draftsman: Mary Shipley, East Lansing, Michigan.

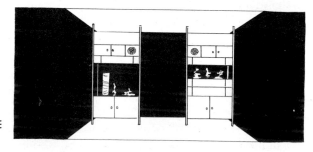

of the living room which is continuous with the dining room may carry the dining room hue into the living room or vice versa. Usually it is wise to put closely related colors on two sections of the same architectural space.

Colored ceilings are likewise to be considered. They frequently add interest. There is a word of caution to suggest in regard to their use but unfortunately it is one which cannot be easily put into practice until it is too late. Sit in the room which has the colored ceiling. Does it become annoying because the eye is constantly attracted upward? There is nothing quite so irritating as being forced to crane one's neck at an uncomfortable angle because of the character of the room decoration. When the ceiling is colorful be careful to use balancing forceful notes at the ground level.

9. Consideration of Lightness-Darkness in the Room Colors

The selection and placement of the light and dark areas in a room is one of the most important decisions which a designer must form. As light-dark contrasts are the most eye attracting which can be made, so the decision about the light-dark scheme must be given a good bit of thought. Most colorists find it to be a good exercise to paint the color of their rooms in monotone first. This helps them to study the light-dark pattern without being distracted by the interesting chromatic colors.

The customary or traditional lightness scheme is like the one which nature often presents. In this the darkest tones are placed on the floor, the middle tones on the walls and the lightest tones on the ceiling. This produces the effect of firmness to the ground and of airiness round about. It is possible to make a recipe which will cover this plan. Floors may be in the range of Munsell values 1 to 5 inclusive.[9] The walls may be Munsell values 5 to 8. The ceiling would of course be very light and might be white.

Attention should then be given to the window treatment. Textiles at the windows attract notice because they cover large areas in several loca-

[9] These values are slightly darker than those recommended for best lighting practice. See Chap. VIII.

tions. Before making a decision about the tone of curtains ask with what objects in the room we wish to relate the windows. One way of accomplishing such an object-window relation is to duplicate the lightness-darkness of the object, in the curtains. Thus, in a very large room the draperies might be related by value to the floor. Or the curtains could be associated with the painted wood trim of the room. For example, in a room painted blue with white wall trim, we could place a figured drapery with white background and with a blue, red, and green floral foreground. Drapery tones may likewise tie in with the furniture colors in a room. Another very good plan is to make the drapery background the same key or a little lighter than the walls. This treatment has the advantage of making the wall plane seem to reach out to the window and therefore of making the room seem larger. It also dramatizes the drapery pattern.

Consider the lightness scheme of the furniture next. The furniture wood establishes an important tone in a room. Traditional furniture is frequently mahogany and thus creates an initial dark color. The contemporary use of lighter furniture woods is often done for the purpose of bringing the room tones closer together. A usual plan for furniture upholstery is the use of several shades for variety, making them repeat or fit by progression into the lightness-darkness patterns already established in the room. An unusual scheme occurs when the tone of the furniture is selected to contrast with the room background. Thus, dark green furniture might be placed against off-white walls. One of the more recent arrangements is to make the furniture similar to the walls in tonality thus making it merge into the background. This treatment is good for a small interior as it seems to create space.

Occasionally dark colors are placed on the ceiling. Dark ceilings, like those of strong hue, are apt to make rooms seem lower. One exception would be the case of a ceiling painted a dark color in the blue range. The visual effect might be similar to that of a dark sky which almost seems to retreat out of consciousness. It is questionable whether a dark ceiling of any hue should be tried on a room which is less than nine feet high.

Why use dark ceilings? One advantage lies in the creation of more interesting plane relations. It might be advisable to use a dark ceiling in a dining room which was adjacent to a living room, or in a library which was adjacent to a hallway. The difference in ceilings between the two rooms would create the illusion that the rooms were of two different heights.

A dark ceiling and dark floor can be used with light walls to give the effect of horizontal extension. As this is the modern effect closely related to the tempo of contemporary life, it is consciously sought by some designers.

A current vogue in designing is to make the ceiling very nearly like the walls in value. In a very close tonal plan the floor may likewise be similar to the walls and ceiling. The middle to light colors are the only ones which are advisable for this. A close tonal scheme produces a restful spacious effect. Likewise it makes us less aware of wall, floor, and ceiling as boundaries. Therefore the room seems to exist in a sort of suspension in space or dream world, so to speak. This is a trick which many stage designers have used.

Dark walls are likewise favored by many designers. Dark walls, as well as ceilings, should only be employed after due consideration of the room illumination. One advantage which comes from the use of some dark walls is the effect of altering the proportions of the room. The visual illusion of changing the position of the wall planes results.

The use of unrelieved dark walls usually makes a room seem smaller. Often this is to be desired as it gives a certain degree of intimacy which we call coziness to an interior. The walls appear to have some weight and importance and not to be just so much light airiness. If we are decorating a very small room which leads into a bright cheerful room, it is often wise to paint the walls of the small room quite dark. The dark walls of this small room will almost seem to vanish, emphasizing the nearby bright room. This same illusion seems to occur when a window wall is dark.

Some designers like to use middle to light tones on the floor. This is often essential when floors are depended upon for reflectance. White floors of course require a lot of cleaning. But a middle tone warm grey carpet does not show soil as readily as a darker carpet does. From the point of view of decorating the modern house, middle tones seem more like a continuation of the out-of-doors. By the same token they make the indoors seem larger.

The woodwork or trim of a room is a very special problem in tonality, the solution to which can make or mar a room color scheme. If a house is old and has much woodwork of poor quality, about the only thing to do is to cover it with paint. If the house is small and a restful, more spacious effect is desired, then paint the trim the same color as the walls. Thus the wall planes will appear unbroken.

White woodwork in a room may be very pleasant but the result is liable to be unfortunate if the woodwork is painted white simply because one doesn't know what else to do with it. Such unpurposeful thinking may divorce the very light color of the trim from any tonal sequence in the room. It must be remembered that white is like a note of pure color and hence must be used as another color factor in design. White can be used successfully to brighten very dark walls on the one hand or quite neutral walls in another case. It will ally itself with very saturated colors to make a vivid room.

Sometimes the room trim is painted a very light or very dark hue as a contrast to walls. If the hue and saturation are wisely chosen, this treatment may be quite interesting. Contrast of lightness-darkness, however, will always make the room seem more active and smaller.

Some older houses have a great deal of very beautiful woodwork which has been left in its natural state. The problem may then be to change the tonality of the wood so that it will fit better into a newer color scheme and at the same time to preserve the wood texture. Stains may be used to darken wood. Simple staining can be quite attractive. We recall a cool-looking house in a wooded setting. The plastered interior was left white. The chestnut trim was stained dark green.

The reverse of the effect of staining wood dark is obtained when a wiping stain employing light toned pigment is used. This is allowed to bite into the grain of the wood and then the excess is rubbed off. Only that which has sunk into the largest wood pores will show.[10] This process makes the grain texture more apparent at the same time that it lightens the wood tone.

In new houses built in the modern manner, the wood trim is or should be of good quality and it is in keeping with the contemporary decorating philosophy to leave it as nearly natural as possible. As the woods are customarily of middle range in lightness the acceptance of this idea suggests the use of wall colors of similar lightness-darkness.

10. The Saturations to Be Used

In many respects a room color scheme is like a painting. The visual area of a canvas responds to the artist's skill and recedes or advances in accordance with his wish. Thus planes of attention such as background, middleground, and foreground are established. The regulation of the saturation of the colors is the most important way to accomplish this illusion.

A typical plan uses weak colors for the background areas of a room, moderate saturations for the middleground and strong saturations for the foreground accents. It is a simpler and modified version of this plan to think of a room as having only background and foreground planes of interest. In this case walls, floors, ceiling, and large pieces of furniture are considered as background. They are then kept of equal saturation which may range from weak to moderate. As a practical guide we have found that rarely should background areas go beyond Munsell chroma 6. It should be remembered that multiple reflections from wall to wall make large areas of color in a room seem much more saturated than a small sample would seem. Small pieces of furniture and accessories provide the necessary saturated accents which are the sparklers of the room scheme.

The accustomed relation of background to foreground, between wall, floor, furniture and accessories, is frequently changed. For instance, background neutral grey furniture is sometimes placed against foreground saturated walls. Patterns on draperies or on upholstery are frequently

[10] Normally these stains are designed for nonporous woods.

vivid and thus a wall and a furniture area become foreground.

Occasionally all the colors of a room are kept similar in saturation. This is done on a strong saturation range whenever white or near white and saturated chromatic color are dominant in a room. The white reflects white light which in turn dissipates the purity of the other colors. Nevertheless this kind of color scheme is dangerous to try in a small area. It requires high ceilings and large rooms to carry it off successfully.

A room where all the colors are dulled (to about a Munsell chroma 4) is the most successful scheme of similar saturations to employ. Then every color really has some of every other color in it (by the process of neutralization). Therefore the colors seem quite harmonious together and a very restful spacious effect may be obtained. Planes of interest may be achieved in this plan by adjusting relative areas of warm, or advancing, and cool, or retreating, colors.

11. Final Check of Color Order

Now our room shapes are endowed with color character and this has affected their visual force. Therefore we must examine our room plan and analyze the present eye movements in the room. Check for visual activity in the rhythms to centers of interest, and in balance, and in the interesting devious routes for visual excursions. Remember there will be only one more visual medium, texture, through which results can be modified.

12. A Suggested Order to Be Used in Planning Living Room Colors

The following is an outline of the order in which we might plan our living room color scheme:

1. Choose the desired emotional effect.

2. Consider the practical characteristics, the expressive characteristics, and the visual room characteristics.

3. Decide upon a dominant color. With this in mind, plan a tentative color scheme with respect to hues, lightness-darkness, and saturation.

4. Sketch, mentally or by simple draft, the places where the colors will be placed.

5. Decide which of these places are to be background, middleground, and foreground. Let us assume a usual plan of treatment using floors, walls, and ceiling as background.

6. Consider the carpet. Assume the usual plan of putting the darkest color on the floor. Place the carpet in the range of Munsell value 1 to 5, chroma 1 to 6. The hue will be the bluest hue of those chosen.

7. Choose the wall color. The hue may be the same as the carpet or it may be any other of those selected. The lightness will be in the middle to light range, Munsell value 5 to 8. The saturation will be the same as the carpet.

8. The wood trim might be the same color or tone as the walls.

9. Consider the draperies. If a quiet effect is desired duplicate the hue of the carpet, walls, or trim in the background of the draperies. The choice of the same hue as the walls will give the most restful and spacious effect. The tone of the background of the draperies will help to unite them to the tone of the room section which they repeat. The saturation of the background of the draperies will be the same as that of the wall.

10. Consider the principal pieces of furniture. The number of hues used will depend upon the line of reasoning outlined in the first part of this chapter. Place the lightness of the upholstery in the middle range, possibly a little lighter than the floor and darker than the walls. The saturations will be similar and about Munsell chroma 4 to 8.

11. Plan the foreground colors, those to be found in small chairs, pictures, drapery pattern, and accessories. The hues will be a repetition of those already used. Or they will be orderly variations of these. The tones will be such as to fit neatly into some of the established tonal patterns. The saturations will be strong.

12. Place the chosen colors on the preliminary room sketch. Observe and check how they integrate and help the room design.

All of this planning helps us to follow an orderly routine for considering and purchasing the colors for an interior. After one has worked in this routine and has planned the more usual color schemes, it is possible to do the more unusual with greater sureness. Having developed a degree of skill we may even feel that some of our most successful results are gained through intuition and are somewhat fortuitous. In the beginning there is need to be more logical in what we are trying to do.

13. Unity of Color Schemes within a Building

Sometimes the colors in a building are annoying because they have not been planned as a whole. The color scheme of an entire place should be something like a symphony. The principal room is possibly the first movement with its statement and elaboration of the first themes. The other rooms use these harmonies as points of departure, always bearing some relation to them. At times they may restate the first color idea in another way, at times they may add something to its development, but rarely should they start off on new channels. The entire edifice should present a unified experience in color but it should not offer a monotonous one.

In a house we proceed from the living room in our color planning to the rooms which can be seen from the living room. Let us take an adjacent library as an example. The colors seen from the living room actually become part of the living room scheme and so should supplement it as well as form a pleasingly unified design of their own. For this there are a great many possibilities. One of the subdominant living room colors may become the dominant library color. The entire hue color scheme of the living room may be altered slightly for the library by rotating the color wheel from the pointers which were used for the living room and gaining an analogous group of colors for the new room. Two of the several living room hues may be used for the library. The library may have a different lightness or saturation scheme from the living room. One room may be treated like the other in color scheme but may have more pronounced shape pattern.

Thought should be given to the special colors most suited to each room. The color scheme of a hallway may act as an introduction to the living room but should never overpower it. Consequently the saturations used in the hall may be weaker than those used in a living room. However, a hall is used for a shorter time than the living area and so can frequently exhibit exciting colors. A hallway is often done in darker tones because it is an entrance to the living room and darkness leads on to light. A library is frequently done in dark somber tones. The books are bright spots of interest and the dark walls help to introduce a cloistered feeling. A dining room on the other hand should be especially cheerful. Consequently the warmer hues, lighter tones, and more saturated colors are appropriate. The kitchen might suggest cleanliness, efficiency, and cheerfulness. Thus sharp clear contrasts of warm hues with white are often used. Yellow used somewhere in the kitchen is enjoyable because it is a hue which is cheerful without being too distracting. Bedrooms can have the most personal of all color schemes provided care is given to their restfulness. Thus more neutral colors with a few accents can be used. Cheer and restfulness are required for the nursery and are accomplished by the use of pale colors, preferably in the warmer hue range.

14. Illustration of Color Design for Specific Color and Space Effects

a. A RESTFUL LIVING ROOM

Let us illustrate these steps of color design by imagining colors in certain rooms. Our first room might be one in which we had considered an effect of dignified and reserved friendliness. Perhaps this is the living room of a mature couple, a retired banker and his wife. Mrs. Banker is very fond of blue and so wishes to use it for the dominant hue selecting it in medium lightness and in a moderate saturation. This blue will certainly express dignity and reserve but would be a little too cold to express friendliness. If Mrs. B were to make the blue quite emphatic in her room by using it as carpet color and in a lighter tone as wall color, then she would be wise to use a quite different and warmer hue in other locations in the room.

Mr. B., we note, has attractive brown eyes and

wears tans and browns and warm rust shades in his country tweeds. Therefore we suggest using tones of yellow-red (orange) to warm up the psychological atmosphere of this living room. As the couple would seem more at home in quiet surroundings, this secondary hue could likewise be used in medium lightness and moderate to strong saturation. These choices may be sufficient to produce the effect desired. The dominance of blue, and medium to light tones with moderate saturations unify the scheme; the contrast of hues serves to enhance the original dominant effect. If greater interest is called for, a small area of a third hue may be used, perhaps a green-yellow which is about halfway round the color wheel between yellow-red and blue. It might be in a light tone and in a strong saturation. The green-yellow then repeats the already existing light tone pattern of the wall but is a unique and contrasting note both in hue and in saturation.

The very unexpectedness of the hue in this relationship makes it exciting. Such a room may be charted on the Munsell system as shown. Notice the greater amount of repetition and variation of dominant traits used in this room and the relatively less amount of contrast. Thus interval relations are small rather than large, adding to the effect of quietness and reserve.

b. A CHEERFUL DINING ROOM

Let us now select a scheme where the total accomplished result is more lively and less reserved. This would call for more stimulating dominant traits and for greater total contrast. To begin our lively effect let us choose yellow walls for our dominant hue. For the carpet we could choose a different hue, not spaced so far away as to detract from the exhilarating effect of the yellow. This might be a darker bluish-red carpet (normal order of color tones). The walls and carpet are in a slightly more saturated tone than was used in the last room because we want a less reserved atmosphere.

There may be introduced into the accents some quite saturated notes of a pure red which would make a natural order of color from the carpet. One or two more accent colors could be

BLUE ROOM

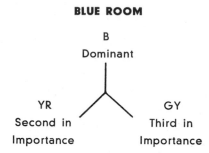

Space	Hue	Value	Chroma	
Wall	B (Repetition)	Light (Variation)	Moderate (Repetition)	Path 1 [11]
Carpet	B (Dominant Hue)	Medium (Dominant value 4)	Moderate (Dominant chroma 4)	
Draperies	B Background (Repetition)	Light (Variation)	Moderate (Repetition)	Path 7
	YR Pattern (Contrast)	Medium (Repetition)	Moderate (Repetition)	
Chairs	B (Repetition)	Medium (Repetition)	Moderate (Repetition)	
	YR (Contrast)	Medium (Repetition)	Moderate (Repetition)	Path 6
Accent	2.5 GY (Contrast)	Light (Variation)	Strong (Variation)	

[11] A few paths are indicated in these rooms to suggest how the colors are ordered. The brackets connect two colors which are related in the manner shown. They form the bond or linkage between one set of color areas and another.

used in this room. But they must be handled skillfully. The first in importance would be an intermediate value and moderately saturated green. This would accentuate the reds by contrast and would seem to make a supporting base for the yellows. If the room were, perhaps, a dining room in a restaurant, the chair seats might be in a broken stripe of red, greenish-yellow, and yellow. Then the table linen or pottery might be in the green. Darker bluish-green notes would be found in the drapery or in a hanging. The eye would be pleased to follow this blue-green to yellow gamut in the same way that it would en-

joy the bluish-red to red cycle. The smallest amount of accent color could be introduced by a series of purples, which, because they were intended for sparkle, could range from the duller, lighter red-purples to the darker and more saturated purple-blues in an unnatural color order. A ceramic bowl or table glassware could pick up the most forceful note in this progression.

c. A DRAMATIC CLUB LOUNGE

Our third color scheme is even more stimulating. It uses strong contrasts and exciting color

YELLOW ROOM

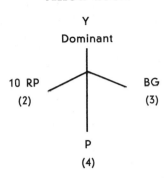

Y
Dominant

10 RP   BG
(2)   (3)

P
(4)

Space	Hue	Value	Chroma	
Wall	Y (Dominant hue)	Light (Dominant value)	Moderate (Dominant chroma 6)	
Carpet	10RP (Contrast)	Dark (Contrast)	Moderate (Repetition)	Path 4
Draperies	Y Background (Repetition of wall)			Path 6
	Pattern: R (Variation)	Medium (Variation)	Strong (Variation)	
	BG (Contrast)	Dark (Contrast)	Moderate (Repetition)	
	RP to P (Contrast)	Light to Medium (Repetition and Variation)	Weak to Saturated (Variation)	
Chairs	Y and R (Repetition and Variation)	Light and Medium (Repetition and Variation)	Moderate and Strong (Repetition and Variation)	
Accent	P (Contrast)	Dark (Contrast)	Moderate (Repetition)	

traits. It could be for a country club in a secondary room which was planned for gay occasions. The woodwork and fireplace are painted white. White gives the emotional effect of a strong saturation. The walls are a darkish moderately strong green. The carpet is a similar toned, bluish-red of the same saturation. Draperies might be chosen with a white background on which are splashy bouquets of saturated cherry red, green, and yellow flowers. In any design, such as the one on the draperies, many minor changes in the principal tones are used in ordered rela-

GREEN ROOM

White (2)

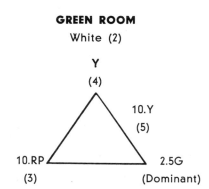

Space	Hue	Value	Chroma	
Wall	2.5G (Dominant hue)	Darkish (Dominant value 4)	Moderate (Variation)	
Woodwork	White (Contrast)	Light (Contrast)	Strong (Dominant chroma)	Path 7
Carpet	10.RP (Contrast)	Darkish (Repetition)	Moderate (Variation)	
Draperies	White Background (Contrast)	Light (Contrast)	Strong (Repetition)	Path 2
	Pattern: 10.RP (Contrast)	Darkish (Repetition)	Strong (Repetition)	
	2.5G (Repetition)	Darkish (Repetition)	Strong (Repetition)	
	Y (Variation)	Light (Contrast)	Strong (Repetition)	
Chairs	10.RP (Contrast)	Darkish (Repetition)	Strong (Repetition)	Path 4
	2.5G (Repetition)	Darkish (Repetition)	Strong (Repetition)	
Accent	10.Y (Variation)	Light (Contrast)	Strong (Repetition)	

tion. This provides added sparkle and interest. The principal chairs might be in slightly more saturated reds and greens. The final accent in upholstery, picture, or ceramic could be lime-yellow. The chart of this room indicates the use of more contrast than variation.

d. A HOUSE OF WOOD AND GLASS WHERE ATTENTION IS DIRECTED TOWARD FIREPLACE AND GARDEN

In this interior the attention in the living room is directed both to the fireplace wall and then to the garden. How do colors cooperate in securing this result?

In the first place the dominant color is chosen with the outdoors in mind. It is similar to the terra-cotta clays of the terrace. This medium light, weakly saturated, yellow-red is placed on the front wall. The fireplace is of brick and thus repeats the wall tone. The ceiling is of natural wood beams and lighter toned spaces. The flooring of wood and carpeting is a tone only slightly greyer than the walls. Thus the background of this room was planned in progressions 1 and 2, in one hue with slight changes in lightness and saturation. This makes an effect of quietness and of greater space.

It likewise leaves the designer free to use accent colors to direct the eye. The room has one large window opening onto the garden and a small high window on the front wall. These windows indicate a line of sight from entrance to yard. This must be aided by color planning. The front curtains can be the same color as the walls but the rear curtains could be an analogous hue. They could be a plain yellowish fabric which would present an orderly variation from the wall tone by being lighter and more saturated. This would turn the eye in their direction but would not keep it from moving outdoors.

There is a wall section which extends from the rear windows through to the dining room. This could be made much darker than the other walls, of equal saturation, and a contrast in hue, a dark charcoal blue, called graphite by Maerz and Paul.[12] This deeper tone would provide a color

[12] A. Maerz and M. R. Paul, *A Dictionary of Color* (2nd ed.; New York: McGraw-Hill Book Co., Inc., 1950), p. 118.

frame, as it were, to help channel the eye movement toward the rear window.

The principal chair upholstery would be attractive in a green which is slightly darker than the walls and similar to the curtains in saturation. This furniture would then be effectual in keeping the eye moving through the room and ultimately toward the window.

Thus far there are three principal colors used in the room: a yellow-red, a blue, and a green. Were we to rotate our color pointers, using a somewhat similar spacing, we would locate the drapery yellow, a cobalt blue and a maroon red. These colors could be used to emphasize the fireplace end of the room in order to make it worth our while to look in that direction when the curtains are drawn at night. The saturation of these accent colors would be aligned with those of the draperies and chairs. All of these colors and a few of the room colors might be located in a picture or art object which would be near the fireplace. If it seemed desirable, they could be repeated in an unobtrusive manner on the drapery so as to spread their emphasis in the room. For anyone who enjoys a combination of green and blue, the latter color might be used in some upholstery, as the color of a chair, or of cushions, or piping. These blue notes should not be scattered throughout the room as this would only serve to make a spotty effect. Our purpose is to create a quiet background and to use accents only as an aid to the prescribed movement.

One other consideration is necessary. There should be some dark note on the fireplace end of the room to balance the visual force of the dark charcoal colored walls. This dark note need not be too extensive in area for the accent hues which we have just placed near the fireplace would provide some of the force necessary to make a balanced arrangement. Some dark green plants or some dark notes in ceramics might prove sufficient.

e. A HOUSE OF STEEL AND GLASS WHICH LOOKS OUT TOWARD AN ENCLOSED COURT

Do you know persons whose entire approach to color is delicate but clear, personalities whose chosen colors are like the thrust of a rapier against a pure white shield? We have planned such a color scheme for a couple whose home is a simple direct expression of the contemporary.

Chalk white does not mix well with city smog. Therefore it would be better to choose a slightly warm off-white background (Munsell 2.5 Y 8/2 or 9/2) for ceiling and walls. No woodwork shows as the house is of steel, glass, and drywall construction. The floor will be made of dark achromatic composition tile with mottle of 10 YR 3/2. Area rugs could be light wool.

It would be interesting to plan this crisp room without draperies in the living area, using only the lightest of bamboo shades of color similar to the walls. A ceiling track could house a drapery which when not in use would hang along the corner of the dining space and could, when needed, indicate a portion of the room used for dining. This curtain could be of crisp cerise colored material shot through with bronze and green.

Furniture supports would be largely of metal or wood. Upholstery might be leather, and firm cotton, and some nubby wool fabric in repetition of wall and floor tones. A panel between the large windows could hold a white sculpture displayed against an electric blue hanging or against a translucent blue glass pane. A large picture in the corner opposing the draperies might be similar to them in color. The frame, if any, could be antique gold with a black casing.

Crispness should permeate this entire ensemble as an expression of the colors. But it should be a crispness allied to wiry softness (as seen in the rug and wool upholstery)—a difficult textural combination to achieve.

Oddly enough this interior need not keep the eye indoors. Its pervading bright tone was planned to give lightness to a house which is partially enclosed. Background colors are likewise neutral to emphasize space. Dark notes provide tonal contrast which accords with the sinews of the structure. The principal furniture is in one of nature's favorite hues. Accents are vivid but well spaced to direct the eye to colored glass and then to the rich greenery of the patio.

15. Summary

To anyone who enjoys color, the creation of lovely color designs is one of the greatest aesthetic experiences. That outstanding lady of the textile world, Dorothy Liebes, once said that people enjoy textiles for three reasons and in the following order, first color, then texture, and lastly pattern. All visual art is enjoyed for these three reasons and color may well be the greatest of the three.

Color design begins with an individual color, its choice the result of many causes. But once chosen, the resolutions can and do wander in many directions in the hands of the skilled colorist. The colors which are added to the first greatly increase its charm. Finally the complete harmony rolls off the color keyboard which, tempered by just the right tempos in the proper places, gives us a perfect color design, not one note to be removed nor one false note added.

With our present methods of producing tremendous brightnesses within very small areas, and controlling these almost completely both as to intensity and as to spatial position, man's triumph over night has been rendered practically complete. . . . Leading illumination engineers are now willing to recognize that their science can no longer be considered as simply a branch of physics. It is realized now that a study of the effects of light on the human organism is equally important, so important in fact, as to constitute a separate branch of illumination engineering.

DAVID KATZ *

Chapter VIII

LIGHT AS AN AESTHETIC FACTOR IN INTERIOR DESIGN

It is necessary to give considerable thought to the subject of light and lighting in any contemporary study of decoration. Light is an essential part of the design of a building. We know that the design of any utilitarian object must be determined by its function. This is particularly true in the case of lighting because light has such a great effect upon our health.

The complete solution to the lighting problem involves the choice and placement of windows, and the means of controlling their light, as well as the choice of equipment for artificial lighting, and the type and color of all surfaces within the illuminated space. Thus many persons, each with a different skill, may participate in the ultimate solution to a lighting problem. It would scarcely be possible for everyone of these persons to have an extensive knowledge of the others' special areas of information. Nevertheless a common understanding of the problem and of its objectives is certainly desirable. Then the decorator will

Horizontal candlepower.

Mean horizontal candlepower.

Mean spherical candlepower.

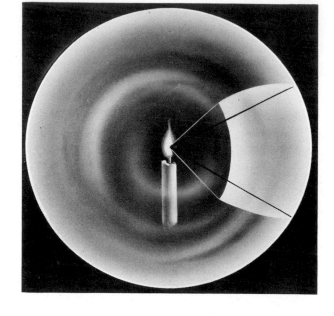

Figure 70. Diagramatic concepts of candlepower.

Photograph: From W. Sturrock and K. A. Staley, **Fundamentals of Light and Lighting,** p. 5, G.E. Bulletin LD-2, January, 1956. Reprinted by permission of the General Electric Co., Cleveland, Ohio.

not tear down what the architect has tried to do. And the architect and the illuminating engineer will work in unison.

A. CHARACTER OF LIGHT AND ITS MEASUREMENT

Color is synonymous with light. When we speak of the latter we are seeing color as the illumination mode of color appearance. The attributes of light are thus the same as those of color. We speak of the brightness rather than of the lightness of light because of the way in which it is perceived. Hue and saturation are the other two attributes of light.

Light can be modified in many ways as it travels from a radiating source to our eyes. The lighting specialist calculates the loss or addition to light every time it is modified and thus analyzes illumination ills.

A photographer measures the light falling on his subject with a small instrument known as a lightmeter or photometer. This measures the amount of localized light or luminous intensity. The basic unit of measure of light intensity is a candle. One candlepower is the amount of light from a standard candle shining equally in all directions on the inner surface of a standard sphere of one foot radius.

Candlepower is the measure of the capability of a light source to produce luminance. As this light travels outward into space equally in all directions, the amount of it which flows in a relatively limited direction is measured on a square foot on the inside surface of the standard sphere which has a uniformly diffusing surface. This unit of measure is called a lumen from the Latin word for light. A lumen is the measure of luminous flux or flow. One candlepower can produce 12.57 lumens, because the surface of a sphere of one foot radius is 12.57 square feet.[1]

The amount of light which shines upon any particular area becomes less the farther that area is removed from the light source. The amount of light at a particular place is expressed in candles per square foot or footcandles. If the meter reads five footcandles, which is a minimum requirement for general room illumination, it means that there is as much light in the room as there would be if a five candlepower light were falling on a square foot area which would be one foot distant from the light. The footcandle is the measure of illuminance.

We need one more unit to measure light. This is called a footlambert (ft.L.) which appraises the brightness or apparent amount of light concentrated on a location. Thus we are engaging in that tricky business of trying to measure a sensation. Light sensation is measured quantitatively

[1] The area of a sphere is 4×3.1416 or (πr^2).

in a similar manner to color sensation. The unknown light is visually compared to a known light the intensity of which has been objectively measured. Just as a visual colorimeter is an instrument for making the comparative evaluation of a chromatic color, so a brightness meter is an instrument for equating brightnesses.

A footlambert is a unit of brightness equal to the uniform brightness of a perfectly diffusing surface emitting or reflecting light at the rate of one lumen per square foot. In order to really understand this relationship we must return to our concept of the standard sphere of one foot radius with the standard candle at its center. One lumen or one footcandle of light shines on every square foot of the interior of that sphere. If that sphere were made of a translucent material which let all of the light shine through with even distribution (a perfectly diffusing surface) then every square foot of the exterior of the sphere would likewise be giving off one lumen of light. By definition such a lighted square foot would have the brightness of one footlambert. Thus any square foot of surface which seemed to have a brightness equivalent to this would be considered to have one footlambert of brightness. Just as tristimulus values can be computed from spectrophotometric analysis, so footlambert values can be estimated from photometric data.

B. GENERAL METHODS OF CONTROLLING LIGHT

Light is reflected, transmitted, or absorbed by materials. Reflected and transmitted light can be accurately controlled in direction. Therefore it is possible through the selection of the media of reflection or transmission to send light forth in definite patterns or to send it forth in many different directions. Reflectors and lenses are examples of reflecting and transmitting instruments, respectively, which direct the light into definite patterns. Matte finishes and diffusing glass are examples of reflecting and transmitting media, respectively, which scatter or diffuse the light and prevent it from having a definite direction. Directional and diffused light each has its use in interior design.

C. REQUIREMENTS OF ADEQUATE LIGHTING

What are the basic requirements of adequate lighting? As with everything else in the art world, there are three sets of interdependent requirements. First there is the functional requirement exacted in the interest of securing adequate light for the physical task of seeing. Then there is the psychological requirement which demands that our lighting contribute its share towards the establishment of the atmosphere of a space. This is the phase of lighting whereby lighting communicates its message to an interior. Lastly there is the design requirement of good lighting. In fulfillment of this requirement the light must directly enhance the visual design of the interior.

1. Physical Functional Requirements

The first functional specification for light is quantitative. There should be enough light to perform a task. Some lightmeters have their footcandle calibration coordinated with prescriptions for desirable amounts of light for a variety of occupations. It is wise to use such a photometer to test the luminous intensity of the light at functional centers in an interior.

Following is a list of footcandles recommended for the performance of various household tasks.

Specific Visual Tasks	Footcandles
Reading	
Books, magazines, newspapers	30
Desks, study	70
Reading music scores	
Simple scores	30
Advanced scores	70
Sewing	
Dark fabrics (fine detail, low contrast)	200
Prolonged periods (light to medium fabrics)	100
Occasional periods (light fabrics)	50
Occasional periods (coarse thread, large stitches, high contrast thread to fabric)	30
Shaving, make-up, grooming	
On the face at mirror locations	50
Work shop, bench work	70

Figure 71. An example of well planned lighting. Diffused light comes from the translucent ceiling and, in dramatic contrast, from the more concentrated area of reflected light off the large, five foot in diameter, dome lights. These latter are important in putting a lid, as it were, on this very high space. The battery of Holophane fixtures directs even light through lenses over the beautiful sculptured wall.

Building: Medusa Portland Cement Company, Cleveland, Ohio. **Architect:** Ernst Payer, A.I.A., Cleveland, Ohio. **Sculptor:** William M. McVey, Instructor in Sculpture, The Cleveland Institute of Art, Cleveland, Ohio. **Photographer:** Hube Henry, Hedrich-Blessing, Chicago, Illinois.

General Lighting	Footcandles
Entrances, hallways, stairways, stair landings	10
Living room, dining room, bedroom, family room, sun room, library, game or recreation room	10
Kitchen, laundry, bathroom	30 [2]

Color schemes should be carefully planned in relation to lighting in order to ensure the necessary amount of illumination. This can be done by calculations from the reflectance charts which accompany a color system. Hue and saturation, as well as lightness, affect reflectance. The type of light source is likewise a factor in reflection. The following reflectances are recommended for the surfaces in a residence: floors 15–35%; walls 35–60%; ceilings 60–85%.[3] These can be translated approximately to Munsell values 4.5 to 6.5; 6.5 to 8; 8 to 9.5, respectively.[4]

[2] *Illuminating Engineering* (August, 1958), pp. 422–432. Reprinted by permission. More extensive tables of recommended levels of illumination can be found in *IES Lighting Handbook*, third edition. Published by the Illuminating Engineering Society, 1860 Broadway, New York, 1959. Pp. 9–76 to 9–88.

[3] *Ibid.*, p. 15–3.

[4] Specific color reflectance should be estimated from the *Munsell Value Scales for Judging Reflectance* (Baltimore, Md.: The Munsell Color Company). A chart of reflectance values for the Ostwald colors accompanies the *Color Harmony Manual* available from the Container Corporation of America, 38 S. Dearborn Street, Chicago, Ill.

The second functional specification for light is qualitative. Light must be of the right quality for comfort while seeing. Such comfort enables one to work with the minimum of nervous fatigue and thus with the least physical exhaustion. Comfortable light is light without glare. Glare may be defined as any brightness within the field of view sufficient to cause annoyance, discomfort, interference with vision, or eye fatigue.[5]

Glare is caused by excessive brightness contrast within the field of vision. This is because eye muscles tire from making severe local adaptations. Glare may result from light coming directly from a source or from reflected light.

Light of good quality may be attained through:

1. A balance of light intensity in an area.
2. Diffusion of light through use of large matte reflecting surfaces.
3. Diffusion of light by passage through diffusing material.

2. Expressive Requirements

Lighting can be an agent in creating the kind of atmosphere which is conducive to carrying out the purposes of a building.

There is a very close relation between light

[5] W. Sturrock and K. A. Staley, *Fundamentals of Light and Lighting*, Bulletin LD-2. General Electric Company, 1949.

and mood. Extremes of light and sound are disconcerting. We shrink from an excessive brightness as from a blast of noise. A pleasurably high level of light is like a paean of music which can stimulate and arouse, while twilight is like the softness of the kitten's purr which ministers to relaxation. Entirely diffused light which casts no shadows is apt to be monotonous and undramatic. At times it is even unsafe light because some shadows are necessary in order to enable us to recognize the shapes of things. Directional light creates highlights and shadows on the various surfaces of a room. These move with the observer and help produce visual mobility and excitement.

Buildings are for shelter. Light and darkness can only provide visual shelter, privacy, and protection. This can be augmented with the psychological feelings of security which derive from various levels of illumination. In terms of house planning, there should be areas of sunlight and areas of shadow, large windows and shaded porches, gardens with sunny flower beds and cool trees, high and low levels of artificial lighting.

Beyond the common need for such lighting as will develop the shelter feeling of an abode, there are specific activities for which the lighting should be planned. One of the most important of these activities is conversation, that social attainment of civilized man. Lighting for conversation should go beyond the negative aspect of not be-

Figure 73. An illuminated ceiling in this apartment foyer diffuses light in such patterns that it appears almost to have texture. Thus texture is kept to floor and ceiling planes. A mirrored wall visually enlarges the space.

Building: Apartment in New York City. **Interior Designer:** Virginia Whitmore Kelly, New York. **Photographer:** Alexandre Georges, New City, New York. **Courtesy: House and Garden,** Copyright, 1959, The Condé Nast Publications Inc.

Figure 72. The lighting in this conference and class room provides adequate localized direct illumination from the many spot lights. This is balanced by the diffused light reflected from the upper walls and ceiling.

Building: Kiva, College of Education, Michigan State University, East Lansing, Michigan. **Architect:** Ralph Calder, A.I.A., Detroit, Michigan. **Interior Designer:** Weger Interiors, Lansing, Michigan. **Photographer:** Lens-Art Photo, Detroit, Michigan.

Building: Church of Maria Königin in Marienburg, near Cologne, Germany. **Photographer:** Courtesy of Mr. G. E. Kidder Smith, A.I.A., New York.

ing annoying. It should create the mood, the psychological set, for conversation.

What kind of lighting furthers conversation? In amount it should be a medium high level of comfortable illumination, neither too high nor yet too low. Thus it will steer between the Scylla and Charybdis of being too stimulating or too depressing. Good conversation is aided by a cloistered feeling, by that atmosphere which is sometimes described as cozy, by those surroundings which accentuate the feeling of shelter and privacy. This can be accomplished by reducing the light in the room areas beyond the conversation group to as low a brightness as is compatible with the recommended five to one functional brightness ratio. Low-placed lighting fixtures aid

Figure 74 (opposite). Light is a most important factor in any interior. It creates a life of movement. It confirms and emphasizes. Above all it is a powerful agent in creating the kind of atmosphere which is conducive to carrying out the purpose of a building.

Figure 75. Directional light from the sun casts shadows on the building and creates highlights on the contours of the sculpture.

Building: Medusa Portland Cement Company, Cleveland, Ohio. **Architect:** Ernst Payer, A.I.A., Cleveland, Ohio. **Sculptor:** William McVey, Instructor in Sculpture, The Cleveland Institute of Art, Cleveland, Ohio. **Photographer:** Hube Henry, Hedrich-Blessing, Chicago, Illinois.

the feeling of intimacy requisite to a conversation area. Particular care should be taken to see that the lighting is warm in tone.

There are occasions when the house is used as the setting for a general festive grouping when a high tea, cocktail party, after-theater gathering or just the preliminaries of a company dinner are afloat. Gaiety and heightened spirits are the order of the day. Pleasantries and chatter fill the air. Greetings are exchanged and a few words spoken without any intent of entering into the give and take of more serious conversation.

What of the lighting requirements? Certainly neither the full brightness of noonday nor yet darkened concentrated lighting would answer. Lighting of a somewhat higher level than that provided for general conversation should fill the room. But it must do so in a dramatic, exciting way. Glareless lighting is certainly required but a pleasurable and exhilarating exchange of light and shadow from directional sources should play its part too in this sort of decoration.

Light for dining should likewise be suited to its program. Dining is eating with ceremony for the purpose of furthering pleasant friendly intercourse. The room lighting should be a mixture of the low diffused lighting needed for conversa-

tion and the more dramatic focusing on the table ceremonials. The general lighting of the room could be low in amount and diffused. But there should be a higher level of more dramatic light directed onto the table. Such spotlighting will make the table appointments gleam and will be flattering to the guests. One should be careful to see that no light shines in the eyes of any person seated at the table. This precaution is particularly important when the table is lighted by candles. Candles burn down and are apt to come to eye level. Otherwise candlelight is soft, warm toned, dramatic light for dining.

Listening to and playing music are pleasurable activities which are benefited by the proper lighting, too. Performance of music, like reading or studying, inaugurates its own set of functional visual requirements. The listener appreciates lighting such as is provided at the concert hall. The general level is never very high—not sufficient to read a program. Every precaution is taken to provide comfortable and restful light. Illumination should be nondirectional and without brightness contrasts. The atmosphere is that of the twilight of a dream world.

Much the same advice as is given for lighting the room for music can be repeated for television viewing. The general prescription is for light of a moderately high level, well distributed throughout the room and having no spottiness or source of glare. The television receiver is a light source in itself and as such should be balanced with other illumination. The surface of the receiver is glass which acts as any other reflecting surface. No room light should rebound to the eyes of the viewers.

That area of the house which is set aside as a reception area or as a traffic artery has unique psychological illumination requirements. The hall area is one which does not function for long periods of time but which is extremely important when it does. It is the main flume and as such echoes the tone of the rest of the house, although it may do so in a more exciting way. As the hall

may be the outsider's only contact with the interior of the house and as it is the guest's introduction to it, lighting of a hall should be especially cheerful. Nothing in the world is as dejected looking as a gloomily lighted hallway.

The private apartments of a house should have thought given to their lighting. When sections of these areas duplicate the functions of the general living room, then the type of illumination should correspond. Sections of these areas serve overtly functional needs and their lighting should be planned to such purposes. For instance, it is essential that adequate diffused light should fall on a person who is dressing.

The sleeping compartment of the bedroom exerts definite lighting demands. During illness the bed is used for long periods of time and every household should plan for this eventuality. The quality of comfort, essential to all good lighting, is of prime importance here. There must not be glare within the angle of vision of the person in bed. It is likewise important that lighting should be cheerful, warm in tone and of sufficient brightness not to be depressing. However,

Residence of: Mr. and Mrs. Ben D. Zevin, Gates Mills, Ohio. **Designer:** Leon Gordon Miller, Cleveland, Ohio. **Photographer:** Denny C. Harris, Cleveland, Ohio.

Figure 76. This stained glass space divider serves visually to enclose the porch and to screen the view of the adjacent house. Tones of green, blue, and purple glass are leaded and set in a blade metal frame.

it must likewise be restful. Therefore, a very high level of light is not desirable. It is necessary to be able to darken a bedroom for sleeping.

In stating the psychological requirements for lighting, no particular mention has been made of the work areas. The basic use of all of these areas is for overt service. Therefore, their primary requirements are for good functional lighting.

D. DESIGN THROUGH LIGHT

Light is an important factor in interior design. In the first place light can be controlled and given a definite shape or it can be reflected or refracted in all directions so as to be shapeless. Allusions are frequently made to the shape of light. We speak of bands, pools, or circles of light. We talk about spotty lighting. We suggest that light sweeps an area.

Spottiness, meaning spots of light which have no apparent relation to the design of the room, should always be avoided. The use of directional light to create definite areas of light for design purposes is another matter. Such light can be given shapes which will aid the shape design of a room, and will act as powerful visual forces in setting up the desired rhythms, centers of interest and balance.

This kind of use of light can be employed in designing both traditional and contemporary interiors. But as the shape organization in the two types of design is different, so the planning of the light will be different.[6] The shapes which contemporary light assumes are large and dramatic. Their placement induces kinetic quality into an area.

Contrary to the traditional emphasis on tangible shapes, modern decoration stresses space, both as spaciousness and as an entity which can be related to other spaces to make a total design. Light can help the designer secure both of these effects. Large sources of diffused light are at his beck and call. Thus amorphous light can flood a room and make it seem more extensive. It is likewise possible to provide light in long bands. These lines of light can relate and unite visual areas.

Attention should likewise be given to the po-

[6] See Chaps. XII and XIII.

tentialities inherent in designing with shadows which have shapes. Considerations similar to those affecting light shapes would hold true for shadows.

Light is also an important design factor because of its color. This is not only important for itself but because of its direct influence on all object colors. Although the extent of this can be accurately determined, a few simple reminders will be useful.

A hue must be in an emitting light if it is to enhance a surface which would normally reflect that hue. That is to say that a light must contain a yellow wave band if it is to reflect yellow from a fabric. The more yellow in the light, the more it can reflect from the fabric. In a similar way yellow light weakens blue. A yellow light, which is normally deficient in blue rays, will not be able to reflect them. A blue pigment absorbs yellow and related wavelengths and reflects blue. The sum of these two facts results in a cancellation in whole or in part of blue colorants by yellow light. Thus a reflected color is weakened by a light on the opposite side of the chromatic color wheel and is strengthened by a light of similar chromatic color. These phenomena occur only to a limited extent because of the normal adaptation of the eye to the color of the prevailing light.

Like achromatic light, colored light can be amorphous or it can have shape. The use of mobile colored light as an art form was developed by Thomas Wilfred with his color organ. He calls his art *lumia*, the art of light. Patterned areas of colored light are played upon a screen so as to make a moving design of light. The effect is interesting and singularly restful to frayed nerves. Such color organs may be found in homes of the future.

Amorphous colored light which can be varied in hue has long been used in the theater to secure changes of scenery colors and to create emotional tones. It is surprising that more use of this fairly simple means has not been made in interiors. Indeed the possibilities inherent in colored light have scarcely been tapped by the interior designer. Consider the potentialities inherent in colored glass or colored filters over windows. Matisse, in his design for the Dominican Chapel of the Rosary at Vence, France, has shown the way. Caution should be given against using too saturated colored light or the room colors may become singularly distorted.[7]

Light alone does not have texture. Yet sharp pinpoints of light seem brittle in their refraction and large pools of light seem soft at their edges. This projection of texture into the light itself probably results from the fact that the character of the visual texture of materials is very dependent upon the character of lighting. Visual texture results from visual nonuniformities in the reflectance of a surface. When light is directional and creates much brightness contrast it enables a textural nonuniformity to throw the deepest shadows and a smooth texture to give the most brilliant reflections. By comparison, diffused light tends to minimize textural differences and thus to soften all textural aspects of a room. It seems good to have a relationship between the textural quality of the light of a room and the rest of its decoration.

E. DESIGN OF LIGHTING FIXTURES

Some fixtures for transmitting artificial light are in evidence in most rooms. It is very im-

[7] The Helson-Judd phenomenon.

portant that they be designed so as to function well and to add to the visual design of the room. There are a great number of impractical and inartistic lamps on the market. At times it is difficult to find a good one. Fortunately they do exist and their number seems to be increasing. This must be one sign of an improvement in taste.

A lamp and all of its housing required to transmit light (technically, luminaire) is first and foremost a functional thing. Later in this chapter there are given some stipulations which a luminaire must fulfill in order to serve its purpose.

In addition to these functional requirements lighting fixtures should be visually well designed. To qualify this statement would require repetition of much of this text. Some appearance characteristics of many lamps on the market suggest that design faults fall into a few easily defined classes. In the first place, many fixtures are too decorative or as we might say, too fussy. As a lighting fixture is simply a housing for light, it is in a sense a decorative design added to the light itself. As such it should not call undue attention to itself and it should be as simple in design as is compatible with interest. Likewise the design of the luminaire should be similar to the shape pattern of its light.

Figure 77. Natural skylighting and a balanced wattage of fluorescent and flood incandescent are well planned to display an outstanding art collection.

Residence of: Mr. and Mrs. Peter J. Lloyd, Moreland Hills, Ohio. **Architect:** Ernst Payer, A.I.A., Cleveland, Ohio. **Photographer:** Bill Engdahl, Hedrich-Blessing, Chicago, Illinois.

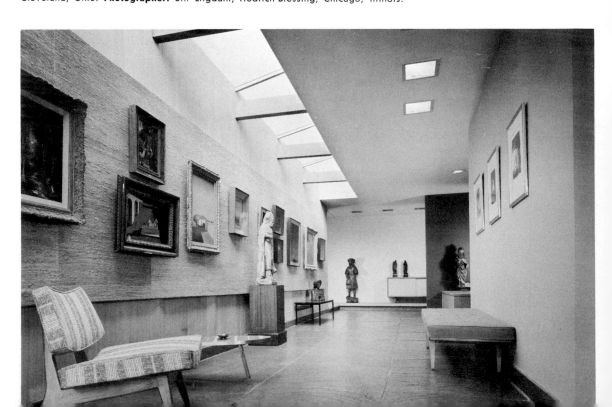

Figure 78. Edge lighting of a transparent mural displays the medium to best advantage.

Building: Golden Bowl Restaurant, Cleveland, Ohio. **Interior Designer:** Leon Gordon Miller, Cleveland, Ohio. **Mural:** Plexiglas® from drawings by Paul Riba, Instructor in Painting, The Cleveland Institute of Art, Cleveland, Ohio. **Photographer:** Denny C. Harris, Cleveland, Ohio.

Most lamps are objects which are intended to be seen in three dimensions. It is a good test to feel around a luminaire in imagination in order to see if the imaginary movement of the hands from part to part is rhythmic. Many fixtures do not have this quality. Modern lamps, like many modern art objects, should be designed so that the movement of the hands is in big broad sweeps or in sharply defined lines and spaces. Older lamps may be more delicate in the movements which they suggest by empathy. Texture and color in lamps can prove to be a helpful ally to this sculptural quality which good three-dimensional design should suggest. Textures should entice one to touch and colors may create a moving or fluid interest.

F. LIGHTING OF ART OBJECTS

Lighting can be planned so as to display art objects to best advantage. The ideal light source for illuminating paintings should be similar in all respects to that under which the painting was made. Care should be taken to see that no reflection of the light source rebounds from the painting to the eye of the viewer. A good position for the light is a high one from whence relatively diffused light falls on the painting at an angle of 45°.

The surface surrounding a painting should be between fifty to one hundred per cent as bright as the average brightness of the picture. This will facilitate visual adjustment to the latter. The background should be quite neutral in tone so that little chromatic light will be reflected to interfere with the colors of the picture.

It is best to place sculpture which was designed to be seen from all sides so that it can be viewed in this manner. Light directed upon a piece of sculpture should create shadows which will display its three-dimensional shape to good advantage. A satisfactory light source is a low brightness unit directing light from an overhead angle of about 45°.

The sculpture should be placed so that reflected light from its surroundings will come from two or three sides and from below. Thus the environment should be light enough to be an efficient reflector but should not be brighter than the sculpture surface.

A translucent or transparent object is best displayed by introducing light through one or more of its edges if it is flat or by illuminating it through opal glass from below if it is three-dimensional. A dark surrounding is advised in order to minimize distracting reflections and to make the sparkle of the transparency more evident.

G. WAYS OF SECURING LIGHT IN INTERIORS

1. Natural Light

Natural light should furnish as much as possible of the illumination for an interior. Contemporary buildings are planned to make the best use of the sun. They have large glass areas oriented to the south, southeast.[8] These windows should contribute to the temperature conditioning as well as to the light.[9]

Large windows help provide glareless illumination. Light from an extensive source falling upon matte reflective surfaces is diffused. It creates less brightness contrast with surroundings than a concentrated beam from a small source. More reflective space is utilized when light enters an interior from a high source rather than from a low. Consequently large window areas reaching to the ceiling are ideal for capturing southern light.

Auxiliary light sources should be designed in other places for balance. Clerestory lighting, which as the term is currently used means lighting from small windows placed high in a wall, is frequently planned to open up the other façades as auxiliary light sources. Skylighting, employing a diffusing material, is another way to light inner areas. Ribbed glass can direct the light which enters. Glass partitions between

functional spaces increase the availability of the light supply.

Even beneficial things sometimes require control. Control of window light becomes a liability only when it is unduly expensive or when decorative considerations [10] negate the functional ones.

Sometimes light is controlled, in the sense of being deflected, before it enters. Because of the heat content of the sun's rays the builder should plan an adequate external eave or eye shade to control direct sunlight during the hot season. If no such control has been incorporated in the building then various devices for this purpose may be utilized. Awnings, with air spaces near their top to allow the hot trapped air to escape, are often used. Screens which have meshes tilted as miniature light reflectors are helpful. Foliage planted near the window will absorb the beneficial but hot rays. Heat repellent glass is about the only solution if, for the sake of a view, large windows face west. The late afternoon sun is so low that eaves are ineffectual.

At times the light must be controlled after it has entered. If the light must be redirected, it can be accomplished by vertical or horizontal reflectors such as Venetian blinds. This sort of control may be necessary when a finely finished piece of furniture must stand near a southern window.

Light may be diffused as it enters. This can give it another emotional tone. The light from a north window may prove too cold or from a south window too warm. A chromatic diffusing medium can change this. Light from small windows is apt to be harsh and to cause a glare if not properly diffused. It is at times necessary to diffuse the light from large, well-oriented, southern windows. The translucent or glass curtain is the usual medium for accomplishing this. Many draw curtains today are not lined and are made of a fabric which is partially translucent. Thus they become useful when it is desirable to exclude some light and to filter the rest. Some other kinds of shades, such as pull shades made from very narrow bands of bamboo, while not

---

[8] In the northern hemisphere.
[9] See Chap. III.

[10] The decorative treatment of windows is discussed in Chap. X.

actually translucent, do modify the light which can enter a room. Translucent glass is excellent when it is not necessary to look out of the window. Translucent Venetian blinds and shades will likewise filter some light into an interior.

Occasionally it is desirable to shut off the window. Privacy or a variable degree of openness may be desired. Here we find the functional value of such controls as shutters, or jalousies, or Venetian blinds which can open to light one minute, deflect it another, and exclude it in yet another. Opaque draperies in the form of traverse curtains and opaque vertical blinds permit a lateral control and opaque roller shades have long been used for up and down control.

2. Artificial Light

Inasmuch as we use or buildings on dark days as well as on bright ones, and after sundown as well as during daylight, artificial light must be provided.

Figure 79. Lighting plan for "A House of Steel and Glass" described on pages 147–8.

Artificial light sources are of two major kinds: incandescent or filament and fluorescent.[11] Fluorescent light has many advantages for the consumer. The first of these is its low operating cost. Once the initial installation is made, a procedure which may involve expenditure in old houses where wiring was arranged to accommodate filament lighting, fluorescent light is economical in current consumption. Secondly, fluorescent light is relatively cool light. The coolness of fluorescent light is of great advantage whenever it is desired to place tubes near inflammable materials such as fabrics. Fluorescent lighting has low surface brightness. This is caused by the diffusing quality of the powders which line the tube

[11] For further information see pp. 98, 99.

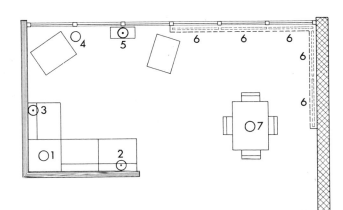

Analysis of Lighting: Courtesy of General Electric Co., Cleveland, Ohio.

(253 square feet) Location	Light Source	Number	Wattage	Total Lumens
No. 1	Table Lamp	1	30/200/230	3700
No. 2	Spot	1	75 R/30	766
No. 3	Spot	1	75 R/30	766
No. 4	Swing Arm Junior Floor Lamp	1	50/100/150	2000
No. 5	Spot	1	75 R/30	766
No. 6	Cornice—20 feet (Cornice Tube channels require dimming Ballasts)	5	40 WWX R/S T-12	9250
No. 7	Suspended Fixture	3	60	2505
No. 8	Spot	1	75 R/30	766

20,519 or
81 Lumens per square foot
(80 Recommended for Living Rooms)

This lumen estimate has not been reduced for reflectance values. The colors used are those indicated in the room on page 148. These very light colors would not materially reduce the total illumination.

and by the relative size of the tube itself as compared with an incandescent bulb of comparable wattage. The linear quality of a fluorescent tube makes it particularly suited to modern decoration.

One of the principal advantages of fluorescent light is its color efficiency. Whereas the chromaticity of an incandescent light is constant and can only be altered by the addition of a selective filter, the chromaticity of fluorescence is dependent upon the phosphors which line the tube plus slight traces of the yellow-to-blue light of the activating mercury vapor present.

The color of light is frequently described in terms of a unit of heat known as a Kelvin unit. When a standard substance known as a black-body [12] is heated to extreme temperatures, it will change color with temperature. As the temperature rises this color changes from red through yellow to white and to blue. When light sources glow to similar colors they are assigned similar Kelvin temperature readings. Thus a K. reading is an indication of the hue of a light. Candlelight is calibrated at about 1,900°K. A 200 watt incandescent light is about 2,810°K.

Fluorescent lamps can be obtained in a variety of colors. Many of these are for specialized uses. The number which are produced for the average lighting needs has been reduced to four. These are divided into two major groups known as the warm whites (about 2,800°K.) and the cool whites (about 4,500°K.).

In each of these classes it is possible to buy a lamp of the standard variety or one known as deluxe. The standard lamps give somewhat better lighting efficiency whereas the deluxe lamps are designed for the best possible color rendition. Thus the decorator has merely to ask himself two initial questions before deciding upon the type of fluorescent tube to prescribe for general use: do I want warm or cool light in a room, and is color rendering of importance in this situation? [13]

Surface colors reflected under the cool deluxe lamps look approximately as they would in daylight. The reds and yellow greens which under the old daylight fluorescence were somewhat minimized, have been restored to their genuine color. Because of the blue phosphors in cool deluxe fluorescent lamps all of the blues are accentuated. Purplish hues and greys take on a pinkish cast under the deluxe cool fluorescence.

Warm fluorescent lamps may be compared with incandescent in the appearance which they will give to surface colors. These lamps contain red or pinkish phosphors in addition to the phosphors used in the earlier types of daylight fluorescence. They are, therefore, very effective in reflecting pinks. They accentuate these more than the yellows in any yellow-reds whereas the incandescent source accentuates the yellows. Moreover, where incandescent filaments are less strong in blue color, the warm deluxe fluorescence is not so deficient. Therefore blues are more accentuated than they would be under the usual incandescent light.

A decorator is interested in the color of light which is generally preferred. The eye, developed under daylight, seems to prefer cool fluorescence whenever artificial lighting levels approach daylight level. This level might be found in a well lighted kitchen or work room. It is likewise true that at low illumination the eye has become accustomed to the warmer flame colors. For much of the artificial light in a home situation, the warm fluorescent or the incandescent lamps seem to be popular. However, lighting experts have predicted that as the general level of home illumination increases, the whiter or cooler light sources will find greater acceptance.[14]

As the color temperatures of incandescent and warm fluorescent lamps are similar, they may be combined successfully in the same room. It is never wise to use lights which are spectrally quite diverse in adjacent arrangements. A person moving from one circle of light to another will be more at ease if distinct color illuminance contrasts are not present.

[12] This is a complete radiator which absorbs all incident energy.

[13] Deluxe warm white lamps are now sold under the name of *home line.*

[14] E. W. Commery and K. E. Leighton, "Fluorescent Lighting in the Home," a paper presented at the Nat. Engineering Technical Conference of the Illuminating Society, August, 1950. The definite analysis of changes occurring in specific surface colors under fluorescence which is given in this paper indicates that general statements are really inadequate to describe the effects of artificial light on surface colors.

Artificial light may likewise need control. This can begin with the lamp, i.e., fluorescent tube or incandescent bulb. Control may be for the purpose of broadening the source and diffusing the light. Such control is usually unnecessary in fluorescent lighting. Many incandescent bulbs are lined with an enamel coating which is designed to alter the hue of the light and to diffuse it. Some of these bulbs are much larger in diameter than the customary bulb. Such lamps take the place of an added diffusing bowl. Special harps (the wire support for a shade) are made to accommodate these bulbs in existing luminaires. Silver-coated bulbs reflect light. When this light is directed to a large reflector, the net result is greater diffusion.

Fluorescent tubes are made in very long slim units and in circular units. Incandescent light in

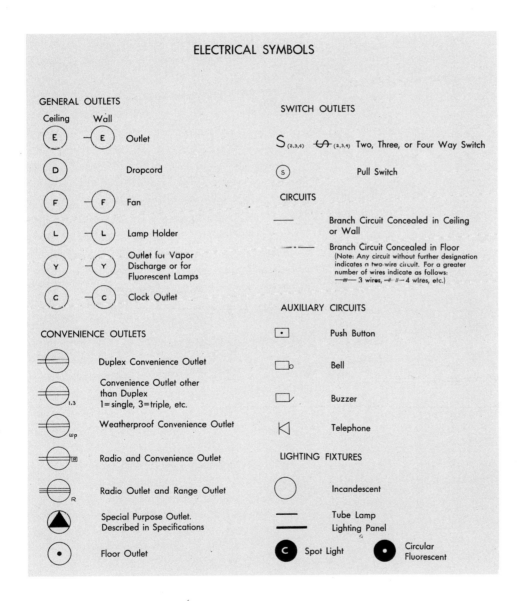

Figure 80. Electrical Symbols.

long coated tubes is available. These are controls on the shape as well as the quality of the light.

Three kinds of incandescent lamps are frequently used even when the major portion of an installation is fluorescent. These are the reflector spot, the reflector flood, and the projector flood lamps. All of these lamps have self-contained reflecting surfaces which redirect the light into a definite path.

In the reflector spot the beam is relatively concentrated whereas in the reflector flood the beam is relatively broad. The projector flood is designed like the reflector flood but has a stronger glass shield and so is more suitable for outside installations. Because fluorescent light is always highly diffused light it is necessary to use one of these reflector incandescent lights whenever it is desirable to have directional light. The spot lamp is used frequently for interior dramatic spotting with light. The reflector flood is often used over the work bench or comparable area. The projector flood frequently illuminates a porch, driveway or garden.

Sometimes a more sharply defined beam than can be obtained by means of the reflector lamps is desired. Such a beam may cover either a broad or a narrow path but it must cut off sharply rather than merge gradually into the surrounding areas. This is frequently desirable for the illumination of art objects or of restricted interior areas. Through it, the most dramatic of lighting can be secured. This is not a usual lighting requirement. When needed it can be secured in a lamp used in a housing similar to that of the reflector type in which the light is further controlled through a condensor lens system.

Diffusing bowls which surround the lamps are helpful in softening the light from filaments. The shade of a luminaire further controls the light. Both bowl and shade should be as large as the light source can justify so as to make the light easier to view.

The color of lamp shades intended to transmit light should be light in tone. The lining of opaque shades must be light for reflection. The outside of the opaque shade may then be planned in relation to the room color scheme. When illuminated, an opaque shade keeps its light confined to a limited pool. As this creates

light and shadow areas it contributes to a dramatic and cloistered atmosphere. Translucent shades diffuse their light and spread its effectiveness over a much larger area.

Even though fluorescent light is diffused light of low surface brightness, it is often wise to conceal the light source further. Sometimes this is accomplished in ways similar to those just described for incandescent light. For example, large diffusing panels are frequently installed between the lamps and our eyes. Shades, too, are used on fluorescent luminaires equipped for circular fluorescent tubes. Because of the relative coolness of the fluorescent lamp, these shades can enclose the luminaire on the top as well as on the sides.

In addition to these expedients, fluorescent tubes are frequently shielded by some system of baffles which prevent us from seeing the tube. They should be designed so that they reflect and scatter the impinging light.

Good luminaires for reading should be about 47 inches from floor to bottom of shade for a floor lamp and 40 inches for a table lamp. Shades on incandescent lamps should be at least 10 inches deep. Floor lamp shades should be a minimum 10 inches across the top and 16 to 18 inches across the bottom. The top of table lamp shades should be no less than 8½ inches and the base of the shade no less than 16 inches in diameter. Adequate control for diffusing the light should be provided. Approximately 300 watts in the floor lamp and 150 in the table lamp should be available. Table lamps should be placed 20 inches to the side and about 16 inches back of the printed page. Floor lamps should be placed 15 inches to the side of the printed page and between 20 to 26 inches from this point to the rear.[15]

H. PLANNING FOR HOME LIGHTING

Much illumination today is architectural. It is planned with the structure of the building and is designed to utilize the surfaces of the building to secure the best returns for the illumination dollar.

[15] E. W. Commery and E. E. Stephenson, *How To Decorate and Light Your Home* (New York: Coward-McCann, Inc., 1955), p. 212.

In planning such lighting it is first necessary to locate the principal pieces of furniture on the plan. This is done to insure that the required light to implement the function of the grouping is provided.

The lighting plan usually starts with provision for local lighting at the major furniture groupings. Much of this may be provided by recessed down lights of the reflector spot type. These provide high wattage and controlled distribution. Trough lighting which is directed downward may also be used for this purpose. Pinpoint refractive spots may be used to dramatize limited areas which are intended for decorative purposes. If down-lighting is extensively used, it is desirable to select a light carpet so as to make a more even distribution of the light through reflectance. When architectural lighting is not feasible, an average size living room will require from four to six portable lamps carrying about 900 watts for this local lighting.

In addition to planning for local lighting, thought must be given to the general lighting of a room. Many structural devices supply large sources of indirect or diffused light. Lighting may be placed behind a dropped ceiling and be diffused through it or be directed towards the walls. Cornice and valance and wall bracket lighting may utilize the reflective value of ceiling, draperies, and walls. Any of these installations can be added to an already existing lighting system. They utilize incandescent or fluorescent sources. If portable lamps must be relied upon for this general illumination, then certainly some of them should have diffusing rather than opaque shades, and walls, floors, and ceilings should be utilized as reflective sources.

The task of supplying adequate light for all of the areas of an interior can be analyzed in the manner just outlined. A careful examination of the current market will show that lighting engineers are constantly improving the means for securing the desired results.

For texture has a unique dimension. The particular rhythm of light and dark that makes up visible texture is beyond our ability to distinguish in any form of visual organization in terms of modelling by shading. It has a fine grain of sensory impact which can be comprehended only in its structural correspondence to other sensory feelings. The surface texture of grass, concrete, metal, burlap, silk, newspaper, or fur, strongly suggestive of qualities of touch, we experience visually in a kind of intersensory blend. We see, not light and dark, but qualities of softness, coldness, restfulness—sight and touch are fused into a single whole.

GYORGY KEPES *

Chapter IX

TEXTURE AND THE MEDIA OF INTERIOR DESIGN

A. MEANING OF TEXTURE

The word "texture" comes from a Latin root meaning "to weave." From this is also derived our word "textile." Today we speak of texture in a broader sense. We refer to the texture of woods and say that oak is coarse whereas satinwood is finely textured. We say that iron is rough in texture and silver smooth. What do we really mean by these phrases?

One aspect of texture refers to the structure of a material. It is the way in which it has been built from the microscopic particles to the mass. In wood, for instance, the structure is fibrous. This is only apparent on the surface but the surface is caused by the inner structure. A microscopic study may help the artist to appreciate the potentialities of a material.

Texture more frequently refers to the outer surface of material. Its qualities may be those which are the natural expression of the inner structure or they may be a modification of these. Thus silver has a silvery grey metallic lustre which reveals its inner character. The silversmith may give it a highly polished surface or he may hammer the surface and make it rough. The weaver may take advantage of the long silk filament with its natural lustre and produce a diapered cloth where the textural reflections are tiny diamond shapes. Surface textures are most lovely when they are developments of inner structures.

B. THE INTERSENSORY CHARACTER OF TEXTURE

The tactile sense is used in an appreciation of textures. This sense of touch is nature's most elemental sense. Through it the earliest living forms recognized danger and food and thus were able to survive. Likewise we are told that the tactile sense is one of the last to depart. Nurses know that pleasant sensations from fine sheets, soft blankets, and smooth china are very satisfying to an invalid. The gratification of the tactile sense may be so basic as to color our other sense impressions. If for this reason alone, it is an important sense to develop.

Textural impressions are conveyed through the eyes as well as through the skin. We see the light, and shade, and indefinite pattern which characterizes the texture. It is through sight that textures acquire a lively quality. The surface of wood grains change with the angles of view. Patterns of light and dark become moving rather than static.

Texture is likewise appreciated through kinaesthesis, the muscular sense. The weight of material, its softness or hardness, these are qualities which we appreciate through the use of our muscles.

There are some textural qualities which seem to require several senses for their comprehension. A texture which is coarse, which has large particles in its structure, seems to be heavy and rough. An open texture seems lighter in weight than a compact texture. A highly reflective texture suggests smoothness to the touch.

Texture is the way a material feels, the way it looks as though it would feel, the way in which our minds interpret an inner structure from its appearance and feel. It is the message which several senses send to our brains, a message which helps us to understand and to enjoy this world. We must learn, as a fine textile firm advertises, "to feel with our eyes." [1]

Because the sense of texture is a sort of intersensory blend using at least half of our senses in its appreciation, a developed textural sense is a very sophisticated sense. It is essential to the work of the interior designer.

C. TEXTURE AS THE BASIC COMPONENT

Texture is basic to artistic work because textures really determine shapes and colors. A sensitive artisan feels that his medium dictates his design. The artist not only knows the workable qualities of his material, he likewise enjoys its texture as a sensuously apprehended quality. The skilled workman may rightfully select sturdy heavy materials as upholstery for large-scale chairs. The artist may choose to substitute materials which have been given the appearance of stoutness.

This, of course, leads to a question which is often asked. Is it permissible by the canons of goods art to imitate one medium with another? What about the artificial graining of material to simulate marble? Should we shun a photographic likeness of one material which has been added to another? Much of fine art is really deception. A picture may be nothing more than paint and canvas which has been given the appearance of a beautiful landscape. In certain periods of art history, notably the seventeenth century or European Baroque period, this photographic deception was frequently employed in interior design. Walls were painted to look like architecture or like scenery. Sometimes the deception was so real as to be given the name *trompe l'oeil*, or mistake of the eye. From this it was only a step to painting one material to imitate another.

Whether this practice should be condemned depends upon a point of view. The modern school of art and decoration is apt to look with disfavor on such imitative processes for two

[1] The Scalamandre Silk Co.

reasons. In the first place, they seem to be examples of faking and hence expressions of dishonesty and not in good taste. In the second place, the result is apt to be less lovely because it is more precision-perfect and less charmingly varied than natural materials. In final analysis one substance can never be as uniquely attractive as another which it seeks to imitate. However to shun all deception in interior design would be to renounce many a fanciful fairyland.

Whether craftsman or artist, the decorator is helped by the knowledge of the practical aspects of his media. Each material presents problems. Will it shrink, dryclean, remain dimensionally stable, craze under heat, resist water and fire? This kind of knowledge is part of the equipment which is necessary in order to create functional interiors. A knowledge of the historical significance of materials likewise helps one to unify his expressions. These are studies in themselves. It is principally the design qualities of texture, however, which is our present focus of attention.

D. THE QUALITY OF MATERIAL

Quality in material is the result of its intrinsic textural nature and of the way in which this has been developed by both the craftsman and the visual artist.

What is good, better, best in intrinsic textural quality? The standards for evaluation must be made in relation to some desired result. One result might be its suitability for a certain physical use. Thus mahogany has a texture which is good for carving. It is better than oak for this purpose because it is softer. Another measuring stick for a texture is its suitability in certain design relations. Thus an artificial leather has a texture

Figure 81. Aesthetic enjoyment secured through appreciation of texture is particularly rich because several senses convey the message. The softer, rougher feel of the textile as contrasted with the hard, smooth ceramic, the similar yet different patterns of the light break-up create a well designed grouping which is in harmony with the proud bearing of the untamed loon.

Textile: Dorothy Turobinski, Instructor in Weaving and Related Arts, Western Reserve University, Cleveland, Ohio. **Ceramic Sculpture:** "Loon," Thelma Frazier Winter, artist and ceramic sculptor, Cleveland, Ohio. **Photographer:** G. Colburn Ball, Cleveland, Ohio.

ATTRIBUTES APPRECIATED PRIMARILY THROUGH TOUCH
—THE FEEL OF MATERIAL

	Physical Expression	Emotional Expression	Character Expression
Surface Contour			
Uneven	roughness		crudity
Even	smoothness		refinement
Surface Friction			
Harsh			brusqueness
Slippery			slickness
Thermal Character			
Hot			friendliness
Cold			austerity

ATTRIBUTES APPRECIATED THROUGH KINAESTHESIS

	Physical Expression	Emotional Expression	Character Expression
Compressibility (resistance to pressure)			
Hard	rigidity		masculinity
Soft	plasticity		femininity
Flexibility (resistance to bending)			
Stiff	unbending		severity
Pliable	yielding		grace
Weight (resistance to lifting)			
Heavy	strength		stolidity
Light	delicacy		imaginativeness

ATTRIBUTES SOMETIMES CALLED THE HAND OF THE MATERIAL
—THE REACTION TO HANDLING

	Physical Expression	Emotional Expression	Character Expression
Elasticity (reaction to stretching)			
Elastic			uncertainty
Inelastic			stability
Firmness (tendency to resist change of internal position)			
Firm			substantiality
Sleazy			fraudulency
Resiliency (tendency to return to position after deformation)			
Resilient	liveliness		youthfulness
Nonresilient	lifelessness		age

ATTRIBUTES APPRECIATED THROUGH SIGHT

	Physical Expression	Emotional Expression	Character Expression
Amount of reflection			
Shiny	activity		ornateness
Dull	passivity		simplicity
Continuity of specular reflection			
Changeable	liveliness, busyness	restlessness	flashiness
Constant	lifelessness	restfulness	constancy
Depth of reflection			
Deep	warmth		luxury
Surface	brittleness		ostentation

ATTRIBUTES APPRECIATED THROUGH SEVERAL SENSES

	Physical Expression	Emotional Expression	Character Expression
Size of structure			
Coarse	heaviness, strength		crudeness
Fine	lightness, delicacy		refinement
Density of structure			
Compact	sturdy		trustworthy
Open	airy		ethereal

which, because of its sheen, may be good for combination with metal furniture. And, again, we may judge the quality of a texture because of its expressive qualities.

Beyond all this, the phrase "good quality material," suggests that a substance has been developed in propitious surroundings. A fine quality oak will grow tall and straight because its growth has been in an open expanse. Finesse of handling by artist and craftsman, likewise contributes to the ultimate worth of goods. It may turn a rough diamond into the Kohinoor.

It is evident that good quality material will cost more than poor quality material of the same type. The rarity of natural conditions favorable to growth, the skill and time required to duplicate these conditions, and the wages of labor involved in processing a material are all contributing factors to its worth. Moreover these conditions make some kinds of materials cost more than others; silks generally are priced higher than cottons.

When artistic handling is given to quality materials then the product is invested with an aura of preciousness. The practical and wise Cinderella of today realizes that she will have to wait for a fairy godmother before acquiring some such precious materials. In the meantime she is secure in the knowledge that there are ways with cottons and with plastics and with silks and that each would lose if it were to deny its own potentialities. It is better to do well with pewter than to do poorly with silver. If Cinderella does not know this she stands in need of Polonius's advice to Laertes to let his standard of worth be "rich not gaudy."

E. THE ATTRIBUTES OF TEXTURE

The successful aesthetic handling of any component depends upon a sensitivity to its attributes. Because the component texture has so many facets no comprehensive listing of its attributes or systematizing of textural traits has

Figure 82 (above). This is a good textural grouping to use with mahogany. The architectural finishes are not too coarse for this wood.

(Opposite) Textiles, while fine, show a careful adjustment of this characteristic to the size of the furniture and to the relation between this room and its natural setting. Reflection from ceramics, glass, brass, and fine leather echo the light from the wood. Carpet and upholstery on the larger chairs offer softness and depth.

been made.[2] Different lists would relate to the physical qualities of the texture and to the aesthetically apprehended qualities. Other lists would be applicable to qualities perceived through various senses.

It is likewise difficult to describe a material with respect to its attributes unless one knows what weight of the material is intended. A steel beam and a steel wire have certain likenesses but likewise certain differences. Similarly it is difficult to find a basis for comparing different kinds of objects. What characteristics would be

[2] Some excellent lists have been made which present textural attributes as they appear to one or another sense. There is, for instance, a list of characteristics of the feel of textiles: the American Association of Textile Chemists and Colorists and Committee D 13 of the American Society for Testing Materials, "Proposed Terms for Fabric Hand." *Textile World* (January, 1941), p. 81.

common to the texture of an oak table and a linen drapery?

The solution to the problem lies in dealing with one sensuous aspect of texture at a time. The lists on pp. 170–71 are an attempt to classify textures and to suggest their expressive qualities.

In describing materials it is apparent that some of the words which we use designate a combination of qualities. For instance, sheerness suggests lightness and openness, crispness suggests lightness and firmness. It is indeed difficult to describe some textures without resorting to these words which defy analysis and which are compounded of several meanings.

Textural traits are especially capable of conveying complex mental characterizations. How easily a room can acquire a feeling of elegance, of honesty, of simplicity, through texture. To this list may be added other character terms. Notice how our language has words for them,—homespun naturalness, polished refinement, ingrained sensitivity, and coarse-grained vulgarity, rugged individualism. These words suggest that through texture similar qualities may be expressed. There is apt to be disagreement as to the exact character quality which a particular texture may connote.

It is this powerful ability of texture to suggest character qualities which makes textural choices such an index to taste. Taste is really the ability to select good character qualities and to make them explicit through good art.

F. TEXTURE DESIGN

The choice of a dominant texture for a room should be made after careful consideration of function, expression, and the existing design character. This decision is complicated by the fact that the expressive character of many delicate appearing contemporary materials belies their practicality.

The dominant texture is strengthened by a textural grouping the members of which have family traits. Contrasting textures should likewise possess some points of similarity. For instance, they may be harmonious in weight but differ in light reflection.

Textures are part of the shapes to which they belong. Therefore textural affiliations may begin with an attribute which can relate them to shapes. This could be size with its suggestion of weight.

A textural grouping to use with heavy oak furniture may serve as an example. Oak has relatively coarse fibers and large pores. Linen is the

Residence of: Mr. and Mrs. R. D. McGranahan, Fox Chapel, Pittsburgh, Pennsylvania. **Architect:** John Pekruhn, A.I.A., Pittsburgh, Pennsylvania. **Photographer:** Joseph W. Molitor, Ossining, New York. **Courtesy: Record Houses of 1956,** F. W. Dodge Corporation, New York.

heaviest of fibers and a coarse linen may be chosen for the initial cloth to combine with oak.

As a substitute for the linen, fabrics could be chosen which had been made to appear heavy even though they were made of finer fibers. Cloths which are compact, or thick, or which have uneven yarns might answer. Sometimes patterns applied to fabrics will give a heavier appearance. Colorful closely drawn designs give this illusion of weight.

Once a certain weight relationship is established, light reflection should be considered. If a hand-blocked linen was chosen for the draperies its reflective character would be constant and luminous. It would be coarse, compact, stiff, and slightly rough. The woods and the textiles are now too similar in texture. Like the old game of fine and superfine, what should the owner do to redeem them?

A couple of chairs may be upholstered in leather. Here is a heavy material which is equally as stiff and unbending as the linen. However it reflects more light and because of the natural unevenness of its pores the light reflections from leather are somewhat changeable.

Note that both the linen and the leather are relatively cold to the touch. Now what does the room need? Certainly some fabric from which the light is deeply reflected. This is particularly true because oak itself, a relatively open-pored wood, has deep light reflections.

Then there is need to introduce the characteristic of softness and perhaps a note of relative sheerness. A textured rayon or synthetic gauze at the window for glass curtaining might seem right. And so on, down the list of needed textiles one goes, never deviating too far from those characteristics which are basic to the texture-establishing woods but frequently using some variety for interest.

A textural grouping with mahogany might be considered in the following manner. Exact materials may be filled in after a study of textiles. Similar harmonies for walnut, pine, and other commonly used interior woods are good textural exercises.

Wood: mahogany—medium heavy—fine grain—
    when given a rubbed-down varnish finish the

light is highly reflected and is changeable due to figure in wood.
Carpet: Wool pile of good quality—repetition of luster and lively character of light reflections due to resilient nature of fiber.
Upholstery: Caning—repetition of lightness and finish of wood.
    Cottons with firm weave, sometimes with glazed finish—repetition of fineness and luster.
    Woven patterned materials—accentuation of changeable character of light reflection.
    Fine yarn pile fabric—repetition of depth reflection of carpet while keeping in family of weights and fineness.
    Nubby or fuzzy yarn occasionally introduced in firm cloth to provide softness contrast.
Drapery: Full hanging gauze of nubby silk yarn —addition of sheerness and crispness with irregular light reflections.

After securing a textural harmony, it should be arranged to aid the design. This means the ordering of textural forces. Intrinsic textural force may be found in extremes of rough and smooth textures. The first will attract because of the contrasts of surface and the second because of the amount of light reflection. Any texture will be made more forceful when it is incorporated in a rhythmic sequence or if it is contrasted with its textural surroundings.

Modern decoration places a great deal of emphasis on texture but this emphasis frequently goes no further than an interest in conspicuous textures. The fact that textural harmonies can be highly developed in a room and that they can direct the eye towards centers of interest or serve to balance the room, often is not recognized. Rhythms might be set up by gradually increasing the unevenness of surfaces or by gradually approaching a more highly reflective surface. A shiny texture on a smaller chair may give it the importance necessary to balance a larger chair in a room.

Textures can be used to create illusions. Forceful textures gain attention and thus increase the apparent size of objects. When wishing to decrease the size of objects and thus to increase the effect of space, steer a middle course be-

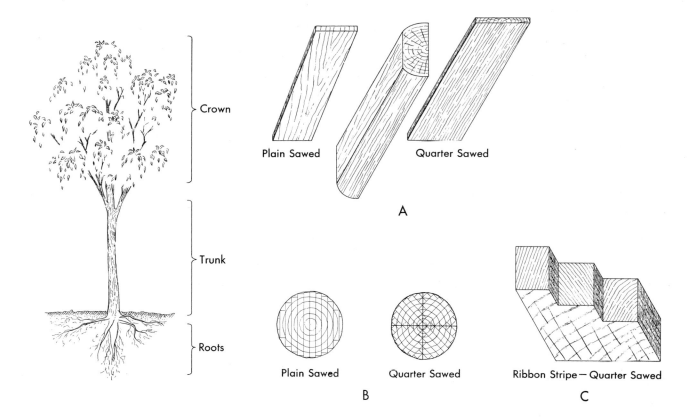

Figure 83.

A. A tree grows as though a conical layer were superimposed each year, thereby extending the new growth upward and outward.

B. Plain sawing and quarter sawing of lumber create parabolic and striped figures respectively.

C. In some trees the changing of cell directions creates ribbon stripe, quarter sawed figure.

tween shiny, sleek textures and rough, nubby, or deep pile textures. Materials should be fine grained with a moderate amount of textural interest. Furniture which has a good bit of exposed wood should be selected. Upholstery fabrics should be firm and a rather hard, definite grain should predominate. Some highly reflective textures, such as mirrors, may be selected, but they should not be used too frequently.

A textural problem which is frequently encountered is the problem of minimizing the apparent coarseness of architectural materials in a room where a fine textural harmony in the furnishing is desired. Much can be accomplished through careful choices of color to minimize the effect of these offending textures. A wiping stain may be brushed into the wood and quickly rubbed off. The pigment will change the texture because it fills the pores and thus makes a closer grain.

G. TEXTURES AND MEDIA USED IN DECORATION

A knowledge of decorative media makes the practice of the art of designing more sure and easy. This information should reach back to the raw state of materials and to the means by which man has fabricated furniture, textiles, carpets, plastics, glass, and ceramics from these.

A   B

(A) **Building:** Industrial Design Offices of Leon Gordon Miller, Cleveland, Ohio. **Designer:** Leon Gordon Miller, Cleveland, Ohio. **Photographer:** Denny C. Harris, Cleveland, Ohio.

(B) **Residence of:** Mr. and Mrs. R. D. McGranahan, Fox Chapel, Pittsburgh, Pennsylvania. **Architect:** John Pekruhn, A.I.A., Pittsburgh, Pennsylvania. **Photographer:** Joseph W. Molitor, Ossining, New York. **Courtesy: Record Houses of 1956,** F. W. Dodge Corporation, New York.

(C) **Building:** Gallery view, McIntire dining room from Peabody, Massachusetts. **Photograph:** Courtesy of the Museum of Fine Arts, Boston, Massachusetts.

(D) **Residence of:** Mr. and Mrs. Peter J. Lloyd, Moreland Hills, Ohio. **Architect:** Ernst Payer, A.I.A., Cleveland, Ohio. **Photographer:** Bill Engdahl, Hedrich-Blessing, Chicago, Illinois.

1. Wood

a. ITS CHARACTER

Wood was one of the earliest materials used by man. It could do so many wonderful things so easily. Moreover it possessed such lovely sensuous qualities that it endeared itself while it served. It has changing color and pattern which pleases the eye, warmth and smoothness to the touch, and odor for the nostrils. A sensitive artist needs only to form wood into useful objects of artistic shape and the wood itself will be its own enrichment. To say this is not to decry carving and inlay and finishing. It is only to say that these embellishments are most lovely when they seem to enrich the natural beauty of the wood.

The knowledge of how a tree grows helps an understanding of this beauty. Wood is composed of both vertically and horizontally elongated cells. The vertical cells contain long cellulose fibers interspersed with hollow pores through which the tree draws its sustenance.[3] The transverse cells of similar but more compact composition are known as the rays. Their function is not clearly defined but they may act as food reservoirs or as binders for the vertical cells. A tree grows horizontally from year to year at the same time that it does vertically. This growth has been described[4] as if the tree were like a huge cone to which a larger and taller cone was annually superimposed.

The outline of these cones is clearly indicated in trees which live in a climate where there are intermittent seasons of growth. A quick-growing warm season will produce large cells and a slow-growing season will make small ones. This difference in cell size is visible in many woods where the more compact cells separate the cross

[3] In the conifers the cells are known as **tracheids**. They resemble closely packed, open-end tubes containing lignified or woody tissue.

[4] M. H. Sherwood, *From Forest to Furniture* (New York: W. W. Norton & Co., Inc., 1936), p. 52.

Figure 84. Plain sawed (A, B) and quarter sawed (C, D) lumber create:

A. Parabolic figure in walnut.

B. Parabolic figure in birch.

C. Ribbon striped mahogany in clock-case.

D. Striped quarter sawed figure in fire-place panel.

section of the wood into what are called annual rings. The age of a tree can be told by counting these.

Figure or pattern in wood is of two main varieties. The first is that which is caused by light reflected from various kinds of cell arrangements and from various angles of the cells. This kind of pattern is one of the chief glories of wood for it has infinite variety. No two pieces of wood, not even two adjacent and thin slices of plywood, are ever exactly alike. This kind of pattern varies with the observer's position because the angle of reflection varies with this position. The second kind of wood patterning comes from color infiltration into wood. The cause for such infiltration is never quite clear but it may well be some kind of harmless fungus growth which has seeped up into the pores.

One of the first variety of configurations occurs because of the way a log is cut. It may be cut so as to produce plain sawed lumber or it may be cut to produce quarter sawed lumber. In plain sawing the log is sliced lengthwise into a number of parallel boards. In so doing the saw cuts the outermost growth rings at an angle which approximates 90°. This angle diminishes as the inner rings are reached until the central ring is cut tangentially. Plain sawed lumber is characterized by large, irregular, parabolic-shaped ring figures flanked by striped ring figures.

Quarter sawed lumber derives its name from the fact that it was originally manufactured by sawing a log lengthwise into quarters and then cutting the board at right angles to the growth rings. This created a figure in which the annual growth rings appear as a series of stripes because the saw is cutting them all at the same angle of 90°. Quarter sawed lumber is usually more expensive because less of it can be obtained from a tree. It possesses the practical advantages of less shrinkage and warpage. Both plain and quarter sawed wood are prized for characteristic patterning.

The rays are conspicuous in some lumber and add to the pattern interest. They appear as wavy lines at right angles to the growth ring figure. Because of its usual light color a ray figure is frequently called a silver flake figure.

Irregular convolutions of growth rings may account for unique patterns. The peculiar structure of the tree at the place where the wood is cut is responsible. Stump wood comes from the location where the root joins the trunk causing distorted grains which are known by such names as curly or mottle.

Tree burls are large excrescences which may occur where a tree has been injured. The twisted grain of burl wood may contain a number of dark piths which are in reality undeveloped seed buds. The appearance of burl grain is often described as oyster burl because of visual similarity to the irregular oyster shape.

A crotch figure occurs where two large branches or parts of a tree converge. The fibers which run in forked directions give rise to a pattern which is variously called plume, feather, or crotch.

Knots, which are the bases of limbs cut off a log, show as irregular darker areas in lumber. Although possessing a decorative value they tend to weaken wood.

One peculiar growth characteristic is that of interlocked grain. Certain trees, usually those in tropical forests, often grow in such a manner that the fibers extend in a right slanted spiral for a certain number of years and then for another span change to a left spiral. When the lumber is quarter sawed, this interlocked grain reflects light first in one and then in another direction. This patterned reflection will look like alternate dark and light stripes which taper off into one another. Hence this type of figure is often called stripe or ribbon stripe figure.

Sometimes unusual distortions of wood grain appear in a tree for no known reason. These might be referred to as sport figures. Some of these show up in plain sawed lumber. Bird's-eye figure, which occurs in some hard maples, is of this type. It is caused by sharp depressions in the growth rings which show in the lumber as a

series of circlets. Some curly and blister figures are likewise of this type.

Other varieties of sport figures show up in quarter sawed lumber. These are usually characterized by areas of light and dark which seem to roll across the grain. Consequently they are often called cross-figure or cross-roll. Mottle, which may occur in places other than in stump wood, fiddleback, raindrop and finger roll are names given to examples of cross-figure.

Pigment infiltration may cause the second major type of figure in wood. Dark streaks in Circassian and black walnuts, pollard or English oak, rosewood, and red gum are caused by such coloring matter.

b. FURNITURE WOODS

Oak, walnut, and mahogany [5] have been our major furniture woods. Although many other woods are used today, these three are still very important and each is used to head a list of similarly textured woods:

GROUP I

1. *Oak:* [6] American white oak which is a light tan color, has the finest grain and is not conspicuously porous due to tyloses or filmlike deposits—red oak, redder and coarser—English or pollard oak, a darker brown.
   a. Size of structure and density—comparatively coarse, large pores at beginning of each annual ring, dense at its end
   b. Contour—relatively rough
   c. Weight—heavy
   d. Compressibility—very little and therefore hard
   e. Flexibility—not easily bent
   f. Firmness—firm
   g. Light reflection—little natural gloss except in very fine grades
   h. Continuity of reflection—interesting characteristic plain and quarter sawed figure—ray figure
   i. Depth of reflection—deep

[5] P. Macquoid, *A History of English Furniture* (4 vols.; *The Age of Oak; The Age of Walnut; The Age of Mahogany; The Age of Satinwood* [New York: G. P. Putnam's Sons, 1905]).

[6] The first wood mentioned in a group is the one described in detail.

2. *Ash:* light grey brown—coarse, large summer wood pores, more dense winter fibers—heavy, hard, and stable—interesting plain sawed figure—rare burl of black ash (as distinct from the more common white ash) shows curly figure used for veneers.

3. *Beech:* light reddish—no particular ornamental figure—thin growth lines, homogeneous texture, takes good finish—hard but bends easily—used generally for structural interiors of furniture—frequently found in bentwood furniture and as a substitute for walnut in European provincial furniture.

4. *Chestnut:* coarse and rough prominent ring figure in plain sawed—prized for worm-eaten imperfections—excellent corewood for veneering, because light, firm and stable.

5. *Cypress, fir, pine, cedar:* soft woods of uniform fibrous structure—aroma of cedar oil kills moth larvae.

6. *Elm:* light and reddish—similar to oak in texture—prominent growth ring figure—English burls prized—good bending properties.

7. *Redwood:* dark red color—natural oil—burl large and prized for figure.

GROUP II

1. *Walnut:* American or black walnut—early varieties a dark brown with occasional dark streaks, recent varieties light; Persian, a general name for European and Asiatic trees (primarily from England, France, and Circassian district of the Caucasus)—soft grey brown, sometimes with darker streaks as in Circassian.
   a. Size of structure and density—comparatively large visible pores—slightly noticeable change in size of spring and winter pores
   b. Contour—smooth
   c. Weight—almost as heavy as oak
   d. Compressibility—little, of a hardness between oak and mahogany
   e. Flexibility—good bending strength, comparable to birch
   f. Firmness—low shrinkage, highly isotropic
   g. Light reflection—lustrous due in part to tyloses

h. Continuity of reflection—changeable in highly figured crotch, burl, or plume figures
   i. Depth of reflection—medium

2. *Apple, pear, cherry* and *fruitwoods:* small pores—figure confined to plain sawed, slightly wavy darker growth ring—take smooth lustrous finish—cherry has the rosiest coloring of the group—frequently used for provincial furniture.

3. *Birch:* light tan color—fine even grain wood—finely marked wavy growth rings—takes a high polish—suitably heavy and hard for furniture.

4. *Butternut:* coarser and softer than walnut which it resembles in plain figure.

5. *Gum:* dense, fine grain wood—sapwood stains easily, heartwood a light reddish brown with darker infiltrations—takes smooth, satin finish.

6. *Harewood* (a species of maple sometimes called English sycamore): dyed silver-grey, fades to light brown—fine smooth texture with ripple figure.

7. *Maple* (soft and hard, or sugar, maples): uniform texture—in good grades lustrous—curly and bird's-eye patterns prized—hard maple, very hard and strong.

8. *Sycamore:* use as cabinet wood limited to veneers showing small rays—frequently used for drawer-lining veneers.

9. *Teak:* fine grain—strong—contains natural oil—yellow brown color with darker brown infiltrations—some fiddle-back figure.

10. *Tulip:* an historic wood from Brazil, known as *bois de rose* because of light color streaked with rose.

GROUP III

1. *Mahogany:* comes from West Indies, Central America (Honduras), upper valley of Amazon, and West coast of Africa.
   a. Size of structure—fine grained
   b. Density—pores are plainly visible, fairly uniform in size and distribution
   c. Contour—smooth surface
   d. Weight—a little lighter than walnut
   e. Compressibility—hard enough for cabinet work, soft enough for carving

(Left) **Designer:** Ursula Meyer. **Manufacturer:** Thonet Industries, Inc., New York.

(Right) **Photographer:** G. Colburn Ball, Cleveland, Ohio.

Figure 85. The bending of laminated wood in contemporary furniture production makes a stronger piece.
  (Left) Shape is created by bending rather than by sawing.
  (Right) Splitting of wood along the straight grain.

f. Flexibility—less than oak or walnut

g. Firmness—very stable with slight shrinkage—comparable to walnut

h. Light reflection—high because of close, fine grain and because pores are partially filled with tyloses

i. Continuity of reflection—lively and changeable—interlocked grain causing ribbon stripe figure—often has beautiful crotch and swirl figures—plain sawed growth rings not conspicuous

j. Depth of reflection—medium deep reflections from visible pores

2. *Rosewood:* a Brazilian and Indian wood—named for faint rose odor—light to almost purplish brown, pigment infiltration lines of very dark brown to black—strong and hard—medium pores, many filled with gum deposits.

3. *Prima Vera:* a Central America hardwood from a species of catalpa—light rosy blond color—closely resembles mahogany—ribbon stripe in quarter sawed.

4. *Satinwood:* beautiful blond wood used extensively in late eighteenth century furniture—hard, close grain—figures rival mahogany.

5. Unusual woods such as *almique, amaranth, avodire, bubinga, ebony, iroko, lacewood, lauaan, padouk, sabicu, snakewood, tanguile* and *zebra wood:* used for inlays and veneers.

6. *Cane, bamboo, reed, rattan, wicker:* parts of long stemmed plants or trees—can be bent in the moist state and become rigid when set and dry. *Reed* and *bamboo* are hollow nodular grasses. *Rattan* is a long vinelike stem of an Asian palm which may be split for cane. *Wicker* is the small twig of the willow.

c. BASIC WOOD MANUFACTURING PROCESSES

Wood is first formed into a desired condition and shaped by processes such as:

sawing—as described on pp. 177, 178, under wood figure.

impregnation—filling the pores of soft wood with resinous material to give strength and flameproof qualities.

lamination—the resin bonding of thin slices of wood with their successive grains at right angles to give greater strength and dimensional stability. Plywood is the board made by such a process.

veneering—the gluing of thin layers of wood, usually figured, to the outer face of core wood—opposed to solid wood which is one piece—if well done veneering is strong and can provide beautiful figure at less cost.

marquetry—veneering done with small pieces of wood to give an effect similar to mosaic in stone.

bending—bending wood grain into a permanent shape under steam pressure in the presence of chemicals.

carving—cutting into the surface of wood for ornamentation.

turning—producing rounded shape by bringing a blade into contact with a block of wood turned on a lathe.

Wood joinery is the putting together or joining two pieces of wood. In observing the joinery and bracing of a piece of furniture an analysis of the stresses must be made to determine the strength of the resulting piece. Methods of joinery include:

dowel joints—attachment by means of a peg or dowel which fits into sockets in each piece.

mortise and tenon, dovetail or *tongue and groove joints*—fitting an extension of one piece into a socket of another. Dowel and mortise and tenon joints are found on well-made furniture of traditional type construction.

wedge joints—inserting one piece through another and forcing a wedge into the joint to tighten it. Sometimes used on contemporary plywood furniture where the thinness of the material makes traditional joinery impossible. Screw joints and other methods of joinery, which were formerly thought unsatisfactory, are now frequently necessary.

The finishing of woods for preservation, dimensional stability, and appearance is an art in itself. Methods for finishes may be outlined as follows:

1. Sanding—to make a smooth surface.
2. Staining or bleaching—to alter the color.
3. Preparing the pores, holes or cracks: to level the surface—done with wood filler or plastic wood.
4. Sealing—to prevent seepage of natural oils and applied stains. A sealer which is fre-

Figure 86. Wood Joinery: A. Dowel; B. Mortise and tenon; C. Tongue and groove; D. Dovetail; E. Wedge; F. Rabbet.

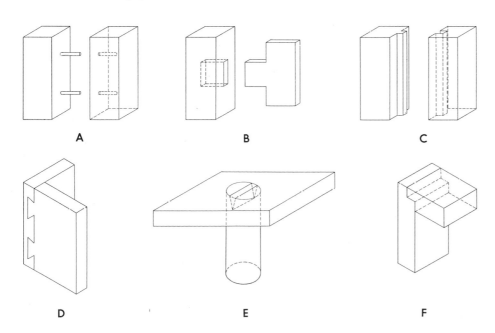

A   B   C

D   E   F

quently used consists of 2 parts shellac and 1
part alcohol.

5. Finish—any of the following
   a. rubbed oil
   b. wax
   c. French finish: many thin coats of shellac,
      each coat hand-rubbed. Shellac may be
      applied in one or two coats for a less per-
      manent finish.
   d. oil varnish
   e. lacquer
   f. paint
   g. antique finish: a stippled application of a
      pigment, e.g., raw umber, in a varnish
      glaze, applied over paint.

d. WOODWORK IN A ROOM

Wood has been a revered finish for interiors
for many centuries. Because lovely veneers are
available and the contemporary style places an
emphasis on natural textures, there is much use
of wood within buildings today. For purposes of
reference the following terms applicable to interior woodwork are given:

Apron—A horizontal board set below the sill of
a window or below a horizontal structural
member in a piece of furniture.

Arch—A curved structural form (usually in seg-
ments of a circle) used to span an opening
and support a superimposed weight. There are
many kinds of arches such as the segmental,
elliptical, and ogival which take their names
from their geometric forms, and others, such
as Tudor, Gothic, and Moorish which take
their names from the particular time when, or
place where, they were used.

Architrave—In classic architecture, the lowest
section of the entablature. It consisted of a
slab or lintel which rested on the column and
which supported the frieze, cornice, and pediment. In later buildings, a flat molding above
any square opening is known as the architrave.

Attic—The portion of an interior wall above the
cornice—used in classically inspired architecture.

Baluster—A small vertical support for a handrail.
A series of balusters is called a *balustrade*.

Baseboard—A board, usually with a finishing

molding, which is at the bottom of a wall.

Beam—A large piece of lumber which spans a
room and is used to support the superstructure.

Boss—An ornament projecting from the intersection of structural members.

Bracket—A flat piece which projects from a wall
and forms a support for some weight.

Capital—The top and most ornamental portion
of a column. The capitals of each of the classic
orders were stylistically different.

Casement—A window sash opening on hinges.

Chair Rail—The top molding of a dado.

Clerestory—Originally the upper story of a Romanesque church which was higher than the
surrounding roofs. Now refers to wall space
above normal room height—frequently contains windows.

Coffer—A recessed panel in a ceiling.

Column—A vertical, free-standing support for a
superstructure. The Greek classic columns
were in three styles—the Doric, the Ionic, and
the Corinthian. The Romans added two more,
the Tuscan and the Composite. The proportions and carving on each of these were eventually prescribed. These five have become known
as the classic orders of architecture.

Cornice—The moldings which decoratively finish
the top of a wall. In classic architecture the
cornice was the top portion of the entablature.
It rested on the frieze and supported the pediment.

Dado—The woodwork on the lower portion of
the walls of a room. It derives from the Italian
word for a pedestal and referred to the central
portion of the pedestal on which a column
rested.

Dais—A raised floor in a portion of a room. Originally the word referred to the raised platform
at the end of a medieval hall.

Dome—A spherical roof.

Dormer—A window projecting from a sloping
roof.

Ear—The portion of the moldings surrounding
some eighteenth century doors, windows, and
mantels which, because of their projection
laterally from the rest of the molding, resem-
bled ears.

Entablature—The portion of a classic building
which rested on the column and which sup-

ported the pediment. It consisted of architrave, frieze, and cornice. A complete entablature was used to finish the top portion of a wall, or was used above doors and windows, in the most exact, classically inspired periods.

Finial—An ornamental end of a structural member.

Frieze—The central portion of an entablature resting on the architrave and supporting the cornice.

Jamb—The side supports of an opening which run at right angles to a wall.

Joists—The supporting members of a floor or a ceiling. These are smaller pieces of wood placed at right angles to any large supporting beam.

Lintel—A straight piece of wood spanning an opening.

Mantel—The woodwork surrounding a fireplace. The word has now come to refer more especially to the shelf above a fireplace.

Molding—A narrow shaped board which is used for a decorative finish to flat boards. In classic architecture exact names were given to moldings of various sizes and shapes. Some of these were the fillet, fascia, ovolo, torus, bead, cavetto, scotia, cyma recta, and cyma reversa.

Mullion—The slender vertical bar which holds areas of window glass in position.

Newel Post—The post into which the handrail of a stairway fits.

Panel—The flat board which forms the major portion of interior woodwork. It is held in place by vertical stiles and horizontal rails.

Parquetry—Intricate patterns made from small pieces of wood, usually used for flooring.

Pediment—The triangular structure in classic architecture which was above the entablature. It is similar to the gable in Nordic architecture. In interior architecture the pediment was frequently used as a decorative feature. During the seventeenth century its pure form was altered to such variations as broken, scroll, and segmental pediments.

Pier—In interior architecture this term refers to the wall surface between doors or windows. In architecture it is the mass of masonry, as distinct from a column, which supports an arch or lintel.

Pilaster—A column form semiattached to a wall.

Plinth—The lowest portion of a column, square in shape. In interior architecture it refers to the rectangular block at the base of a door trim.

Rail—The horizontal banding which holds a panel in position.

Riser—The vertical portion of a stair step.

Sash—The framing into which the glass of a window is set. The term has come to refer especially to the kind of window frames which slide vertically upon one another.

Sill—The horizontal member which forms the lowest part of a frame for a window or a door.

Soffit—The underside of a doorway, archway, window, or subordinate architectural member. Used as opposed to ceiling which refers to the overhead lining of a room.

Stile—The vertical banding which holds a panel board in position.

Transom—The horizontal crossbar of a window or door. The term frequently refers to a small horizontal window above a door.

Tread—The horizontal portion of a stair.

Trim—The wood finish around doors, windows, and fireplaces.

Vault—An arched covering over a corridor.

Wainscot—The name originally referred to wood panelling completely lining a room; now, generally refers to panelling which is below the dado.

e. CONSTRUCTION OF WOOD FURNITURE

Wood joinery should be doweled or mortise and tenoned for the furniture made from larger wooden pieces. Wedge and screw joinery is frequently used to join the laminates. New materials introduce new methods of joinery which should be analyzed for performance.

In upholstered furniture of traditional construction, the unexposed frame should be made of thoroughly seasoned hard wood. A base of strong interlaced cloth webbing is tacked to the under side of seating furniture as a support for the springs. Heavy gauge spiral steel springs are usual. A wave shaped spring, called No-sag,® is sometimes used. A small helical tension spring

® Registered trade mark.

may be attached by one loop to the furniture frame and by the other to a fabric base. Coil-springs are arranged close together and are attached to one another and to the frame and webbing with sturdy hemp cord.

The springs are then covered with a firm fabric to prevent dust and seepage from the padding. The best upholstery padding was made of curled long horsehair. Other padding materials such as moss, palm leaf fiber, tow (from flax fiber), coco fiber, sisal, and cotton are frequently used. Some of these may be preferred to low grade hair. Additional cotton padding is applied at the edges of seats and arms in order to soften them and to make the upholstery wear longer.

Muslin covering is attached over the padding and the final upholstery material is fitted. The latter is usually put together with welted seams or with some finish such as brass tacks which is appropriate to the piece. Cushions made with one seam for closing are generally known as loose or squab construction. Cushions which are built up like a rectangular box are called box cushions.

New developments used in place of springs to give resiliency to the body support are nylon and other resilient synthetics in the form of cords or webbing, laminated wood on rubber shock supports, spring steel structure. Products used for seating buoyancy are rubberized hair, hair impregnated with foam rubber, or any of the synthetic plastic foams finished with a plastic spray which acts as mattress and covering, foam rubber which may be bonded to fabric, spun glass fibers enclosed in a muslin pad. Technology will certainly introduce more such innovations.

Bed upholstery is similar to that used in seating furniture. In much contemporary construction box steel springs are placed on top of slats to form a lower layer of support. A box spring is made as a platform of wood or steel. Then the coiled springs are set into a slot of the frame and are firmly attached to it and to one another. The final covering consists of padding and a firm ticking.

The inner-spring mattress is placed on the box springs. Such a mattress is formed by units of coiled springs which are laced tightly together and covered, or which are individually encased in muslin pockets. They are then covered with a padding of cotton, curled hair, or wool. Firm mattresses must be equipped with ventilators to allow air to circulate within. The springs in both springs and mattress should be capable of independent action so that they can flex with the varying weights of different parts of the body.

Some of the new padding materials which are used in chair upholstery are likewise used in mattresses.

Pillows are a customary part of bed equipment. The best pillows of the past were filled with down or feathers, preferably of waterfowl. Foam rubber, solid or in small pieces, is used quite extensively today for pillows. Synthetic fibers are likewise used. A suitably firm ticking is the final covering for mattresses and pillows.

2. Textiles

The large number of names associated with decorating textiles is frequently confusing. A textile is referred to sometimes by several different terms. For instance, a patterned heavy linen may be designated as a crash, or a cretonne, or a textured linen. Of the many names some are fairly standard ones for staple fabrics, some are more recent trade names, some are current fashion labels which may be changed in a few years.

It is important to know the standard terms for basic decorative textiles. It is even more important to appreciate how one fabric can differ from another and to comprehend how these differences affect performance and appearance. The basic differences in textiles occur in several stages. First there are the fiber differences, then the yarn, the construction, the embellishment, and the finish differences.

a. FIBER DIFFERENCES

A textile fiber is the fundamental material from which a textile is made. Therefore fiber characteristics predispose a textile towards its final quality. No subsequent treatment can entirely erase or change the nature of a fiber. Each textile fiber has unique and admirable qualities which make the cloth containing it particularly suitable for certain uses.

For thousands of years all textile fibers came from natural sources. The chief of these natural fibers are:

A. Cellulose fibers—from vegetable sources.
 1. Cotton
 2. Flax—made into linen yarn
 3. Others less frequently used such as hemp, jute, ramie, kapok, sisal, and coir.
B. Protein fibers—from animal sources.
 1. Wool and hair
 2. Silk
C. Mineral fibers: asbestos.

1) Cotton Fiber

How does it feel and handle? How does it reflect light?

Cotton in the boll is composed of short fuzzy fibers which form a protective covering around the seeds. The cotton thread formed from spinning is dull because of these protruding ends. Longer fibers, known as long staple cotton, form a more lustrous yarn. Special processing and finishes can likewise give cotton more luster.

Cotton feels softer and more pliable than flax and it is not so heavy. Therefore a cotton cloth will drape in softer folds than a linen cloth. But in comparable size a cotton cloth will not stand up in as straight line folds.

Cotton is not very resilient. Therefore a cotton cloth is apt to wrinkle. A fabric with a cotton pile should be thick so that it will not mat down.

Cotton is a firm strong fiber. It is dimensionally stable and holds its shape well against stretching or shrinking. Moisture, heat, or cold do not easily affect it. It likewise takes dye readily and retains it well. Therefore although its short ends may catch dirt, it launders well.

One of cotton's biggest assets is its availability and relatively low cost.

2) Flax Fiber—Linen

The flax fiber is the inner bast core of the flax plant. It has a unique feel which may be described as similar to that of chamois or leather. There is a toughness about it even though it can be bent.

There are various grades of all of the natural fibers and there is considerable difference in the qualities shown by these various grades. The finer grades of flax are the longest and the smoothest, thus reflecting the most light. As a class, however, there is a natural smoothness and luster to linen which nothing can alter.

Flax, being a good conductor of heat, is the coolest fiber to touch. Moreover its luster makes it look cool. What an ideal fiber to weave into all manner of summer cloths!

The fineness of the best quality of flax is comparable to silk. Most manufacturers of linen cloth capitalize on the weight rather than the fineness of linen and produce cloths which can hold their own with furniture of larger scale. Linen with its natural luster, its body, and slight irregularity, is a desirable fiber to use to express the naturalness of contemporary decoration.

Flax is the least resilient of the fibers. Therefore it is seldom seen in a pile weave. Carpets made from it are of thick matted construction. Many linens, even in interior decoration fabrics, are specially treated to make them crease resistant and more resilient.

Flax is not easily dyed and does not readily retain color, a fact which should be remembered when choosing linen draperies. It was for this reason that most linen draperies in the past were lined. Today many beautiful linen cloths which are intended for curtains are made in a natural color and owe their interest to the texture introduced into their weaves.

Linen is not easily destroyed by heat. Because of its smoothness it does not soil readily. It absorbs moisture and dries quickly and thus is especially suitable for napery.

Flax is a very strong fiber. Irregularities in spinning may weaken it and should be watched for.

Flax of good quality is costly to produce and fine linen is expensive. Coarser linens are now procurable in the moderate price range.

3) Wool Fiber

In addition to the various quality levels of the wool fiber there are different kinds of wools which come from different varieties of sheep. The wool of each kind is prized for its special characteristics. Mohair, the wool of the angora goat, is strong, lustrous, and wiry. Cashmere, from the

Kashmir goat, is soft and silky. Hair, which is straighter than wool, can vary from coarse horsehair to the finer camel hair. Despite these great differences there are some qualities which wools and hairs possess in common.

Wool, in general, is not smooth to touch. The tiny scale-like character of its structure catches the fingers and makes the fiber seem uneven.

Wool is a poor conductor of heat and therefore is the warmest fiber. As such it is a good insulator. Woolen draw curtains make excellent winter protection. Moreover the wools look warm, the sleeker hairs less so.

It is not always recognized that wool is both a very light and fine fiber with great pliability. This characteristic allows gossamer wool gauzes to fall in the loveliest of folds.

Wool is both the most elastic and the most resilient of the natural fibers. It is almost impossible to wrinkle a good wool and it will spring back into position after bending. This quality accounts for its important role in the pile carpet industry.

Because the tiny wool scales become enmeshed, it is easy to spin wool evenly and the resulting yarn is firm and strong. Wool can be easily injured through excessive heat and it may lose many of its desirable characteristics if it is not properly cleaned and handled. As wool is similar to hair it can be washed if handled as carefully as one would hair. Oriental carpets are customarily washed. Thorough rinsing is essential.

Wool is characteristically dull rather than shiny. The hairs and the best quality wools which are cut from the most protected portions of the animal are more lustrous. Long wool fibers are sorted and given careful preliminary treatment and are made into the fine quality yarns known as worsted. The luster of such yarn is very lovely for it is not too high and it does have a depth reflection which introduces myriad shadow overtones. Wool is dyed readily and these multiple reflections soften the light from its colors. Hence there is a certain richness of color tone which wool can give to a room which is difficult to obtain from any other fiber source.

A fine quality wool is difficult and expensive to produce. However, it is strong and should wear a long time if well treated.

4) Silk Fiber

Silk from the cultivated silk worm as well as from the wild (tussah silk) caterpillar is comparatively smooth to touch and lustrous to look upon. Its light reflection is always pearly and never harsh. This is possibly due to the fact that the filament is semitransparent. The entering light is undoubtedly refracted and reflected from within.

Silk takes dye readily and with modern technological methods holds it well.

Silk is the lightest, finest, and longest of the natural fibers. Woven into fine glowing cloths it looks cool although actually it is not a good heat conductor. The greater unevenness of the tussah yarn is due to the breaking of the silk cocoon by the moth with the consequent cutting of the filament length. Douppioni silk filaments are reeled from double cocoons which have become enmeshed during formation. They make heavier and rougher yarns.

Silk is similar to wool in pliability, elasticity, and resiliency. All of its qualities make silk luxurious. It is costly to produce. However it is one of the strongest of materials. If cared for as the other animal fibers, it is extremely durable. Wild silks are produced in the moderate price range.

5) Man-made Fibers

The manufactured fibers are called the synthetics. They are chemicals of high molecular structure which are fluids in one stage of their development and solid filaments in another. They are thus one kind of plastic. Several of the recent arrivals in the field of synthetic fibers are well known in another form as commercial plastics.

Some of the synthetic fibers are made by simply altering the physical form of a natural substance such as wood pulp. Rayon is an example of this type. The acetates are examples of fibers which are made from natural substances which have undergone chemical as well as physical change. Nylon is a third type of synthetic which is actually built from more simple chemical ingredients.

There are three types of names which are given to these fibers. The most particular designation is essentially a trade name. It is assigned by a manufacturer to a particular fiber which his company manufactures. Many of these names are registered in the United States Patent Office; "Celanese" is an example of such a name.

Some of these particular fibers are similar in source or manufacture. A group of manufacturers making similar fibers may propose a class name for their fibers. They likewise propose what are called fair trade practice rules for the manufacture and sale of these fibers. These they present to the Federal Trade Commission which has power to accept these rules and to enforce them. In that manner, for instance, the acetates were established as a class of man-made fibers. Celanese is one of the acetates.

The most inclusive group name which can be assigned to fibers returns to the natural source from which they were derived. The following classification is primarily made on this basis. It is not all inclusive.

I. MODIFIED NATURAL POLYMERS
   A. Those derived from a cellulose base [7]
      1. The rayons, e.g., Bemberg,® Avisco,® Fortisan,® Jetspun,® Coloray.®
      2. The acetates—Celanese,® Avisco,® Chromspun,® Celaperm.®
      3. The triacetates—Arnel.®
   B. Those derived from a protein base (no trade practice name)
      1. Animal source—Caslen® from milk casein.
      2. Vegetable source—Vicara® from corn zein, and Ardil® from peanuts.
   C. Those utilizing a metal base—Lurex,® Melton,® Mylar.®
   D. Those utilizing a rubber base—Lastex.®
II. POLYMERS SYNTHESIZED by man from simple chemical compounds. (Classification of synthesized polymers made on basis of similarities of chemical structure and thus of performance. The classification is usual to advertising literature.)
      1. Acrylic fibers—Acrilan,® Dynel,® Orlon,® Verel.®
      2. Polyamides—Nylon.
      3. Polyester—Dacron.®

[7] The major classification headings are those assigned by a subcommittee of the American Society for Testing Materials. See *American Fabrics* (Spring, 1956), p. 103.
® Registered trade mark.

      4. Polyethylene monafilament.
      5. The vinyls:
         a. Basically vinylidene chloride—Saran, Velon,® Lumite.®
         b. Vinylidene chloride and acetate—Vinyon.®

III. THE GLASSES
   Fiberglas.®

Each of the man-made fibers has many valuable qualities of sensuous character, performance, or price. None is suited to all purposes. Combinations of fibers are frequently made in order to provide more nearly universal satisfaction.

In general the synthetics have achieved the practical advantages of strength and ease of care for a moderate price. Their textural character can be controlled within wide limits. They can provide fineness and luster with pliability. Textile technology is directed towards processes which will improve existing fibers. Signal advances have been made quite recently in improving dimensional and positional stability, elasticity, resiliency, and color retention.

The following particular excellences for decorative use may be noted:

1. The rayons and acetates: suited to many decorative uses—fineness—good draping quality—controlled luster—good color range—in new developments exceptionally good color fastness, launderability, and qualities similar to synthesized polymers.
2. The protein derived polymers: particularly useful in blends—softness—moisture absorption—deterrent to static.
3. The metallics: useful in blends—metallic luster with launderability.
4. The acrylics: suited to winter bedding, felts, sturdy as well as light sheer curtaining—light weight coupled with warmth and bulk—fire resistance in dynel—dimensional stability—ease of washing with quick drying.
5. Nylon: suited to carpeting, light sheer fabrics—strength with great abrasion resistance—resiliency—dimensional stability—ease of washing, quick drying and no-ironing.
6. Dacron: suited to light sheer fabrics—also used for felts and fillings—strength with abra-

sion resistance—dimensional stability—fluffi-
ness—ease of washing, quick drying and no-
ironing.

7. Polyethylene monafilament: used in blends to
induce pucker—high shrinkage with maximum
control.

8. The vinyls: suited to heavy duty upholstery—
useful in blends—strength—stainproofness—
color fastness.

9. The glasses: suited to curtains—fireproofness—
luster—weight—ease of washing and no-ironing.

b. YARN DIFFERENCES

Yarn is the name given to a fiber after it has
been spun or thrown. *Spinning* consists in combining fibers, drawing them out to proper thickness and giving them the requisite amount of
twist for strength. Silk and synthetic yarns result
from the twisting together of several filaments
(single elements of silk or synthetics). They are
not drawn out. The process of making these yarns
is known as *throwing*.

The most distinctive character of a cloth may
lie in its yarns. Yarns may combine several kinds
of fibers. They may vary in their number of filaments. They can vary in ply (the single yarns or
strands twisted together to form a ply yarn).
They can differ in size. Interesting novelty yarns
are likewise produced through variations in twist
and tension. Long filaments may be cut into
shorter staples and spun to secure controlled
luster. Permanent crimping introduced into filaments gives enough added strength to lessen the
need for twist, thus providing lightness with
added coverage and stability. This process is
another means of controlling luster. Chenille
yarns introduce depth and softness.

Mercerized cotton yarns, made by the process
of immersion in an alkali bath under tension,
give added strength and luster.

c. CONSTRUCTION DIFFERENCES

Yarns are made into cloths. The simplest cloth
construction is known as felting. Fibers, rather
than yarns, are matted together to make felt. The
wool fiber is customarily used in making felt
inasmuch as it is especially adapted to this purpose because of its natural crimp and tendency to
bend towards its roots under heat and pressure.
Some new felts are constructed on a net base for
added durability.

Cloths are usually made from yarns. They may
be constructed from a single element or thread.
Knitting, crocheting, and similar techniques are
methods of looping one thread on itself to form
a mesh. Plaiting and braiding are means of forming cloth by intertwining long lengths of multiple elements or threads. Many of the basic nets
and laces are constructed of single elements or of
long lengths of multiple elements by processes of
interlacing. Square-meshed filet laces are made
by knotting threads in the manner of making a
fisherman's net. Bobbin laces are the result of
interlacing bobbin wound threads. Sometimes
they are known as pillow laces because a small
bolster anchors the lace as the work progresses.
Nets are made by intertwining threads to form a
regular mesh. These results may be machine
produced by complicated mechanisms which
seem quite miraculous as they manipulate yarns
by vertical and horizontal movements.

The major portion of the fabrics used in interior decoration are woven textiles made from
several sets of threads on a loom. A loom is essentially a very simple artifact consisting of a rigid
frame on which the lengthwise (or warp) threads
of a fabric may be strung and held taut while the
crosswise (or weft) threads intersect them at
right angles.

The essential warp threads are wound on
beams or rollers. One of these becomes the cloth
beam for the finished textile. The other is called
the warp beam from which the length of warp
is fed. Sometimes a loom is equipped with more
than one warp beam and can hold more than one
set of warp threads. This enables the weaver to
adjust the tensions of separate warp groups and
to control a wider range of patterning.

Looms have equipment for raising specific
warps. The smallest unit of this equipment is a
leash. This consists of a loop or opening in a
cord or metal bar through which one or several
warp threads may be strung. A group of leashes
fixed side by side in order to be moved at the
same time is known as a heddle. The total of
heddles which take part in one function in the
execution of a textile is called a harness. Two or

TEXTILE WEAVES

BASIC WEAVES

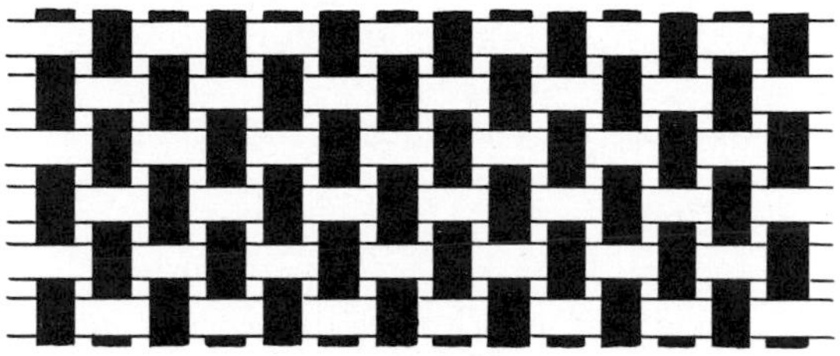

Plain Weave

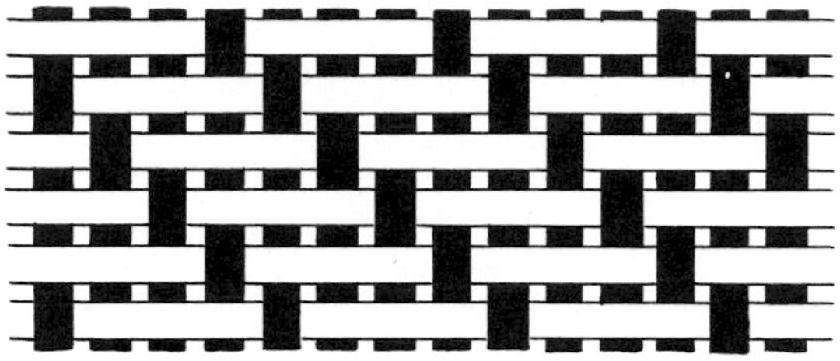

Twill Weave

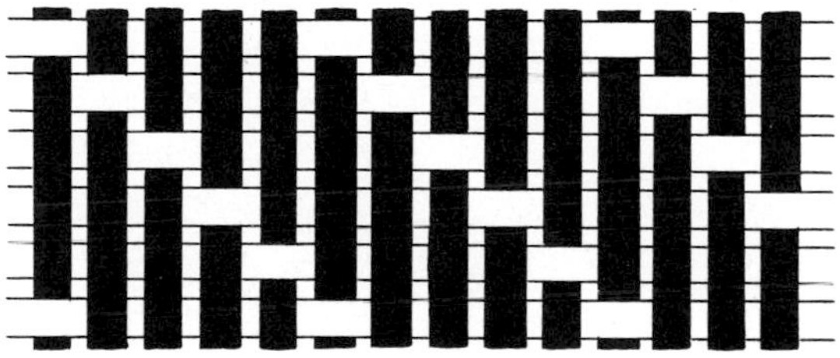

Satin Weave

VARIATIONS ON BASIC WEAVES

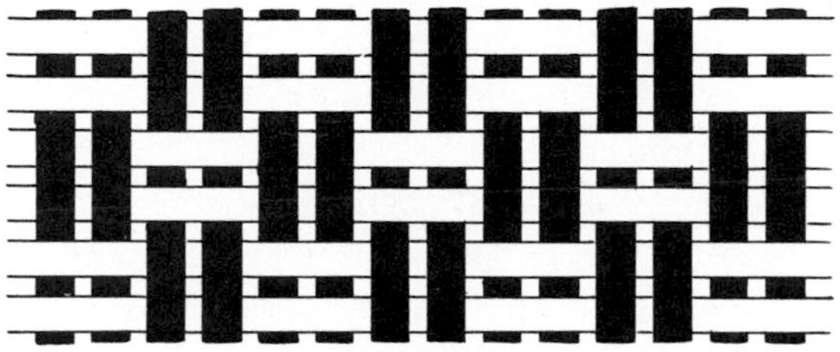

Basket Weave

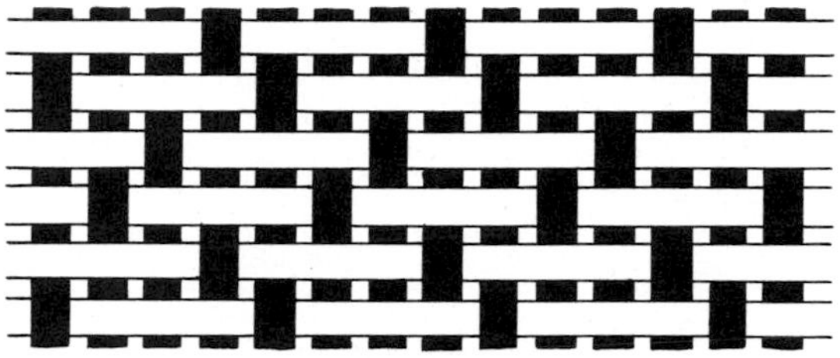

Broken Twill Weave

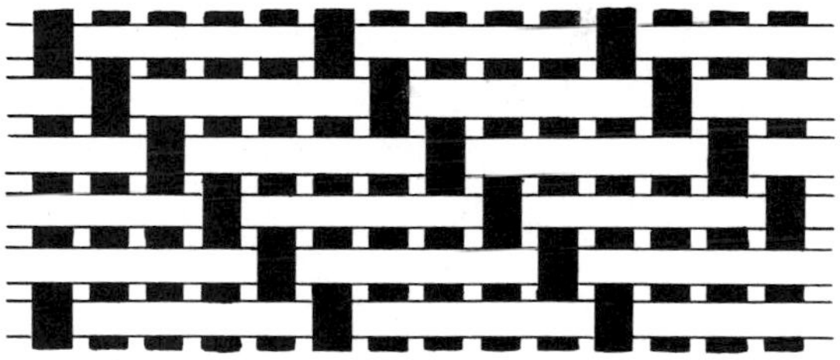

Sateen Weave

CROSSED WARP WEAVES

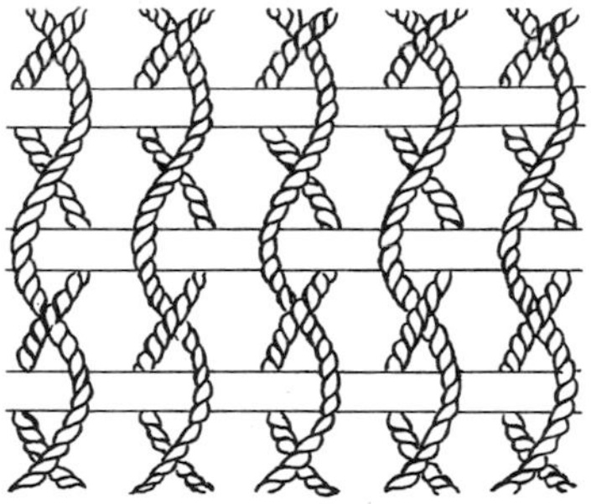

Leno Weave

VARIATIONS AND EXTENSIONS OF THE BASIC WEAVES

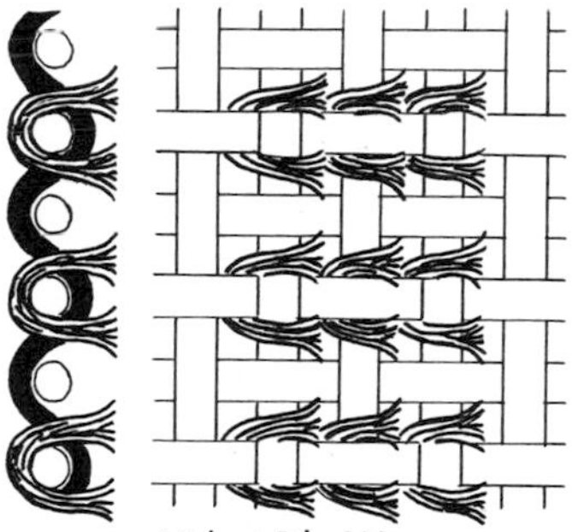

Velvet-Pile Weave

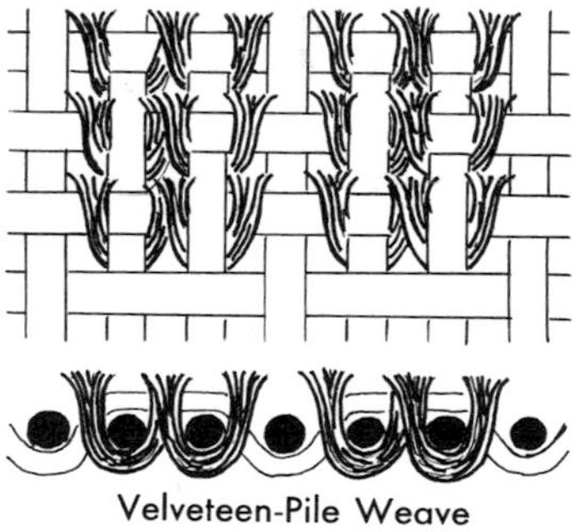

Velveteen-Pile Weave

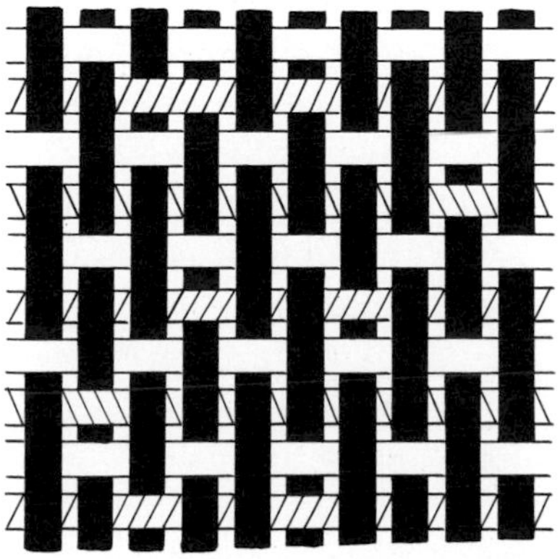

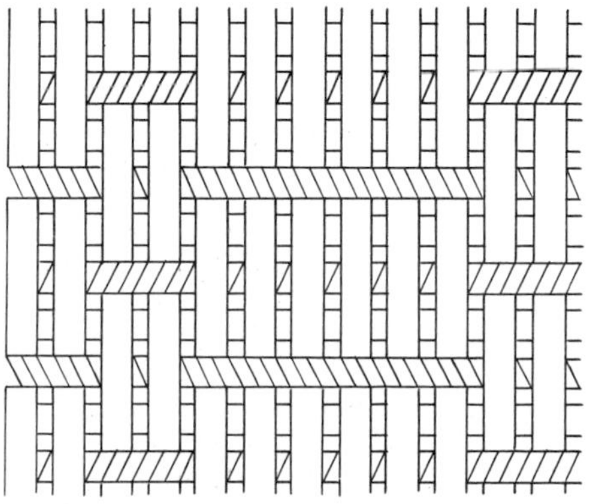

COMPLEX SINGLE WEAVE—Another Variation and Extension of the Basic Weaves

Back
(without extra set
of warp thread)

Front
(without extra set
of warp thread)

Front
(with extra set of
warp threads covering
the base warp threads)

Draftsman: Mary Shipley, East Lansing, Michigan.   **Figure 87.**

more heddles constitute a harness.[8] The raising of the heddles is controlled by a series of bars and levers of a degree of complexity related to the particular type of loom.

When a group of warp threads is raised it forms a shed much as the fingers of our two hands form a shed when they are placed between one another and then pivoted open. Through this shed a shuttle holding a wound length of weft thread can be passed. Such a passing is known as a shot or pick of weft. A reed (so called because originally made of reed), comb, or batten is likewise an essential part of a loom. Its purpose is twofold: to space the warp threads, and to beat or batten the weft threads into position. Every skill has its own language and this is the essential language of weaving.

There are a number of different ways to classify cloth weaves. Some of these names are inferior because they are not based upon any real concept of how the weaving is done. For instance, it is misleading to classify a carpet as a broadloom weave because many kinds of carpets can be made on broad looms. Their weaves are no different from carpets made on narrow looms (the original width of carpet looms was twenty-seven inches). We have seen advertisements for silk weave or linen weave fabrics. These terms are likewise ambiguous. Certain weaves may be used frequently with silk yarns because they utilize the potentialities of silk. But silk can and has been used in every kind of weave.

Weaves

It is helpful if a classification of weaves fits both historical (museum) and current (industrial) usage. The following is a suggested classification.

[8] The nomenclature for weaving lacks standardization. Different meanings are assigned to equivalent words in different countries and among different textile groups. The C.I.E.T.A. (trans. International Center for the Study of Ancient Textiles, Headquarters at Lyons, France) is an organization which is working for standardization. We are indebted to the C.I.E.T.A. for the classification and definition of historic weaves, such as compound and lampas weaves. The terminology in the descriptions of historic weaves on the following pages is essentially that of the provisional C.I.E.T.A. manuscript, which we were kindly permitted to use.

I. BASIC WEAVES

A. PLAIN WEAVE (sometimes called tabby weave)

1. WHAT LOOM? A plain weave can be made on any loom because it requires only two heddles. One raises warp threads 1, 3, 5, 7, etc., and the second raises 2, 4, 6, 8, etc.
2. WHAT CHARACTERIZES THE REGULAR INTERSECTING? The weft threads go over and under adjacent warp threads and alternate this intersection every alternate row.
3. WHAT ARE SOME VARIATIONS OF A PLAIN WEAVE? The basket weave, where the intersection is of alternate blocks of threads.[9] Historic tapestry weave (this is not machine-made tapestry cloth), where the weft threads carry the pattern. In this, a weft thread goes as far as one color is needed, where it either interlocks with a continuing color, or returns on itself.
4. WHAT ARE THE DECORATIVE CHARACTERISTICS OF THE PLAIN WEAVE? The plain weave is firm, easily constructed and therefore relatively inexpensive. Its surface is not particularly interesting. It makes a good background for printed designs. It can be given a great deal of textural interest through yarn combinations.

B. TWILL WEAVE

1. WHAT LOOM? A twill weave can be made on any four heddle loom. Actually a twill could be made with three sets of heddles but because the loom will have a greater range of utility if an even number of heddles is available, the four heddle loom is used. Any fabric woven on such a loom and taking advantage of the possibilities which it affords can be called a variation of a twill.
2. WHAT CHARACTERIZES THE REGULAR INTERSECTING? A weft thread intersects from one to three warp threads. In the next weft row it makes the same kind of intersection but progresses one warp thread to the left or right. It progresses in this manner until it returns to a repeat.

[9] This is defined by C.I.E.T.A. as extended tabby.

3. WHAT ARE SOME VARIATIONS OF A TWILL WEAVE? Irregular or broken twills in which the progression in successive weft shots is not regularly one thread to the left or right. Frequently the intersection in a four heddle twill is over warp 1, 3, 4, 2 in successive shots. Patterned twills such as diaper and herringbone twills are variations produced by varying the direction of the binding rib.

4. WHAT ARE THE DECORATIVE CHARACTERISTICS OF THE TWILL WEAVE? In a regular twill a diagonal wale or rib is produced across the cloth. This will vary in sharpness and slant according to the relative sizes and count (number per square inch) of the warp and weft yarns. Regular twills when made from tightly spun yarns have precise regular surfaces. Patterned twills likewise have a neat exactness. Broken twills are often used to display yarns in a more interesting way than a plain weave can do. Regular twills are intrinsically strong fabrics. The interweaving is frequent enough to be firm and the same warp thread takes the load in only one shot out of four.

C. SATIN WEAVE

1. WHAT LOOM? A satin may be woven on a loom of any number of heddles greater than five.

2. WHAT CHARACTERIZES THE REGULAR INTERSECTING? In the eight heddle satin, one weft thread binds down one warp thread and then goes under the next seven warps. The same binding principle extends throughout the weave, but the bound warp moves three threads to the right with each shot of weft. This makes a warp face satin. The reverse of this process, where the weft thread goes under one and over seven warps would produce a weft face satin. Most weft face satins are made of mercerized cotton and are known as sateens. It is always possible to float a thread over or under a number of intersecting threads which is one less than the number of har-

nesses. The thread going through this last group of heddles is needed for interlocking. In some of the satins the binding threads advance by more than three threads to the right in each shot. In a regular satin they always advance in regular fashion.

3. WHAT ARE SOME VARIATIONS OF A SATIN WEAVE? Irregular satins in which the points of binding are spaced unequally. Patterned satins may be produced, as in the other basic weaves, by an interruption in the regular binding system resulting in a contrast of effects and a regular pattern.

4. WHAT ARE THE DECORATIVE CHARACTERISTICS OF THE SATIN WEAVE? A satin weave results in a surface which will display long lengths or floats of yarn. It is capable of revealing the luster inherent in a fiber.

II. VARIATIONS AND EXTENSIONS OF THE BASIC WEAVES

When these weaves require the elaborate Jacquard loom to control the patterning they are frequently called Jacquard weaves.

A. PATTERNED BASIC WEAVES (cf. "patterned" under basic weaves)

B. VARIATIONS USING MORE THAN ONE SET OF WARPS OR WEFTS OR BOTH

1. COMPLEX SINGLE WEAVE. Appears as one web only, which may be backed or faced with an extra yarn, which may have pattern sections raised (as in piqué), or which may have pattern threads brought to the surface to produce color effects (as in machine-made tapestry).

LAMPAS WEAVES (an historic variety of the complex single weave)

a. WHAT KIND OF LOOM? The looms are normally equipped with ground and figure harness (Jacquard looms).

b. WHAT CHARACTERIZES THE REGULAR INTERSECTING? The lampas weave is made by two sets of warps and two sets of wefts which are interwoven in such a way as to produce a design effect superimposed on a ground effect. The main warp and weft combine to form the ground effect and the second warp and weft combine to form the design effect. The ground effects may be formed by any of the basic weaves or variants thereof. Pattern wefts are bound in plain or twill or are floated on the surface without any apparent binding system.

c. WHAT ARE THE DECORATIVE CHARACTERISTICS OF THE LAMPAS WEAVE? This weave creates a thicker fabric with a three-dimensional patterned effect which appears embossed.

2. DOUBLE WEAVE—APPEARS AS A TUBULAR CLOTH OR AS TWO SEPARATE CLOTHS JOINED AT INTERVALS

a. WHAT KIND OF LOOM? Any loom with four or more heddles may be used for a double weave. Because at least two harnesses are required to perform one function in the weaving, a four heddle loom is the simplest one which can produce a double weave. In the simplest of double weave cloths where two plain weave webs are attached only at the edges, the warps for the two webs are entered alternately through the reed. The looms required for double weaves, where the two webs are separate in some patterned portions but are interwoven in background portions, are equipped with long-eyed leashes. Because the ground warp threads function in two sets of harnesses it would be impossible to raise these independently were it not for the special leashes.

b. WHAT CHARACTERIZES THE REGULAR INTERSECTING? The warps are separated into more than one series which during the process of weaving are raised one above the other and alternately woven by the wefts. Two fabrics are thus formed one above the other. They may be entirely separate or joined in parts.

c. WHAT ARE SOME VARIATIONS OF A DOUBLE WEAVE? Patterns may be formed in double weave. This normally requires the addition of a figure harness (Jac-

quard loom) to control the weaving of the pattern while the ground harness controls the shedding for the interweaving of the warps and wefts according to one of the defined binding systems.

d. WHAT ARE THE DECORATIVE CHARACTERISTICS OF THE DOUBLE WEAVE? The double weave in its regular form has the additional bulk of a double fabric. It may also produce a raised effect of padding or quilting. (Actually quilting is the stitching of two fabrics together in patterns.)

3. PILE WEAVES. In these weaves a three-dimensional effect is produced upon a foundation fabric. The pile, composed of the thread at right angles to the basic fabric, may be a warp or a weft thread. The foundation fabric may be formed by one of the basic weaves. Pile weave fabrics are classified in the following manner.

a. WARP PILE WEAVES (VELVETS)

1) WHAT KIND OF LOOM? This loom must contain two warp beams because of the enormous difference in the amount of warp used for ground and pile. The pile beam is above the ground warp beam. A velvet must be woven on a loom with a ground and pile harness (Jacquard loom). It requires special cloth beams designed to keep the pile from being crushed. Carpet looms made on this principle are more intricately constructed.

2) WHAT CHARACTERIZES THE REGULAR INTERSECTING? In a true velvet, the ground harness weaves the ground web which may be in any one of the simple weaves. This ground interlacing binds the pile yarn into the body of the cloth. Then the pile harness is raised and a rod or wire is inserted in the shed. When the pile harness is lowered and after more ground is woven, the pile wire may be removed. If it is equipped with a sharp edge, or if a cutting tool releases the wire by cutting

along the loop, a cut pile fabric results.

3) WHAT ARE THE VARIATIONS OF THE PILE WEAVE? Patterned pile fabrics can be made by voiding the pile in the ground. It is then woven into the ground as described above and is only brought up as a pile where the pattern dictates. Patterns can be made apparent in pile by using different height piles, cut and uncut piles, solid and voided pile and by the use of different colors. Frequently a combination of several of these is used. A recent method of making patterns in pile weave has been to cut out the pile in the background (carved or sculptured pile). This is frequently done in carpet.

4) WHAT ARE THE DECORATIVE CHARACTERISTICS OF A PILE WEAVE FABRIC? Pile weave fabrics are valuable for obtaining deep reflections in textural combinations.

b. WEFT PILE WEAVES

Weaves in which an extra weft, the pile weft, is floated over several warps and then cut to form the pile. Its decorative uses are similar to those of the warp pile velvets. As the weft pile is usually cotton the material is less rich in effect than the warp pile.

III. CROSSED WARP WEAVE

Two crossed warps are used in making the body of the cloth.

A. WHAT KIND OF LOOM?

Crossed warp weaves can be made on an ordinary loom with a leno [10] attachment. This is an extra harness having U-shaped leashes. Through these leashes the extra set of warp threads is strung. The ground warp is passed between the uprights of the doup harness (so-called from Italian word for double) and is threaded through its own leashes. The doup yarns are shifted to one side and then to the

[10] Thus often called a leno weave.

other side of the ground yarns as the weaving progresses.

B. WHAT CHARACTERIZES THE REGULAR INTERSECTING?

The alternate warp threads cross each other between the wefts, and the wefts hold the crossing in place.

C. WHAT ARE SOME VARIATIONS OF THE CROSSED WARP WEAVE?

There are none, although the leno weave is often embellished to make more interesting fabrics.

D. WHAT ARE THE DECORATIVE CHARACTERISTICS OF THE CROSSED WARP WEAVE?

Gauze or leno weave fabrics can be relatively strong and sheer.

Weaves such as the compound weave, a variety of the complex single weave, and others such as the tapestry, tablet, and soumac weaves are of special interest to the textile historian. The specialized knotted pile weave will be described later under carpets.

Machinery has made weaving easier but has not assured more beautiful fabrics. The hand weaver made many of his intricate patterns, color, and texture changes by manipulating his weft threads. It is less costly to set up patterns in power loom weaving by manipulating the warp threads, because once the tie-up of the loom is made, an essentially mechanical operation can complete the process. As the warp must be the heavier of the two threads used in weaving, the exquisite weft brocades and tapestries of the hand loom era are largely things of the past. The general bulk of fabric which is produced is tending towards the simplest of weaves with texture introduced through yarn, and color introduced through printing.

d. DIFFERENCES DUE TO EMBELLISHMENT ADDED TO THE BASIC FABRIC

1) Added Yarns

Fabrics may be enriched by the addition of yarns, integral coloration, or applied colorant pattern. Yarn can provide textural interest. Embroidery is one way of introducing yarns onto the body of a cloth. It is done with a needle stitch upon fabric. An effect of a small embroidered figure can be machine produced by a loom attachment which contains a set of warp threads in needles.[11] It produces a weft-wise pattern.

Some early laces were made from embroidery by cutting away the cloth background. "Point" (derived from an old French word for prick, hence, stitch) laces are made by embroidering over a skeletal network of threads sewed to a firm pattern. The pattern is then detached.

Extra yarns may be added to glorify a basic textile while the cloth is woven. Brocading is the introduction of a pattern weft which is inserted between the ground wefts. In historic brocades the movement of the brocading weft was limited to the width of the motif produced. Similar effects today are produced by patterning in a complex single weave or by special weft bobbins,[12] which produce a small weft figure.

2) Added Color

Color may be added to cloth through dyes and paints. Dyeing is a complex process. Colorants and fibers interact in physical and chemical ways. In some cases dye can be applied to the fiber directly. In other instances a mordant is needed to fix the dye. Some dyes, viz., the vat dyes, are insoluble and must be made soluble during the dyeing process. Sometimes the dye is developed through several stages of treatment of the cloth.[13]

Color can be acquired at any stage of fabric manufacture. Some of the man-made fibers are now dyed in the solution stage, a development which improves their color quality and color fastness. The use of yarns dyed in different colors can produce colored stripes, plaids, and mottled effects. A cloth can be woven of different fibers which will react differently in a dye bath. Thus one dye bath can produce several colors. Some nonabsorptive fibers cannot be directly dyed.

[11] Known as a lappet attachment.

[12] Known as swivel bobbins.

[13] There is an excellent account of dyes from the standpoint of their dyeing properties: Z. Bendure, and G. Pfeiffer, *America's Fabrics* (New York: The Macmillan Co., 1947), pp. 464–488.

They must have their color bonded with the aid of film forming materials. Dispersed pigments [14] are applied to cloth in this manner.

Color is often introduced with pattern. This can be done in the process of weaving with various colored threads. Color and pattern can likewise be applied after the cloth is woven. There are many ways of accomplishing this, some as old as weaving itself. One method stems from the batik process of the East. The parts of the cloth which are not to be colored with a particular dye are handled in some way so as to resist the dye. Hence this is often called resist dyeing. In batiks the surface is covered with wax to hinder impregnation. Later this wax is taken out with a solvent. Another resist dye fabric is the tie-dye fabric. Numerous small pattern areas of the fabric are tied with cord so tightly that they do not take the dye into which the cloth is immersed. Both our modern stencil and screen fabrics are offshoots of the resist process.

Screen printed fabrics have become so popular today that the decorator should appreciate something of their special value. They are made by a resist process whereby a large frame is covered with a very fine meshed material. This is called the screen. The parts of this screen which are to be resistant to the dye are covered with a moisture-repellent material. Then the dye, in pasteform, is forced through the open parts of the screen onto the cloth. A limited number of impressions can be made from one screen pattern. Therefore a screen printed fabric is comparatively exclusive. It is indeed not too expensive to have fabrics made with a unique design for the purpose of repeating motifs or colors found in other furnishings. Many firms specialize in just this sort of custom work.

Discharge printing is the reverse of resist printing. After the cloth is woven, a design is put onto the fabric by impressing parts of the fabric with a chemical which will eradicate or discharge some of the dye.

Direct printing is different from either resist or discharge printing in being a direct application of colored pattern to a fabric. This process originally stemmed from wood block printing. On a

[14] See Chap. VI.

wooden block the portions not intended to take the color are cut away. The paste dye is then applied to the raised portion of the block and thence to the cloth. Wood block printing of fabric is still practiced. It is possible through this technique to produce an original fabric at nominal cost. One virtue in hand-screened and hand-blocked fabrics lies in the fact that one color can be superimposed upon another thereby giving depth of color tone. This is not practical in a machine print process because time cannot be allowed for the necessary drying of one color before applying the next. Wallpapers as well as textiles may be printed by hand screening and by hand blocking.

The bulk of fabric printing today is done by direct printing from engraved or etched copper rollers. Each color as a dye paste or as a pigmented emulsion [15] is applied directly from a roller. Even the background is roller printed.

The preparation of these rollers is very expensive. Therefore many impressions must be made if the finished fabric is to be reasonably priced. As each additional color adds to the expense, the less expensive fabrics are printed in a limited color range and in one which the manufacturer expects will make volume sales.

Sometimes a design is printed on the warp threads only. Different colored warp threads used with one color wefts may produce a similar muted effect. These latter fabrics are sometimes known as jaspé or strié fabrics.

A limited number of fabrics are made by a photoengraving process. They are executed in the same manner as a large volume photographic reproduction. The design is transferred to sensitized copper rollers from a photographic film. It is then etched and printed. This method can produce the most personal of fabrics because the impressions may be of favorite scenes. This need not result in a naïve pictorial representation. It can be productive of a tonal effect which is much the same as that found on the old French toiles.

Glass fibers, with their possibility of being both reflective and translucent, can be printed to produce many unusual effects of pattern versus

[15] See Chap. VI.

ground. Reversal of tones may be accomplished as a pattern is viewed as a lustrous surface or as a diffusing screen.

e. FINISH DIFFERENCES

The finishes which are applied to cloth may alter its textural character. In today's manufacturing the number of these finishes is legion and a cloth may be indebted to them for much of its visual beauty as well as for added practicality.

Some finishes make one fiber resemble another. Napping may be done to rough up cotton so that it resembles wool. Some finishes introduce the crispness of linen or the suppleness of silk. Glazing and calendering give duller materials a silk- or linen-like sheen. Moiréing is produced by embossing portions of a cloth so that it reflects light in swirling patterns. Panneing is a finish which lays pile flat so that it will reflect more light.

Flocking is the adhering of small pieces of fiber onto a finished cloth to change its texture or to give it a raised pattern. Various processes are used to give a crinkled effect to fabrics. True crepe is produced by using tightly spun yarns of different twists in a cloth. Pucker can likewise be obtained by using various tensions during weaving. Finishes which produce three-dimensional effects may be the result of controlled shrinkage of various types of fibers used in one cloth.

Many finishes provide some practical advantage. Sizing is a well known method of giving smoothness and body. Crease resistant, flame retardant, mildew resistant, moth repellent, water, spot, and dirt repellent—these qualities suggest ways in which the usefulness of cloth is improved. Continual effort is made by industry to treat cloths so that they will be dimensionally stable and will retain plaiting. Finishes are improving color fastness to sun and to gas fumes. Metalized finishes insulate cloths.

From the standpoint of the consumer several questions about finishes are important: How enduring is the finish? Has the finish harmed the cloth in any way? Are the claims for its performance exaggerated? Will its cost be offset by its benefits? If special finishes are selected wisely, they may add many desirable qualities to the original textiles.

f. GLOSSARY OF DECORATING FABRICS

The following listing of decorating fabrics with respect to their textural character may be helpful in making textural groupings.[16]

1. *Armure*—A plain weave fabric characterized by heavier weft threads (rep) and a small warp pattern. Appropriate for informal, provincial type furniture. Sometimes called a tapestry which it superficially resembles.

2. *Batik*—A fabric in which the pattern is made by wax resist process. Javanese batiks are frequently used as wall hangings.

3. *Batiste*—A fine, sheer, soft, mercerized long staple cotton fabric in a plain weave. Frequently embroidered or screen printed. Used for sheer curtains.

4. *Brocade*—A patterned fabric made by an extra weft yarn floated to resemble embroidery. Usually of fine silk or synthetic yarns. Appropriate for fine upholstery.

5. *Brocatelle*—A lampas weave material in which the pattern is in warp-faced satin and the ground is in any simple weave. The pattern appears embossed due to manipulation of tensions. Historic brocatelles used a coarse linen ground weft. Appropriate for fine upholstery on chairs of heavier scale.

6. *Buckram*—A stiffened, plain weave cotton. Used for stiffening.

7. *Burlap*—A coarse, jute, plain weave fabric. Used as covering for upholstery springs, for coarse wall covering or upholstery.

8. *Calico*—A plain weave printed cotton made in imitation of an obsolete textile. Patterns are small and colors simulate those of natural dyes. Suitable for use with provincial furnishings.

9. *Cambric*—A plain weave cotton or linen of light weight. It has many uses such as linings, underflounces, etc.

[16] Pronunciation is the preferred one in *Webster's New Collegiate Dictionary* (Springfield, Mass.: G. and C. Merriam Co., 1956). In some cases in the pronunciation of foreign words the dictionary has adopted a pronunciation which is part English and part of the language from whence the word came.

When no special designation of the weave is given it implies that any basic weave may be used. When no specific designation of fiber, yarn, color, or finish is given, the fabric is not definitely prescribed in these respects.

10. *Canvas*—A heavy, plain weave cotton or linen. Used as base for embroidery. A sized variety is used as a support for oil paints. *Duck* is finer and lighter but similar to canvas.

11. *Casement Cloth*—A name given to a group of light weight plain, twill, or leno weave fabrics which may have small monotone patterns incorporated in the weave. Frequently used for draw curtains.

12. *Chenille*—(pron. shĕ-nēl) (the French word for caterpillar). The name of a yarn which is made by first weaving a leno fabric with widely spaced warps. Cutting between the warps provides a yarn from which a pile protrudes. The use of this yarn in a fabric makes a chenille fabric. Suitable for upholstery or draperies where softness and depth are needed.

13. *Chintz*—A fine, plain weave cotton usually with a printed design. Frequently glazed. Suitable for upholstery on light-scale furniture, or draperies, where reflections and crisp lines are needed.

14. *Corduroy*—A cotton weft pile fabric showing warp-wise ribs. Comes in various weights suited to upholstery or hangings. Useful to introduce a fine soft texture with straight line pattern.

15. *Crash*—A name frequently applied to plain weave coarse linens. Often used for upholstery of contemporary furniture.

16. *Cretonne*—A plain or twill weave unglazed printed cotton or linen fabric which is heavier and larger in scale of pattern than chintz. Used in much the same way as chintz but with furnishings of larger scale.

17. *Crewel Embroidery*—Wool embroidery done on linen crash principally with crewel or chain stitch. Suitable for use with sixteenth and seventeenth century furniture.

18. *Damask*—A fabric in patterned satin weave which comes in all fibers. Characterized by a flat reversible pattern. In true damask the background is warp face and the pattern is weft face. Single damask table linens are five heddle, warp-faced satin with ground in weft satin. Double damasks are eight heddle weavings. Elaborate damasks may require many

more heddles and special figure harnesses. Suitable for many uses where flat patterned reflections are required.

19. *Denim*—A heavy right hand cotton twill. Suitable for sturdy slip covers, curtains, bedspreads.

20. *Dimity*—A plain weave cotton with heavier threads introduced to make stripes or bars. Tightly spun finer threads result in crisp sheer fabric. Appropriate for curtains especially of informal type.

21. *Faille*—(pron. fīl) One of the reps, a plain weave with heavier weft than warp threads. Synthetic or silk warp usual. Loosely spun cotton weft. Used for draperies. Lighter weight failles used for draw curtains.

22. *Felt*—Fabric of matted fibers sometimes on a net base. High per cent wool content desirable. Used as pads for lamp bases, drawer linings, etc. The softer felts which are now manufactured have more extensive uses.

23. *Fortuny Prints*—Handblocked prints on basic weave cottons. Made by Mariano Fortuny craftsmen of Venice. Color overlays give a rich textural effect. Used for hangings, draperies and fine coverings.

24. *Frisé*—(pron. frĕ-zāy, as it is more generally known in interior design) or frieze (pron. frēz). Pile weave fabric with uncut loops. Pile is frequently mohair or linen. One of the sturdiest of upholstery materials.

25. *Gauze*—A thin, open-mesh fabric, originally in leno weave. Name now applicable to plain weave fabrics with similar characteristics. Theatrical gauze is linen. Used for curtains.

26. *Gingham*—Plain weave, yarn-dyed fabric usually patterned in plaids. Typical ginghams of light weight mercerized cottons. Well suited for provincial and informal interiors.

27. *Guimpe*—(pron. gămp). A narrow braid or edging with a heavy cord running through it.

28. *Haircloth*—Plain or twill weave fabric made of mohair or horsehair (often synthetic) mixtures. Nineteenth century fabric made of horsehair weft and used for upholstery. Contemporary mohair fabric used for draperies.

29. *Homespun*—A loosely defined group of fabrics characterized by soft, loosely spun yarn in a plain weave.

30. *Honeycomb or Wafflecloth*—A plain or twill weave fabric with the patterning in small squares.

31. *Imitation Leather*—A plastic coated fabric which resembles leather. Many varieties, each with its own trade name.

32. *Indianhead*—Trade name for a medium weight plain weave cotton. Slightly heavier and less smooth than cambric. Many uses. Substantial enough for slip covers.

33. *Lace*—An open mesh fabric made by intertwining threads in some manner other than by intersection on the loom. Machine laces designed to imitate the appearance of the hand made laces. The nets are classified as laces.

34. *Lampas*—An historically important elaborate silk fabric in a lampas weave.

35. *Leather*—Treated animal hide used as a fabric. Top grain or top cut from the hide is most desirable. Used for sturdy upholstery where sheen and depth reflection are required.

36. *Madras*—Name for small patterned cotton shirting material and likewise for a leno weave patterned (extra weft thread woven in) curtain material.

37. *Marquisette*—A leno weave fabric of tightly twisted yarn. Used for curtains.

38. *Matelassé*—Figured double weave cloth. Raised design made of two webs which can be separated. Used for fine covers and upholstery where some thickness is required.

39. *Mohair*—Name given to fabric the fiber of which is largely mohair, the fleece of the angora goat. Yarn is wiry, resilient, and lustrous. Excellent drapery fabric for large window expanse.

40. *Monk's Cloth*—Fabric made in the basket weave variation of the plain weave of loosely spun coarse cotton yarns. Used for inexpensive hangings and covers.

41. *Muslin*—A generic name for plain weave cottons of medium weight. Frequently refers to a sheeting material which is not quite so fine as percale. Many utilitarian uses.

42. *Needlepoint*—Originally referred to needle laces, now designates an embroidered material made by a half cross-stitch on canvas.

Petit point (little stitch) is finer than *gros point* (big stitch). Name frequently applied to a plain weave upholstery fabric in which the twist of the yarn creates a superficial resemblance to the embroidered material.

43. *Nets*—Varieties of laces characterized by regular meshes:
   a. Bobbinet—hexagonal mesh.
   b. Filet net—square mesh.
   c. Point d'esprit (pron. pwan desprē)—a bobbinet with small dotted design.

44. *Oilcloth*—A cotton plain weave material coated with linseed oil and pigments or with synthetic coatings. Used as a waterproof covering for tables, etc.

45. *Organdy*—Sheer, plain weave material made of tightly spun cotton yarns. Specially processed to preserve crispness. Used for curtains.

46. *Paisley Shawl*—(pron. pāz′-lĭ) Hand-woven soft, woolen shawl made in Scotland in the nineteenth century in imitation of Kashmir shawls (woven in tapestry twill sometimes with added embroidery) of India. Used today for decorative "throws."

47. *Percale*—Plain weave, fine quality cotton. Used for best quality sheets and pillow cases.

48. *Piqué*—(pron. pē-kā′) Cotton material characterized by a raised rib now customarily running lengthwise. Bedford cord is the name now given to a similar but heavier fabric. Cord is made with extra warp stuffer yarns held in place by extra wefts. Useful in producting stiff, linear, tailored effects.

49. *Pongee*—(pron. pŏn-jē′) Name derives from a dress fabric of plain weave in wild (or tussah) silk. Heavier weight known as shantung or rajah. Other names for similar appearing cloths of varying weights are shikii silk, antique taffeta, and douppioné (pr. dūp-io-nā) silk.

50. *Quilted Fabrics*—A fabric in which a surface fabric, cotton batting interlining, and a sheer cotton lining are stitched together in patterns giving a padded effect. Italian name for historic hand-quilting over a corded pattern was *trapunto*. Used to give thickness with fineness.

51. *Rep*—A generic name for a class of fabrics characterized by heavier weft than warp threads.

52. *Sailcloth*—Heavy, plain weave cotton material of the type originally used for sails. Sometimes called canvas or duck. Used for furniture seats and covering.

53. *Sateen or Satine*—A weft satin weave fabric made from mercerized cotton yarns. *Glosheen*® is a trade name for a fine sateen with printed figure, often used for draperies. Natural color sateen is used for linings of draperies.

54. *Satin*—A material made in a warp satin weave. Cotton, silk, and synthetics are usual fibers. Antique satin made from textured silk. Used to introduce fineness and high reflections.

55. *Scrim*—An open mesh plain weave fabric made from tightly spun yarns. Coarser than a Swiss. Practical curtain material.

56. *Seersucker*—A plain weave medium weight cotton with puckered warp stripes. Pucker caused by varying warp tensions. A utilitarian textile for curtains, bedspreads, etc.

57. *Swiss*—A sheer crisp plain weave fabric made from tightly twisted cotton yarns. Usually figured with dots applied in one of the following ways:
   a. Chemical—printed on the fabric.
   b. Woven dots—done with extra weft. Loose ends cut on each pattern weft.
   c. Woven dots—applied by *lappet* weaving in which an extra warp thread is lifted above the loom as for pile weaving. However, it is directed horizontally and when bound down by ground weft, produces an effect of weft floats. Cut from pattern to pattern.
   d. Embroidered dots—done by intricate embroidery attachment to loom; not bound down by weft.
   e. Swivel dots—imported Swisses made on a swivel loom. Dots made by individual shuttles, ends of dots hand-tied.
   Swisses are used for curtains, covers, and flounces where a crisp, sheer effect is desired.

58. *Taffeta*—A fine light weight, compact, plain weave fabric in which the warp and weft are

® Registered trade mark.

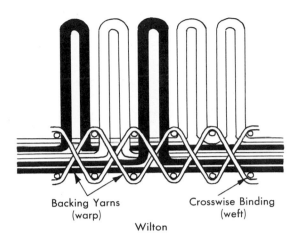

Backing Yarns
(warp)

Crosswise Binding
(weft)

Wilton

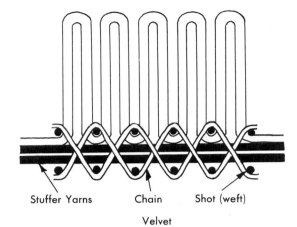

Stuffer Yarns   Chain   Shot (weft)

Velvet

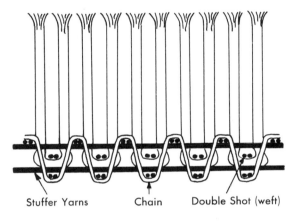

Stuffer Yarns   Chain   Double Shot (weft)

Axminster

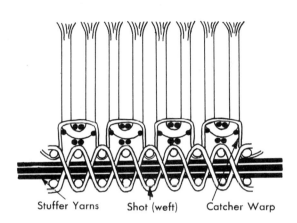

Stuffer Yarns   Shot (weft)   Catcher Warp

Chenille

OTHER TYPES OF CARPET CONSTRUCTION

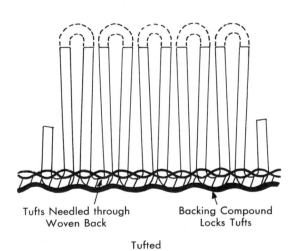

Tufts Needled through
Woven Back

Backing Compound
Locks Tufts

Tufted

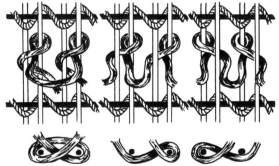

Ghiordes
or Turkish

Lefthand Sehna
or Persian

Righthand Sehna
or Persian

Oriental Knots

Figure 88.

Draftsman: Mary Shipley, East Lansing, Michigan. **Carpets drawn from material courtesy of:** American Carpet Institute, E. Moon Fromm, Public Relations Director, and The Hoover Company, "Carpets and Rugs," Eleanor Delany, Director, Hoover Home Institute.

of the same size. Made of silk or fiber resembling silk. Cotton taffeta contains a percentage of cotton and synthetic fibers. Antique taffeta is made from wild silk. A light weight silk taffeta is known today as *silk gauze*. Used for curtains, etc., where crispness, linear draping quality, light weight and luster are required.

59. *Tapa Cloth*—A decorative cloth made in the South Sea Islands by pounding tree bark to paper thinness and applying block printed designs. Largely used for hangings.

60. *Tapestry*—
   a. The original type was a ribbed material produced on a heavier warp by finer wefts wound on bobbins. One color weft was carried only as far as needed in the pattern and then another color was introduced. In the historical pictorial tapestries the weft is usually wool and the warp linen. The weft threads run vertically in the finest tapestries when the tapestry is hung. Tapestries were intended for wall hangings and for upholstery.
   b. Machine-made tapestry cloth is a complex single weave fabric. Designed to imitate some of the effects of the hand-loomed tapestries. The yarns are frequently woolen for the face with cotton or linen for the back. Used for upholstery on heavier pieces.

61. *Terry*—An uncut warp pile fabric with the loops extending on both sides of the fabric. No so heavy as frisé. Appropriate for hangings.

62. *Ticking*—Closely woven cotton fabric in twill weave. Used for pillow and mattress coverings. Occasionally used for upholstery.

63. *Toile De Jouy*—(pron. twäl-de-zhoo-y). Plain or twill weave cottons produced from 1760–1815 in the town of Jouy, France. Delicately engraved monotone printed designs. Good imitations on today's market. Applicable for hangings and coverings on fine scaled furniture.

64. *Tweed*—A name now given to a loosely woven woolen twill weave fabric. In a strict sense, a cloth of single ply woolen yarns woven in some variation of a twill.

65. *Velvet*—A name loosely given to all pile fabrics produced by some adaptation of the velvet weave.
   a. Velveteen—a weft face cotton velvet.
   b. Corduroy—a weft face cotton velvet with warp wales.
   c. Panne Velvet—A velvet with pressed pile.
   d. Velour—A velvet with a short compact pile.
   e. Plush—A long pile velvet.
   The velvets are useful for introducing deep reflections.

66. *Voile*—A plain weave, sheer, open fabric made from tightly twisted yarns. May be any fiber. Used for durable sheer curtains.

3. Floorcoverings

a. CARPETS

The average layman possesses very little technical knowledge of floorcoverings. Yet he spends a relatively large amount of his furnishing budget for them. This lack of information is understandable because carpet construction appears very complicated.

1) Materials

Much that has been learned about fabrics in general can be related to carpets in particular. The quality of fibers and yarns is important. If a fiber is resilient and strong it is suitable for pile carpeting. Luster is an added advantage. Softness in the blend adds a desirable textural quality. Abrasive strength is especially required for a matte or flat surface floor material. Backing or ground fibers should be as durable as surface yarns and they should be permanent to the same kind of cleaning.

In addition to the use of cotton, linen, wool, and synthetics, many flat weaves are made from some of the more unusual fibers. Sisal, wild grass, and rushes are used. A fiber known as Kraft Fiber, which is made from fir wood, is made into fiber rugs.

The ground or backing for carpets is of various less expensive materials. Cotton and jute in combination are usual, although linen and wool are used. Jute is strong and stiff but not particularly pliable. It is usually incorporated as stuffer yarns to give extra bulk.

2) Construction

The quality of carpets is likewise related to their construction. Many floorcoverings are not entirely woven. The Eurasians make felted rugs. *Braided rugs* are made by sewing together braided strips of cloth. *Hooked* and *tufted rugs* are constructed by inserting loops of yarn or cloth into the body of some coarse, compact material such as burlap. Embroidery on a ground material produces fabrics which vary from the elegant rugs of France to coarser embroideries coming from places like Spain and Africa.

The plain weave is frequently used for floor coverings. In the Orient it is used in the making of Khilims and Soumaks. The *Khilim* is woven as are hand-woven tapestries. A *Soumak* is made on a similar principle but there is a ground weft thread in addition to a pattern weft thread. The latter is manipulated like an embroidery half back-stitch going over four warp threads, back under two. The *Aubusson* and *Beauvais* are the great tapestry carpets of France, taking their names from the places of their production. The American Indian rugs, some of which are beautifully designed, are tapestry weavings. Simple plain weave rugs made on hand looms using a cotton warp and strips of cotton cloth for weft are known as *rag rugs*.

The first power loomed carpets made in this country about a century ago were basic weave fabrics made in wool. They are known as ingrain carpets because the pattern is in the body or grain of the weaving.

Many carpets are made in the pile weave. Pile carpets were first made in that great wool raising belt which extends from Asia Minor to the plains of China along the 35°N. latitude. These hand weavings are still known as Oriental rugs.[17] French historic hand-woven pile fabrics were called *Savonnerie* from the place of their manufacture, the previous location of a soap factory. Modern hand-woven and hand-tufted pile carpets come from a number of sources in addition to the Orient. Puerto Rico, Finland, Spain, Holland, Africa, and America are producers.

[17] Discussed further on p. 203.

Whereas all hand-loomed pile carpets are constructed on the simplest of looms, power loom fabrics are made on four different types of looms each of which has been developed for the weaving of a particular type of carpet. The first of these carpets to be originated was the Wilton carpet (1745). This carpet weave goes back to the days when carpet weavers of the town of Wilton, England, devised a method of obtaining a pattern pile carpet by a quicker method than that of the old hand-tieing of knots. This was made feasible because of loom attachments which provided pattern threads when needed. Later Joseph-Marie Jacquard (1752–1834) of France more completely mechanized this process.

The *Wilton carpet*, the better grades of which are always made of worsted yarn,[18] has been called the weave with hidden value. This is because every colored yarn in the warp pile is embedded in the body of the cloth and is only brought to the surface when needed in the design. The selection of the colors for the design is accomplished by the elaborate mechanism of the Jacquard loom. In this loom the control of the shedding is accomplished through a series of perforated cards. A highly simplified explanation of the principle is that a hole in a card will allow a warp thread to rise and thus come to the face of the cloth. The Jacquard mechanism and its tie-up is very costly. Therefore many carpets must be woven in order to make such effort profitable.

The colored pile yarns in a Wilton are limited in number by the pile beams or frames which are placed above the ground warp beam. Six is the highest number of colors which are usually found although extra tones can be planted. As many as nine frames may be used in weaving special Wiltons of added durability for areas receiving much wear. Wilton looms can likewise produce piles of different heights and types.[19]

The chain warp is the one which intersects the weft shots to hold in the pile. In a top quality Wilton the chain warp may be linen or wool.

[18] Some Wiltons are now made with cotton pile.

[19] Originally Wiltons were always cut pile. A carpet with uncut pile woven on a Wilton loom was called a *Brussels carpet*. These are referred to now as uncut Wiltons.

In other quality carpets it is cotton. Most carpets carry what are known as stuffer warps. These do not intersect with the weft but are merely carried along to give body to the cloth. In some Wiltons there may be as many as five stuffers and in the top grades these are cotton or linen rather than jute. The number of the weft shots binding in the pile is important. A Wilton may have as many as five weft shots for each row of pile. It would then be referred to as a five shot Wilton. A Wilton carpet should provide a fine compact texture and a deep pile.

A *velvet* carpet does not have any warp pile yarns embedded and hidden in its body. It can be woven on one of the simplest of carpet looms, similar to that used for the weaving of unpatterned velvet fabrics. Most velvet carpets rely upon textured and colored yarns to provide interest. The pile may be cut or uncut and by means of a profile cutting wire may be of two heights. Colored pattern can be introduced into a velvet by printing. This is done by an ingenious method of printing the colors on the warp pile before it is woven into the fabric. The colors are estimated and the yarn dyed on large drums as it would be needed for the pattern. It is, of course, just about impossible to get this color register perfect in alignment. Therefore a patterned velvet will frequently be stepped off just enough so that it will resemble the diagonal steps made between adjacent colors in the hatchings of handwoven tapestries. This resemblance has given the name of tapestry velvet, or loosely just tapestry carpet, to a printed velvet carpet.

What are some standards for a velvet carpet? It is customarily made of a heavier yarn and therefore has fewer points (pile tufts) per square inch than a Wilton. It may have a slightly higher pile than a Wilton although many velvets do not. It will frequently have several jute stuffer yarns to give it added body. Warp chains are usually cotton. Weft shots are frequently two although more may be found.

A velvet is a reasonably priced carpet of much worth. For plain or yarn textured carpet it is an excellent buy if care is given to obtain a good quality.

Axminster carpets are produced on quite a different principle from the Wilton or Velvet carpets and the result which should be expected design-wise is also quite different. An Axminster weaving is one of the most economical ways to make a patterned rug. It may contain innumerable colors and it is designed to have a luxurious deep pile look for a lower price. Consequently the number of points is not large but the pile is high and the yarns are woolen rather than worsted in order to give that soft textured look.

In an Axminster carpet the chain warp may be wool or cotton, the stuffers cotton, but the weft is jute. Therefore this weave is clearly recognized because it results in the only carpet which can be rolled lengthwise but not crosswise. These jute weft shots are chained down by the warp. There is frequently a stuffer yarn above and below the level of the pile interlacing. One set of wefts may tie in the topmost stuffers, one set tie in the pile and another tie in the lower set of stuffers. This makes a deep bodied carpet which feels firm underfoot.

In weaving an Axminster, long spools are first set up on which are wound, in order, every warp pile color which is needed for a particular weft row. The winding of these spools is a very expensive process inasmuch as it is necessary to have as many spools as there are pile rows in one warp-wise repeat of the pattern. Once the spools are wound the weaving is relatively easy and inexpensive. When a certain spool comes up in the pattern it comes down into place in front of the loom and the necessary wool to make one tuft of pile is removed from each of its threads. Then it goes back out of use until required again by the pattern. The next spool then comes into position and functions in similar manner.

Axminster looms make a high percentage of today's carpets. The only rival for producing many toned deep textured woolen carpets is the *tufted carpets*. These are machine-made on the principle of hand-made hooked rugs where a pile loop is hooked or needled into a base fabric. Such carpets are frequently coated on the back with a plastic to prevent ravelling.

The most expensive of the carpets is the

chenille. The first step in its construction is just like that of a chenille fabric. A chenille yarn is woven on a separate loom. This yarn is so planned that the colors for a row of weft pile are made on one yarn. When this yarn takes its place in the carpet it becomes a particular weft pile row. As many colors as are desired can thus be incorporated.

The difference between a chenille fabric and a chenille carpet lies in the fact that the weaving for the latter really consists of two parts. There is first the weaving which binds down the chenille weft. This is done with fine linen yarn in the best chenilles. At the same time that this binding is being accomplished the body of the carpet is being woven. In this the chain warp is usually wool or cotton, and the stuffers may be cotton. The weft which binds in the chain warp may be wool or cotton.

It is no longer necessary to use the chenille construction for the purpose for which it was originally devised, namely for custom patterns. Chenilles have advanced along lines of being very compact deep pile luxury fabrics. They are frequently embossed by cutting a design into the pile, creating a sculptured effect. These special weavings are expensive.

Carpets in which inexpensive chenille yarns are bound into plain weave fabrics using jute binding wefts and cotton warps are called machine Smyrna rugs and are inexpensive. They should not be confused with chenille carpeting.

Because of the many new technical developments, construction alone can no longer be considered the determining factor of quality, as was apt to have been the case in the past. Rugs and carpets of all grades are constructed by each method today. Each method has certain advantages in producing certain types of effects at a specified cost level. These are utilized by the manufacturer to offer the consumer wider choice.

b. ORIENTAL CARPETS: MATERIAL, CONSTRUCTION, AND DESIGN

No study of carpets would be complete without an understanding of the hand-knotted carpets of the East known as *Oriental* rugs. There are many different ways to approach this study.

Their history is interesting, for all of the conquests of the Orient have left imprints on their designs. The symbolism in their designs tells us much about the culture of their weavers. Their manufacture, identification, market value, original use, and the great museum collections of Orientals—each of these could be a subject for special study.

Oriental carpets are woven in six districts, all lying in the great wool belt of the East. They are usually called by the name of the district from which they come, and are known as Turkish (from Turkey), Persian (from Iran), Caucasian (from the district in Southern Russia called the Caucasus between the Black and the Caspian Sea), Turkoman (from the district in Southern Eurasia lying roughly between the Caspian Sea and the Himalaya Mountains), Indian (from Northern India) and Chinese (from Western China).

The pile of most of these hand-loomed carpets is often said to be a knotted rather than a looped pile.[20] A knotted pile is made with an extra weft thread which is twisted or knotted around two warp threads before being brought to the surface. There are two kinds of knots which are used. The first is the Ghiordes knot which is named for a town in Turkey. In the Ghiordes knot a weft goes over two warps and then is brought up between them to form a pile. In a carpet woven with a Ghiordes knot there is a pile tuft between every two warp threads. This makes a coarser fabric characterized by more widely spaced piles than does the Sehna knot. This latter knot, named after a city in Persia, is made by crossing the pile yarn under one warp and over an adjacent warp, returning under this warp to project beyond the surface. Thus the cut pile ends are next to adjacent warps and there is a tuft between every warp. This makes a finer more compact body.

The ground of Oriental carpets is made either of wool or of cotton, the former being customary in the great sheep-raising districts like the Caucasus and the latter being more frequent in the lower lands of Persia and China. The wool

[20] With the exception of a limited number of Soumaks and Khilims already mentioned.

pile is softer and finer in the countries which depend upon the fleece of lowland sheep. As the lower lands lie in the path of more advanced civilization, there is a marriage of fine medium and more sophisticated artistry in the work of the Persian, Indian, and Chinese weavers. The carpets woven by rugged mountaineers have strong designs like the architecture of the land. As the entire character of Oriental carpets is variable within its unity, so their decorative uses vary. Such rugs as the Turkoman, Caucasian, and many of the Turkish, are appropriate for interiors of large-scale and coarse textures; whereas the Persian, Indian, Chinese, and many of the remaining Turkish rugs look best with finer ensembles.

Chinese Orientals are woven with the Sehna knot and have a deep luxurious soft woolen pile. All but the oldest have a cotton ground. Some have designs outlined with clipped pile. Many Chinese rugs are characterized by narrow border designs and symbolic central medallions. The field in some Chinese carpets is plain, quite unlike the customary field of other Orientals. Other fields contain small designs consisting of such Chinese symbols as the peony, the dragon, the cloud band, the wave, and the swastika. Colors are predominantly blue, ivory, and saffron yellow. A few Eastern Turkoman rugs have a character which is Chinese with the inclusion of Turkoman symbols.

By contrast with the lighter tones of its Eastern rugs, the real *Turkoman* weaving is austere and somber. The generic name for the largest class of these rugs is Bokhara. The knot is almost always Sehna and the pile yarn is wiry and not very deep. The ground is wool and goat's hair is used for the overcast selvedges. The ends are plain woven. Designs in Turkoman rugs are regular, prescribed tribal designs known as guls. These are compounded of diamonds, hexagons and octagons. The colors in these Northern Turkomans are distinctive. Their reds are a subdued yellow or blood red. This is coupled with a great deal of black and some spotting of an almost white tone. Turkoman carpets are masculine in design character. Yet their thinness of body renders them appropriate for use with fine furniture. They are good choices

for libraries and for contemporary rooms with straight line designs.

Situated between India and Persia, the countries of Afghanistan and Baluchistan (modern Pakistan) make carpets of small geometric designs which combine Persian blue with Turkoman reds. A deep brown is more customary than the Bokhara black in these rugs.

Indian carpets in the great tradition of Oriental rug manufacture are no longer made. They were the weavings of the sixteenth and seventeenth centuries during the reigns of the Moghul Emperors. Indian design is frequently realistic but it is so in such a light-hearted, dainty sort of way that it never seems crudely pictorial. The individual motifs may be arranged in rows or within a latticework design. Indian colors are far from somber. Light blue-reds and yellow-reds combine with other pastels to form a crisp feminine palette.

The *Persian* rug is frequently called the queen of the Orientals. There are many varieties of Persian carpets and superficially they seem quite different. Traveling across the South of Persia one finds the realistic floral patterns of the Kermans contrasted with the large geometric medallions of the Shiraz. In the Western mountains the tribesmen favor rows of small formal motifs such as pears, fish, or flowers. These rugs are the Sarabands, Lorestans, Bakhtiari and Kurdish carpets.

Farther north we come to towns which are in closer contact with the former capital cities of Tabriz, Herat, Ispahan, and the present capital, Teheran. The carpets woven for the court are frequently characterized by large central medallions which are masterpieces of formalized pattern. Among these are the Saruk, Kashan, and Kermanshah (named after an alien Shah from Kerman!). Larger and bolder medallions characterize the Hamadan (on a camel's hair ground) and the Gorevan, Serapi, and Herez weavings of districts adjacent to the Caspian.

The central Persian plateau, the seat of most present day weaving, produces the Saruk, Kashan, Lilihan, and the old carpet known as the Feraghan bearing a small stylized flower and leaf motif known as the herati (from the old capital of Herat) on a deep blue ground.

For all their diversity the Persian carpets stand out as being masterpieces of skillful craftsmanship and design. They show a mastery of color in relation to pattern and texture. They are fine weavings. An old Sehna (similar in pattern to a medallion Saruk) may have four hundred Sehna knots to the square inch. Persian carpets are distinguished by a deep ruby red and a rich indigo blue, against which is found ivory, saffron, blue-greens, and some green. It fits best into a blue dominated scheme. The Persian motifs are frequently flower inspired but they are formalized and admirably contrived into a flat pattern suitable for flooring.

The best *Turkish* rugs, like the Caucasian, are masterfully designed. The general level of production, however, is somewhat uneven. Many of the Turkish patterns are geometric adaptations of the Persian. The prayer rug, on which Mohammedans kneel in prayer, is characterized by a formalized niche or mihrab which is to be turned toward Mecca, the sacred capital of the Islam empire. The majority of Turkish carpets use the Ghiordes knot and coarse wool yarn. Colors are similar to the Persian but are somewhat lighter and more saturated. Green is more frequent. Varieties are the Ghiordes, Bergamo, Anatolian, and Oushak. Turkish carpets can be strong and beautiful accents in a room.

Caucasian carpets no longer are marketed in the West. Such names as Kazak (Cossack), Karabagh, and Daghestan suggest the wildness of the Russian steppes and Kara Dagh mountains. The Shirvans and Khubas come from the shores of the Caspian Sea. Persian influence is seen in some of these carpets but in general the Caucasian carpet is at its best when allowed to be the most untamed of the Oriental weavings. The fiber and ground is coarse wool. The knot is Ghiordes. Stylized human and animal figures, the swastika, latchhook, and medallions shooting tongues of flame are characteristic patterns. Colors are daring but sure, with much use of blood red and black with yellow, blue, and green.

If an Oriental rug is several hundred years old it merits being called antique. Carpets of more than fifty years of age are merely called old or semiantique. More recent carpets are contemporary. Age is venerable in the East. If one studies the Oriental weavings with a discriminating eye and learns to choose between the superlative, the good, and the poor, one will find rich rewards for use today. In the process of this study there will come a new appreciation for the art and history of those peoples whose civilization is far older than ours and who have given us so much enrichment.

c. CARPET FINISHES, PADS, AND OTHER FLOOR COVERINGS

Pads under carpets make them seem softer and protect them from abrasion. They are sometimes made of sponge or foam rubber which is made from latex or the milky fluid from the rubber tree. Other pads are made from felted cattle hair, or jute, or similar fibers.

The backs of carpets are frequently treated with a plastic coating which is intended to strengthen the fabric and to keep it from ravelling. Carpets are sometimes given a finish to dull their color and to give them a sheen.

Many floors are covered with types of flooring such as linoleum, rubber, cork, asphalt, or synthetics. These may come as strips or in tiles. Linoleum is made from a mixture of linseed oil, gum, wood or cork dust, and pigments, applied to a canvas backing. It should be laid on a special felt paper lining. It comes as inlaid linoleum where the pattern goes through the entire thickness and as printed linoleum where the pattern is printed on the surface. Inlaid linoleum is more economical for heavy traffic use.

4. Ceramics

The word "ceramic" describes any object made from clay and hardened by fire. An earthen flower pot and the finest piece of Ming china are both ceramics. What are their essential similarities and differences?

a. COMPOSITION TYPES

The basic chemicals in any clay are hydrogen, silicon, aluminum and oxygen combining to form a hydrous silicate of aluminum. The average clay likewise has many impurities. These ingredients combined in the clay account for its color, texture, and plasticity. They likewise determine the temperature at which it can be fired and thus set the body characteristics of the ceramic.

Pottery is that ware which is made from clays which cannot be fired at an intense heat (which porcelain clays can withstand). The body is therefore opaque and porous. It was a long time before man developed the art of making glazes to coat pottery and make it nonporous. The majority of pottery glazes have a composition similar to that of glass and contain lead. Many glazes are therefore transparent. Many of these transparent glazes contain colorants which modify the color as well as the texture of the pottery on which they are placed. Some of the greatest masterpieces of the potter's art have been produced through his mastery of glazes.

Not all glazes are transparent. Pottery clays vary in color from a red known as terra-cotta through buff to a cream color. Opaque glazes were desired to cover some of the darker clays. The introduction of oxide of tin was an early discovery which the potters of the Near East found would make the glaze opaque. Such glazes are frequently called enamels.[21]

The customary glazes on pottery clay are not fired at the temperature necessary to harden the body of the ware. Therefore a first or so-called biscuit or bisque firing, and a second or glost firing is required. This creates a separation of body and glaze which may cause the glaze on pottery to chip off or to craze. Unglazed pottery is known as bisque ware.

Pottery made from the coarser red and buff clays is often called earthenware although all ceramics are made from earth and are, strictly speaking, earthenwares. The term *faience* (from the town of Faenza, Italy) became associated with colorful glazed European pottery. The term *majolica*[22] is given to that type of faience which added metallic lusters over a painted tin glazed pottery. Majolica was named for the Island of

[21] Transparent glazes may likewise be called enamels. Nomenclature is not standard. The distinction of regarding enamels as colored low fired glazes is often made.

[22] Warren E. Cox, *The Book of Pottery and Porcelain* (New York: Crown Publishers, Inc., 1944), p. 332. Authorities disagree on the difference, if any, between faience and majolica.

Figure 89. This is good ceramic design because the essential shapes, the glazes, and the added color and pattern provide enhanced sensuous enjoyment. This is especially true because of their suitability to their respective media.

   A. Pottery tea service.
   B. Pottery and stoneware pieces.
   C. Porcelain plates and bowls.

C

(C) **Article:** Porcelain bowls, bottles, and jars. **Artist:** Charles Lakofsky, Associate Professor of Art, Bowling Green State University, Bowling Green, Ohio. **Photographer:** The Cleveland Museum of Art, Cleveland, Ohio.

(A) Article: Pottery tea service. **Artist:** Charles Lakofsky, Associate Professor of Art, Bowling Green State University, Bowling Green, Ohio. **Photographer:** The Cleveland Museum of Art, Cleveland, Ohio.

(B) Article: Pottery and stoneware bowls and jars. **Artist:** Toshiko Takaezu, Honolulu, Hawaii, and Cleveland, Ohio. **Photographer:** The Cleveland Museum of Art, Cleveland, Ohio.

Majorca from which it was exported from Spain.[23]

Stoneware is the next development in ceramic manufacture. Fine stoneware is often called iron-stone china on the contemporary market. Some manufacturers call it semivitreous china. This, together with the better grades of pottery, is occasionally advertised as dinnerware. These latter are general terms and do not have as definite a meaning as the words pottery and stoneware.

When a clay body can be fired to such an intense heat as to become hard and stonelike and nonporous, it is said to be vitrified. *Stoneware* is made of such clay, a clay that contains a higher percentage of aluminum silicate than do the pottery clays. Stoneware clay is light grey or cream in color. If stoneware is made very thin it is almost translucent. True china is generally translucent.

As stoneware does not need a glaze to make it nonporous, much stoneware is unglazed or biscuit ware. The famous products of the Wedgwood factory which are known as Jasper ware (integrally colored blue or green with white figures) and Basalt ware (black) are all unglazed stonewares which are named for their resemblance to the natural stones. Some glazes can be applied at the same time as the biscuit firing of stoneware. Ordinary salt is frequently added in the kiln when stoneware jugs are first fired. This produces what is known as a salt glaze which sometimes runs down a jar in a hit or miss fashion which adds to its interesting quality.

China or *porcelain* is the highest refinement of ceramic manufacture. As this fine ware first came from the Orient it was known as china. The Italians, seeing in it a resemblance to a shell known as porcellana, gave it a name which has been translated to porcelain.

Porcelain is made of light colored clay known as kaolin. This clay, which is largely pure aluminum silicate, is almost infusible. To it is added petuntse or a feldspar rock which makes the kaolin fusible at an extremely high temperature. This petuntse likewise acts as a glaze and therefore porcelain can be glazed as an

[23] Italy likewise produced historic majolica.

integral process with the biscuit firing. Sometimes an additional glaze is placed over any applied decoration which is then known as underglaze decoration. The high firing of body with glaze in porcelain creates a highly vitrified ware which is frequently translucent when held up to the light and which has a bell-like ring when struck.

Contemporary chinas are divided into hard paste chinas (to differentiate from a soft paste china which was an early European ware attempting to duplicate the Oriental chinaware) and bone chinas. Most European chinas are hard paste and English chinas are bone. The latter is made with the addition of calcined bone, which acts like the feldspar to make the clay more fusible. Not requiring so high a temperature it is not quite as hard or vitrified as the European chinas. The added materials give it a creamier body and greater translucency than hard paste china. Bone china is given a second or glaze firing. The glaze is similar to glass in composition.

b. FORMING

The processes by which ceramics are formed are an influence upon their shapes. A primitive method recently reutilized by many potters is that of carving or hewing out a bulk of clay to make it hollow. Hand-carving of clay is a technique which is used today in making large free form bowls in the contemporary manner. Some ceramics are made from coils or ropes of clay which are entwined to a form.

Potters learned to give symmetry to their work by throwing the clay onto a revolving wheel which held a convex form on which the piece could be shaped. As techniques influence design so many potters today feel that a true pottery shape should indicate the roundness of wheel throwing. China pieces are likewise made in molds in which the clay can be placed and from which it becomes loosened as moisture evaporates. Molded ceramics may have their inner surfaces stamped into form. In fine mold work the potter's hand and instruments can subsequently shape the thicknesses of the vessel's walls and considerable skilled artistry can enter at this point.

c. EMBELLISHMENT

The smooth surfaces of ceramic vessels have always been a great temptation to the painter or the sculptor. He has experimented with applying decoration under the glaze and over the glaze. He added color through colored slip (moist clay), transparent glazes, enamel, and luster coats. He modeled or carved the surface of the clay or added thick slip to create decoration. He incised through a slip coating to form what is known as sgraffito or intaglio decoration.[24] Sometimes he put decoration of superb quality on ware of inferior body, as is the case in much Persian ware. Sometimes he placed decoration of poor quality, judged from the point of view of good decorative design, onto wares of good body. Rarely in the total array of the world's ceramics, has he been content to rest his case on structural shape, color, texture, and glaze without added pattern. Some of the pieces so made have been the finest that the ceramist has ever produced.

d. CONTEMPORARY FACTORIES

The bulk of our utilitarian ceramics are the product of our contemporary factories. What choices are available? It is not possible to state exactly what the body and glaze of each type of contemporary ware is because such formulas are the ceramist's secrets. An acquaintance with historical wares gives a good clue to the character of contemporary wares. In the first place much contemporary work is the product of factories which have been in continuous existence since the eighteenth century and which are following along with wares of traditional fineness of body and with some use of contemporary design. Newer factories can be related to the old and an appraisal made.

Many of the central European factories cannot produce for the western market at this time. However, hard paste china of the character of historic Dresden and Meissen (East German) china is being exported from West Germany. The patterns frequently stem from eighteenth century rococo forms and are dainty

and fanciful. Other patterns are freer and more contemporary in feeling. Arzberg and Rosenthal china from Bavaria are interesting contemporary hard paste chinas.

The fine china of the northern countries, Denmark and Finland, is available. Royal Copenhagen Danish china has long been known as a hard paste china of excellent quality. From Finland and from various centers around the Baltic comes good pottery which is hand-painted under a glaze in wares similar to the old Delft (Holland) pottery. Shapes and patterns are both traditional and modern and, as with so much northern design, are done with a light rather than a heavy hand.

The French firm of Haviland at Limoges in south-central France, produced some of the world's finest table china. Closed before World War I it was reestablished in the United States. Some of the old patterns are available although many new ones are made. The body of the ware is creamier and has a more lustrous glaze than the French Haviland had.

One center of European hand-made pottery is Vallauris. Here many Spanish and French artists such as Picasso and Chagall design for the modern market. Italian potteries are exporting heavy wares intended for garden and buffet meals. Their works are often marked with an individual touch, no two pieces being exactly alike. Some of the patterns are most delightful. Similar pottery of traditional provincial pattern comes from the French provinces.

English bone chinas of superior quality are available. Spode, Wedgwood, Royal Worcester, Royal Doulton, Minton, Coalport, and Royal Crown Derby are factories well known for several centuries for the excellence of their product. Spode and Wedgwood likewise make fine quality pottery. There are many other English potteries located in and around Staffordshire making good tableware. The shapes and applied designs of the British wares are largely traditional and frequently the patterns are delightful floral pieces or chaste classical designs. Quite recently some excellent modern designing has been done.

Ireland produces small amounts of a china of great translucency and of soft creamy color

---

[24] The former usually consists of incised linear patterns whereas in the latter the background is cut away around the pattern.

known as Beleek. Small wares such as tea sets are the only pieces available.

Japanese ceramics are exported. The Japanese ceramic tradition, like the Chinese, is in hard paste china. It is to be hoped that a combination of Oriental artistry with fine ware will create lovely ceramics in the future.

America's ceramic factories have gained much ground in the last seventy-five years. Lenox with its lustrous sheen and high translucency; Syracuse, one of our oldest fine chinas; American Haviland and Franciscan are but a few of the well known names. The Ohio china kilns have produced very good dinnerware of all types at reasonable prices for many years. Chinas and pottery are made in the Southern mountain areas. Many new California kilns are coming into existence making everything from gay colorful potteries to finer chinas.

e. CONSIDERATION OF CHOICE

What are the qualities in ceramics which make for excellence and for desirability for use? Practical considerations come first. Thus we note that pottery, although it is heavier than china, is more susceptible to chipping and to the crazing of the glaze. China is hard and it will shatter with a blow, but it will not chip easily. It can be subjected to great heat without harm because of the nature of its clay. Chinas are now made which will withstand intense oven heat. Underglaze decoration is usually more serviceable than overglaze decoration.

Grade for grade a china is more expensive than a pottery. However, a fine grade of pottery may cost more than a poor grade of china and may be a much more desirable product from all points of view.

We are most concerned with the aesthetic qualities of ceramics. Although in this chapter our topic is texture, we cannot forget that ceramics have shape which is important to the real artist potter. First he must consider the usefulness of this shape. Will a pitcher hold liquids, be easy to clean and to pour from? Contemporary pieces are lower and broader so that they will not tip. Surfaces must be smooth for easy cleaning. Plates are frequently without an inner rim so that there is greater surface for serving.

Aesthetically minded, we notice certain things about the inner space of a vessel in relation to its volume and the walls which enclose it. Is this space beautifully designed with just that amount of variety in its concavity which will make it interesting and not enough to ruin its unity of form or its usefulness?

The walls of clay vessels may be of various thicknesses. Pottery is normally thicker than porcelain. If we observe closely we will note that just as an interesting line varies in its thickness in an orderly fashion, so do the walls of some of the most exquisite ceramics vary. To observe this is a source of aesthetic pleasure. Interrelations between space enclosed and wall thickness are often carefully adjusted by the artist.

Color in ceramics can be one of its greatest sources of appeal. In order to secure beautiful color for our enjoyment the potter has need for much knowledge and skill. Ceramic colors may change with kiln temperatures. For instance, a copper salt which at one temperature will produce a blue color will turn to green at another. Many colors, including gold, cannot be fired at the heat of the china kiln and must be added after the first firing. Ceramics are both translucent and reflective media and their color therefore varies with the nature of the ware. In the exquisite china from the Orient, color may be reflected and refracted through several glazes. A piece of Ch'ing dynasty porcelain with a "peach bloom" glaze is considered by many to be the pinnacle achieved in color in relation to the ceramist's art.

Texture likewise contributes much to the aesthetic pleasure derived from ceramics. China responds to touch with the coolness and smoothness of quartz and the crispness of flint. Stoneware has a touch which is more like granite. Pottery glazes possess their characteristic tactile qualities.

When china became forgetful of its own values and became loaded with too much pattern and with heavy overglazes, modern potters turned away from porcelain to the down-to-earth beauty of the potter's clay. Having rediscovered its sensuous appeal, they are turning to stoneware and even porcelain for contemporary accessories.

Pattern on contemporary ceramics should be like the quality of good decorative design of all time. It supports and contributes to the beauty of an artistic contemporary shape.

5. Glass

a. COMPOSITION TYPES

Glass is another remarkable invention of man. The principal ingredient of glass is sand as a source of silica. Various alkalies, usually a combination of two or more of the following—soda, potash, lime, lead, or aluminum, are added as modifiers and act as flux. Specialized ingredients impart other desirable qualities. Glass is heated before forming. In its molten state it is referred to as the metal.

Glass is customarily classified as one of three compositional types depending upon which alkalies are predominant. The commonest glass is frequently called soda or potash glass. Where color impurities remain this is sometimes known as green glass. It does not possess great clarity, weight, or resonance. Its uses are many with a range dependent upon its refinement.

An increase in the amount of calcium in the formula results in a clearer glass which is sometimes known as lime glass. When lead oxide is added to the batch, the glass becomes heavier, more resonant, and has greater ability to refract light (sparkle). It is of a desirable softness to engrave or cut and of plasticity to form. Lead glass is sometimes called flint glass, flint being a vary hard glass-like form of quartz. Fine lead and lime glass are both currently known as crystal.[25]

b. FORMING

What the potter's wheel is to ceramics, the blowpipe is to glass. The shaped glass resulting from use of the blowpipe is said to be blown or off-hand glass. This latter term implies that the glass has come from a hand rather than a

[25] G. S. and H. McKearin, *American Glass* (New York: Crown Publishers, 1944), p. 7; J. C. Harrington, *Glassmaking at Jamestown* (Richmond, Va.: The Dietz Press, Inc., 1952), p. 47; F. V. Tooley (ed.), *Handbook of Glass Manufacture* (New York: Ogden Publishing Company, 1953), p. 455.

mechanized process. Every child knows that the soap bubbles which he blows have a spherical shape. So to the glass blower the spherical shape is basic. As the glass cools or anneals, the craftsman may further elongate or flatten this shape, he may give it a flanged or a depressed edge.

Glass called blown-molded is likewise shaped by being blown into a mold. The mold may be of one or several parts. The latter type may leave a slight imprint on the glass along the line where the parts of the mold are hinged. One method of classifying blown-molded glass is through the number of these marks and the glass may be correspondingly known as two or three mold.

A quicker and less expensive method of forming glass is by pressing. In this process the glass is poured into a mold which makes the outer surface. The inner surface is made by a plunger which presses down into the first mold.

A newly reestablished method for forming glass is called the plastic glass process. Bits of broken glass are fired in a refractory fireclay mold. The glass fuses perfectly and after cooling is removed from the mold. This method is usually reserved for solid pieces and for large bas reliefs.

Each of these forming techniques is best suited to a particular type of metal. Whenever artisans understood this relationship the finest styles in the art of glass resulted.

c. EMBELLISHMENT

Something may be done to glass at every stage of its manufacture with the intention of making it more attractive. Color may be added to the batch and, as with glazes, quite different colors may emerge from the furnace. A small amount of gold and tin in the batch created the famous ruby color of the old Bohemian red glass. Irridescent color, such as characterized the Tiffany glass of the late nineteenth century, was the result of added body color. Milkglass contains an opaque white colorant. Much of the color of early American glass was the result of impurities in the metal.

Glasses of different colors may be combined in distinct patterns. Sometimes one color glass will be contained within another. It is always intriguing to see threads of white glass within

(A) **Article:** "The Catch," Glass vase. **Artist:** Clare Leighton. **Manufacturer:** Steuben Glass, Corning, New York. **Photographer:** Herbert Smit.

(B) **Article:** "St. Francis and the Birds," Glass vase. **Artist:** Vicke Lindstrand. **Manufacturer:** A. B. Orrefors Glasbruk; Orrefors, Sweden. **Photograph:** Courtesy Potter and Mellen, Inc., Cleveland, Ohio. **Courtesy:** Fisher, Bruce and Company, Philadelphia, Pennsylvania.

(C) **Article:** Glass vases with black orbit lines. **Artist:** Vicke Lindstrand. **Manufacturer:** The Kosta Crystal Works, Sweden. **Photograph:** Courtesy Potter and Mellen, Inc., Cleveland, Ohio. **Courtesy:** Ebeling and Reuss Company, Philadelphia, Pennsylvania.

(D) **Article:** Glass bowl. **Artist:** Tappio Wirkkala. **Manufacturer:** Karhula-Iittala, Finland. **Owner:** The Museum of Modern Art, New York, Phyllis B. Lambert Fund. **Photographer:** The Museum of Modern Art, New York.

a form of colorless glass or to see a tear drop or a series of bubbles snugly ensconced within the stem of a goblet. Occasionally the container and the contained shape may be of the same color but their different thicknesses and separate walls make them appear to be different tones. The secret of accomplishing these glasses within glasses is the same as that used by a cook in making a marble cake. It is to keep the layers separate until they are set. As glass is more viscous than cake dough, this is not difficult. Some examples of this type of work are merely a tour de force. Others are genuinely artistic and create an aspect of fantasy.

Color in the form of enamels or of colored glass may be added to the finished glass product. Gold and silver and other metals may be encrusted on the surface for added enrichment.

Much decoration on glass is sculptural in the sense that it affects the plane of the glass surface. Molded and pressed glass may be of this nature. Sand blasting of glass produces a sculptured effect with the broadest strokes. This is done by preparing a shield for the parts of the glass which are to be protected and by cutting away the unprotected portions with a blast of sand.

Etched glass is acid-eaten. The entire glass is covered with a resist through which a design is cut. Then the glass is immersed in an acid which cuts deeper into the design. The resist is then removed. Both in sandblasting and in etching the background is sometimes the part which is cut away leaving the glass design intact. Cameo glass where the design is in one color glass and the background of another, may be made in this manner.

Figure 90. This group of outstanding glass pieces was selected because each piece of superb crystal illustrates the relation between the fluidity of the medium and that of the finished shape. The copper wheel engraved designs of "The Catch" and "St. Francis and the Birds" emphasize the respective rhythms of the structural shapes. The black orbit lines on the pair of vases serve a similar purpose. It is especially noteworthy that the body of the glass varies in thickness, thereby creating different depth refractions and beautiful edge lines.

Cut or engraved glass is actually cut deeply or engraved shallowly with stone and copper wheels respectively, revolving at great speed. Both cutting and engraving require the utmost skill on the part of the craftsman.

As in glass forming, the greatest artistry results when the embellishment of glass is suited to its composition and method of forming.

d. CONTEMPORARY FACTORIES

Glass is a plastic which this century has produced in abundance and with merit. The Italians have followed one Venetian tradition of blowing glass into interesting plastic shapes. All Italian glass is apt to be called Venetian on today's market. Likewise all central European glass may find itself labeled Bohemian. This latter glass probably comes from either Austria or Bavaria today and is remarkably clear glass, frequently cut or engraved.

France has made signal contributions to the contemporary glass market. The Daum Cristallerie, in addition to other types, creates a crystal which is not blown into shape but which is pulled and molded like warm taffy. The result of this handling is glassware in lovely forms each varying slightly from the other. The designs are fluid and essentially French in character. The Baccarat factory (Cie des Cristallerie de Baccarat) is likewise in the eastern part of France near Nancy. Baccarat glass is often without added decoration, depending upon the purity of the crystal for its effect.

The Leerdam (NV Koninklijke Nederlansche Glasfabriek) factory in Holland and the Belgian firm, Val Saint Lambert, produce fine glassware. The Eda Glass Works, the Kosta (A. B. Kosta Glasbruk) factory, and the well known Orrefors (A. B. Orrefors Glasbruk) factory in Sweden manufacture contemporary glasswares. Karhula (Karhula-Iittala Glassworks) and Nötsjo (A. B. Nötsjo Glasbruk) glass come from Finland and have exceptional clarity. Holmegaards (Holmegaards Glasvaerk) glass is Danish and Hadelands (Hadelands Glasverk) is Norwegian.

The English today make much fine lead glass as they have since the seventeenth century. They are scientists in the art of glass cutting and know just where to cut in order to gain the greatest brilliance from the refracted light. They make very fine table glass which is frequently in the eighteenth century design tradition.

America is producing much of its own glass. For perfect off-hand lead glass none can excel Steuben glass made at the Steuben Division of the Corning Glassworks, Corning, New York. The shapes are contemporary and adhere closely to spherical derivations. Many of the pieces are unornamented and some have well designed engraving.

The center of the American glass industry is in Ohio, western Pennsylvania, and West Virginia. Here in numerous factories, such as the Westmoreland Glass Company, the Fostoria Company, the Libby Glass Company, the Tiffin Glass Masters, and the Blenko Glass Company, fine table glass of all types is made. The lovely colored ware of Blenko is noteworthy. The designs of these factories have begun to develop along contemporary lines. Large structural glass is likewise manufactured by the Libby-Owens-Ford Company and the Pittsburgh Plate Glass Company.[26]

e. CONSIDERATION OF CHOICE

Durability of glass is a functional consideration. Any incising of the surface should be examined to see that the remaining glass is not too thin for use. The glass composition affects its fracture but there are no general rules which can be given for this consideration. A hard glass may nick but it can be ground smooth again. Shapes should receive the same practical consideration as was indicated for ceramic shapes.

In judging the shapes of glass it would seem that rhythm between the masses should be especially important. Glass is a plastic and we should sense the flowing quality in its finished form. As glass is blown, the curved forms coming from the bubble shape seem most appropriate, although other shapes are possible.

Flawless glass needs no adornment. When it is patterned the greatest restraint is necessary in order to enhance rather than to detract from the body of the glass itself. Cutting should be restrained and where it is deep it should be planned to aid the natural ability of glass to refract light.

On the other hand the vagrant bubbles, the natural color, and the less than perfect shapes of some glass, such as Mexican, has its own appeal.

Color can at times add to the enjoyment of even the finest glass. In fine heavy colored glass the beauty of a dichroic or two-tone effect is possible when the vessel walls vary in thickness.

Texture of glass is an indescribable thing, perhaps more appreciated through touch than through sight. The heavy thin edge of lead crystal has a different feel from the edges of other glasses. The surface of bottle and of soda glass actually feels waxy.

6. Silver and Other Metals

The metals are of great functional and decorative use in furnishing. Silver is one of the soft metals which has been in demand for artifacts as well as for coinage since early times. Its use as coinage gave it an established value and its durability and beauty gave it an intrinsic value.

a. SILVER COMPOSITION

Silver must be alloyed or combined with a harder metal to make it strong. One of the first indications of law and order in any land is the enforcement of a standard percentage of silver to alloy which is permitted for coinage. This is known as the coinage standard. Silversmiths would not exceed the coinage standard although they might fall short of it. Coinage standard is expressed as eighteen dwt. (or eighteen pennyweights) of alloy to eleven oz. two dwt. of pure silver. This is Troy weight which is standard for measuring precious metals. Twenty pennyweights equal one ounce (oz.) and twelve ounces equal one pound (lb.) Troy weight. Ever since 1856 American silver of coinage standard has been labeled sterling. Sterling silver is said to be 925/1000 pure which, if your mathematics is good, can be figured from the above. The term solid silver means that the piece is of sterling silver throughout.

---

[26] Plate glass is the name given to glass formed in large sheets by pouring onto a metal table and flattening with a metal roller.

Article: Group of silver pieces. **Artist:** Frederick A. Miller, Cleveland, Ohio. **Photographer:** The Cleveland Museum of Art, Cleveland, Ohio.

Figure 91. A group of contemporary silver pieces which illustrates well the tenets of excellent design in this medium.

Plated silver is the name given to silver applied through electroplating silver onto a harder metal by means of electrolytic action. The base metal is usually an alloy of copper, zinc, and nickel. In the plating process bars of pure silver (the anodes) are placed in solution in tanks with pieces of the base metal (the cathodes). By the use of an electric current molecules of the pure silver are deposited on the base metal. The duration and strength of the current determines the thickness of the silver deposited. The purchaser should be assured of a plate which is sufficiently thick for the use intended. Some silver plated objects have inlaid blocks of solid sterling silver at the points which receive hardest wear. Plated silver of comparable size is always heavier than sterling silver. It frequently bears, along with the maker's name, some kind of indication of the quality of the plating.

Some silver is combined with gold in tableware. The fineness of gold is expressed in carats which is likewise a unit of weight for precious metals. One carat signifies a twenty-fourth part of a grain [27] and therefore fourteen carat gold means that the metal has fourteen parts gold to ten parts of baser metal. Alloys of metals other than gold and having the color of gold are made into tableware.[28] They are attractive and durable.

b. SILVER FORMING

Much of silver manufacture is still a hand process and methods are centuries old. Silver ingots are rolled into sheets of various thicknesses or gauges depending upon the article to be made. From this a blank of the article is cut. This blank is then further rolled so that the silver is formed into varying thicknesses depending upon where the greatest strength is needed. From the blank a rough pattern of the article is cut much as a cooky cutter would cut dough. It is then pressed between an upper and lower die or hammered over a form to give it its pattern of convexity or concavity. Finally it is smoothed up and given a buffed finish. All of these processes have been somewhat mechanized today.

c. CONTEMPORARY SILVER

There are a number of firms in America which have been manufacturing sterling for over a hundred years. The center of this craft is in New England and upper New York, localities which produced our famous Colonial silver-

[27] The grain, which is equivalent to .0648 gram, is common to all tables of weight.

[28] Dirilyte is the trade-name of one such product.

smiths. Some of the well known firm names are Gorham, Lunt, Reed and Barton, Alvin, Towle, Wallace, Heirloom, and Oneida, and there are a number of others. Each company produces a number of designs some of which are traditional in inspiration and some contemporary.

Silver is exported from Norway, Sweden and Denmark as well as from France. This silver is heavy in weight. The designs of the northern silver are typical of a long heritage of silver design. A characteristic is a large area of plain surface with pattern concentrated in one area. French silver likewise follows its tradition which leans toward more ornate patterns.

d. CONSIDERATION OF CHOICE OF SILVERWARE

If sterling silver is all of one quality and if the quality of plated ware is reasonably assured, what then are criteria for silver choice? In the first place there is a practical appraisement. There may be difference in the weight of pieces even within the production of one company and of one pattern. Heavy silver will cost more than light silver. The weight selected should be practical and appropriate to its use.

Functional standards should be closely observed. Most silver is made for use. Table silver pieces are tools. When buying a table knife analyze it as a cutting and spreading tool; a fork as a skewer, pusher, and sometimes a cutter; a spoon as a scoop, stirrer, and partial cutter. Examine the shape of these pieces to see if they can perform these tasks well. Take them in your hand and see how they feel. Are the weight and balance of the instrument right? Is the handle shaped to suit the hand grip? Table silver is going to be used for many years. It would be wise if the masculine eye with its focus on functionalism could be consulted in the valuation of such an important purchase.

Silver is good to possess because of its associational value. It is well to be on guard, however, lest a glamorous historical name which has inspired a silver pattern, blind us to the intrinsic merit of the design. Neither should family pride,

associated with the possession of valuables such as silver, become inordinately important.

The visual design of silver is very important. The three-dimensional shape of a piece of silver is part of its pattern. Silver should be beautiful from whatever angle it is viewed. However we see the top surface of table silver most clearly. Therefore it should be particularly lovely as seen from this angle.

The texture of silver is important. Silver has a porous but very fine texture. It can be given a very high or low polish. As any highly reflective surface blanks out the apparent texture of an object, contemporary silver is frequently given a satin rather than a high gloss finish. This satiny patina comes to old silver with use and is another argument in favor of constant use of household silver. If properly cared for the patina of silver should grow more lovely with age. Many feel that ornate silver becomes too darkly oxidized with use. Ornate patterns are usually designed with the idea that silver oxidation in the shadows contributes to a more interesting surface.

e. OTHER METALS

Interiors are enriched by many other metals. These are so numerous and various as often to cause textural incompatibles to be grouped together. Therefore a study of the textural character of the various metals is important.

Iron is abundantly used for interior work. Iron is characterized by a coarse compact structure, a rough cold surface and considerable weight. Its surface is dull and in its most common form is black. Cast iron is the coarsest variety and is usually restricted in use to fireplace accessories. Wrought iron contains less carbon than cast iron and, being less brittle, it can be made into many shapes. Its textural character is a little finer than cast iron. Its present day use as furniture or as parts of furniture seems most appropriate to woods of the medium fine category. Wrought iron can be burnished to a satin finish and in this form is used for ornamental grilles, rails, lighting fixtures, and hardware.

Steel is a variety of iron which is finer grained

and can be given a higher polish. When chromium is combined with steel an alloy can be made which will not tarnish. Stainless steel is made into various pieces of tableware for the modern household.

There are two reasons that steel must be used carefully in any ensemble. In the first place the light reflected from burnished steel seems too intense and specular to group it with any wood where the light comes from large deep pores or with woods which have a too similar high reflection and fine grain. Steel ensembles well with woods of medium grain and natural finish and with firm sturdy cloths and with leather. Steel has a bluish grey cast, "cold as steel." It must therefore be combined cautiously with warm hued furniture woods. A matte finish on steel often makes it congruous in settings where it would otherwise be unsuitable.

Aluminum is a comparative newcomer to the decorating field. Its important qualities of very great lightness coupled with soft metallic luster make it very desirable. It is cast into furniture and is extensively used in lighting fixtures and tableware. It can be integrally colored or enameled in lovely tones. Used with discrimination it makes a pleasing contrast with wood graining.

Among the softer metals, copper, pewter (a combination of tin and lead), bronze (a combination of tin and copper), and brass, (a combination of zinc and copper) are used. Copper and brass can be given a high metallic sheen but are often used in satin finish. Copper, bronze, and brass are all used in contemporary lighting fixtures. Pewter was the metal which was originally used for table utensils which were less expensive than silver. Its soft grey glow and fine porous surface is fashioned into lovely contemporary objects. Holland is exporting beautiful pewter. Contemporary metals are often lacquered to prevent tarnishing. This finish may be a source of high reflection. Because these metals appear in a variety of forms and textures and even of colors it is important in using them to see that the objects made from them have suitable shape pattern and surface treatment to make them harmonious for a particular grouping.

7. Stone

Stones, in natural form or in the form of glazed clay tiles, are reappearing as decorative media. Mosaics of stones or tiles afford an opportunity for interesting color and texture patterns. Marble is again used for table tops and for interior finishes where its beautiful coloring is lovely.

8. The Plastics

Plastics are becoming increasingly important in modern decoration. In a broad sense a plastic is any material or group of materials which can be formed in one physical state and then can be processed so as to give permanency to that form. Defined thus, plastics are not new. Glass and pottery are plastics. Rayon and nylon are plastics.

The term plastic is used now in a more restricted sense to apply to a group of synthetics which have plasticity in one state and rigidity in another. Many plastics are chemically similar to the man-made fibers but are utilized in different physical form. They are sometimes used as finishes to make fabrics water and stain resistant, to make metals tarnishproof or to give wood a permanent finish. Sometimes they are used in unseen ways as when they bond the strips of laminated wood or make soft wood hard by impregnation. Plastic curtaining, plastic flooring, plastic table tops, plastic upholstery, plastic dishes—the uses of plastics are legion.

The practical advantages of these new materials are so outstanding that they have invaded the furnishing field. A careful estimate of their textural quality is necessary in order to give them artistic affiliations. Plastics are not resonant as are the metals. They are relatively smooth and generally lustrous. If they are accompanied by materials which repeat their compact and glossy nature, there would seem to be need for some hard metals and for some deep soft materials of a resilient character. Open meshed materials if they are firm, break up light in a manner which provides a foil for the more constant reflections from the plastics. Thus fine bamboo curtains or strong nylon nets seem suitable.

Not once beat 'Praise be thine!
I see the whole design,
I who saw power, see now love perfect too:
Perfect I call thy plan:
Thanks that I was a man!
Maker, remake, complete,—I trust what
thou shalt do!'

ROBERT BROWNING *

Chapter X

TOTAL DESIGN AND CONCRETE DESIGN PROBLEMS

A. REVIEW

In the preceding chapters we have studied shapes, colors, and textures. Each of these components creates a minor plot in the total design. These parts must cooperate to form a whole.

Notice how our design outline is affected by this interweaving.[1]

1. *Decide* on the general *effects* desired.
   —some colors are harsh in a shiny texture, pleasant in a soft texture.
   —some textures seem functional in one color, impractical in another.
2. *Choose* the principal shape, color, and texture *qualities* to gain effects.
   —these must support one another—a curved line and pink may both suggest femininity; the

---

[1] The examples following are merely suggestive of many other similar cases.

* From "Rabbi Ben Ezra" by Robert Browning. Reprinted from the **Complete Poetic and Dramatic Works of Robert Browning** by permission of Houghton Mifflin Company.

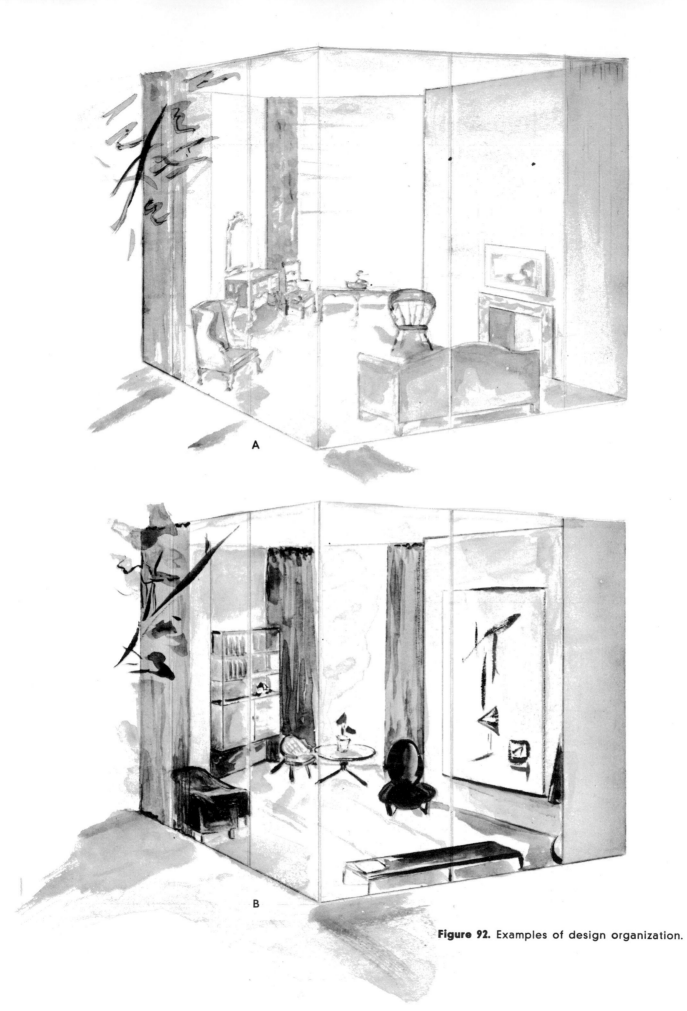

Figure 92. Examples of design organization.

combination of some bold curves with pink may prove inharmonious.

3. *Consider the development* of these basic qualities for purpose of *intensification.*

a. Which are to be most emphasized?

A contemporary house in a natural setting might curb color development in the interest of texture—an old, nondescript city building could play up color—a great architectural conception might emphasize shapes —rarely will all three be prima donnas.

b. How is the enhancement of a quality to be accomplished?

1) Through its original importance (using a large amount of the quality either in one or repeating units)?

—a stone fireplace wall speaks of natural textures in no uncertain terms. A dominance of quite natural colors makes the textures more noticeable.

2) Through an importance gained by a variety of expressions of the quality?

—straight line planes become dramatic when horizontal, vertical, and even diagonal directions are counterposed. Color can aid this drama.

3) Through an importance gained by contrasting the quality with quite different qualities?

—a Baroque three-dimensional curved frame can be a foil to a straight line flat designed painting. It can correspond in color to other notes in the room.

4. Plan *the arrangement* (alignment of forces) of the various visual themes (larger groupings) to create desired movement and rest.

a. Simple activity.

—a curved line may call attention in one direction while a flash of red may pull in another.

b. Directed movement or rhythm.

—grey colors to gay shapes with bright colors may create background to foreground interest.

—compactly arranged furniture groups may be further integrated through repetitive color.

—climaxes to centers of interest may be built up in one direction through progres-

sions of color, in another through shapes— interesting tensions are thus set up which make the ultimate resolutions more vital.

c. Choices of various alignments through interlockings (complexity of design).

—a piece of furniture may figure in a straight line theme, a blue color theme, and in a texture progression, sending the attention wandering down any of these quality paths.

d. Rest or stability (equalizing forces and tensions around a visual center or axis).

—a dark wall may balance an expanse of nature seen through a large window.

5. Resulting integration—a unity of coordinated forces.

B. TWO EXAMPLES OF DESIGN ORGANIZATION

The architecture in both rooms shown in Figure 92 is the same and is contemporary. Room *A* has traditional furniture, room *B* modern. The atmosphere of *A* is mellow; the feeling in *B* more forceful and there is no breaking ranks with an assured new world.

QUALITIES AND THEIR DEVELOPMENT

I. Shape

Room A. Active shapes very important. Graceful curve dominant.

Room B. Relation of active shapes to background shapes important.
Straight line dominant. Strong curves for contrast.

II. Color

A. Small intervals. Quiet tones.

B. Large intervals emphasizing lightness contrasts.

III. Texture

A. Small intervals. Medium weight. Luster of fruitwood dominant, accompanied by that of linen, pewter. Softness in carpet.

B. Large intervals. Medium weight. Dullness of wood, metal, and upholstery. Sleekness of slate. Concentrated depth and resiliency in rug.

IV. Alignment
   Background to foreground movement.
   A. Subdued background. Shape activity
      in foreground.
   B. More active background because of
      shape placement.
   Lateral movement to centers of interest.
   A. Through active shape, color, texture
      rhythms.
   B. Through space relations, tone rhythms.
   Choices.
   A. Color interlocking with various shapes
      and textures.
   B. Dark tones an interlocking force.
   Stability.
   A. Established by equality of tensions
      around a central axis.
   B. Established around axes crossing at
      acute angles.

Each room is well designed from the standpoint of presenting a unified whole which enhances the effect of the chosen qualities in an interesting way.

C. CONCRETE PROBLEMS

The following emphasis upon concrete design problems presupposes a thought for the part which each plays in an enlarged scheme.

1. Floor Treatment

Problem 1. Extent of covering. Should it extend over the entire floor or a portion of it?

Room is enlarged by uniform wall to wall treatment or by coordination of floor covering with room shape. On the other hand, space is contracted if pattern is prominent or texture is shaggy. Smooth texture of plain wood or tile floors may contribute to space illusion.

Problem 2. Plain or patterned floor coverings. Which should be chosen?

Absence of pattern enlarges space. Plain covering aids designing in planes. However, pattern relieves monotony of much space. Accent rugs may be centers of interest. Floor pattern may balance wall pattern or texture. Pattern can be practical in concealing uneven floors and in

places subject to wear and soil. Most historic coverings have pattern.

Problem 3. Choice of pattern. What are the considerations?

Floor patterns should first be good design by all standards. Specifically, a floor pattern, because it is to be walked upon, should be nondirectional, stylized, flat pattern.[2] Pattern and background should be similar in tone to avoid too much forward or backward movement. In special cases such as in the use of Oriental prayer rugs, directional patterns can be appropriate for directed emphasis. Accent rugs may be regarded as a floor picture and may have insistent pattern.

Problem 4. Color. What color should be placed on the floor?

This question was analyzed in Chapters VII and VIII.

Problem 5. Texture. What are the considerations?

A relatively close even texture will increase the effect of space. Advancing and receding movement will be created in carpets of various depths of pile. This should be related to the overall room movement. High and low pile floor coverings should be compact in order to avoid destruction of the high pile. Softness is desirable underfoot but cushioning which is too soft and springy may be difficult to walk upon.

2. Wall Treatments

Problem 1. Plain or patterned wall covering. Which should be chosen?

Unpatterned walls enlarge space. They keep the wall plane intact. They are the appropriate choice where pictures are to be hung. On the other hand, a room with prominent architectural features (such as panelling to a dado) may

[2] For explanation of terms, see wall treatments on the pages following.

Figure 93. In this contemporary home a Moroccan deep pile rug provides just the right amount of pattern interest to balance the attention factors of books and art objects.

Residence of: Mr. and Mrs. Irving Richards. **Interior Designer:** George Nelson and Company, Inc., New York. **Photographer:** Scott Hyde, New York. Reprinted by permission of **Progressive Architecture.**

Building: Early 19th century dining room, Mansion House-Museum, Oglebay Park, Wheeling, West Virginia. **Photograph:** Courtesy Oglebay Institute Oglebay Park, Wheeling, West Virginia. **Photographer:** G. Colburn Ball, Cleveland, Ohio.

need pattern on the plain surfaces for balance. A room with irregular wall areas (such as a recess) may have pattern used for disguise or, conversely, to set the irregularities apart. Pattern may camouflage poor walls. Pattern may be necessary to balance a busy floor. Mural decoration may be an interesting substitute for a movable picture or screen.

Problem 2. Choice of pattern. What are the considerations?

Wall pattern must be good design by all standards. Because a large mural pattern is constantly in view it is important that its design possess a degree of complexity, so that the eye may find several paths along which to travel. However, the pattern should not be as intricate as that of a painting because it would present too much busy work for the attention.

A good mural design should likewise contain rest positions. These are especially necessary because a wall design is usually repetitious. Without these quiet centers a wall becomes disturbingly restless.

Some persons make the mistake of thinking that a wall pattern should always be inconspicuous. The degree of insistence of the pattern is dependent upon its function in the total design and bears no relation to its intrinsic merit. Inasmuch as many wall patterns can be bought in papers in several different color combinations, it is often a good practice to examine a particular design in its most contrasting color relationship. If it stands up as a good design under this kind of examination, then it can safely be used in the tones which would give just the right amount of emphasis for a particular area.

In general wall patterns should be scaled to the size of the space. However, this is not a blanket rule. In the first place a pattern which is too diminutive, especially if it is a design which would be better suited to a larger scale, may merely appear trivial. Again the compressed size

Figure 94. A scenic wallpaper designed with depth of space seems the right accent to use in this early nineteenth century dining room. The delicate yet prominent architectural features are enhanced by this treatment and the lovely portrait is not eclipsed by its surroundings.

of a pattern may result in an exaggerated and quick movement which will make the room seem smaller than a larger pattern with more restrained movement would. Other factors such as the pattern design quality, insistence, and flatness will modify its scale potential.

The flatness of a pattern relates to its treatment of depth. First there are the flat designs in which there is no three-dimensional modeling. Most linear designs fall into this category although area designs may also be flat. These designs hold their positions in a wall plane in the tradition of much mural painting. They fit in best in the treatment of any wall as a plane because they hold their place in the plane. Since they do not advance noticeably from the wall surface they can be used to great advantage in a small room. A flat design can be larger in scale without reducing apparent room size.

Many designs have three-dimensional modeling on a flat background. Here the design stands out in solid form from its background. Thus it is best used in a space which can stand some reduction in size.

Lastly the depth treatment in a design may be one which utilizes all the known laws of perspective to create the illusion of recession in space. Here the background recedes into distance. This kind of design may be used effectively to enlarge space. One must be very careful, however, that the force of pattern activity on a wall does not bring it forward more than the perspective vista pushes it out.

Closely related to a consideration of depth treatment in wall patterning is the study of the degree of stylization in the pattern. A highly realistic pattern is one in which an illusion of reality is accomplished by the use of many devices known to the painter. He duplicates the colors that appear in nature; he depicts the lights and darks so as to simulate the three-dimensional modeling of nature; he makes use of linear perspective to reproduce the natural positioning of objects in space. From this illusion of reality the artist designer may depart as far as he wishes.

A pattern which deviates from nature but which uses a natural subject as its point of departure is frequently called a stylized pattern. The artist does not alter nature merely for the

(A) **Article:** "Glass Candelabra," wallpaper. **Designer:** John R. Denst. **Manufacturer:** Denst and Soderlund, Chicago, Illinois. **Photographer:** Kranzten Studio, Evanston, Illinois.

(B) **Article:** "When in Rome," wallpaper. **Designer:** Clarence Hawking. **Manufacturer:** Denst and Soderlund, Chicago, Illinois.

(C) **Article:** "Clouds," wallpaper. **Designer:** Donald K. Soderlund. **Manufacturer:** Denst and Soderlund, Chicago, Illinois.

(D) **Article:** "The Common," wallpaper. **Designer:** John R. Denst. **Manufacturer:** Denst and Soderlund, Chicago, Illinois.

sake of being different. He alters nature because he wishes to create more developed design relationships.

When a pattern deviates quite markedly from nature to the extent that nature becomes merely an inspiration for the design, it is frequently called an abstract design, meaning that it has been abstracted from reality. A step further on this path away from realism would be a nonobjective or nonrepresentational design where no reference to any natural object can be observed. Because there is a kind of relation between this kind of design and the scientific character of today's world, nonobjective design seems appropriate to modern buildings.

There are other ways to depart from nature in making a design. Realistic motifs can be arranged into a larger designed composition. Here it is the arrangement which deviates from reality. Represented objects may be altered in scale, some large, some small. They may be changed in position, some upright, some upside down. They may be unrealistically colored or textured. They may be enclosed within a designed frame.

The type of reality produced and enjoyed in art is closely related to the culture (including the technical processes) of a people. For instance, folk pattern is liable to be composed of many somewhat unrelated motifs each individually stylized. It resembles children's art in this respect. Early American wallpaper pattern, although it stems from European work, is influenced by the simple stencil and block processes used, which did not lend themselves easily to the

C D

Figure 95. Each of these three wallpaper designs shows a different treatment of depth.

A. Flat design where the wall plane is unbroken.

B. Modeled design where objects show the shading which light gives their contours.

C. Vista where the horizon recedes in space.

D. The last wallpaper design illustrates the interest which is obtained through complexity. This mural can be viewed as a combination of dark trees, a grouping of shadow foliage, or an assemblage of light buildings. Common pattern qualities unite these various objects. Spatial rest positions occur in the low lying areas.

nuances of realistic portrayal. The most characteristic contemporary design, for all of its abstraction, is marked by a strong rhythm. More conventional or formal period designs are frequently marked by bisymmetry or by enclosure within a restricting framework.

Several suggestions seem to come from these observations about design types. There is no direct correlation between a type of design and its intrinsic excellence. The character of the design should be chosen with great sensitivity to the character of the room and its occupants. In a group of closely associated spaces there is greater unity when one type of design character predominates.

In general the character of a wall is best preserved by a flat design which is at least stylized to the degree which is necessary to support the room structure. There may be times for deviation from this. If the planes are complicated, as in slanting ceilings and dormer niches, the wall designs may have to be nondirectional. If the architectural treatment has a provincial air then disconnected patterning may be in character.

Problem 3. Color. What colors should be placed on the walls?

This question was considered in Chapters VII and VIII.

Problem 4. Texture. What are the considerations?

Smooth matte textures will increase apparent size. Highly reflective textures may cause brightness glare. Imitative textures used on walls are a matter of taste. Natural textures such as wood veneer and grass cloth, seem appropriate for architecture which is closely related to natural settings. Three-dimensional textures present some cleaning problems.

3. Window Treatments

Window treatment is a major problem. Windows are functional[3] as well as decorative. Their utility and enjoyable qualities should be increased by proper handling. Hangings are for the purpose of modifying the light, softening the window edge, or for added privacy.

Problem 1. How is the window treatment related to the room design?

a. When the window is a focal point:—visual forces should be arranged to carry the eye to the window. Then the consideration is one of relative emphasis. If the view from the window is desirable, the window treatment should be unobtrusive. If there is only modest interest in the view, the decorative treatment should not obstruct vision outwards but it may be intrinsically more interesting. If the view is poor then it may be desirable to shut it out and concentrate interest on the window location. Questions of lighting must be carefully considered here.

b. When the window is not a focal point:— give it a treatment which will make it less forceful than other centers of interest. Similar considerations about the quality of the view enter here. Where the view is present of necessity then it must be considered as an attention factor and stronger interests should be placed elsewhere.

Problem 2. Plain or patterned window treatment. Which should be chosen?

Plain material, except when greatly contrasted with surroundings, is less emphatic. It may provide an opportunity for textural interest. It can provide an interesting play of light and shade through the relative compactness and openness of weave. It can provide a contemporary feeling of wall plane designing. Pattern, on the other hand, may provide interest. It can supplement room design. When helped by color it may unite a number of unrelated factors into one large pivotal detail.

[3] See Chap. VIII.

Problem 3. Choice of pattern. What are the considerations?

Pattern should be good design by all standards. If the window treatment is accomplished through a taut material, such as screens, then the principles of wall patterning are relevant. If the treatment introduces folds of textiles then the following considerations are very important. Pattern should be closely related to the texture and processes of production evident in the textile. Some textures will hang in stiff folds and so seem to require bolder linear patterns made by such processes as weaving or block printing. Some fabrics fall in soft folds and seem suited to fragile designs made possible through roller printing or photoengraving.

Pattern should be such that it will be effective when hanging. Its rhythms should be observed in this position. At a window where patterned draw curtains are used, the material must be considered in two positions—first when the curtains cover the window and again when the draperies are pulled open and are thus concentrated at the sides of the window. The conspicuousness of the pattern in these two situations should be carefully considered.

Textile patterns may be for the purpose of simulating texture or for the purpose of imposing a tapestry effect of color. Both of these kinds of pattern give the illusion of greater fabric weight.

Problem 4. Color. What colors should be placed at the windows?

This question was considered in Chapters VII and VIII.

Problem 5. Texture. What are the considerations?

That aspect of fabric texture which is commonly known as the hand or the handle is exceedingly important to the linear treatment of draperies. The fabric cannot be too sleazy or the weight of abundant folds will drag it down. If the fabric is intended to support a straight line theme it must have the backbone to do so. If it is intended to drape into soft curves it should have the necessary pliancy for the purpose.

Many a drapery treatment has been spoiled because there was not enough of the material used either in length or in fullness. Window treatment in cloth is designed to display the

(A) **Article:** Wood, Maternity Fetish, African, Bambala, XVIII Century. **Owner:** The Cleveland Museum of Art, purchased by the African Art Sponsors of Karamu House. **Photographer:** The Cleveland Museum of Art, Cleveland, Ohio.

(B) **Article:** "Coryell's Ferry, 1776," oil on canvas. **Artist:** Joseph Pickett (1848–1918). **Owner:** Collection of the Whitney Museum of American Art, New York.

(C) **Article:** Standing figure. **Artist:** Bernice Kussoy, Cleveland, Ohio. **Photographer:** The Cleveland Museum of Art, Cleveland, Ohio.

(D) **Article:** "Rumination," white marble. **Artist:** William M. McVey, Cleveland School. **Owner:** The Cleveland Museum of Art, Norman O. and Ella A. Stone Memorial.

A

C

B

D

Figure 96. Various degrees of reality are enjoyed in art. When exact representation is sacrificed it is usually because the artist is more interested in some other aspect of the subject. This is not only true in the case of the individual artist; it is frequently characteristic of an entire epoch or civilization.

A. Maternity fetish, African symbolic sculpture.

B. American so-called "primitive" painting.

C, D. Contemporary sculpture in metal and marble which closely relate stylization to the medium.

Residence: in Hawaii. **Photograph:** Courtesy **Honolulu Advertiser,** Pat Millard, Building Editor.

Figure 97. The window treatment should be unobtrusive when the view, such as this of the Pacific, is desirable. Here a ceiling track allows the textured gauze curtaining to be drawn when necessary.

sensuous character of the cloth—its texture and color as it relates to line. For this a liberal expanse is required.

Any textural play of opaque and translucent areas should be carefully considered both in taut and in loose treatments. If the purpose of a window covering is to modify the light, its patterning should not create blotchy shadows or attract undue attention.

In treatments using any variety of slat blinds, the textural relation between the body material and the draw tapes and cords is important. One designer is careful to see that the warp threads of lattice wood shades are of a soft nubby material. Plastic slats, on the other hand, would seem more related to a hard twisted cord.

Problem 6. Positioning of window coverings.

Contemporary windows have a minimum of architectural framing. The apron has virtually disappeared along with the elaborate entablatures of classically inspired periods. The customary precepts about how to hang shades and curtains must be modified to suit the new simplicity.

Glass curtains were originally planned to modify light and to aid privacy. Their original use dictated a simple treatment. They were gathered onto rods which were attached to the upper sash and they extended to the sill. Glass curtains today, however, are frequently related to the drapery treatment and derive their positioning from the latter.

Draperies are curtains which are hung at the side of the window for the purpose of softening the sharp edge of light made between the window and wall. Although draperies are frequently of an opaque material, the new treatment of combining drapery and glass curtaining in one fabric has led designers to create a number of translucent materials for this purpose. It is not intended that these be lined. The usual drapery material, however, looks better if it is lined. Some new drapery textiles are complex single weave cloths so designed as not to require lining. They should be handled as lined fabrics.

A lined drapery should be hung in firm pleats (French pleats are one variety) or it may be looped up onto a rod. It is usually too thick to be gathered on the rod. Unlined curtains of an informal character may be gathered. The use of a heading or fold of cloth above the rod casing, depends upon the character of the fabric and the position of the rod. Very soft fabrics may look better without a heading.

When the trim possesses an elaborate architectural character, the draperies may be hung entirely within the frame or they may be designed to cover only a portion of the trim. On most wood framed windows the rods are placed so that the top of the curtain will come to the top of the trim and so that the side framing will be covered. The rods may extend out onto the wall to convey an impression of added width. On windows which have a complete wood surround draperies should reach either to the bottom of the apron or to the floor. The latter length is preferable for formal treatments.

Many curtains today are hung from an inconspicuous track which is placed close to or on the ceiling. This positioning is frequently used even though the window itself does not have that height. The length of contemporary curtaining should be related to the character of the room design, the positioning of the upper rods, the fabric, and the window. Curtains usually extend to the sill, just below the sill, or to the floor.

Traverse or draw curtains are those which can be pulled back or drawn over a window. Such curtains were originally suspended behind draperies and were only pulled across the window for privacy. They were frequently made of a plain casement cloth. With the greater simplification of modern window treatment, the functions of drapery, traverse curtain, and glass curtaining are often combined in one hanging. If it is drawn by pulley cords it must be pleated or looped onto the traverse fixtures. If there is a great expanse of window to be covered, a pocket should be planned in the wall to take care of the voluminous material when the curtain is drawn back.

The simplification of window treatments has quite generally eliminated the use of valances. The purpose of a valance is to conceal the mechanism from which curtains are hung, to make an ornamental finish for the top of the window and to harbor light fixtures. It also shortens the apparent length of high windows. Valances may be designed as tailored coverings for a valance or cornice board (wooden frame) or they may be of elaborately draped material. The latter type are often called swags or lambrequins. They were traditionally used in many of the elaborate window treatments of the past. If valances are used today they should be carefully considered in relation to the rest of the window and room design. It would seem undesirable to design them of any shape, color, or texture which would call undue attention to the upper part of a room.

The process of simplification has likewise removed many other parts of window treatments such as curtain knobs, tie backs and floor hooks (placed in the floor to fasten curtains in place). All of these additions may be desirable for specific window treatments.

Curtains are frequently divided horizontally into two sections, thus creating what is frequently called a cottage or café curtain. This is a current modification of a very old device. It is a very useful scheme for it enables one to secure privacy without completely blocking out the upper light, or to modify the upper light without obstructing the lower view. Such curtains are usually of an informal character. Design-wise they do break a window height into two parts and are thus more visually busy.

The placement of shutters, roller shades, Venetian blinds, and screens must be dictated by the design of the window in relation to the room.

4. Upholstery

In furniture upholstery there is a very close relation between the basic object and added material. The piece of furniture has a shape and a color and a texture, each of which should harmonize with the chosen upholstery.

Problem 1. Choice of texture. What are the considerations which should influence our choice?

In a consideration of upholstery material, texture seems more important than pattern. In addition to the fundamental textural affinities of structure, apparent weight, and amount and depth of light reflection, the following textural qualities are especially important.

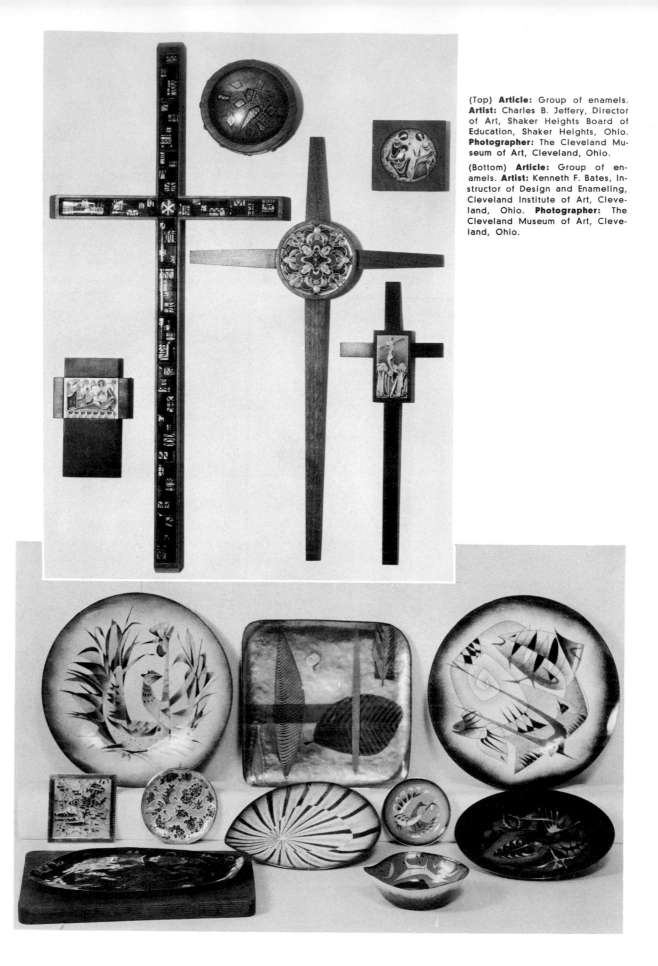

(Top) **Article:** Group of enamels. **Artist:** Charles B. Jeffery, Director of Art, Shaker Heights Board of Education, Shaker Heights, Ohio. **Photographer:** The Cleveland Museum of Art, Cleveland, Ohio.

(Bottom) **Article:** Group of enamels. **Artist:** Kenneth F. Bates, Instructor of Design and Enameling, Cleveland Institute of Art, Cleveland, Ohio. **Photographer:** The Cleveland Museum of Art, Cleveland, Ohio.

The compactness and precision of grain, the surface contour, and the changeable character of the light in materials influence upholstery selections. A trim, sleek frame requires a taut appearing fabric. It may possess a directional grain such as is found in a twill or a rep. Surface contour and light breakup should be relatively even so that there will not be too much activity in the reflections.

On the other hand a piece which is informal in shape and thick in its contours will require a firm material but one which does not possess a right or left directional character in its weave. A certain unevenness of contour is desirable for correspondence with the lack of definition in the frame. A firm plain weave fabric with nubby yarn may be suitable.

All chairs which are designed in three dimensions, meaning that their backs, seats, and arms deviate considerably from their respective planes, likewise require nondirectional weaves. The surface contour of the material is dependent upon the thinness and general attenuation in proportions of the furniture's structural members, as well as upon the amount and quickness of their curvature. A finely etched damask might be suitable for one wing chair and another would require a puffier matelassé. If the break up of light in any material causes quick visual motion, the material may prove too active and forceful for a small chair and too busy for a large one.

Problem 2. Pattern. What considerations?

The over-all precept in any consideration of upholstery pattern was covered in the discussions of shape design. Certain special pitfalls can be indicated.

In giving thought to scale, it is the scale of every part of the pattern which is important. Scale in relation to linear character should be noted. A fine line drawn with grace may be used on smaller chairs even though the complete fabric pattern is large in scale. A pattern with a

Figure 98. Two outstanding groups of enamels of religious and secular nature indicate the fine artistry which is available for accessories in an interior.

quick nervous line movement may prove more forceful than a larger pattern with more poise. A large scale chair may require a pattern which is composed of area rather than linear relations.

The arrangement of the patterning is also an important consideration. As in wall patterning, a compact, compartmental pattern is more formal than one which bursts its bounds. If such a compact pattern is small in relation to texture scale it is liable to suggest a conventional, even a smug kind of character. Thus a small chair of provincial feeling would look right in a neat diamond patterned armure. A large formal Chippendale cabriole leg chair might require a bisymmetrical formalized pattern where an informal Queen Anne chair of similar curvature would look better with a sprawling pattern.

Problem 3. Color. What considerations?

The principal aspects of this problem were considered in Chapters VII and VIII. A suggested relation between color and shape may impose lighter colors on fragile shapes and darker colors on heavy pieces.

Tonal changes in upholstery should be carefully considered. Great contrast in tone accentuates pattern activity. It is seldom wise to break up a furniture shape by using different tones in the upholstery. When this is done it seems best to divide the furniture at the structural points. These suggestions may be nullified if the furniture is so huge and architectural in character that it is necessary to camouflage its extent.

5. General Consideration of Decorative Accessories

Decorative accessories are among the most important objects chosen for an interior. Too often they are considered only as an afterthought. In a household they may be the result of the accumulation of acquisitions. If this collection has been thoughtfully chosen and has some real meaning in the experience of the owners, there can be no sounder aesthetic practice than to use such items. There should be an occasional reappraisal of the aesthetic value of accessories in the light of changes which occur in personal taste and in styles.

A decorative accessory is any object which can be omitted without depriving a space of its essential practical function. As they are fundamentally unnecessary, their excuse for being must be that of added convenience, interest, or beauty. For this reason what volumes they can speak about what a man values.

Problem 1. What place in the room design will the decorative accessories take?

The extent of the attention which a decorative accessory should command is determined by the role it is meant to have in the total room design. Is it the focal point of the room decoration? A painting could well be a major center of attention. Is it intended to serve as an interesting accent in the room? A green plant or a set of book ends enclosing interesting books might be useful in this capacity. Is it needed to make some visual transition from one piece of furniture to another? A screen might accomplish this.

An accessory may be intended merely as an enrichment or embellishment wherever it is placed. Then it should not attract too much attention. We recall a lovely enameled ashtray which usually reposed on a walnut table. It had been made to special order with the request that it should not stand out conspicuously as a spot against the walnut. The artist had selected dark bronze-like tones and the mosaic blending of these caused one to look at the tray with great pleasure.

Problem 2. What other considerations should govern selection?

If an accessory, such as a candlestick, has a practical purpose, then a consideration of its suitability to perform this function is of first importance.

An accessory should be selected with great care for the quality of its medium. This is not the place to traffic with values. There can be no room for the shoddy or the fake in those objects which are chosen solely for embroidery. If economy is necessary then one may consider a less expensive kind of material, or one requiring less expensive manipulation, or one where the quality of the material is not sacrificed for added ornamentation. A good plain crystal is preferable to an inferior glass which is heavily decorated.

Careful thought should be expended upon the design quality of an accessory. It need not be a definite or highly developed design. It may please simply because of its shape, color, or texture. If a complex form is incorporated in the object then one should seek the best possible artistry.

The expressiveness of a decorative accessory is important. It should relate to the interests of the owners with such modification as will be necessary to fit the meaning of the room. It is doubly expressive if it has been hand-crafted. Thus accessories placed in a home should suggest pleasant, although not necessarily sentimental matters. The quality of this expression in its relation to design, material, and possible function is a certain index to the quality of visual experience which is enjoyed.

6. Tableware

One of the most rewarding ways to make a lovely picture is to set an attractive table. This should prove true whether the occasion is a family dinner, company entertainment, or a restaurant meal.

It requires careful planning to have suitable table appointments for a variety of circumstances and at the same time not to spend time, money, or space disproportionately. Social customs and styles of entertainment change constantly. Their purpose is unchanged. It is to be hospitable in such a manner as our lives will permit. Lives seem to be very busy today and help is less available. Therefore there should be greater simplification of table service. Each of us, in solving his own hospitality problems, must decide at what point ease of service and aesthetic nicety quarrel.

Today's manufacturers create wares of fewer pieces and of multiple uses. The body of contemporary ceramics and glass is both attractive and durable. Shapes are designed with an eye to function.

Many young moderns select a ware which is not so expensive that it must be reserved only for occasional use. There is certainly something to be said for the purchase of an expensive lodestar in the form of tableware for a family's life. It may be of the stuff that dreams are woven and life should sell dreams to us all. However, many considerations of relative value should enter into their purchase.

Little need be added to a well selected nucleus of dinnerware. Possibly a few pieces are needed for more general usage. If they are chosen to be harmonious with the finer ware, then the inventory is enlarged when the guest roster unexpectedly rises.

Problem 1. Shape of tableware. What considerations?

The structural shapes of contemporary dishes are frequently lower, broader, and less complicated than the shapes of traditional pieces. This trend is in the interest of greater practicality. There is less danger of tipping or of breaking. There is more surface to use. Many designs, particularly in metals, are organic three-dimensional forms. These are frequently beautiful manifestations of the modern spirit. A critical eye should appraise their functional qualities.

Decorative pattern on tableware should be carefully suited to structural design. The range of choice in linens, flowers and candles may be restricted if dishes or glassware are highly patterned.

It is particularly advisable that the weights of a table ensemble correspond. Fine crystal is harmonious with both china and fine pottery but the weight selected to go with the latter would be heavier.

The term table linen is somewhat a misnomer today because we use many kinds of fibers and materials on our tables. Table linen meant nothing but damask linen tablecloths not so long ago. There was thus no problem of shape except in the decorative pattern of the damask itself. Table linen is expensive in money and care. Traditional table damask was spotlessly white and had to be kept so. It is customary to place cloths over pads for softness. The table damask was ironed without a crease and kept free from wrinkles by placing on rollers for storage. Many homemakers today are unwilling and unable to expend this amount of care on table linen.

Lace cloths have proven easily cared for. They should be chosen only when their quality is appropriate to their use and to the other table appointments. Their open pattern should likewise correspond to the surrounding shapes and should not call undue attention to itself.

Table mats are frequently used in place of large cloths. Their shapes and applied designs should correspond to the shape of the table. In deviating from this it must be recognized that a busier picture results.

Problem 2. Color of tableware. What considerations?

A table may now be a colorful sight. This possibility is a challenge which is fraught with pitfalls. Where economy of time, money, and space is desirable it is wise to play around a key color. Accessories which are selected for daytime or summer use will probably be chosen in lighter tones while those intended for informal late evening or winter use might be darker. Many persons still feel that formal dining requires a near white cloth. The important factor is that the table ensemble and the room should be a unified color design.

In a consideration of color it should be remembered that various metals possess slightly different colors which should be considered in using them together.

Problem 3. Texture of tableware. What are the considerations?

This question was considered in Chapter IX. New textures appear constantly in tableware. An artist's eye should appraise their visual qualities and a knowing hand their practical ones.

Problem 4. The ensemble. Is it sacrosanct?

Because table appointments are used together they should be selected so that the ensemble will seem harmonious. This point of view can be carried to extremes, however. The table is an especially appropriate place to portray another kind of unity, that of associational temporal continuity. Heirlooms from the past often give more character to an arrangement than would be found in too neatly matched contemporary pieces. Loveliness will always delight even though its style of appeal is different from ours. Sometimes it is good to see a visible strand of family history in the appointments of our homes.

7. Pictures and Sculpture

Choosing pictures and sculpture is the most important decision about an object of visual art that we are called upon to make. These things contribute nothing to the physical utility of an interior. Their value is solely aesthetic and they should incorporate all the values which we ascribe to beauty. Else why?

Therefore our choice of any piece of fine art to live with is an index to our sense of beauty. Moreover through their relative importance in the decorative scheme pictures and sculpture disclose the importance to us of a spiritual quality divorced from a practical quality.

Problem 1. Where is a picture or a piece of sculpture needed?

As such objects are in themselves focal points of aesthetic value, they are needed wherever a space is barren of these values or where it needs the aesthetic emphasis which a particular picture or piece of sculpture can bring. For instance, in one contemporary house there is a corridor flanked by louvered windows. The corridor obviously leads the eye to its end, a meaningless space until illuminated by a fine piece of sculpture.

Sometimes a furniture grouping may be eminently useful, the individual pieces may be well designed but the whole grouping may not be integrated design-wise. The right choice of a picture may complete an aesthetic whole.

Occasionally the expressive tone of a room is deficient. The rich contribution of a well designed picture which can convey ideas may add immeasurably.

The reverse of all this is also true. Not every blank space calls for a picture. Blank space in proper relation to visual activity can be both restful and suggestive. It is in part a measure of the success of the hanging of pictures that their positioning serves to create such meaningful spaces.

Problem 2. The general character of the work of art. What considerations?

The first decision relates to two-dimensional (pictures) versus three-dimensional (sculpture) art. When pleasure can be derived from seeing and feeling around an object then sculpture is called for. This usually negates chromatic color although much of the great sculpture of the past used color. Pictures, however, are the great vehicle for giving joy through color, space, and texture relationships as shown on a two-dimensional area.

The choice of the medium used in a painting or piece of sculpture is another important consideration. The various media are discussed next. The use of several media in one room is a matter of personal taste and of consideration for scale and textural attributes.

The choice of design is based on principles such as those which have been the subject matter of this book.

What style is indicated? There is no dogmatic answer to this question. Good art transcends time. The man who lives in a good contemporary house will probably enjoy good modern art and want it. He will be equally appreciative of the eternal qualities in art whatever its date. The artist designer will seek to harmonize all aspects of a setting but only where strict purism prevails need, for instance, a Colonial interior be restricted to the use of early American paintings.

What subject matter is allowable? All subjects are transformed into beauty through great art. However, taste [4] may eliminate some subjects from some settings. Likewise subjects which are generally unpleasant in their suggestions might well be erased from rooms which are intended for happy social life.

Problem 3. The medium. What are the considerations relative to its choice?

The answer to this question requires study and a constant effort to keep up to date. Techniques change with time. New ones are developed and old ones are revived and come back into fashion.

The following serves merely as an introduction:

a. Oil painting—similar media are fresco and encaustic.[5] Support is wood, plaster, or canvas.

All of these media have great visual force and are preferably chosen for any location where the painting must carry for a distance. Encaustic painting is a particularly useful medium for this purpose because of the textural effects obtained through its use.

b. Watercolor—a similar medium is tempera. Support is paper.

Due to the fluidity of the solvent, the effect of a good water color should be spontaneous and fresh. It should not look worked over in any sense. Watercolors can contribute this bracing quality to a room. As their carrying power is usually not great they seem best suited to smaller spaces. Tempera paintings can be more forceful.

---

[4] Discussed in Chap. XI.

[5] For definitive description of all processes using colorants, see Chap. VI.

c. Pastel—a similar medium is crayon. The support is paper. They are similar in effect and use to tempera.

d. Pencil—similar techniques are pen and ink, silverpoint (made with a silver stylus) and scratch board work (incised drawing made through a coating on a composition board). This is linear work of varying degrees of delicacy, scratchboard probably being the coarsest. These are examples of the so-called graphic processes to which all of the prints belong (e through k following). They are usually dependent for their effects upon linear character and achromatic tone rather than on chromatic color. They are best suited to locations where these qualities can be observed at close range.

e. Wood block—the support is paper or fabric.

This is another graphic process. It is likewise a print. The valuable block prints are known as artist's proofs as is the case with media e through k. Each of the artist's proof prints is made by the artist. The edition is usually limited (the print number and the number in the edition together with the artist's name appear in the lower corners) and the block or plate is subsequently destroyed. Some of the processes most suited for the making of artist's proofs are likewise used for larger editions.

A wood block is made by cutting grooves in the block of wood or its coating and then inking the block. The ink is then transferred to the paper from the surfaces which are not incised. Due to the difficulty of cutting, the lines are comparatively thick, and strong contrasts in tonal areas make a wood block one of the more forceful prints. Oriental artists have used a more delicate line.

f. Engraving—a similar product is a mezzotint. The support is usually paper or perhaps fabric.

An engraving is first cut on a copper or steel plate by an instrument known as a graver which is pushed by the artist and thus makes a very even, clean line.

A mezzotint is like an engraving except that the plate is pricked by an instrument. The resulting dots make the tones.

The plate is inked and an impression made.

g. Etching—a similar medium is an aquatint. The support is paper.

A plate is covered with a soft resist through which the artist draws his lines with a stylus. An acid then eats out (German—"Etsen") the line. The resist is removed. The plate is inked and an impression is made. As a resist is easily pierced, the lines of an etching can be sensitive to the artist's style of calligraphy.

An aquatint is like an etching for tonal effects with the tones accomplished through rubbing down areas of a porous ground resist before the work of the acid begins. When several plates are used an effect similar to a tempera painting can be produced.

h. Drypoint—the support is paper.

A drypoint, made by pulling rather than pushing a sharp instrument over a plate, has a line which has a soft velvety edge. This is because the instrument leaves a burr on the plate.

i. Lithograph—the support is paper.

A crayon sketch is made on a plate (originally on a stone). Water is added which adheres only to the background. Ink then adheres only to the crayon. A lithograph print closely resembles a charcoal drawing in its broad effects. It is a flat reproduction not bearing the imprint of the pressure of the plate.

j. Serigraphy or silk screen [6]—the support is usually paper or fabric. When several screens are used an effect can be produced which is similar to a tempera painting.

k. Photographs—the support is paper.

Original artist's proofs owe their quality to skillful handling by the artist. Many kinds of tonal effects can be produced. Color is possible today.

l. Reproductions.

These are unlimited edition prints. The process is quite mechanical. There are many processes such as halftone screens, collotype, and photogravure. Some contemporary processes go further and reproduce the exact texture of the original painting.

A copy should be judged on the basis of its accuracy of reproduction. A wide variance will be found between different facsimiles in this respect.

m. Sculpture.

[6] The process is further explained in Chap. IX, under textiles.

Figure 99. Comparing this oil by Vincent van Gogh with the one by Salvador Dali in Figure 110, the contrast in technique is apparent.

Figure 100. In this oil Dufy has conveyed to us some of the excitement of sailing.

The original meaning of the word sculpture implied something cut away, as in the chiseling of stone. Indeed the great French workers in brass and similar metals cut away the metal after the initial form was molded. They were known as *chiseleurs.* Sculpturing of this nature is done today in many materials. The purpose is not only to create a form where mass and space are organized into a good three-dimensional design, but also to bring out the natural structure of the material through this design. Wood sculpture has forms which seem to grow from the grain of the wood.

Plastic sculpture or modeling creates forms which show the hand-forming rather than the hand-cutting process. Such objects are first made in clay or in a similar pliable material. They are then given permanent form either by firing or by casting a plaster replica from a mold. As several copies can be made by the latter method, such pieces are similar to artist's proofs in prints.

The design might well indicate the original plasticity of the medium.

Three-dimensional design is now utilizing many new materials and processes. Sculpturing is done with a blow torch on metal. Wire and plastic are utilized.

Unlimited reproductions of sculptured pieces are likewise produced. These are divorced from the artist's supervision just as are the unlimited replicas of two-dimensional art. Many artists, however, will not allow duplicates to be made without their approving the result. The work of many firms includes such a quality guarantee.

Problem 4. How to develop taste, especially as oriented towards modern art, in selection?

The following are some suggestions:

Try to realize that fine art can have various kinds of appeal and may even be one-sided in its appeal.

For instance, a craftsman is frequently interested in the material and its handling. The con-

Article: "Composition (3)," 1914, oil on canvas.
Artist: Wassily Kandinsky. **Owner:** Collection of
the Museum of Modern Art, New York, Mrs. Simon
Guggenheim Fund. **Photographer:** Soichi Sunami
for the Museum of Modern Art, New York.

Article: "Composition in White, Black and Red,"
1936, oil on canvas. **Artist:** Piet Mondrian. **Owner:**
Collection of the Museum of Modern Art, New
York, gift of the Advisory Committee. **Photog-
rapher:** Soichi Sunami for the Museum of Modern
Art, New York.

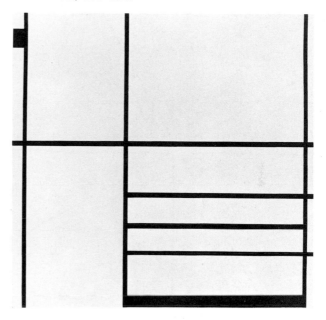

Figure 101. "Composition (3)" by Wassily
Kandinsky.

Figure 102. "Composition in White, Black
and Red" by Piet Mondrian.

sistency of a technique in any artifact indicates deliberation and skill which may initiate our admiration. One approach to appreciation is through attempting to do. It is soon seen that much modern art revolves around technique experimentation. This leads to an understanding of how and perhaps why the craft of Dali is different from that of van Gogh.

Then, too, while experimenting and learning about technical matters try to set down sensuous material in various kinds of order. The order may not be analyzed, but colors, linear tracks, spaces, imitated textures—all of these in juxtaposition may provide interest. Doodling is fun and some artists seem able to preserve this simple expression of joy through free rendering. Does something of the excitement of creation come across to us from their work? Can anything which is too contrived and finished ever convey the full meaning of the universe? Do we begin to appreciate Dufy who can tell us with

what appears to be a few swift brush strokes, why it is that people like fairs and race tracks?

On the other hand, our approach of experimentation with order may create an interest for art which has been done with meticulous care, with isolation, and concentration on the potentialities of one or two components. This sort of art may intrigue a scientific-minded person, one who wishes to find the perfect solution to a problem of limited range. Does Mondrian, for example, with his black and white proportions, begin to take on meaning?

If we are sufficiently inquiring in the study of visual order, we may find ourselves sitting before a Kandinsky and following the routes of the more complex thematic relations. Many realignments of the visual material are possible and are interesting to trace. We may find ourselves appreciating what the critic often calls plastic organization.[7]

[7] Our familiar design precept of "several alignments."

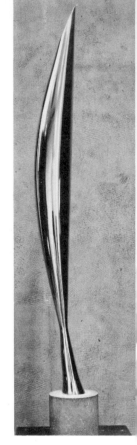

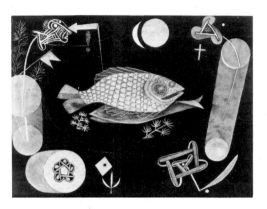

Figure 103. Oil painting, "Viaduct" by Lyonel Feininger.

Figure 104. "Around the Fish" by Paul Klee. (The titles of Klee's paintings are part of the fun.)

Because most contemporary art emphasizes design it is desirable that an appreciation of its other qualities, when present, should come through this doorway. It is a stodgy onlooker who cannot sense that the expressive power of the shapes, colors, and textures tell us about the artist's world today. When this communication is succinct and unlabored we often find a delightful form of wit. Much of Klee's painting is such.

The views of foreign cultures which Gaugin provides, of social upheavals seen in the work of Orozco and of disjointed psychological conditions which Wood suggests—these are straightforward portrayals which capture aspects of the contemporary scene.

It is surprising if the leaders in the scientific world do not appreciate another sort of imagery. Scientists deal in concrete symbols for abstract relations. The symbols of visual art merely derive from the basic matter of experience, the components of sensation, and are used to make an idea understandable. Let the physicist and the chemist attempt to explain the taut explosiveness of the atom, the engineer try to show the motion which has conquered the air, the sociologist to draft a conception of the majesty of our cities and the psychologist to chart their nervous energy. If they should then fail to appreciate Feininger, Brancusi, Sheeler, and Marsh, there is doubt that they are creative scientists.

If one still finds that he likes a picture only if it is an exact representation of something, let him look for that. Observe the variety of ways of portraying a subject. It is sometimes a good idea to take an interesting topic and see how it has been depicted by artists. Thus if one man likes the sea he might like the oils of Waugh. Looking at a Marin watercolor he finds a completely different treatment. What of the mood of the sea in a painting by Mattson and how different is the work of Ryder? Which would be chosen and why?

Out of such a study of one subject treated in

Figure 105 (opposite). Bronze "Bird in Space" by Constantin Brancusi.

241

Figure 106. Oil painting, "American Landscape" by Charles Sheeler.

Figure 107. Tempera painting, "In Fourteenth Street" by Reginald Marsh.

different ways by different artists comes the idea that there is more than one way to show the same subject and still get the idea across in a very likable manner. It can be represented just as our two eyes would see it if we were at a fixed distance from the object. Every camera enthusiast knows that he can vary this representation by varying his lens or his station point. Therefore it is interesting to note how the painter has exercised the same prerogative.

The painter has more freedom than the camera in his representation and he has imaginatively utilized this freedom since the beginning of art. He can inject the idea of relative importance of objects by their size and position in space. We accept this idea very easily in advertising art. The artist can convey the idea of motion or mobility of objects by representing one object as seen through another object which conceivably has just taken up its position in front of the first object. He can let us see two scenes at once through a montage. This is a favorite technique of the motion picture. In short the painter can tell us many things about objects through his visual sign language. And it is enlivening to discover them.

The subject matter of today's art is as varied as our world; the interpretation of this subject matter is as varied as human experience. If the artist is worthy of the name he will employ his medium to give the message of the joy which the eyes can bring, to show the order which man can find in the visual world, and to convey something of the human struggle to keep in harmony with the universe. The contemporary artist is apt to consider these accomplishments in this relative order. But the meaning which is asked for in a work of art is indivisible.

The artist is the perpetual foe of regimented unity—a fact for which our syndicated culture should give thanks. The artist is likewise forever conscious of the links that bind experience. Our specialized civilization has lost these. When found again, art will be different.

Problem 5. Where should we seek good art objects?

   a. Museums. They contain the best art of all ages. Most museums sell good reproductions of their possessions and will mail lists and prices.

   b. Artist's exhibitions. Almost every community has them. When the exhibition material is judged by a competent jury, there is some assurance of artistic merit. Juries, however, are human and fallible. Try an occasional work of a neophyte, if it pleases.

   c. Illustrated catalogues. Most libraries have the following:

      1) UNESCO, Paris, France.
         Catalogue of color reproductions prior to 1860.
         Catalogue of color reproductions 1860–1952.[8]

      2) Raymond and Raymond, Inc., 40 E. 52nd St., New York 22, N.Y.

      3) Museum Pieces, Inc., 114 E. 32nd St., New York 16, N.Y.

      4) The Williamsburg Prints. The Craft House, Williamsburg, Va.

      5) Artext Prints, Westport, Conn. (Miniatures which can serve as a catalogue of their large prints.)

      6) The Metropolitan Museum of Art, New York, N.Y. (Postage stamp-like reproductions which can be used as a catalogue.)

      7) Museum lending collections. These are not generally available to private individuals. A request to view a particular print may be honored.

   d. Reputable art dealers. They can assist in the procurement of any desired object.

   e. Good artists who will work on order. (Which is not the same thing as on dictation!)

Problem 6. What kind of "trial run" of an art object is desirable?

The best way to test any work of art is to live with it for a time. Most dealers will permit one to take a picture out for a short period loan. Some art clubs allow their members to borrow works of art for yearly loans. Membership in such clubs is for a fee but it is a very good way in which to gain the message of a work of art and to see which art is the wisest personal choice.

Should the work of art be left in position ad infinitum? Sometimes the answer is yes, sometimes no. A happy change of scene makes one the more eager to return. In the Oriental home pictures are placed like flowers, in a changing order. This enables the family and its friends to look with a fresh eye. Sometimes this can be accomplished by changing pictures, like slipcovers, with the season. Sometimes it can be accomplished by rotating pictures in the same frame. An additional storage space is required for such a procedure but with a bit of ingenuity it can be contrived. On the other hand there are permanent satisfactions which accrue from some possessions because they are continually available.

If art objects, when placed in position, seem to lift rooms out of the impersonal, ordinary class and to give them that vitality which some personalities give to a gathering, the expenditure in time and money that went into their purchase is warranted. If art continues to do this over the years it is worth more than stocks and bonds on which we collect a dividend only every quarter. Our dividend comes daily.

Problem 7. How should a picture be framed?

First, why frame a picture? The most obvious reason is to protect it from knocks. If the painting cannot be cleaned we likewise cover it with glass to keep it clean. There are other purposes that a frame may serve. It helps to isolate a picture from its surroundings—gives it a little world all its own. While doing this it may enhance the picture just as a lovely dress flatters a pretty girl. A frame may likewise merge a picture with a background on which it is hung.

The framing of a picture is an imaginative work of art in itself. A frame need not be orthodox but it should never be in the category which we might call stunt framing. The frame on a picture is there to do a particular job and if it becomes exotic at the expense of its function, it is not good framing.

---

[8] These catalogues are of incalculable worth, for in addition to illustrations and prices, they list the best sources of reproductions. This last list was made after careful consideration by authoritative museum connoisseurs.

Certain injunctions may be given for all good framing. The frame should complement the expressive character of the picture. This is in large part a question of textural harmony. For example, a picture which suggests the American rural scene, such as one of Grant Wood's, might be framed in a simple frame of oak.

The expressive character of the painting also plays a role in determining the shape of the frame. A French landscape as done by Utrillo, may be largely composed of straight lines. But it has a certain elegant and fairy-like character (due perhaps to its tones and its technical handling) which seems to require some curvature in its frame.

The shape design of a picture must likewise be considered in choosing the shape of the frame. Generally speaking, this would call for similarity in the design elements of picture and frame. However, some contrast may be required for emphasis. A van Gogh picture of a countryside, because of its agitated brush strokes, would seem out of place in a smooth straight frame. On the other hand, a curved line painting such as Matisse's "Blue Window" seems to incorporate so many curves in its design that a straight line frame might, by emphasizing the straight lines in the picture, provide a suitable foil.

For a similar reason of providing contrast, many contemporary paintings are framed in elaborate curved line frames so as to be different from the more stark lines of the modern room.

The size of a frame is likewise important. So often a picture is spoiled by a frame which is too scanty or too large. An oil painting may be framed in the simplest of narrow wood moldings such as are usually reserved for water colors and artist's proofs. Le Corbusier finishes his paintings with a metal band which merely acts as a finish at the edge of the picture. In framing an oil these simple moldings are placed close to the picture. In media of less aesthetic force it is customary to place a mat between the picture and such a frame.

When a frame is broader than this simple edging it should be wide enough to carry the visual weight of the picture. This forcefulness may be compounded of many things. The agitated strokes of van Gogh require a wide deep frame. A landscape with large dark masses in the foreground may require a broad frame. It is a somewhat safe guide to say that such a frame should be at least one-sixth to one-eighth the width of the picture.

The depth of a frame is another aesthetic problem. The framer must decide whether to strengthen a flat painting by repetition of this flatness or whether to accentuate it by a deep contrasting frame. Deep frames do break up room space more than flat ones. They may cast troublesome shadows on a picture. They likewise may relieve a room which has too many flat textures and surfaces. Frames which are flat in themselves but which advance the plane of the picture or which use a deeper molding adjacent to the picture, are one solution.

The tone of the frame is of utmost importance. In most cases the frame should not be lighter than the lightest tone in the painting. This suggestion is sometimes set aside in the interest of fitting the frame into the color scheme of the room or of lightening a somber painting. If a painting fades out to very light tones at the edges, a border molding of dark tone may be placed on the frame adjacent to the painting. This border or the entire frame is frequently rubbed with one of the colors of the painting. A liner used with a mat achieves the same purpose.

Frames may be of the so-called button back variety. This means that the picture is held in place by a flexible hasp which permits the interchange of pictures in the same frame. Obviously this kind of frame is best suited to a group of pictures with similar design characteristics.

Problem 8. Should a picture be covered with glass?

The answer to this question is just a matter of common sense. Glass protects a picture from dirt and is therefore an essential covering for any picture surface which would soil easily. All pictures made on paper should be covered with glass.

Some artists prefer to cover their oils with glass. There are two objections to this practice. In the first place glass may reflect light in a manner not intended by the artist.[9] This is an

[9] Picture glass which corrects this fault is now available.

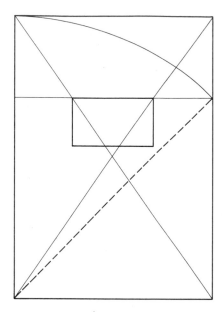

Figure 108. A root 3 horizontal rectangle in a root 2 vertical.

objection to its use over any painting. In the second place, glass detracts from the textural effects of an oil painting and so it would seem wiser not to use it over any painting which utilized three-dimensional texture for part of its appeal.

Problem 9. How should a picture be matted?

A mat is a flat piece of material, usually a flat cardboard which has an opening (a very carefully cut hole with a beveled edge) for the picture. It is advisable to use a mat on any picture which requires greater importance in its position.

Any picture which is finished with a mat really requires little else in the way of a frame. An unobtrusive molding or corner brackets should be sufficient.

Some mats are integral with the frame of the picture. They are merely flat extensions of the picture frames and are made of the same or similar material. This is a favorite method of framing opaque water colors and occasionally oil paintings.

The shape of the picture, its design, its expressive character, and the nature of the surroundings are all important determining factors for the nature of the mat. Only a few guide posts can be given.

The first suggestion is that the shape of the mat should correspond to the shape of the pic-

ture but that for the sake of interest it may vary from it slightly. For example, a root three horizontal rectangular picture might be placed in a root two mat.[10] The mat is frequently less elongated than the picture.

The absolute size of a mat should be large enough to accomplish its purpose of isolating and dignifying the picture. Frequently the marginal areas bear a rhythmic relation to the picture size and thus determine the absolute size of the mat. Occasionally very small prints are placed in very large mats. The mats of a group of pictures of various size may be planned to be uniform in size.

The American Museum mat for artist's proofs is a hinged mat of standard size 14½ inches by 19½ inches. Frames are uniform and have button backs. An artist's proof should never be pasted down solidly to the back mat. The print

[10] See Chap. V.

Figure 109. Mats on pictures and other proportional relations are not always best solved by a rigid adherence to a proportional system. Many complicating factors such as linear or tonal movements, which create new relations, may suggest that proportions be adjusted by the eye—a most sensitive instrument.

Residence of: Mr. and Mrs. Peter J. Lloyd, Moreland Hills, Ohio. **Architect:** Ernst Payer, A.I.A., Cleveland, Ohio. **Photographer:** Bill Engdahl, Hedrich-Blessing, Chicago, Illinois. **Painting:** Salvador Dali.

Figure 110. This room was planned so that the focus of interest would be the painting by Salvador Dali. The room colors, subtle white and silver greys, are those which are emphasized in the painting. The placement of the canvas Is such that there is visual opportunity to pick up its rhythms and to move to the windows and to the outdoors.

should be loose so that the texture of the paper, the identification and the plate mark can be examined. This plate mark is the depression made in the paper by the metal plate from which the print is taken. These are all of interest to the connoisseur.

The relation of the marginal sizes surrounding a picture is decided by the artist's understanding of their purpose. If visual stability is desired the bottom margin is frequently the widest.[11] In a vertical picture the top margin may be next in size and the side margins the narrowest. They may decrease in accordance with dynamic ratios. In horizontal pictures, if width is to be stressed, the side margins may be larger than the top. If a more static effect is desired then these three or possibly all four margins may be the same.

The tone of a picture mat should be carefully selected. As a general rule it should not be more saturated then the background of the picture nor lighter than its high lights. The tone of a mat is frequently one of the cooler, lighter, duller tones of the painting. Occasionally one of the darker tones will create greater enrichment. A warmer tone may accord well with a symphony of warm hues.

[11] Even this so-called rule of margins may be changed when the design of the picture requires a different proportion.

The French, in framing graphic prints, frequently used a dull blue mat of medium tone. This blue seems to bring out the richness of the velvet-like black tones and the middle lightness seems closely related to the middle tones of the picture. Such a mat is often surrounded with a narrow gold frame. Frequently a few color lines are drawn close to the opening of the mat and a wash of harmonious color is placed between the lines. This is customarily known as a French-lined mat.

The opening in a mat for artist's proofs, is usually cut to show a margin from the plate mark of about one-quarter of an inch on the sides and one-half of an inch at the bottom. This bottom margin should provide space for the numbering of an artist's proof and for the signature of the artist. The edge of the opening of the mat forms an additional line around this plate mark which increases its emphasis.

A reproduction of a painting may be framed with or without a mat. If the reproduction is made by a process which simulates the texture of an original oil and if no glass covering is required, it would be better not to use a mat. Even though a facsimile is done on paper and only apparently duplicates the original texture and does require a glass covering, it may be framed close and without a mat. This close framing is possible when and to the degree that the forcefulness of the painting can successfully compete with a close frame. When such a facsimile is framed close, the frame chosen would probably not be as heavy or large as might be placed on the original painting. If a mat is used over a facsimile of an oil, its texture may be heavier than that of a mat for a water color or graphic print.

Problem 10. How and where to hang pictures?

Perhaps the most troublesome problem in decorating is the problem of how and exactly where to hang pictures. It is one of those problems of taste about which there certainly should be no disputing and yet, with a certain kind of self-assurance, there must be wonder that everyone else does not agree.

Pictures are chosen for many different reasons but there is one common denominator to all of these, which is that a picture is meant to be a focal point of attention. It was the focus of the artist's attention and now it is to be of ours. Therefore viewing conditions should be arranged with this in mind. If the picture has something to say it should be allowed to say it.

This will rule out all tricky plans where the machinery of hanging becomes more important than the picture. The usual position for a picture is flat on a wall. Experimental setups on free standing supports are only reasonable when the two-dimensional character of a picture is not violated.

If the picture is then hung so that the wires and hooks which give it support are inconspicuous, the how of hanging will be fulfilled. Occasionally there may be a decorative reason for showing these. The French customarily hung their oval pictures with elaborate silk cords from which tassels were appended. This gave verticality which fitted the picture into the room panel.

Were there no other consideration to alter the case, a picture should be hung at the best eye level for viewing while standing. That would mean that the center of interest of the picture would come about five feet five inches above the floor, or at the eye level of the average man. Deviation from this should be downward rather than upward because it is easier to look down than up. Moreover pictures are quite frequently viewed from a seated position.

The design of a room may place its demands upon the positioning of a picture. The furniture near a picture becomes of great importance in placing it satisfactorily. Greater coordination of spaces is accomplished when isolated objects such as pictures are rhythmically grouped with other objects such as furniture so as to make a larger whole. With a little careful planning this usually can be accomplished without hiding the picture or making it too low for viewing. If the furniture is extremely high it would be best not to hang pictures above it.

The entire wall plan of a space enters into a decision about where to hang a picture. If walls are well defined in panels the picture placement should be considered in relation to the panel on which it is hung. It will ordinarily please if the picture proportions vary slightly from those of the panel but are related to them. In placing the picture in the panel the margin of space below the picture is generally smaller than that above the picture. That may seem to be a violation of the rule given for margins in picture matting. Here, however, larger areas are being handled and the guiding factor becomes the fact that the eye muscles are less strained when the picture is hung low. Some wall spaces are similar to panels and impose similar conditions upon the hanging of pictures.

Few walls are broken into panels. Quite the reverse is true. An attempt is made today to treat the entire wall as one unbroken plane surface which may even project beyond the boundaries of the room. Thus walls are given a horizontal emphasis and are connected rhythmically with all the other wall surfaces in view. In such a situation a picture is placed so as to aid the kind of rhythm and balance which is planned for the area.

Occasionally one sees unique arrangements. For instance, several pictures are hung as a group. This is sometimes done when one picture is not sufficiently large for a position. The pictures should be hung quite close together if they are to be seen as a group. The space between the pictures should be narrower than the width of an individual picture. In grouping pictures in this manner it is clear that the expression of the individual picture is somewhat lost in the expression of the group. Therefore pictures so grouped should be similar in character, and the import of the picture will be less obscured if its character is more decorative than meaningful.

Sometimes pictures are arranged in a vertical or a horizontal border. In such an arrangement the value of any individual picture that falls outside the range of vision, is practically nullified. The whole arrangement must gain in pattern decorativeness if this loss is justifiable.

A stepladder arrangement of pictures should be handled with extreme caution. The pictures are apt to become stepping stones to carry the eye toward the ceiling. If a larger picture is placed in the center and a step-down as well as a step-up arrangement is planned then the eye may be kept where it belongs. Pictures placed on the wall adjacent to a stairway are, for obvious reasons, an understandable exception to this precept.

The trouble with some picture arrangements is not that the pictures are poorly placed but that they are of the wrong size for their design purpose. To make a picture more sizable for a space it may be hung on a cloth wall hanging of larger size. Such a hanging can make a good backdrop for a piece of sculpture. Sometimes a wall stencil can be used to frame a group of small pictures.

Something was wrong in our set-up, we were off the true somewhere, if we would behave like that. My reaction had nothing to do with the ethics of the occasion: it was the discord that worried me. It jarred as I believe the first misfire, indicating a fault in some smoothly running machine, must jar on the ears of an engineer.

LAURENS VAN DER POST [*]

Love is a flower
     Forever blooming
Life is a fountain
     Forever leaping
Upward to catch the golden sunlight,
     Striving to reach the azure heaven.
Failing, falling,
Ever returning
     To kiss the earth that the flower might live.

EUGENE O'NEILL [†]

Chapter XI

DESIGN AND EXPRESSION

A. WHAT AN INTERIOR DESIGN CAN SAY

What do the surroundings we have created communicate? They reveal more than our ability as artists of visual design and the expressions which are related to the separate visual qualities. They become an exposition of character in a very special kind of way.

B. WHAT IS VALUABLE?

Character is related to a personal set of values. It shows that to which we give top-drawer space in life's bureau of accounts. When character is shaped so as to capitalize on the highest values in a civilization its possessor may be called cultured.

The fields of relative values have been classified as the good, the true, and the beautiful. It

[*] From **Venture to the Interior** by Laurens van der Post. Copyright 1951, William Morrow & Company, Inc., and reprinted by permission of the publisher.
[†] From **The Fountain** by Eugene O'Neill, taken from **The Great God Brown, The Fountain, Moon of the Caribbees and Other Plays.** Copyright 1926 by Horace Liveright, Inc. Reprinted by permission of Random House Inc.

Residence of: Bertha Schaefer, New York. **Photographer:** (Below) Bill Jackson, New York. (Opposite) Ernest M. Silva, New York.

Figure 111. This New York apartment speaks eloquently of an owner who has such a highly developed aesthetic sense as to be able to choose and combine the finest art of many periods and to create that which is both timeless and of the present. Moreover, this interior possesses that quality, essential to great art, of bearing the stamp of a personality.

is a fundamental purpose of education to inculcate standards of excellence in these.

The value cabinet of life is larger than its subdivisions and thus represents a transcendent worth which, for want of a better name, may be called the right. This is not just the ethically right, nor the scientifically right, nor the aesthetically right. Yet if it neglects goodness, belies truth, or fails beauty, it is never perfection.

C. WHAT IS WISDOM?

This kind of equity of values frequently eludes those who focus too narrowly on filing material in one of the small pigeonholes of existence. To discover this kind of rightness is really to acquire wisdom. The first of its servants is knowledge—not of one kind of thing but of many kinds. Knowledge, which can only be attained through the exercise of judgment, is a masculine servant possessing the masculine trait of perspicacity, that ability to see through a situation and winnow the chaff from the wheat, the false from the true. The second servant is a handmaiden, sensitiveness. She possesses the feminine trait of circumspection, that ability to see around a situation and to reflect on its many facets. The third personage in the retinue of wisdom is imagination, that farseeing friend who envisages the image of the finished picture and who knows the best way to effect it.

Education attempts to convey knowledge directly. Sensitivity and imagination must be taught by indirection. It is the supreme responsibility of the arts to develop these qualities. Those who possess these attributes are potential artists. A work of art is fundamentally brought into being by a way of life. Moreover, once created it shapes a way of life.[1]

D. WHAT IS TASTE?

Taste, when we imply distinction and grace in its use, is the abiilty to make wisdom explicit

[1] J. Dewey, *Freedom and Culture* (New York: G. P. Putnam's Sons, 1939), pp. 9–11; S. Giedion, *Space, Time, and Architecture* (Cambridge, Mass.: Harvard University Press, 1946), p. 20.

through art. It is, therefore, a preeminent art. Living is the most complex of arts and the one to which the general term "good taste" is frequently applied. Although each specific art is meaningful to the man of taste, it becomes a particular prerogative of an art like interior design, because of its close association with life, to express taste.

As there is no art which can be learned by rule, there is no book which has ever been written which can go farther than the kindergarten in giving the answer to questions of taste. Decisions of taste, however trivial their manifestations may seem, must be based on a scale of values. These decisions are most difficult when standards of excellence in several arts seem to conflict. When and where is a painting vulgar? When to use clever but harm dealing wit? What is the line of demarcation between conventionality and pedantry, self-expression and eccentricity? Reaction to such issues can be called the real measure of taste.

E. OF WHAT VALUE IS TASTE?

Persons of cultured tastes have developed a certain finesse of action which speaks in every detail of their daily life. This kind of taste is such a real thing that it can be counted upon to function in a very definite way. That is the reason that in the employment field it is actually a marketable commodity.

Beyond its economic value it possesses a social worth. One characteristic of taste is its awareness of and respect for the various influences on a culture. Creative artists and scientists are not the sole producers of a civilization. Pilots cannot steer a ship which harbors a mutinous crew. There must be directive from both the helm and the hold. Leaders learn from keen observation of the world.

However necessary both parties are in a boat race, a coxswain cannot reach the oarsmen without a megaphone. This interpreter in the artistic world is the person of taste. Taste is the creative force which can alter the common mind to adjust to new levels of culture.

F. HOW CAN A HOUSE TEACH TASTE?

Each of us strives to improve his taste and wishes to inculcate excellent standards in the next generation. In this wise, although the instruments and musicians of old may be lost, their music lives on.

Taste is first born of preference. Our preferences are almost subconsciously acquired. They come from indirect messages so transmitted through the complex telegraphic network of existence that they become largely emotional in character.

Artistic preferences come from music which a child hears almost as soon as he is born. Needless to say his earliest impressions and thus his earliest preferences are formed at home. Training in sensitivity and imagination may thus be

Figure 112. This home speaks of its interest in books. The library wall has been extended into the living area thus creating a visual extension of space. The folding partition insures quiet when desired.

Residence of: Mr. and Mrs. Ben Zevin, Cleveland, Ohio. **Designer:** Leon Gordon Miller, Cleveland, Ohio. **Photographer:** Denny C. Harris, Cleveland, Ohio.

taught by the house itself. A house tells us a very great deal about the culture of its occupants. And what it tells us it teaches its children.

What are some ways in which a house can influence? Honesty or the esteem for integrity is of a piece with the honest use of materials. Genuineness is learned from objects which are unostentatious. Graciousness is acquired in a house which is designed, not just to put a friend at ease, but to make him realize his value. Love can be taught by a well cared for home. Courage can be learned from a cheerful emotional tone. Spirituality becomes easy to one whose house provides a sanctuary for those qualities which, like flowers, are most ephemeral and most eternal in worth. Open-mindedness can be taught by a house which has come to terms with time.

G. CONSCIOUS TRAINING FOR TASTE

Taste is likewise born of discernment which is a rational process seeking to determine the values in a situation. It is on this conscious intellectual level that taste can be improved. The undertaking is as difficult, however, as the proverbial task of lifting oneself by one's boot-straps. It is hard to operate on a member which must function in performing the act.

There are a few guideposts which have seemed helpful. Start as students of this fast-moving, changing world. If it becomes boring for one second—look out. That is the sign of stalemate. Seek excellence in the pattern of today. It is exhilarating to find that it is always there.

The integrity of personal taste must be respected. If our taste and that of the best of the surrounding culture are homogeneous, then we fortunately inherit good taste in our culture. If we move to another culture, respect for our basic preferences is still essential. It is the past and the only firm ground on which we are able to build the future.

In formal training the curriculum must be broad as well as specialized. It must seek to understand our civilization which certainly requires a knowledge of its history, its philosophy, and its science. It likewise requires specialized study in the arts in order not only to appreciate artistic excellence but likewise to obtain that fullest comprehension of the relations between the physical and the human experiential world.

Some years ago, I chanced to visit the house of a collector in London and without preparation, after admiring the pictures, stepped from the modern house into a room designed and built by Inigo Jones, which the owner had bought entire and had set up afresh as an adjunct to his house . . . It is strange how suddenly one can change one's mental climate. I seemed to have stepped straight into the seventeenth century; into England as it was when a plain majesty of style, the style of the Authorized Version of the Bible, came naturally to speech and pen, when also the glories of the Italian Renaissance were beginning to impress their forms upon art and architecture, as they had already coloured with flame the poetry and drama of England. It was like, I thought, inhabiting for a moment the mind of Milton. Those simple yet stately proportions, that austerity of ornament, that disdain of the trivial which yet communicates no sense of emptiness but rather of latent richness—these belonged to Milton's native air, to the time in which he lived.

LAURENCE BINYON *

Chapter XII

DESIGN AND PERIOD STYLES —HISTORIC EXPRESSION

A. OUR USE OF HISTORY

The interior designer should be an ardent student of history. Careful study of authentic design of the past and careful correlating of this design with its cultural epoch will show how closely the two are related.

Through such study one learns to respect the integration of good design with human needs. He accustoms his eyes to good quality in design because the most successful designs of the past have been those which survived. He is enabled to wander in the realm of the mind into associational lands and centuries which are closed to the traveler of only today.

* From **The Spirit of Man in Asian Art** by Laurence Binyon. Copyright 1955, the Harvard University Press, and reprinted by permission of the publisher.

Figure 113. This room from a mid-seventeenth century Massachusetts house is in that style often called early or provincial American. It is similar in feeling to simple rooms of the English Renaissance.

Building: Parlor of the Thomas Hart House, Ipswich, Massachusetts, built about 1640. **Photograph:** Courtesy Metropolitan Museum of Art, New York, American Wing.

This book cannot treat decorative history as exhaustively as it should be studied. It is hoped that through further study, and through visits to museums and to old buildings, the student may really learn to appreciate the beauty and richness of the past and to understand better the relation of all great art to its own time.

B. MEANING OF STYLE

One of the marks of a person of good taste is his ability to adjust to change at the same time that he respects tradition. Change and continuity are both seen in the phenomenon of style in art. A style in interior decoration is a distinctive way in which people of a particular time and place designed the interior of their buildings.

Styles in interior design change because the human race learns to adapt to changing conditions. Modes are the expression of an evolving universe. Styles in some types of architecture such as homes and churches change with relative slowness because of the expense connected with building and because of emotional associations.

Any change in style is most drastic and rapid in those centers where wealth is concentrated. These locations become style centers from which new style influences emanate. A style as it develops in such a center is frequently referred to as a *mother style*.

Styles merge gradually into one another. There is no sharp break between them. However, there are times when a particular style is at the height of its popularity, and finds its finest and most characteristic expression. We then say that the style is in fashion.

When we speak of decorative periods we are dividing styles arbitrarily. A period is often said to begin in a certain place at a definite time and to end with as prompt dispatch. We all know that styles do not work this way but it is useful to assume that they do. Likewise it gives the student dates to remember.

Actually styles overlap and we can refer to *style cycles.* These may be visualized as waves having long gradual upward surges, and brief crests. Their force is dissipated like that of breakers which recede in the wake of another wave. A period is usually dated from the time when a style becomes firmly established to the moment before its complete dissolution.

Periods which show similar style influences in different countries may overlap in time. For instance, the Baroque period began in Italy before the Renaissance influence died in England.

The pace of a style becomes slower the farther one goes from its energizing center. In remote localities, style movements may be so slow that their influence rarely dies and new styles move in to mix with the old. The resulting hybrid style is given a local expression by local craftsmen in local materials. Such styles are sometimes called *provincial,* in the sense that provinces are distant from metropolitan style centers. Often a provincial style is very charming and may be suited to our use because it came out of living conditions which were similar to ours.

When a district or a class of society has very little contact with a changing world it creates its own style. This is compounded of primitive forms, local techniques, and of the peculiar emotional flavor of a people. These styles are often called *folk styles.*

C. DESIGN CHARACTER OF THE STYLES OF INTERIOR DESIGN SINCE 1500

1. Renaissance Design

The name *Renaissance* is given to a cultural period which began earliest in Italy and from there its style traveled to France, and subse-

quently to England.[1] Inclusive dates might be given as 1400–1650. The word *Renaissance* means rebirth. The Renaissance succeeded an era of approximately one thousand years, known as the *Medieval* period, which extended back to the downfall of the classic Greek and Roman civilizations. The Renaissance was characterized by a reawakened interest in all aspects of the ancient classical civilization. Thus it was marked by a rational, humanist approach to life. The Renaissance likewise inherited some characteristics from Medieval culture, such as the quality of exceptional vigor which had marked the Nordic races and their art. Renaissance culture was therefore a new culture. Its architecture and interior design paid close respect to the formal aspects of the classic but they possessed a largeness and a grandeur which spoke eloquently of a new and vital civilization.

The Renaissance art period is usually divided into the following minor architectural and interior design periods. A study of the accompanying illustrations will show distinguishing characteristics in these various sub-styles. However, the general family likeness in all Renaissance work, as in the work of subsequent major periods, far exceeds any differences.

Italy   No essential subdivisions.

France   No essential subdivisions although the periods are sometimes named after monarchs, including the early Renaissance styles of Charles VIII, Louis XII, and Francis I; the middle Renaissance styles of Henry II, Francis II, Charles IX, and Henry III; and the late Renaissance styles of the first Bourbon Kings, Henry IV and Louis XIII.

England
   Tudor, during the reigns of Henry VII, Henry VIII, Edward VI and Mary, who were of the House of Tudor.
   Elizabethan, during the reign of Elizabeth I. This style might likewise be properly called Tudor.

[1] Discussion is limited to Italy, France, England, and Northern America. Italy is not a leading style center after the seventeenth century and America becomes more important in this respect as we approach the twentieth century.

Early Stuart or *Jacobean,* during the reigns of James I and Charles I who were of the House of Stuart.

The Commonwealth or *Cromwellian,* during the brief interlude between the reigns of Charles I and Charles II.

The rooms of important Renaissance houses and the furniture which they contained were of large size. The shape of the furniture was dominantly rectangular and straight lines were emphasized. The Italian and French designers, with a keen eye for comfort and for luxurious effects, introduced curved arms on chairs and utilized the curve for embellishments.

Colors in Renaissance decoration were few and there was much use of the primaries. Saturations were strong and tones were medium to dark. Some contrast of tone occurred in the light relief of plaster or stone used against darker woods. The use of gold enriched the color palette.

The silk velvets of Italy, the tooled leathers of Spain and France, the woolen tapestries and embroidered linen cloths of France, the Netherlands, and England afforded the Renaissance interior rich but heavy cloths. Their luster was moderate and much of it was of that quality which comes from deep reflections. The principal woods were heavy oak and walnut. The fact that they were frequently left without finish or with only an oil or wax treatment, gave them a natural luster and a porous surface which fitted in well with other Renaissance textures. Wood paneling which was combined with stone and plaster gave the walls the same textural qualities of relative coarseness, apparent weight, and dull or lustrous light.

Furnishings were comparatively sparse and arrangements possessed a formal dignity.

The feeling conveyed by Renaissance interiors must have been one of sturdiness and richness. A room done in Renaissance feeling might be charted as follows:

Walls: Oak and smoke-toned plaster.
Floors: Oak in random width planks, covered with deep oriental rugs in tones of blue, red, and cream.

Davenport: Sturdy, straight line shape—walnut wood—green wool Jacquard tapestry covering of medium lightness of tone and moderate saturation.
Chair: Shape similar to davenport with the introduction of curvature in wood arms—walnut, oak, or similar wood—leather covering held with brass tacks—color, one of the floor colors.
Other Pieces: Planned to remain in the same general design family.
Curtains or Draperies: Fabric with weight sufficient to create strong, straight folds—uneven texture and slight luster—colors to fit into color design—textured suggestions might be linen or wool gauze, coarse blocked linen, or linen damask.
Fireside Equipment: Iron, copper or unburnished brass.
Ornaments: Copper, heavy colored glass, glazed pottery.

2. Baroque Design

The name *Baroque* is given to the cultural period which followed the Renaissance. Inclusive dates might be given as 1650–1750. In America the Baroque influence continued longer. The origin and the meaning of the name Baroque is not clear. It now refers to a cultural epoch which did not break completely with the Renaissance but which indicates some realignment of emphases. During the Baroque, strict adherence to classical canons was generally abandoned in favor of freer interpretation. Although the wall surfaces of most Baroque interiors possess impressive simplicity and scale, they are finished with bolder use of classic ornament. Sometimes concentrated embellishment in overdoor pediment or in furniture design is executed with an exuberant flourish. This freedom on the part of the designer must have resulted from a sensitive awareness of the exciting geographical and scientific discoveries which were beginning to disclose a new modern world. In America the architecture and interiors of the early Baroque were provincial derivations of former European forms. In the late Baroque they were largely developed from contemporaneous English prototypes.

Figure 114. This room is an outstanding example of that flowering of the Baroque style which in England might be called Georgian and in America is known as Colonial. Most of the furniture is of Chippendale design and was made by men such as William Savery, Benjamin Randolph, and John Elliott who were members of the famous group of Philadelphia craftsmen of the mid-eighteenth century. On the floor is a superb Oriental carpet of Persian Feraghan weaving.

Interior: The Marlboro Room from Patuxet Manor, Calvert County, Maryland, c. 1744. **Owner and photograph:** Courtesy Henry F. du Pont Winterthur Museum, Winterthur, Delaware.

The Baroque art period is usually divided into the following minor architectural and interior design periods.

Italy   No essential subdivisions.

France   The periods are sometimes named after the monarchs, including the high Baroque style of *Louis XIV*, and the later Baroque style of *Louis XV* which is also sometimes called *Rococo*. During the early years of Louis XV's reign, due to his youth, a regency was established. The style of this period is sometimes called French Régence or Regency.

England

The *Restoration, Carolean* or *late Stuart*, during the reigns of Charles II, James II, William and Mary, and Anne who were of the House of Stuart.

Early Georgian, during the reigns of George I and George II who were of the House of Hanover. The furniture style of this early Georgian period is sometimes called after its principal designer, Thomas Chippendale.

America

Provincial or early American.

Colonial.

Rooms in early Baroque homes and the furniture which they contained were still of comparatively large size. There was greater vertical emphasis than had existed in Renaissance shapes. After seventeen hundred, both scale and verticality were considerably diminished. Moldings and decorative ornament which had been in bold relief during the early Baroque became flatter in profile. Throughout the history of interior design, French furniture is lighter in scale and more delicate in proportion than the corresponding English pieces. The curved line was very conspicuous in Baroque furniture design. Broken lines are frequently noted. Early Baroque utilized the geometric *C* and *S* curves. Later Baroque featured the continuous organic or *cabriole* curve.

Baroque colors were at first similar to those of the Renaissance. As the period progressed, intermediate hues of less somber cast with medium lightness and moderate saturation were much in evidence. Many rooms had painted paneling in these tones. Lighter tints were used for pan-

eling earliest in France and the moldings were frequently embellished with gilt. Gilt decoration was not so common in England. After seventeen hundred, French coloring tended towards a light, close value interval. English and American interiors assumed a dominantly light color scheme with dark notes used in the furniture.

Baroque textures were more refined than those of the Renaissance. In elaborate homes they were sumptuous. As the period progressed, textures with great depth were exchanged for those having more surface sheen. Walnut was the principal wood of the early Baroque. Later mahogany took its place in England and America, with painted and lacquered woods being popular in France and England. Provincial furniture in France was frequently made of fruitwood. In England and America local woods were used including maple, cherry, and the conifers.

In important decoration, the arrangements in interiors adhered to a classic formality. The number of pieces of furniture was greater and their character was more diverse than in former periods.

The best of Baroque decoration gives an impression of restrained, if free, use of power. The feeling is one of richness without gaudiness, homelike quality without instability, gaiety without restless frivolity. In the hands of an inept designer, Baroque design frequently crossed from these desirable to the undesirable qualities.

A room of about 1725 done in the spirit of Baroque might be charted as follows:

Figure 115. This hallway is typical of the early Neo-Classic period in design. In England it might be named the Adam period after the outstanding architect Robert Adam. In America this style is frequently called the Federal period as it flourished during the early years of the Federation of States. Such an elliptical flowing stair is typical of the freer forms which were finding favor and which were indicative of things to come. The furniture seen in this illustration, whch is in the style called late Sheraton, came from Boston and was made by the English-trained cabinet makers John Seymour and his son Thomas.

Interior: Montmorenci Stair Hall, Montmorenci, Warrenton, North Carolina, 1822. **Owner and photograph:** Courtesy Henry F. du Pont Winterthur Museum, Winterthur, Delaware.

Interior: The Empire Parlor, Rufus King house, Albany, New York, c. 1839. **Owner and photograph:** Courtesy Henry F. du Pont Winterthur Museum, Winterthur, Delaware.

Walls: Paneled and painted yellow of medium lightness and moderate saturation.

Floors: Walnut parquet, covered with an oriental rug of fine texture and subdued coloring of deep blue, rose, and gold (i.e., red and yellow, medium lightness, moderate saturation).
Unfigured velvet carpet of blue or gold might be substituted.

Davenport: Typical Chippendale design with cabriole leg and ogival (double S curve) back —mahogany wood—silk or linen damask covering duplicating one of the hues in the rug.

Chair: Large wing chair with straight legs— mahogany wood—linen cretonne covering in subdued tones of blue on cream.

Other Pieces: Planned to remain in the same general design family—shapes might feature organic curves or the simpler turnings inherited from the Dutch-influenced William and Mary style—woods might be walnut, mahogany, maple, or fruitwood—coverings could be damask, matelassé, twill, or velveteen.

Curtains and Draperies: The same linen cretonne that covers the wing chair could be used— organdy curtaining would be a possibility.

Fireside Equipment: Polished brass.

Ornaments: Silver, china, fine glass.

A more informal version of this room might be:

Walls: Wood paneling on one wall left in natural state or painted blue, green, or yellow of medium lightness, moderate saturation—other walls cream or white plaster.

Floors: Random width boards—hooked or braided rugs or linen plain weave carpet—colors restricted throughout to a few primary hues of medium lightness and moderate to strong saturation.

Figure 116. The formal social room known as a parlor is shown here as an example of the late Neo-Classic style which is sometimes known as the Empire or Greek Revival style. The furniture in this room is attributed to New York craftsmen such as Roswell Hubbard and Charles Honoré Lannuier. The rug is an Aubusson-type, contemporary with the period.

Davenport: All of the furniture in general design character of straight line American provincial relieved with some Baroque curves, or in the design character of curved line French provincial—walnut, maple, or fruitwood—covering, cotton damask or plaid gingham or an armure.

Chair: Covered in monotone chintz in color of the walls.

Other Pieces: Planned to remain in the same general design family.

Curtains: Chintz, organdy, or gingham with white or cream background.

Fireside Equipment: Brass or copper.

Ornaments: Heavy silver or pewter, or fine pottery.

3. Neo-Classic Design

The name *Neo-Classic* is given to the cultural period which followed the late Baroque. Inclusive dates might be given as 1750–1840. The name Neo-Classic implies a newly revived interest in classic design. During the earlier stages of this revival interest centered upon late classic design such as was to be seen in the newly excavated, late classical city of Pompeii. The character of this design was influenced by late Greek culture and was elegant and urbane. In the later stages of the Neo-Classic revival inspiration was found in earlier, simpler, and bolder classic forms. The art of ancient Egypt influenced French decoration. Neo-Classic design was not a repetition of classic design. It was a use of classical forms to interpret the life of the late eighteenth and early nineteenth century. The principal style center during the first part of the Neo-Classic period was England and the style was suited to an aristocratic way of life. The principal style center during the latter part of the Neo-Classic period was France and the style was suited to a way of life which centered around the newly created Emperor, the commoner, Napoleon.

The Neo-Classic art period is frequently divided into the following minor architectural and interior design periods:

France
Louis XVI.
Revolution and *Directoire,* during the period of political upheaval.
Empire, during the political ascendancy of Napoleon Bonaparte. No essential styles ascribed to the reigns of Louis XVIII, Charles X, and Louis Philippe.

England
Late Georgian, during the reign of George III. The decorative styles of this period are sometimes called after the architect Robert Adam or the furniture designers, George Hepplewhite and Thomas Sheraton.
Regency, a name given to the decorative style of the last portion of the reign of George III when, due to his insanity, a regency was declared. The decorative design during the reigns of George IV and William IV is usually associated with the Regency style.

America
American Federal. The furniture style of this period is often associated with the furniture designer, Duncan Phyfe.
Greek Revival

Neo-Classic rooms retained vertical emphasis. Their size was proportionate to the grandeur of the building. More rooms of modest size were to be found. Previous to 1800, the scale of furniture was very light. Later it became much heavier. Early proportions were attenuated and there was delicacy in the handling of ornament. Later Neo-Classic was characterized by extensive plain surfaces and concentrated bold relief. Lines in early work were dominantly straight although the good designers used subtle curves for interest. In later furniture the straight contours were combined with unbroken geometric curves. Large architectural pieces retained the straight line.

Figure 117. This bedroom corner is typical of the Victorian period as it was exemplified in a manner modifying the exuberant expression of the era.

Building: Mansion House-Museum, Oglebay Park, Wheeling, West Virginia. **Photograph:** Courtesy Oglebay Institute, Oglebay Park, Wheeling, West Virginia. **Photographer:** G. Colburn Ball, Cleveland, Ohio.

The earlier Neo-Classic used a light, pale color scheme and the later used a predominantly dark, strong scheme. Early Neo-Classic English furniture, frequently being of mahogany, introduced dark notes among otherwise light colors. American decoration used more moderation in color schemes.

Textures in the early Neo-Classic interiors were fine. Woods were satinwood, mahogany, and light painted woods. Mahogany was the dominant wood in later furniture. Textiles were at first light in weight, fine, and with high reflections. Later heavy cloths of both deep texture and surface gloss were used.

Classic formality dominated the arrangements in all but the simplest of homes.

As the late eighteenth century was revolutionary in political life, so the two sections of Neo-Classic decoration were opposed in feeling. The early style gave the impression of formal elegance of an extremely delicate sort. The latter style gave the impression of conventional grandeur of a ponderous order. Neither extreme was reached in America.

A room done in American Neo-Classic of about 1820 might be charted as follows:

Walls: Plaster or wallpaper in a moderate blue tone of medium lightness—white moldings.
Floors: Oriental rug on walnut parquet floor, or carpeting in tones of red, blue, and green interlaced with blacks.
Davenport: Typical Duncan Phyfe design using Greek curves—mahogany wood—covering of dark blue or green silk damask with a rigid bisymmetrical design in gold.
Chair: Sheraton straight-legged type of American design, slightly heavier than corresponding English chairs in scale—mahogany wood—covering of striped linen or of silk damask—gold color.
Other Pieces: Planned to remain in the same general design family—some woods might be hard maple or satinwood—some coverings might be velveteen—caning could be used.
Curtains and Draperies: Curtains, a fine embroidered swiss—draperies, a velvet, velveteen, or self-patterned silk.
Fireside Equipment: Polished brass.
Ornaments: Fine silver, china, mirrors, and brass.

A

B

C

D

E

G

F

H

267

4. Victorian Design

The name *Victorian* is given to the design of that long period covered by the reign of Queen Victoria of England. Inclusive dates would then be 1837–1901. The cultural epoch suggested by the name indicated a civilization engrossed in expanding a materialistic way of life made possible by applied science and mercantile capitalism. It was consequently a civilization with little time for art appreciation. Designs were largely revivals with small knowledge of or regard for authenticity. The inspiration for the architectural revivals derived sequentially from Gothic, Romanesque, and Italian Renaissance styles. The inspiration for furniture revivals came in the mid-century from Louis XV styles. Much design is called eclectic, a name which implies a poor borrowing from several past styles. After the middle of the century, most manufacture was by machine and there was little use made of the sensitivity of a designing artist. Craft revival styles which forecast the simplicity of the modern began in England.

The Victorian period is frequently divided into the following minor architectural and interior design periods:

France
   Second Empire, during the empire of Louis-Napoleon Bonaparte.
   Republic—no essential styles ascribed to this source.
England
   No essential subdivisions.
America
   John Belter style, a name frequently given to the mid-century furniture style as done by its principal furniture designer.

Victorian rooms were smaller in scale but retained emphasis on verticality. Furniture of the mid-century was comparatively low. The line of much that the Victorians designed was curved.

Although the prototype of these curves was the organic Louis XV curve, the nineteenth century examples were flamboyant. Later furniture was heterogeneous in shape.

Colors of mid-Victorian rooms were strong and deep. They were frequently used against a neutral background. Much use was made of gold. Later Victorian rooms were less colorful.

The finest mid-century furniture was rosewood. Furniture of the sixties and seventies was usually walnut. Marble tops were common. Oak stained a golden color appeared in the eighties. Cloths were heavy. Some were deep textured; some, such as horsehair cloth, were shiny. Open lace texture was used at windows. Heavy draperies and deep valances framed the openings.

Arrangements were no longer so formal. An effect of hominess in simple interiors and of vigor and exuberance in important rooms was established. The easy access of all people to goods of poor design quality resulted in some interiors which were both ostentatious and ugly.

A room similar to a Victorian interior might be charted as follows:

Walls: Floral wallpaper in monotone cream or grey with design created by a slightly darker value or by a shiny texture.
Floor: Printed velvet carpeting with large rose designs on black background.
Davenport: Typical John Belter design with curved legs—black walnut or rosewood—horsehair covering in black.
Other Pieces: The shape patterns would be similar throughout—textures in materials might vary from velveteens to heavier satins—small patterned armures could be used.
Fireside Equipment: Highly polished brass and iron with marble fireplaces.
Ornaments: Much use of gilt ornaments and mirrors.

Figure 118 (pages 266–267).

A. Hickory and ash Brewster type armchair, American, XVII century, Massachusetts. Similar in characteristics to certain early English chairs.

B. Maple armchair, American, late XVII century, in style derived from English Carolean.

C. Walnut Philadelphia side chair, 1725–1750, in style often called English Queen Anne.

D. Mahogany side chair, American, c. 1750–1775, in style of English cabinet maker Thomas Chippendale.

E. Federal period chair, American, made in Salem, c. 1783–1802, in style of English cabinet maker George Hepplewhite.

F. Chair, carving attributed to Samuel McIntyre, American, made in Salem, 1800–1805, in style of English cabinet maker Thomas Sheraton.

G. Chair by Duncan Phyfe, American, c. 1795–1815, based on styles of Sheraton and French Directoire.

H. Rosewood Settee, part of a parlor suite, attributed to John Belter, American, middle XIX century, in style often called English Victorian.

The modern is the eternal viewed in terms of the present.

ascribed to LUIGI PIRANDELLO *

Chapter XIII

DESIGN AND MODERN STYLE —CONTEMPORARY EXPRESSION

A. WHY THE MODERN STYLE?

All great art has come from the necessity which each age feels to create beautiful forms which serve its needs and express its culture. Only if a contemporary style comes from this age in this manner will it live as great art.

A civilization is a complex organism based upon the union of life and matter at a particular time and place. Because fundamental human needs and the basic ways of supplying them do not change, all cultures are similar. This constant character of the world enables one age to enjoy good art of other times.

Time, however, alters some things. The geographical and ethnic relations of peoples may be shifted. The American continent is now the home of many groups whose character had been established through long sojourn in other parts of the world.

* Reprinted by permission of Mr. Enzo Scipioni, Administrazione degli redi di Luigi Pirandello, Rome.

Man's artificial environment likewise changes. This is the outcome of technology which includes social, political, and economic systems (in themselves a form of technology); and man's ideology. This created background can, in turn, shape the future world.

When a culture is analyzed, its present forms can be evaluated and its future forms predicted. Twentieth century culture is responsible for twentieth century art. If we read the stars in our skies correctly we should be able to create buildings and their interiors which will not be outmoded before they are paid for.

The following is a partial suggestive analysis of the culture of twentieth century America. Each of the following factors will play its part in determining modern architecture and furnishings. Careful study of these determinants will suggest ways in which they will shape the building art of the future.

Figure 119. The plant-like form of this Tiffany vase shows the influence of L'Art Nouveau on the design of its time.

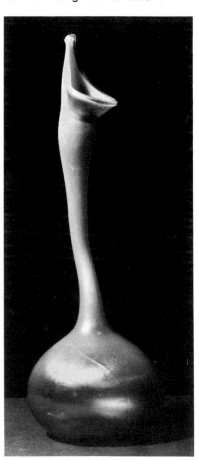

Article: Vase. **Artist:** Louis Comfort Tiffany. **Owner:** Collection of the Museum of Modern Art, New York. **Photographer:** Soichi Sunami for the Museum of Modern Art.

1. Natural factors.
   a. Land unchanged but frontiers gone—results: higher land and natural commodity values, greater economic competition.
   b. Mixed peoples with variety of backgrounds —results: diversity and possible lack of surety of taste.
2. Created factors.
   a. Technology marked by
      1) New sources of power—results: labor-saving machinery, accelerated transportation and communication; therefore, more free time and wider intellectual horizons. Nuclear fission, therefore, fear of destruction.
      2) New physiological discoveries—results: longer life span.
      3) New materials and accurate knowledge about materials—results: new forming-potentials.
      4) Greater technological complexity and potentiality—result: greater need for skilled and understanding workers.
   b. Social, political, and economic structure marked by revolutionary social and economic movements—results: rapid changes in levels of society, rapid changes in location of population, developing attitude of social interdependence and responsibility.
   c. Ideology influenced by scientific thought which currently places emphasis not on matter itself but rather upon energy and relationships—results: a reappraisal and reaffirmation of values in these terms.

B. THE TAPROOTS OF THE MODERN

The roots of any new movement are to be found underneath the apparent surface. For more than one hundred years prophetic writers have been criticizing the imitative quality of building art. For instance, the American sculptor Horatio Greenough, of the early nineteenth century, said that the mechanics of the United States had outstripped the artists in inventiveness. Some Englishmen, like the writer John Ruskin and the artist craftsman William Morris, felt that only if man turned his back on the machine would a great creative art develop.

Figure 120. Villa Spitzer, Vienna, the photographic studio of Joseph Hoffman. This room illustrates the dramatic use of straight line geometry and light-dark contrast which was characteristic of the Viennese contemporary design.

Building: Villa Spitzer, Vienna, photographic studio of Joseph Hoffman. **Photograph:** Courtesy Museum of Modern Art, New York.

In the midst of this dissatisfaction with the visual aspect of their world, a small group of men, using the Paris exhibition of 1900 as a proving ground, attempted to create a new style arbitrarily. It was self-christened *l'art nouveau* and was doomed to failure because its characteristic sweeping curves and ornamental floral forms were too weak and unstable for either architecture or furniture. No movement which divorces one aspect of art from its alliances will long survive. L'art nouveau died because a novel appearance was its only asset.

Similar new stylistic movements were developing almost simultaneously in other parts of Europe. Painters in the Netherlands such as Piet Mondrian and Theo van Doesburg, and the Belgian architect Henri Van de Velde (who had likewise been a leader of l'art nouveau) correlated painting and architecture in a style which evolved largely from a straight line break-up of space.[1]

[1] The "whiplash" line of l'art nouveau was sometimes added for embellishment.

In Austria the stylistic approach to new forms was important. It coincided with a native feeling for color and texture and with an equally characteristic respect for sound craftsmanship. This dual point of view marked the work of the Vienna *Werkstätte* group. This was one of the first artists' organizations to develop a school and merchandising outlet competent to deal with every facet of the building complex. Thus the barriers between architect, builder, designer, and craftsman were removed.

A construction problem involves many skills and the Werkstätte united these under one planning discipline. The architectural style of this group from its early leadership by Otto Wagner to the days of Joseph Hoffmann, was characterized by a simplification of form, a concentration of color decoration relieved by large areas of plain surface, and a qualification of shapes through material texture. The Scottish artist and builder, Charles R. MacKintosh, who exhibited interiors in Vienna in the early years of this century, introduced a Gallic-influenced note of dramatic black and white simplicity into the Danube style.

Another approach to a twentieth century style developed in Germany. Here the industrial revolution had come late. This gave its leaders a chance to learn from the mistakes of their competitors. German industry from its very inception attempted to ally good art and the machine. In 1907 the first Werkbund was organized, a coalition of industrialists, artists, and workmen dedicated to the production of honest, useful, and beautiful things through industrial processes.

A Viennese-trained architect, Peter Behrens, became an early leader in this cause. The most influential leaders of twentieth century European architecture came under his influence. Le Corbusier (Charles Édouard Jeanneret-Gris), the Swiss-born French architect, is one. Others are Walter Gropius and Mies van der Rohe who became directors of the famous school at Weimar (later at Dessau and Berlin) known as the *Bauhaus.*

The purpose of the Bauhaus curriculum was to establish a standard by which buildings and all enclosed artifacts could be made by twentieth century processes and still be beautiful

Figure 121. This famous interior of Tugendhat House, Brno, Czechoslovakia, which the architect Mies van der Rohe designed in 1930, was one of the first successful demonstrations in a building of many characteristics of contemporary architecture. It has an open plan and an exposed supportng framework with glass exterior walls.

Building: Tugendhat House, Brno, Czechoslovakia, 1930. **Architect:** Mies van der Rohe. **Photograph:** Courtesy Museum of Modern Art, New York.

Article: "Bamboo in Fine Weather After Rain," twofold screen, ink on paper. **Artist:** Ikeno Taiga (1723–1776), Japanese. **Owner:** The Cleveland Museum of Art, The J. H. Wade Collection, Cleveland, Ohio. **Photographer:** The Cleveland Museum of Art, Cleveland, Ohio.

Figure 122. Many characteristics of Oriental art such as a respectful love of nature, a dynamic movement with a mete subordination of detail to this rhythm, and a meaningful and suggestive utilization of empty space, have evoked sympathetic admiration in the Occident.

and functional. The basic instruction involved experimentation with a wide variety of materials and techniques. Because of its academic sanction the school was an important influence in promoting the structural use of steel, glass, and ferroconcrete.

The forms, largely originated by the Bauhaus designers, became known under the name of the *International Style*.[2] The significance of the architectural package so described was that it derived from contemporary materials and processes, which made possible new planning potentials, which in turn influenced its appearance. Mechanized fabrication of lighter, stronger materials lead on the one hand to greater regularity of structural modules and to larger interior spaces. On the other hand, greater plasticity of materials and large sheets of glass added the potential of organic rhythms and of visual ex-

tension of the interior to outer space. Most Bauhaus artists have accepted the discipline of a regular precise framework within which to develop a moving sequential order.

Certain stylistic aspects of oriental art, particularly the art of Japan, have influenced modern occidental architecture. This is true because these qualities have been a concrete expression of exactly those characteristics which the Bauhaus advanced. However, oriental art exemplified these through works which were hand-formed of natural materials. Thus the expression was emotionally appealing. The respect for the natural world, the preference for organic rhythms (built in architecture from regular modules), and the utilization of space as a design factor have been easily translated from the East to the West.

While most oriental art is characterized by a subtle and subdued color palette, Mexican art, so close to our border, uses strong colors and patterns. There is every indication that its spirit

[2] H. R. Hitchcock and P. C. Johnson, *The International Style, Architecture Since 1922* (New York: W. W. Horton Co., Inc., 1932), p. 14.

Residence of: Mr. and Mrs. C. K. Reynolds, Jr., Hudson, Ohio. **Photographer:** William A. Wynne, courtesy of the **Cleveland Plain Dealer,** Cleveland, Ohio.

276

Figure 123. American architecture comes from American soil. It possesses a straight-forward vigor in design and a close association with nature. This is shown in this home built in the mid-nineteenth century. Its interior planning is by no means stereo-typed. The hallway occupies a center and side of the building and living areas are freely planned around this position. It creates a charming setting and a way of life for an interesting and busy family of today.

(Above) **Building:** Farmington Museum (Stanley-Whitman House) Farmington, Connecticut. **Photographer:** G. Colburn Ball, Cleveland, Ohio.

(Opposite) **Building:** Monticello, Charlottesville, Virginia. **Photograph:** Courtesy Thomas Jefferson Memorial Foundation, Curtis Thacker, Superintendent of Monticello.

will supply the kind of excitement which many enjoy. Even current Japanese art seems influenced in this direction.

Any new building art which is to grow on American soil cannot be solely an import. It must come to terms with indigenous American predilections. Despite the fact that many nationalities settled this continent, America primarily has been a crucible which poured out the individual contributions as new forms. Expansion into nature has been part of our heritage. As soon as safety would permit we spread outdoors onto porches. We rambled indoors with a free plan even though the exteriors of buildings were clamped into formal façades. We simplified and made more forceful and dignified the classicism of the eighteenth century. We approached structure from an experimental angle.

Louis Sullivan, the Chicago architect of the turn of the century, was an outstanding exponent of an American building art which developed from American roots. His pupil, the great American architect Frank Lloyd Wright, restated this dream of a native architecture in terms of the American house.[3] He felt that a house must be related to the earth both in form and in materials. Broad eaves, providing a sense of shelter, contribute to this effect. The disposition of walls and spaces should make movement between the outdoors and the indoors easy. While glorifying nature, man's dwelling should likewise

[3] F. L. Wright, *An Autobiography* (New York: Duell, Sloan and Pearce, 1943), pp. 123–149.

Figure 124. These two famous houses, one of the seventeenth and one of the eight-eenth century show how the character of simplicity and vigor in design and close relation to the earth persist even as styles in American architecture change.

dignify his own stature. This is accomplished through functional planning and through scaling to the human size. Nevertheless the scope of human powers should be granted room for development. Inner spaciousness is desirable and is in part accomplished through opening up inner space and in part by the avoidance of inner clutter, i.e., all that is visually or practically unessential. Mr. Wright was likewise a consistent experimenter with new techniques.

This then is the background. The path ahead is not just any man's guess. We anticipate that American designers will appreciate and develop those aspects of the building art of other peoples which will implement our way of life. Whatever may be its worth, it is impossible for art to deny this way and survive.

C. THE VISUAL DESIGN OF THE MODERN INTERIOR

1. The Over-all Picture

The visual design of the modern interior is more than an artist's whim. He has used the structural, mechanical, and planning techniques of today to create a pleasing design which he intends to be useful and expressive of our way of life. Although no style can be regimented unless it is dead, nevertheless it is not a contradiction to say that certain characteristics of a living style can be analyzed. The limitations which define the style do not act as restrictions. Actually they serve to stimulate rather than repress creativity.

279

The composite picture made by contemporary interiors is one of such simplicity that it gives the impression of having no calculated design. This is far from being the truth. The casual effect of the contemporary is certainly not fortuitous.

Modern interior design seems more complex than compound. It is made by developing a few rather than many visual traits. The number of different shapes, colors, and textures which are used is restricted. Their development is largely by repetition and slight variation. Contrast is reserved for bold relief.

An examination of such an interior will show a relation between modern architecture and its furnishings. This may be further illustrated as follows.

2. Shapes in the Contemporary Interior

a. GENERAL EMPHASIS ON SPACE AND DYNAMIC MOVEMENT

The emphasis in all modern architectural design is upon the space rather than the mass of its volume. This is first accomplished by opening up interior space (called open planning), rather than dividing it into a number of small rooms.

Various structural methods may be used to create these larger spans of space. Usually there is dependence upon a number of visible and regularly placed supports which in turn impose their modular rhythm upon the interior.

A second and dynamic kind of movement pattern is frequently part of both the architecture and furnishings. Mass and void may be related to each other so as to create a visually apprehended flow of space in two or in three directions.

Such plastic organization gives a temporal aspect to the space experience of a good modern interior. Actually and imaginatively one must move through the spaces and movement involves time.

Because it is desirable to sense an equilibrium from every visual angle of this journey through space, the resulting design is a fluid unified organization wherein mass exists primarily for shaping space and creating spatial relations.

b. SHAPES IN FURNISHINGS

The separate pieces used in modern furnishings are designed with an emphasis on space. The structure of furniture permits strength without bulk, therefore scale need not be large and edges can be thin. Furniture which takes its place as part of the fixed architecture of a room may be an exception although much of this is designed so that its planes are suspended in space.

One large piece, however, which is related to the architectural room divisions, will look less busy than several small pieces. With similar logic, decorative focal points are frequently overscaled in comparison with traditional usage. Large pictures, lamps (which are usually more functional, too), plants—these accents are few and must carry proportionately more emphasis.

The dominant direction in which contemporary furnishings are organized is horizontal. Gone are the highboys of the eighteenth century. Length is more in evidence than height. Tables and chair seats are low. This low horizontality is sometimes strikingly opposed by vertical thrusts. There is often a prominent diagonal direction which is essential to the joinery of some furniture, or which is part of the functional angle of some seating furniture, or which is undoubtedly added for verve in some instances.

Line becomes a most emphatic type of shape in modern design. In an art where mass is minimized, where planes are principally used to mark relations between spaces, line remains the only type of shape which can be used as a pattern tract. Line will not interfere unduly with the illusion of space. A line can epitomize a character quality most succinctly. As modern character is so allied to movement a moving line almost becomes its symbol.

The lines most in evidence in modern furnishings possess a vigorous and flowing quality. Straight lines and either the strong organic or regular curves are suitable. Oblique angularity is likewise expressive of today's construction where steel may be drawn taut over a three-dimensional grid, and thrust and counterthrust are so clearly resolved. The delicately scaled organic curve of French eighteenth century

Figure 125. The Hickox House, Illinois, 1900. Frank Lloyd Wright, architect.

Building: The Hickox House, Illinois, 1900. **Architect:** Frank Lloyd Wright. **Photograph:** Courtesy Museum of Modern Art, New York.

furniture, as well as tenuous tracts such as are found in a Klee painting or a spray of twigs, are frequently used with modern furnishings. These lines are flowing but are not forceful. They may suggest something of the quizzical state of the modern artist's mind when contemplating the thin and easily snapped thread of modern existence.

In order to give the lines and planes of modern shapes full rein, they are usually stripped of added decoration. Embellishment will probably come in due time. Surface decoration which takes on the character of surface texture is already seen. Later it may be expected to appear less random and to strengthen structure.

Furnishings are sparse in modern interiors and their placement is related to the spatial rhythms of the room. Such restraints and disposition requires the most sensitive feeling for proportional relations. It necessitates leaving any space which is vital to the design, either unfilled or unobtrusively occupied.

Articles are used in the contemporary style not for themselves alone. They break space into purposeful divisions and may cause vision to move from the object to the space beyond.

c. PRACTICAL SUGGESTIONS FOR SHAPE ORGANIZATION

There are practical ways of obtaining these contemporary shape effects. The following suggestions may be given:

1. Simplify the wall and floor surfaces in older structures by removing heavy moldings, baseboards, and any projecting fixtures.
2. Furnish as sparsely as considerations of function will allow.
3. Select furniture which is functional but which is light in scale.[4] The emphasis should be on space rather than on mass.
4. Select major furnishings with an eye for quiet, unobtrusive design.
5. Utilize built-in furniture whenever it fits into the functional plan.
6. Whenever possible use one larger furniture unit which coincides with the architectural spaces in preference to several small units.
7. Arrange the furnishings in functional groupings but try to keep the groups related to the architectural spacing. An exception to

[4] Furniture which is too small for a space is likewise to be avoided as it detracts from a forceful effect.

A

(A) **Residence of:** Mr. and Mrs. Norman Everest Weaver, Scottsdale, Arizona. **Interior Designer:** Mary Jane Manning, Interiors for Solar Living, Scottsdale, Arizona. **Photographer:** Albert Summers, Phoenix, Arizona.

(B) **Residence of:** Mr. and Mrs. Robert A. Boone, Pepper Pike Village, Ohio. **Interior Designer:** Robert A. Boone, A.I.D., Irvin & Co., Inc., Cleveland, Ohio. **Photographer:** Robert A. Boone, Cleveland, Ohio.

(C) **Residence of:** Mr. and Mrs. James Kelso, Kent Woodlands, California. **Architect:** Wurster, Bernardi and Emmons, A.I.A., San Francisco, California. **Interior Designer:** Maurice Sands, San Francisco, California. **Photographer:** Roger Sturtevant, San Francisco, California. **Courtesy: Record Houses of 1956.** F. W. Dodge Corporation, New York.

(D) **Residence of:** Mr. and Mrs. Frank B. Evarts, Kailua, Hawaii. **Photograph:** Courtesy **Honolulu Advertiser,** Pat Millard, Building Editor.

B

C

Figure 126. Americans will live as America lives. The structure and the design will be of today and tomorrow created by men of vision. The flavor will differ over the expanse of territory and with regional tastes. But the spirit of this way of life has roots in yesterday.

A. In Arizona;

B. In Ohio;

C. In California;

D. In Hawaii.

D

this is when space is large enough so that furniture may be arranged free from the wall and thus give the feeling of free circulation through space.

8. Respect glass walls whenever they are used. Do not obstruct them by placement of furniture in front of them.

9. Keep the furniture as low as is functional.

10. Keep the horizontal level as uniform as is compatible with interest.

11. Arrange the furnishings so that the eye is carried from group to group and finally to centers of decorative interest and, in many cases, outdoors.

12. Use decorative objects and pattern as proportion spacers and for emphasis. Be certain that they are aesthetically worthy and sufficiently important for their purpose.

3. Colors in the Contemporary Interior

a. POTENTIALITY OF COLOR TODAY

Color is one of the most exciting tools which the modern artist can command. Contemporary pigments offer possibilities far beyond yesterday's palette. Modern painters frequently desert both perspective and chiaroscuro to give greater play to color. Because their work is not dictated by an imitation of nature it is frequently flatter in design and more related to wall surfaces. It is not mere chance that modern painting has suggested the possibility of relating color to architecture [5] in new and exhilarating ways.

b. SPACE AND MOVEMENT IN RELATION TO COLOR

Modern color must supplement the spatial effects of the building in which it is incorporated. All of the suggestions [6] to enlarge space through color may need to be followed. In addition, color can emphasize the spatial rhythms. Highly repetitive color sequences can echo repetitive architectural modules, and close, progressive color sequences may implement the dynamic rhythms of spaces. Color contrast is sometimes of use to position a plane or to emphasize an accent.

c. COLOR AS RELATED TO LOCATION AND STRUCTURE OF BUILDING

Because of the differences of location of contemporary buildings, various types of palettes are found suitable. In a situation where the interior is closely related to a natural outdoor setting, the earth colors may set the tone. The reduction of the principal saturations and lightness-darkness to the intermediate range will give the greatest illusion of space in this situation because these tones will suggest a continuity with the setting.

Whenever a structure utilizes steel and glass rather than natural materials such as wood and stone, another type of palette may be indicated.[7] To the extent that the steel is evident, colder or more achromatic colors are suggested. In order to reestablish a warm emotional tone, contrasting hues or contrast in lightness-darkness is almost requisite. When such a structure is located among urban surroundings there is no particular reference between the structure and nature. Thus an achromatic background with the most brilliant color accents may be the solution. Brilliant hues as well as black and white are somehow akin to the taut sinews of the building. When such a building is in a natural setting its color scheme would be necessarily more restricted. Backgrounds could be nearly achromatic but not completely so. Grey toned, light-filtering curtains are frequently required in order to effect a tonal unity between the indoors and the outdoors. Accents should be carefully adjusted so as to give first place attention to the scenery. Warm slightly less greyed tones would be good.

Occasionally a contemporary room is found which shows little reference either to its structure or to its surroundings. The palette of the

---

[5] H. R. Hitchcock, *Painting Toward Architecture* (New York: Duell, Sloan and Pearce, Inc., 1948).

[6] Considered in Chap. VII.

[7] New buildings, such as the Seagram building in New York City, designed by Mies van der Rohe and Philip Johnson, are in bronze and dark glass. These materials would appear to require a warmer, deeper suffusion of color.

Figure 127. A high degree of artistic skill is required to create the effect of simplicity achieved in this living room.

Residence of: The Architect, Moreland Hills, Ohio. **Architect:** Ernst Payer, A.I.A., Cleveland, Ohio. **Artist:** Ceramic plant holder, Lisa McVey, ceramic artist, Cleveland, Ohio. Marble figures, sculptor unknown, Northern Spain, late 15th Century. **Photographer:** C. W. Ackerman, Cleveland, Ohio.

(A) **Article:** Form-wire, "Small Diamond" chair. **Designer:** Harry Bertoia. **Manufacturer:** Knoll Associates, Inc., New York.

(B) **Article:** Upholstered, molded cup-like shell chair. **Designer:** Eero Saarinen. **Manufacturer:** Knoll Associates, Inc., New York.

(E) **Article:** Molded plywood chair. **Designer:** Charles Eames. **Manufacturer:** Herman Miller Furniture Co., Zeeland, Michigan.

(F) **Article:** Pedestal chair, molded plastic. **Designer:** Eero Saarinen. **Manufacturer:** Knoll Associates, Inc., New York.

(I) **Article:** Classic chair, wood. **Designer:** Hans Wegner. **Manufacturer:** Georg Jensen, Inc., New York.

(J) **Article:** Lounge chair. **Designer:** Folke Ohlsson (President), Dux, Inc. **Manufacturer:** Dux, Inc., San Francisco, California.

(C) **Article:** Low wood armchair. **Designer:** Jens Risom. **Manufacturer:** Jens Risom Design, Inc., New York.

(D) **Article:** Plastic shell, molded chair. **Designer:** Charles Eames. **Manufacturer:** Herman Miller Furniture Co., Zeeland, Michigan.

C

D

G

(G) **Article:** The "Barcelona" chair. **Designer:** Mies van der Rohe. **Manufacturer:** Knoll Associates, Inc., New York.

(H) **Article:** Occasional lounge chair. **Designer:** Finn Juhl. **Manufacturer:** Georg Jensen, Inc., New York.

H

(K) **Article:** Metal upholstered chair. **Designer:** Paul McCobb. **Manufacturer:** B. G. Mesberg Corp., New York.

(L) **Article:** High back lounge chair. **Designer:** George Nelson. **Manufacturer:** Herman Miller Furniture Co., Zeeland, Michigan.

K

L

Figure 128. Contemporary chairs showing emphasis on space.

Residence of: Mr. and Mrs. Lewis Dowell, Seattle, Washington. **Architect:** Paul Hayden Kirk, A.I.A., Seattle, Washington. **Interior Designer:** Del-Teet Furniture Company, Seattle, Washington. **Landscape Architect:** William G. Teufel. **Photographer:** Dearborn - Massar, Seattle, Washington.

Figure 129. The opening of space in three dimensions has been artistically achieved in this interesting home.

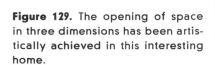

interior designer then is less restricted. It need only consider the kind of atmosphere which is intended.

d. COLOR SUGGESTIONS FROM MODERN PAINTERS

Whatever the conditions, it is possible to produce an interesting modern color scheme without having it out of character or garish on the one hand, or drab on the other. A study of the color of modern painting might provide many practical suggestions. Here are a few relations which have been noted.

The Mexican painters frequently use hues which are close together, in strong saturation, and in duplicate lightness-darkness.

Matisse combines colors in which the lightness-darkness relations are different from those found in the rainbow. He then reestablishes the natural order in the same painting.

Utrillo is master of elegant work in a nearly achromatic scale.

In some oriental painting a small dark area will be a counterpoint for an entire moving sequence of lighter tones.

Picasso is apt to divorce his color organization from his spatial organization. He arranges his colors in amorphous areas and over these he superimposes an unrelated grid of linear pattern.

Both Bracque and Picasso frequently keep their color within the confines of an enclosing shape but break up the latter by subtle alterations of the enclosed color.

The contemporary painter creates the illusion of transparency through color. This effect is produced by designing two shapes so that they overlap one another. The overlapping section is colored with a tone which would result if a transparency of the color of the one space were laid over the other.

Impressionists' use of color in small areas which becomes mixed by the eye, is part of modern technique.

Aerial perspective, or the utilization of color to suggest location in space is frequently seen.

e. PRACTICAL SUGGESTIONS FOR COLOR ORGANIZATION

One good formula for a buying guide for a modern color scheme might be:

1. Start with a carpet which is medium in lightness and moderate in saturation.
2. Buy unfigured carpet and upholstery unless for some reason this is the spot where concentration of accent is intended.
3. The major wall areas can be like the carpet in hue and saturation. It may be necessary to make the wall light for reflection.
4. From this basic wall color other walls may move by short color intervals to whatever is the room's focal point.
5. Balance and rest may be secured by the weight of some tonal contrast.
6. The upholstery colors are frequently restricted to one hue which may be a wall or floor tone, or to one hue plus a neutral, or to one hue and a wall or floor hue.
7. Drapery colors are frequently similar to wall colors. They may be lighter and brighter and contain more yellow. This is along a recognized path for eye movement.
8. Saturated accent hues may be concentrated in some significant focal point, rather than scattered about the space.

Another good formula for a buying guide for a modern color scheme might be:

1. Start with walls which are very light and greyed (any hue almost achromatic).
2. Use dark floors with light rugs. Occasional patterned rugs in bold light and dark accents may help to preserve balance with bold accents to be used elsewhere.
3. Curtains can be similar to walls or, occasionally, to floors.
4. Upholstery may be of several bright, saturated hues used in some contemporary visual order relationship, for example an orange cushion on a red chair. Or most of the upholstery may be in one dark unsaturated hue played against a rhythm of more saturated closely related hues seen in areas of upholstery or of decorative objects.
5. Furniture may be of achromatic toned steel, black iron, or dark wood.

4. Textures in the Contemporary Interior

a. SPECIAL NEED FOR QUALIFICATION BY TEXTURE

Because modern architecture designs with planes and uses plain surfaces there is need for textural as well as color qualification of the shape design. The contemporary designer knows that an expanse of beautiful texture can bring its own aesthetic thrill.

b. TEXTURE AS RELATED TO LOCATION AND STRUCTURE OF BUILDING

What kinds of textures seem most in keeping with the modern interior? The answer depends upon the location of the building and upon the kinds of texture which are in its structure. The building which is closely related to nature in material and location will require textures which are not too fine and which break up light into irregular patterns. Light reflection should not be excessive and it would seem harmonious to have reflections which are not hard off the surface.

The contemporary house which is built of harder materials, which uses steel and a great deal of glass in its structure, which may not be in close contact with a natural setting, generally requires finer textures. Softness with resiliency is likewise needed—the first trait supplying contrast, the second fitting the texture into the scheme because of its suggestion of strength. Depth textures are required to soften the effect of hardness created by the structure itself. Soft, resilient, and deep textures are likewise suggested for use with plastics.[8]

c. TEXTURAL PROGRESSIONS FROM EXTERIOR SPACES TO INTERIOR SPACES

Because many contemporary builders grade the textures with which they build from coarse to finer as they move from the exterior to the interior of the house, so the interior designer will do likewise. This gives greater opportunity for the use of fine textures than was formerly

[8] See p. 217.

thought to be possible in the decorating of the contemporary house. The contemporary house of more formal character may likewise use finer textures.

d. IMPORTANCE OF TEXTURAL DESIGN

Creating a design from textural variations and contrasts is an important part of decorative work today. This is an advance in contemporary design beyond the early days when a room filled with shaggy rough textures was considered to be the only trademark of the modern.

D. THE DESIGN USE OF THE OLD WITH THE NEW

Many designers like to use the old with the new. In many instances this is benefit born of necessity which creates a homelike interior.

The successful alliances of the traditional with the modern are usually a matter of shape harmony. Color and texture differences can be modified through finishing. Expression relations are very important.

It is not possible for the old to be exactly like the new. Therefore, whenever a modern focus is intended it should be planned and should predominate. Older pieces will be suitable because they provide some design similarity or a great deal of contrast with the new. Contrast pieces would probably be reserved for important emphasis and therefore would need to be of especially good quality.

The following notations indicate some of the design alliances between traditional and contemporary furniture.

1. Renaissance, including early American:
   a. Repeats straight line vigor and integrity of expression of the modern.
   b. Contrasts with the contemporary in greater size and mass.
2. Baroque:
   a. Repeats aspects of modern curves. Early Baroque, specifically English Restoration, repeats modern geometric curves but contrasts with the modern by breaking these in ornate fashion. Early Baroque likewise contrasts in greater size.

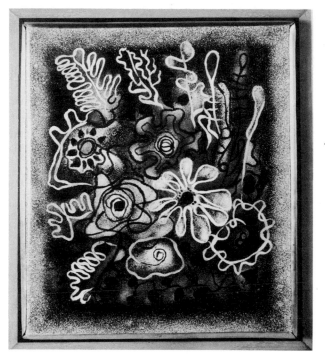

(Left) **Article:** "Delineation," enamel plaque, 1950. **Artist:** Kenneth F. Bates, Instructor in Design and Enameling, Cleveland Institute of Art, Cleveland, Ohio. **Photographer:** The Cleveland Museum of Art, Cleveland, Ohio.

(Right) **Article:** "Unicyclists," sculpmetal. **Artist:** John Clague, Instructor, The Cleveland Institute of Art, Cleveland, Ohio. **Owner:** The Cleveland Museum of Art, gift of the Cleveland Art Association, Cleveland, Ohio. **Photographer:** The Cleveland Museum of Art, Cleveland, Ohio.

Figure 130. In all phases of contemporary artistic expression we note the prominence of linear shape. A line is a succinct way of spelling motion and has been a notable characteristic of the art of many peoples who have lived in vigorous climates.

b. Late Baroque, especially Louis XV, repeats general scale and lowness of modern. Its continuous and silhouetting organic curves repeat this quality in contemporary work. The French curves have smaller scale.

3. Neo-Classic:
   a. Repeats the straight line or the unbroken geometric curves of the modern.
   b. Early Neo-Classic, especially Sheraton, repeats the modern emphasis on space rather than mass. It repeats the modern in its use of plain surfaces. It may contrast with the modern because of its sometimes smaller scale and its expression of formality.
   c. Later Neo-Classic, especially Empire, repeats the general scale of the modern. Some larger pieces of this style may provide impressive contrast.

4. Victorian:
   a. Repeats the lowness, organic curves, and general size of the modern.
   b. Repeats a general expression of informal hominess.
   c. Contrasts in its flamboyant ornateness.

E. CONTEMPORARY FURNISHINGS

1. The Road Recently Traveled

The development of modern applied art parallels the history of contemporary architecture.[9] Middle Europe became the first center for that clear thinking which allied the machine to good

[9] The data for this section was obtained from many sources. One of the most complete sources is R. Rosenthal and H. Ratzka, *The Story of Modern Applied Art* (New York: Harper & Bros., 1948).

Figure 132. This residence, another view of which is seen in the frontispiece, is a city apartment. Its interior textures are finer and harder than those of a building with exposed wood. Metal and glass are used to repeat the hardness; leather and tile, the light reflection; and porcelain and silk, the refinement of the room textures. Deep firm pile in the carpeting affords the necessary relief.

Building: Apartment in New York City. **Interior Designer:** Virginia Whitmore Kelly, New York. **Photographer:** Alexandre Georges, New City, New York. Courtesy **House and Garden,** Copyright 1959, The Condé Nast Publications, Inc.

Figure 131 (opposite). When a building is closely related to nature, the textures used in the interior show an appropriate correspondence in respect to fineness.

Residence of: Mr. and Mrs. Bruce M. Walker, Spokane, Washington. **Architect:** Walker, McGough and Trogdon, Architects, A.I.A., Spokane, Washington. **Photographer:** Morley Baer, Berkeley, California.

design through the training of the designer.

This approach to furnishing design which was dictated by contemporary resources never found great favor in France. French industry was built on the luxury trade and it was slow to adopt measures which might jeopardize a traffic in suave, elegant, expensive wares.

Nevertheless it was the French government which made the world conscious of modern furnishing. In 1925 it sponsored an exhibition devoted to modern industrial and applied art produced since World War I. The Austrians through the Werkstätte were able to contribute the most consistently unified expression of architecture and furnishings. The United States turned down the invitation to participate because of lack of material.

During the first quarter of the twentieth century there had been little applied art produced in the United States which might be considered to belong to any concerted modern movement. Sporadic craft enterprises such as that of the

early twentieth century community, the *Roycrofters* at East Aurora, New York, under the leadership of Elbert Hubbard, attempted to follow the English handcraft movements and to link a hand technique to good design. Unfortunately much of their furniture output, which was similar to that of the machine-made so-called American mission style,[10] was uninspired in design.

There had been a few modern innovations seen here. In 1904 modern furnishings designed by Peter Behrens and the pavilion designed by Joseph Olbrich of Vienna were shown as an important contribution to the St. Louis Fair. In 1912 the Newark Art Museum, under the directorship of John Cotton Dana, organized the first American exhibit of modern utilitarian articles which had been designed abroad. The famous show of modern European painting in New York, known as the Armory Show, occurred

[10] So named because of a presumed design relation to the furnishings of the missions in our West.

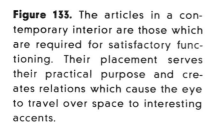

Figure 133. The articles in a contemporary interior are those which are required for satisfactory functioning. Their placement serves their practical purpose and creates relations which cause the eye to travel over space to interesting accents.

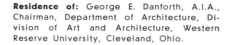

Residence of: George E. Danforth, A.I.A., Chairman, Department of Architecture, Division of Art and Architecture, Western Reserve University, Cleveland, Ohio.

in 1913. It introduced America to changes in the European fine arts horizon. The Russian Ballet, which came in 1916, showed an entirely new gamut of saturated colors.

Despite these prefaces to a new design world, the Paris Exposition of 1925 came as a shock to many Americans. When travelers saw examples of the best modern which was produced in Europe, they were made aware of the fact that any American contribution was noticeable by its absence. Store buyers who went to Paris to look, eagerly bought of the new. They returned to America and introduced the modern style through that great medium for the creation of popular taste, the American department store.

American industry when it sensed a demand, made a belated attempt to produce. These first American wares were very poorly designed. Except for the work of the relatively few European designers who had come to America, there was no directive for the new turn in style preference. Soon however, American schools began to train modern designers. The Cranbrook Academy of Arts at Bloomfield Hills, Michigan, became a prototype for American schools patterned after the advanced institutions in Europe. Its approach is similar to that of the Bauhaus and its program combines training in the fine and applied arts. The Chicago Institute of Design carried on the Bauhaus principles under the leadership of Bauhaus personnel.

Outstanding American museums, especially those whose charters included clauses permitting a relating of the arts to daily life, began to present exhibitions of the best designed American products. The Metropolitan Museum in New York appointed Richard F. Bach as associate in Industrial Art. In his dual capacity as educational director, also, of this great museum, he worked for artistic integrity and for creativity.[11]

In 1929 the Museum of Modern Art was founded in New York City and erected its permanent building ten years later. Through its exhibitions, contest for good furniture design (1940), and Good Design Awards sponsored jointly with the Chicago Merchandise Mart, the

[11] Mr. Bach is now the educational advisor of the American Institute of Decorators.

museum has made the American public conscious of good modern design. In 1956 the Museum of Contemporray Crafts was opened in New York City.

By the mid-thirties the early educational efforts were bearing fruit in America. There were a number of industrial designers who were leaders in the modern movement and who hold the front ranks today.

At the middle of the century modern applied art may be said to have arrived in America. It has gained public approval as those antennae of public taste, the home furnishing magazines, clearly indicate. Art in the schools has joined its ranks. One sign of its maturity is the fact that many of its practitioners are now anonymous as contrasted with those earlier who were singularly well known. Designers and craftsmen work for excellence in the modern style. Their work stands on its merit and industry has no need to sell modern furnishings solely on the value of a name.

American industry does not stand alone in production of well designed modern furnishings. The Scandinavians come very close to the heart of the modern movement in the applied arts. They have of necessity produced the major portion of what they needed. They have a tradition of simplicity in living and of honesty of craftsmanship that reaches back toward antiquity. Their contemporary arts are derived from but are not copies of their folk art. Their forms are thus both indigenous and original, expressive of the taste of a sensitive, sturdy, nature-loving people. Such furnishings please similar persons in other lands. In 1954 four Scandinavian countries joined in sending an outstanding exhibition of contemporary arts and crafts to the United States. This exhibition was seen in many of the leading art museums of this country.

Italy has been the most recent European country to join the fashion front in production of contemporary furnishings. Italy's artistic past had been so glorious that she found it difficult to break with it. Not being a strongly centralized nation, manufacture was largely handcraft and localized. Gio Ponti, through his publication *Domus,* did much to encourage the modern style in the decorating arts. The Triennale exhibition,

Figure 135. For many households an older residence may seem the best answer to the housing problem. Old buildings can be given a contemporary look without doing harm to the original architectural character.

Building: Apartment in New York City. **Interior Designer:** Virginia Whitmore Kelly, New York. **Photographer:** Ben Schnall, New York. **Courtesy: Interiors,** Copyright 1957, Whitney Publications, Inc.

Figure 134 (opposite). The owners of this beautifully designed contemporary residence had for some years enjoyed their association with their fine traditional furniture. How at home it seems in its new setting and how much more the house must mean to them because of its presence.

Building: Residence in northern Ohio. **Architect:** Ernst Payer, A.I.A., Cleveland, Ohio. **Photographer:** Bill Engdahl, Hedrich-Blessing, Chicago, Illinois.

Residence of: Mr. and Mrs. Leon Gordon Miller, Shaker Heights, Ohio. **Interior Designer:** Leon Gordon Miller, Cleveland, Ohio. **Photographer:** Martin Linsey, Shaker Heights, Ohio.

Figure 136. It frequently seems desirable to alter the entire interior design of a building so that its purposes and the wishes of its occupants may be better served.

which has been held every third year in Milan for a period of over twenty-five years, has shown a consistent advance in the modern creative work of the Italian designers. In 1950 an exhibition entitled "Italy at Work" began a tour of a group of leading American museums.

This new Italian Renaissance covers a diversity of objects from furniture to clothing. It is characterized by a dramatic quality which, although it has a counterpart in French design, seems more spontaneous and more expressive of the sheer joy of living. Although its fun gets somewhat out of hand and capricious at times, it never seems pretentious. The absence of this quality gives it a spirit of truly sophisticated gaiety.

Oriental countries are producing for the modern home furnishings market. With modern architecture so strongly marked by design similarities with the East, the decorative objects of the orient find favor in Western eyes. It would seem that they could be best used to supplement our way of life rather than to imitate an eastern mode.

2. Furniture

a. AN APPRAISAL

Modern furniture has grown to maturity. Good modern furniture can be secured at a range of prices. It utilizes many new techniques and materials and it is humanly serviceable.

Certainly there are poorly designed pieces on the market. The least insidious of these is the furniture which to any cultivated taste is just plain ugly. The most dangerous pieces are those which are lovely to look upon but which belie their own claims to functionalism and efficient fabrication. Newness of design is not always progress but newness often creates sales. Therefore the young designer may become its slave. There are some pieces of faulty construction, those wherein physical balance is off, where lateral stresses are ignored, where bonding is not strong, where upkeep is too difficult, where comfort in use is only given advertising lip service. Wherever there is humbug in modern designing it should be criticized. Fortunately the good

seems to be getting better and the poor to be less in evidence.

b. THE PRESENT MARKET

Although change is no guarantee of progress there can be no progress without change. A look at the significant furniture achievements (most of which are still on the market and continue to be pacesetters) of the past twenty-five years' production will indicate the sources and direction of change.

The contemporary designer seems to have done especially well with the chair. In modern chair design we see a new form, typed with a certain homogeneous style quality and yet mixing gracefully with its ancestors. First came several pieces by Mies van der Rohe and Marcel Breuer. Breuer made the first modern tubular metal chair at the Bauhaus in 1925. In 1927 Mies van der Rohe produced the steel tube frame chair which utilized the spring quality of the steel. In 1930 he made the frame of resilient flat metal strips, the so-called "Tugendhat" chair. In 1929 he designed his famous "Barcelona" chair, with its separate leather upholstery. This chair probably has the most subtly designed curves in its cold steel frame that furniture has seen since the days of Louis XV or of ancient Greece.

Le Corbusier was also one of the early designers of steel furniture. He designed chairs which would accommodate themselves to the various positions of the sitter without any mechanical adjustment. Marcel Breuer in 1933 made a chair of aluminum strips which was designed to fit the body. The idea behind contour chairs is not new. These chairs represented solutions using modern techniques.

Following the designing trend set by steel, Alvar Aalto, the Finnish architect, designed his first chair with a laminated bentwood frame in 1928. Many of his designs were produced subsequently by the Finnish firm of Artek and by the American firm of Pascoe. Some of Aalto's pieces are ingeniously designed to stack in large numbers. The material used is largely birch. They are now sold by several prominent firms.

Thonet Industries, Inc., a firm which dates back to Michael Thonet who designed bentwood furniture in the Rhineland at Boppat, Germany, over one hundred years ago, was a pioneer firm in the making of bent plywood and tubular steel furniture in this country. The Thonet firm is still making excellent furniture in this tradition of a character especially suited to institutional wear.

Another new structural technique used in furniture design is the use of a rigid metal frame from which fabric is suspended for back and seat upholstery. The old suspended hammock is the ancestor of this idea. Designer Vietti first made a chair using this technique in 1939, suspending netting from an iron bar frame. A removable canvas or saddle leather back and seat suspended in similar manner was used by designer Hardoy in 1941.

This chair, as well as Mies van der Rohe's "Barcelona" chair, is procurable through Knoll Associates, Inc. Knoll Associates and the Knoll Planning Unit is in itself a clear exposition of coordinated designing in the field of interior architecture and design. The planning unit undertakes the development of interiors and furniture for special projects much as the Werkstätte did. Knoll Associates is headed by Florence Knoll and a group of outstanding designers, who design, produce, and merchandise modern furnishings.

It is a healthy sign that many other such cooperative associations of designers are to be found. The firm of Laverne, Inc., which is under the direction of Estelle and Erwine Laverne, is one of these. Dan Cooper Design Corp., is a prominent designing firm headed by Mr. Cooper.

One of the Knoll designers is George Nakashima, whose respect for and expert craftsmanship with wood has resulted in chairs possessing the sturdy quality of early American design and the lightness of modern.

Residence of: Mr. and Mrs. Bruce M. Walker, Spokane, Washington. **Architect:** Walker, McGough and Trogdon, Architects, A.I.A., Spokane, Washington. **Photographer:** Morley Baer, Berkeley, California.

Figure 137. Isamu Noguchi has shown his talents, which are so well known in other types of sculpture, in the design of his "Akari" lamp.

Article: Laminated wooden bowls. **Artist:** Tappio Wirkkala. **Owner:** Collection of the Museum of Modern Art, New York. **Photograph:** Courtesy Museum of Modern Art, New York.

Figure 138. Laminated wood can be the medium for artistic, individual creation as seen in these pieces by Tappio Wirkkala.

Eero Saarinen's shell chair is another one of the famous chairs which Knoll produces. Eero Saarinen, son of the late director of Cranbrook Academy, is an architect of note. The shell chair is constructed of molded plastic covered with foam rubber and fabric. It has metal legs. There is a separate cushion on its back and seat. This chair is sometimes described as a leaf chair because in its three-dimensional character it resembles a bent leaf. It features easy sitting in many postures and a lightness of handling.

In 1940 Saarinen collaborated with architect Charles Eames of Cranbrook to produce the so-called "Organic Design" chair which won the Museum of Modern Art contest for good design in modern furniture. The chair designed by Saarinen and Eames was a shell of laminated bent plywood designed to fit the contours of the body in seated position. The finished chair weighed twenty pounds whereas the usual upholstered chair weighs about forty-five pounds. Padding was of foam rubber, placed directly over the frame. Legs were inserted by wedge construction. This chair is the antecedent of the many Eames chairs which are now sold on the market and which are currently produced and sold by the Herman Miller Furniture Company.

The architect George Nelson is the present design director as well as designer for the Herman Miller Company. He has been responsible for the further development of the firm's modular unit furniture system. The Werkstätte was first interested in the functional possibilities of modular furniture and made studies in an attempt to standardize sizes. The name of the German designer, Bruno Paul, is associated with the production of early unit furniture. Marcel Breuer designed standardized enamel furniture for one of the apartments of the housing development in Stuttgart in 1927. Gilbert Rhode designed unit furniture for Herman Miller during the thirties.

Paul Lazlo is a well known Hungarian designer whose work is produced by the Herman Miller Company.

It is through the industrial production of Isamu Noguchi's free form table by the Herman Miller Company that the public has become acquainted with the work of this sculptor and designer. Noguchi's sculpture seems to accomplish that sound balance between abstract form and expression for which great artists strive. His free form furniture reflects his mastery of three-dimensional form. The famous Noguchi table has walnut or ebonized birch legs and a glass top.

The work of the Finnish craftsman, Tappio Wirkkala, who is as renowned for his wood as he is for his glass, is also characterized by beautiful free sculptural form. His approach to design through technique is similar in both of these media. In wood he works with lamination. He builds up a block of thin laminated layers and from this hews his tables and other pieces. None of the results is rigidly prescribed nor haphazardly fortuitous. The hand of the artist utilizes the grains of wood in the same manner that it utilizes the hollow bubbles of glass to create exquisite three-dimensional rhythms.

Edward Wormley is among those designers who are associated with large producing companies. He designs for the Dunbar Company. His current group of Dunbar pieces are in ash, walnut, or mahogany and they are frequently ankled in brass. Wormley's furniture has a knack of being elegant in a masculine sort of way.

The Widdicomb Furniture Company (now

Widdicomb-Mueller Corporation) of Grand Rapids, Michigan, produced furniture designed by the English-born T. H. Robsjohn-Gibbings. Gibbings made custom designed furniture both in London and in New York City before his work for a more extensive market. Working largely in light colored woods, he designs pieces with elegant proportions and suavity of line, which seem compatible with chaste classic English designs. The older firm of John Widdicomb, which had specialized in traditional furniture, is now likewise making modern pieces.

In a somewhat bolder vein was the work of Paul T. Frankl, a native of Vienna and eminent teacher of design in California. He designed furniture for the Johnson Furniture Company. He had an Austrian feeling for the sensuously decorative, often employing large scale, rich materials, and light and dark contrast for accent in furniture. Frankl was one of the first designers to make good rattan furniture. This highly flexible material can lend itself to contortioning so easily that much restraint is required in its handling. Several well established firms dealing in this medium are listed at the end of the chapter. Tommi Parzinger designs for the firm of Willow and Reed, Inc., as well as for his own custom outlet.

Paul McCobb designs for Directional Showrooms, Inc. His furniture has a classic quality without being traditional either in design or technique. He combines metal with wood and synthetics in a highly satisfactory manner.

Harvey Probber uses metal supports in combination with upholstered furniture. Metal furniture is made by a number of specialty firms listed at the end of the chapter.

Hendrick Van Keppel and Taylor Green are two California designers who have made well designed modern furniture frequently using steel tubing and redwood. Upholstery is of foam rubber. Many seats are cotton cording, rattan weaving, or metal mesh.

The Scandinavian designers are prominent on the modern market. Bruno Mathsson, Hans Wegner, Carl Ekselius, Ib. Kofod-Larsen and Finn Juhl furniture can be seen at Georg Jensen, Inc. George Tanier, Inc., is another New York City outlet for the Baltic designers. Oak and teak are currently favored woods. Cane, leather, or cloth upholstery is used.

Juhl's work illustrates a dual sort of enterprise which is not uncommon. He designs for both the industrial and for the handcraft market. The latter pieces are made by the Danish craftsman, Niels Vodder. The former are made by Baker Furniture, Inc. The alliance of one designer with two production fields should place exacting requirements on each.

One of the most interesting types of contemporary furniture is that designed by Folke-Ohlsson and others of Sweden for Dux, Inc. This furniture, known as "Dux" is available through several New York City outlets for Scandinavian furniture and also through the firm's California warehouse. It is literally knock-down furniture. Legs fasten by means of a patented quickly maneuvered dovetail. Bolts are used for some of the attachments. Woods are walnut, birch, and mahogany. Upholstery padding is either foam rubber or rubberized hair. Loose cushions are slipcovered. It comes neatly crated. Other firms are entering this market of easily transported articles.

Jens Risom is a Danish-trained designer who came to America in 1938 and in 1941 went into business for himself in New York City.

Count Sigvard Bernadotte, son of the King of Sweden, designs furniture produced by the firm of John Stuart, Inc. It has won several good design awards and should rank very high for its consummate subtlety of proportion and line. The firm of John Stuart produces much contemporary furniture which is the work of other distinguished designers.

The furniture of the Italians Gio Ponti, Carlo de Carli, Franco Albini, Ico Parisi, Carlo Mollino, and many others, is sold through various American outlets. The firm of Altamira concentrates on presenting modern Italian interior design; and M. Singer and Sons produces furniture designed by the Italians.

The above necessarily incomplete account has attempted to suggest some of the beacon lights in the contemporary furniture market. The list must be added to as the years move on. The names here listed, however, will not go out of date as a record of achievement.

3. Accessories

a. IMPORTANCE

Accessories may be the enrichment of the modern home as they are of the traditionally furnished one. They are particularly important to the modern scheme because they can introduce the quality of self-expression into a style which must be organized from industrially standardized furnishings. Likewise the modern style, which is almost ascetic in its emphasis on sparseness, makes each individual accessory item relatively more significant.

b. KINDS OF SOURCES

Accessories may be purchased from three kinds of markets—mass production, custom production, and the unique, or one-of-a-kind production. Obviously many things which are used in furnishing must, for economy, be mass produced.

Today the majority of firms producing objects of applied art use designers for their products. Sometimes these same designers work for the custom trade and likewise make individual objects of art. Such a tie-up creates a degree of insurance against a trade standard on one side and an ivory tower point of view on the other. However, adjustments are necessary for the industrial processes, even though they are adjustments in favor of greater regularity rather than toward greater mediocrity. Therefore the custom-produced or the artist-produced object is the only way to breathe individuality into a setting.

It is a mistaken idea to imagine that in the industrial field every object which is offered for sale with a designer's name attached is necessarily well designed. Good art is only found where there is a good artist and some so-called designers are not good artists. Therefore the responsibility for choosing artistic articles still rests firmly on our own shoulders no matter what market we have used.

Any résumé of contemporary accessories could be endless, even were it limited to individually created objects. Every locality in this country possesses a local group of artists who do work of surprisingly good quality. These regional markets should be depended upon for many articles. Purchase of art objects from local sources stimulates creative activity and gives a unique regional quality to an interior. Moreover, art is more interesting when related to the artist.

In any account such as the following, limitations must be imposed. The work included here has been that produced for a somewhat limited market and in most cases has been that of designers who have been pacesetters. The decision to include designs and designers is a personal one. Even so, many notable persons have been omitted for lack of space. Therefore this discussion should be regarded as suggestive and each should exercise his personal discrimination in compiling a list of his own. Some outlet firms are included to indicate the availability of the products.

c. WORKS OF FINE ART

Works of fine art are, of course, the most priceless objects. In the category of visual art these include pictures and sculpture. It is our belief that money spent for such objects, even though it were the price of a car (which it probably wouldn't be) would be money well spent. That is, it would be well spent if it bought a good work of art and not just an expensive one. A discussion of quality in and sources of contemporary fine art is included in Chapter X.

d. FABRICS

Good modern textiles are made for our decorative use by every type of production. One of the first leaders whose work has bridged several areas is Dorothy Liebes. In the textile world she is generally known as the "First Lady" of the loom. She works in the hand-weaving, the custom-weaving, and the industrial-weaving markets and feels that this diversity is good. Hand-weaving keeps her experimenting with her art, custom-weaving helps her to focus upon a particular problem, and industry keeps her in touch with the needs of people. Dorothy Liebes is also interested in research in and development of specialized fabrics and yarns. Her fabrics are characterized by subtle elegance and are frequently outstanding for their dramatic color brilliance.

Article: "Blue Waterfalls," woven textile. Artist: Dorothy Turobinski, Instructor in Weaving and Related Arts, Western Reserve University, Cleveland, Ohio. Photographer: G. Colburn Ball, Cleveland, Ohio.

The weaving department of Cranbrook Academy of Art pioneered in directing hand-weaving into contemporary design channels. Loja Saarinen and Marianne Strengell, both from Finland, fostered a tradition for experimental work which has crystallized in the fine modern work of many students. Jack Lenor Larsen of New York City came from Cranbrook. His hand-woven and custom-woven fabrics are characterized by great textural interest. He believes that there must be a strong relationship between architecture and weaving, therefore his fabrics seem always to suit the particular type of building for which they are planned.

The Black Mountain College Weavers, who were directed by Anni Albers, have likewise been a creative force in contemporary textile design. The Black Mountain College in North Carolina is organized along Bauhaus lines.

Contemporary rooms with their large glass areas have need for a light filtering fabric screen. Such textiles are well produced by Michael D. Belangie of Menlo Textiles, Menlo Park, California. Casements of restrained texture and design are woven frequently on a mohair warp with wefts of wool or other fibers. Some are left in their natural tone; others are yarn- or piece-dyed to pale neutral colors. James West of Tiburon, California, hand-blocks the fabrics with motifs which are oriental in character. These textiles are all custom-loomed on power looms. This system of production brings exquisite cloths within a reasonable price range.

Coming into the area of power-loomed fabrics which are not exclusively custom produced, an outstanding contribution is made by the firm of Boris Kroll. Kroll began his textile career by weaving on a Jacquard power loom, which he considers the greatest creative instrument of modern times. He seems to have a particular ability to forecast trends and his fabrics are, among industry produced fabrics, especially indicative of the way the wind blows.

The latest development in the house of Boris Kroll is his fabric library. This was established

Figure 139. Wall hangings are an interesting and, at times, almost necessary way to secure softness and depth texture, along with pattern and color in a contemporary interior.

to help the decorator coordinate his color and texture problems. In the library are thousands of actual fabrics in variations and combinations of color arranged in orderly fashion with respect to variations of hue, saturation, and lightness. If this range is not adequate for choice, samples can be experimentally produced on a hand loom which he maintains for the purpose.

In printed fabrics, designer Ruth Reeves has consistently been a leader. She prints her own fabrics and designs for quantity production. Her designing skill has kept pace with changing modes. Currently her nonobjective designs are masterpieces in dynamic color movement. Indeed, much of her work is so forceful that a pattern motif can be isolated and used successfully as a nonobjective picture. Marion Dorn has been a leading designer of printed fabrics and

wallpapers both in the industrial and in the custom market.

The firm of Ben Rose has specialized in contemporary hand-printed textiles. Patterns are kept in stock and can be made up to order. Colors may be mixed to suit the customer. This sort of special order work is done by a number of very good design firms throughout the country. Among them are Angelo Testa and Company, Chicago; Elenhank Designers, Inc., Riverside, Illinois; Adler-Schnee Associates, Detroit, and Laverne, Inc., New York City. It is not too costly to have a special design prepared for an individual use. Stock designs may be spaced on the textile according to a customer's wishes.

Many firms such as Herman Miller (fabrics designed by Alexander Girard) and Knoll Associates design their own fabrics to be used with

Figure 140. Fabric hangings have embellished walls through time. Here a Fortuny fabric made in Venice today has reproduced an Italian Renaissance design and provides a background for Renaissance and Baroque art in the Metropolitan Museum of Art, New York.

Building: Gallery in the Metropolitan Museum of Art, New York. **Textile:** Fortuny fabric. **Courtesy:** Elsie McNeill Lee, President, Fortuny, Inc., New York. **Photographer:** Henry Fullerton, Westfield, New Jersey.

their furniture. Many designers such as Dan Cooper design and print fabrics for the interiors they plan.

Hand-woven fabrics are coming to the American market from other lands. These fabrics are noteworthy because the entrepreneurs do not attempt to kill the native designs in favor of a pseudo-Western product. For example, Mauretania Fabrics, Inc., imports hand-woven wools from North Africa. Margit Pintar, who lived in Africa for a number of years, found the woolen fabrics of the natives so adaptable to use in her own home that she came to the United States and imported them for sale.

On the Pacific Coast the firm of Kneedler-Fauchere, San Francisco, carries a number of sturdy Mexican hand weaves in their stock. The Mexican color gamut introduces a vibrant note which is not garish.

No account of imported fabrics is complete without mention of the decorative silks which are now coming to these shores from the non-communist orient. One of the firms which is importing the silks of Thailand (Siam) is that of Thaibok Fabrics, Ltd. This interesting enterprise owes its success to the work of architect James Thompson, who went to Bangkok on a mission for the government. Seeing the gorgeously colored silk garments worn by the natives on festival days, he returned to America and organized the firm of Thaibok to distribute these silks here. Following in the same trend, other houses are importing beautiful silks from the orient.

Printed fabrics are coming to America from foreign lands. From Venice the firm of Fortuny Inc., is now exporting prints done in a contemporary manner as well as those done in a traditional way. The tonal variations which are contrived through the Fortuny method of manufacture create fabrics which are adaptable to many modern uses. This is particularly true of those textiles with small patterns giving a textural effect.

The Scandinavians are outstanding contributors to the storehouse of modern textiles. The very unusual merchandising firm of Nordiska Kompaniet in Sweden has sponsored hand-woven and hand-printed fabrics for its customers. A collection of these, designed by such well known

Figure 141. The exquisite artistry of this glass which is made by engraving and fusing silver and gold foil on ten thin laminations of glass, can only be suggested in a black and white photograph. Other colors are turquoise, cobalt blue with shadings of violet and rose.

Article: "Vision in the Blue Grotto," laminated gold glass. International Ceramic Traveling Show, 1958–1960. **Artist:** Edris Eckhardt, Glass artist and instructor, Cleveland Institute of Art, and Lecturer in Art, Western Reserve University, Cleveland, Ohio. **Photographer:** The Cleveland Museum of Art, Cleveland, Ohio.

artists as Astrid Sampe and Viola Grasten, are available through American outlets.

The Italians are likewise contenders in the production of decorative textiles. Their printed designs lean toward fantasy and whimsey but are also important for their daring use of color and rich tonal qualities. There is much work done in Italy on hand looms. Much of this production is designed for table use and includes fabrics incorporating native materials such as hemp.

Ireland and Belgium are doing significant work in hand-blocked and hand-loomed linen fabrics.

Textile designing for wall hangings, both in the nature of tapestries and of prints, is being revived. It is only natural that, as textiles are used less at windows, they are used more on walls where their softening character is often needed for acoustical as well as for visual reasons. Jean Lurçat, the French artist and painter, is perhaps the master mind behind the tapestry renaissance.[12] Under his direction the State Looms of France have produced tapestries made from cartoons designed by Dufy, Gromaire, Matisse, Picasso, and Lurçat. These, of course, are beyond purchasing price. But they have indi-

[12] J. Lurçat, *Designing Tapestry* (New York: The Macmillan Company, 1951).

cated the way for such designers as Martta Taipale of Finland to make lovely smaller pieces. Lurçat himself has created many small tapestries which are suitable for homes.

Some of Lurçat's early work was embroidery, especially petit point for chair upholstery and similar uses. Cloth as a design support seemed to interest him. It remained for Mariska Karasz to lift embroidery into the position of a major decorating medium. Her embroidered wall hangings and screens, the latter made with embroidered cloths inserted between translucent bindings, introduce lovely, one of a kind, textural, and color qualifications into contemporary interiors. Her works are sold through the Bertha Schaefer Gallery, New York City, and are owned by many of the leading art museums of the country.

e. FLOOR COVERINGS

Custom loomed floor coverings have been beautifully designed for a number of years by

Figure 142. A hand blown light fixture of Italian Venini glass has been effectively used in the reception area of this country club. From its stripes of wine, red, white, blue, and green the room color scheme was developed. Walls are white plaster and mahogany paneling. Carpet is wine. The large wall diamonds duplicate the Venini colors in high gloss enamel on metal.

Building: Bookcliff Country Club, Grand Junction, Colorado. **Architect:** Day and Thorson, Van Deusen and Bliska, Architects, Grand Junction, Colorado. **Interior Designer:** Ann L. Thorson, Grand Junction, Colorado. **Photographer:** Midwest Photo, Grand Junction, Colorado.

Stanislav J. V'Soske. Many of his carpets feature carved patterns. Some of his most significant textural achievements are those carpets which combine piles of slightly different heights, thus giving the effect of varying color. These are subtleties in design which indicate the work of the artist.

The custom designing of floor coverings is done by several other prominent firms listed hereafter. Many fabric weavers, such as Jack Lenor Larsen, likewise weave carpets.

The hand-made carpets of George Wells are unique accents.

From foreign shores such as India, Africa, Spain, the West Indies, and Ireland, come interesting carpets to be used in modern interiors.

f. CERAMICS, GLASS, ENAMELS, AND PLASTICS

One of the finest potters and creator of some of the earliest modern forms was the painter Henry Varnum Poor. Poor has operated his own kiln in New York since the twenties, when he added ceramics to his other media.

The modern forms in tableware ceramics probably owe more to Russel Wright than to any other person. His lower, less complicated shapes in many subtle colors, which he designed in 1939, began a vogue which many other firms have followed. Wright has not confined his talents to ceramics. He has consistently approached design from the point of view of suitability of product to use and has created many articles intended for daily living which illustrate this approach.

One of the constant leaders in the designing and hand-crafting of pottery and glass has been Marianne von Allesch who came from central Europe as one of the first of our modern designers.

The ceramics at Cranbrook Academy of Art, under the direction of Maija Grotell, have achieved well merited recognition.

Modern hand-crafted ceramics have progressed from pottery exclusively, through stoneware, to the use of porcelain clays. Eva Zeisel was the designer of some of the first translucent dinnerware of contemporary design. Her production

was the result of a collaboration between designer, manufacturer (Castleton China), and the Museum of Modern Art of New York. Many artist potters are learning to work with the more difficult of the clay media. For example, Anne Siimes of the Arabia Factory, Finland, designs white porcelain vases and bowls which have fragility of shape and slight patterning in tones which are exquisite developments of the ceramic sculptor's art.

Many modern ceramic accessories come from abroad. We have already mentioned the French pottery activity in and near Vallauris, a small Mediterranean village. This work is, however, a "great name" enterprise and the prices are accordingly high.

The Italian potters work most naturally in their traditional low fire faience technique. With this they have a sure touch which results in a kind of forceful, colorful, sculptured work of ceramic art. The exhibition, "Italy at Work," showed some examples of the work of Leonardi Leoncillo and Pietro Cascella, both of Rome, and of Lucio Fontana of Albisola. The Etruscan-like forms of the figures of Guido Gambone of Florence, which come closer to stoneware in amalgamation of body and glaze, should be mentioned.

Unlike ceramics, glass does not easily lend itself to work by individual artists. The plastically formed or heavily etched glass of René Lalique of France and the sculptured pieces of the Leerdam factory of Holland are the combined work of both designers and craftsmen. The designs of Edward Hald, Edvin Öhrström, and the late Simon Gate, of Orrefors and of Sidney Waugh of Steuben Glass have been executed by expert blowers and engravers. Some of Öhrström's designs which necessitate a control of bubbles in a highly refractive glass (ariel glass) require the closest partnership between designer and craftsman. Oriental artists have likewise created designs which have been given a glass embodiment at Steuben.

The recent work of Tappio Wirkkala, who does his own glass blowing at the Karhula-Iittala Glassworks in Finland, is significant. The work of Edris Eckhardt in gold laminated between sheets of glass, reviving lost techniques of

Figure 143. The scintillating quality of this sculpture in metal by Harry Bertoia holds attention without being too dominant in this living area.

Residence of: Mr. and Mrs. Stanley J. Winkelman, Detroit, Michigan. **Article:** Metal Sculpture. **Artist:** Harry Bertoia. **Photographer:** Stanley J. Winkelman, Detroit, Michigan.

the ancient world, adds the glories of changeable color to the translucent medium. The Italians who work outside the large industries, do their own blowing. The Italian glass metal assumes fanciful, colorful, modern shapes which can be grace notes to any composition. Stained glass, which introduces color with translucency, is being revived as an art. The recent room dividers made by Joseph Escuder are noteworthy.

Enamels are exceedingly important as enrichments of modern decoration. They range from the large enamel plaques such as are designed by Edward Winter for the Ferro-Enamel Company, Cleveland, Ohio, kilns, to the many smaller pieces designed with artistry and skill by artists throughout America. The work of Kenneth Bates is important. It is difficult, however, to choose even a few names from the legion of enamelists although some are great artists in this technique.

Occasionally a worker in a unique material such as plastics, elevates his medium to the realm of good visual art. The free form creations of Naum Gabo and the mobiles of Alexander Calder would come under this head.

g. METALS AND STONES

There are likewise many artists working in metals. The work of Frederick Miller (Potter and Mellen, Inc., Cleveland, Ohio), and Hudson Roysher in silver, and John Paul Miller in gold, is outstanding. Harry Bertoia's sculptured metal on steel as well as his designs for mesh metal chairs (Knoll Associates, Inc.) is pacesetting.

The Danish silversmith, Georg Jensen, designed silver and began a firm which has stood for excellence in silver work. Pieces by many Danish artists are to be seen in the current collections. The suave, graceful shapes made by Johan Rohde of Denmark are modern clean forms. Among the Italians the more realistic and yet stylized pieces of Argenteria Finzi of Milan are to be noted.

Italy may be credited with beginning a vogue for stone work, especially as mosaics. The American Richard Blow, who lived part-time in Florence, had the vision to revive the native stone craft. He opened a workshop on his property at Montici for workers in hard stone or *pietra dura*. The impetus given to the art has encouraged other Florentine artisans to work in this medium. American outlets for this native Italian work and for similar work of American craftsmen are now located in such places as Italian Marble Mart, New York City.

h. LIGHTING FIXTURES

Lighting fixtures become an enrichment accessory when they are handled in an imaginative way. That is the manner in which Paavo and Helena Tynell, the Finnish designers, worked. Their earlier designs featured the play of light and shadow. Paavo Tynell's more recent work is more functional in emphasis. Helena Tynell is likewise designing glass for Riihimaki Glassworks in Finland.

The Italian glass manufactories, Arte Luce and Fontane Arte, have made glass and brass chandeliers which successfully combine grace with function. The Italians have added color to glass globes and to glass in general in a free form way under the supervision of the late Paolo Venini.

The inspiration for Noguchi"s "Akari" (meaning *light* in Japanese) lamps came from the orient. These are paper and wire structures, made in Japan, which are direct descendants of Japanese lanterns. They are simple solutions to low cost, low brightness lighting. Some of Noguchi's "Akari" are in fantastic shapes and add an imaginative aspect to lighting. They are procurable through Bonniers in New York City. George Nelson has designed so-called bubble lamps which emit a diffused glow. Other designers have taken up this same idea.

Kurt Versen and Walter Von Nessen are designers of modern lighting fixtures. Hansen Lamps is an outlet for Orrefors glass fixtures. Other firms dealing with contemporary designing are listed at the end of this chapter.

i. SCREENS

Screens are movable walls which play an important utilitarian and artistic role in the modern house. Many screens are made of translucent cloth or plastic. Opaque forms may be fastened between the plastic layers to create a shadow effect. Mariska Karasz's embroideries are made into screens as has been mentioned. Natural foliage is often designed into screen panels. The work of the Van Loons, William and Victoria, of the Gaillard Press, Mentor, Ohio, is outstanding. Oriental screens may be priceless possessions. Oriental type translucent screens are known as shoji screens.

j. WALLPAPERS

There are some contemporary papers which, like the hand-painted oriental and French papers of the eighteenth century, are of sufficient merit to enrich portions of an interior. Ilonka Karasz and Marion Dorn have designed such. The firm of Katzenbach and Warren has produced panel papers from designs by Calder and Matisse. Other firms making fine wallpapers are listed in the directory on page 321.

Humpty Dumpty sat on a wall
At three o'clock he had his great fall
The King set the Time Machine back to two;
Now Humpty's unscrambled and good as new.

FREDERICK WINSOR *

Chapter XIV

THE TOTAL ART FORM— A PLAN FOR ACCOMPLISHMENT

A. EXAMPLES OF ART FORMS IN INTERIOR DESIGN

Analysis of interior design may be fruitful. The whole, however, is worthy because its enjoyment is such a delightful unity of practicality, sensuous organization, and essential manifestation of character. A few examples come to mind.

We are reminded of the Jones family with four small children. They bought a century-old house in a small town near the metropolitan area where Mr. Jones works. In this way more space was purchased at less cost. What a location for an antique flavor, some decorators might have thought. The Joneses, however, had their own needs in mind when they furnished. Stripping the house for action, they laid dark mottled linoleum on the floors. The walls were painted light tones. The children were allowed to draw on their bedroom walls but a careful line was

* From "The Space-Child's Mother Goose," **The Atlantic Monthly,** December, 1956. Reprinted by permission of **The Atlantic Monthly.**

Figure 144. This house, the plan of which is seen in Figure 33, looks different from the many galleried, high ceilinged Louisiana houses of yesterday only because it was produced within today's economics and technology. Its essential flavor is that of a New Orleans urban residence—a patio garden home.

Residence of: Mr. and Mrs. John T. Upton, New Orleans, Louisiana. **Architect:** Curtis and Davis, A.I.A., and Associated Architects and Engineers, New Orleans, Louisiana. **Photographer:** Frank Lotz Miller, New Orleans, Louisiana.

Figure 145. The many objects chosen from broad interests, the art studies and paintings, the rich dark colors of walls and floor—all result in an interior which is very warm and inviting in the home of a prominent artist.

Residence of: William C. Grauer, "Grassmere," East Claridon, Ohio. (Associate Professor of Art, Western Reserve University, Cleveland, Ohio.) **Photographer:** G. Colburn Ball, Cleveland, Ohio.

made between liberty and license. Not a mark was to appear on the walls of the family room! In this were placed low tables, child-height. These were painted harlequin colors and provided work and play surfaces. Large colorful cushions made seats. Adults were not forgotten. For them there was one very large davenport done in dark tones and several metal pull-up chairs which were comfortably contour-fitted. Bookshelves contained children's materials below and books and a few plants above. Curtains were simple and accented the light and dark patterns of walls and upholstery. The planning of all this was dictated by function. The result had a character that said workability first but was pleasantly expressive none the less.

Then there are the Kenilworths. Theirs is a snug-little-harbor sort of house. It is decked with gay chintz and the dainty china and silver of their native England. Flowers seem inspired to bloom everywhere. How different from the home of a Scottish shipbuilder of our acquaintance. His house looks out to sea. With its high paneled living room, its plain large windows with an expanse of monk's cloth framing the bleak surf, it has a majesty like that of its owner. Incidentally, this house has a huge hearth with benches close by, which is as heartening as the family proves to be when one knows them.

The home of an artist also comes to mind—a modern house made warm and friendly by earth colors shading to mauves on the painted walls, brown carpet, light tones in contemporary furniture, beautiful oil paintings on the walls, several easel paintings in process of construction, taper candlelight. This house has the design character of a rich tapestry.

Imagine, too, the tiny apartment of a pleasant quiet woman. How drab it appeared when she first moved in. What a change she accomplished. A grey wallpaper with a narrow irregular stripe was used. The carpet and woodwork were the same grey. She chose a few fine old mahogany pieces upholstered in a greyed green together with an old and very lovely gilt mirror. Somehow there were always current books and magazines—a precisely etched design of cameo quality.

All of these houses seemed to have character—a good character. They were pleasantly and well designed without seeming "done." This is to say that each of them had a social instinct. These houses suited their inhabitants. They expressed the unique timbre of their taste so well that they only seemed complete when their people were present. The house, you see, really needs its inhabitants, not the other way round—that is, if it is a good house. Moreover, these houses worked for their inhabitants. The spaces functioned in their lives, they were active in their interests. Lastly, each of these houses respected the pocketbook of its owner. These pocketbooks were of various sizes but none was too meager. We sometimes wonder what pocketbook would be too small to prevent character from creeping in. We have memories of a clean neat whitewashed cabin where an errant child was always welcome. Somehow the character of that little house has a way of flashing across our memory at the most inappropriate times and frequently to the detriment of more pretentious habitations.

B. AN ART QUALIFYING PROGRAM FOR A FACTORY

All buildings would be better if more thought were given to their artistic form. Here is a design consultant's program for a factory. It is complete in its outline plan. Details are merely suggestive.

1. What work is to be done? Planning for practical efficiency.
   a. plant layout:
      best equipment and personnel
      best organization of spaces and work
   b. color and lighting:
      best light conditions for performance
      best surface colors for performance, i.e., working areas in light dull tones—safety colors a factor
   c. textures:
      carefully considered in relation to tasks, i.e., fireproof fabrics, splinterproof desks, easily maintained materials
2. What message is to be conveyed? e.g., reciprocal loyalty and regard, efficient service.

a. physical connotations:

straight shapes used where sturdiness or precision is to be suggested

some warm colors for rooms with northern exposure

b. emotional connotations:

some curved shapes used in departments largely occupied by women

soothing colors in areas of great activity

c. character designations:

contemporary shapes with clean-cut lines, no inferior decorative design

some use of good quality textures in spaces used by all of the workers, essential honesty of all textures

d. preference or evaluative considerations:

for such a general use the shapes, colors, and textures should be those which are generally liked. However, there should be a freshness of approach which speaks of foresight.

3. What thought should be given to design?

The best possible design will be the most rewarding. Through it the perception of function, expression, and enjoyment of visual qualities is enhanced.

C. PRACTICAL PLANS FOR ACCOMPLISHMENT

From a practical point of view how may one plan for this kind of accomplishment? It will cost money certainly, but money without sincerity of motivation is impotent. Every commodity exacts its own price in kind and the price for a work of art is caring enough to plan.

This is equally true for a big business enterprise or for a modest home. The latter, however, will be chosen as an example.

What are several approaches to planning? Some persons are advocates of the frontal attack. They make a list of everything that seems necessary for equipment and complete a preliminary investigation of cost levels. After deductions are made for possessions on hand, then a decision can be formed about the price range to adopt. This results in a spic and span new production. However, this kind of buying is price buying and

it often happens that satisfaction value in the individual article is sacrificed.

Price buying frequently dictates the style into which the furnishings must fall. Some modes of furniture, for example, were produced in periods which commanded the most expensive materials, techniques, and artistry. To attempt to duplicate these styles at a price results in a gaudy effect.

There are some styles which lend themselves well to the restricted purse. Frequently the country or provincial styles are well done at a medium cost. These styles have a way of fitting nicely into improvised backgrounds now, and into large informal houses later. Also in this type of informal designing, the addition of heterogeneous hand-me-down pieces can often be made congruous by the use of some paint or covers. A pleasing comfortable-appearing home frequently results.

It is likewise true that well designed modern furniture can be secured on the budget price market. This, after all, is the mass market and many good firms and good designers are producing with it in mind.

Some people, with little money for furnishing, plan a style which has a humorous twist to it. This has often been referred to as the tongue-in-cheek type of decorating. Not having money to pay for a really good sofa they improvise one from purchases made at a secondhand store. Seats are made of nail kegs, padded and covered with petticoats. Silver is replaced with tinware. Pictures are frequently chromos set into improvised frames.

The logic behind this kind of attack is to be admired. It turns up with a gay, brave answer to the cold world of dollars and cents. Even this smile-and-shoestring decorating costs some cash and a deal of effort. Unfortunately this kind of furnishing does not form a satisfactory nucleus for growth. We question whether purchases dictated by this sort of planning could ever be companions for life.

At the opposite pole from the purchase-all-at-once school of thought, there is the project where standards of quality are chosen and no quarter given. This is buying for satisfaction value rather than price. This may leave us in the hypothetical

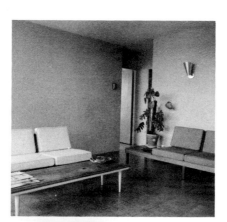

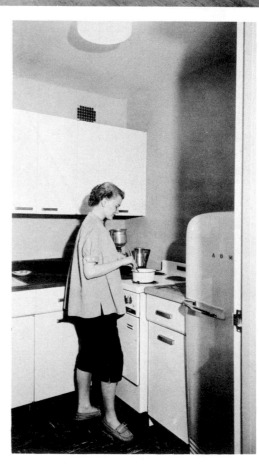

position of the woman who spends so much for her dress that she cannot afford shoes. It may procure a davenport and four blank walls. Or it may—judging from the frailties of your present company—result in a good painting and no table. Which, at best, is making unbalanced preparation for the needs of a household.

The wisest course probably lies somewhere between the two extremes of immediate purchase of everything and deferred purchase of too many articles. Some purchases should be initial. Others can wait and can be arranged for over a period of a few years.

Which purchases should come first? Before making this decision let us think about what we wish to attain. We are not buying pots and pans and pictures and bric-a-brac. We are buying something beyond the material, as every advertiser of home furnishings knows. It is the ultimate values such as health, social prestige, enduring memories with which he intrigues us.

Self-preservation is the first obligation. The first necessities serve health, such as facilities for bathing, cooking, refrigeration, and sleeping. Although it would be sheer folly not to provide a young mother with labor-saving devices, much of the equipment can be adequate without being the latest models. The best quality sleeping equipment is a positive health insurance. The stores of linen need not be large. The visual design of the work and sleeping areas can be contrived at little cost. Storage furniture can be made. A sewing machine may be a money saver in the hands of an ingenious craftsman.

After these most necessary purchases, the next articles of importance are those having definite

Figure 146. Domestic interiors are created at first by young people. Today the quarters are frequently temporary, and may even be on a college campus. Wisely planned purchases should provide the nucleus for satisfactory living later in life.

Building: Carman Hall, lobby of campus apartments for students and faculty housing, Illinois Institute of Technology, Chicago, Illinois. **Architect:** Mies van der Rohe. **Photographer:** Hedrich-Blessing, Chicago, Illinois.
Interior photographs: Courtesy Public Relations Department, Illinois Institute of Technology, Chicago, Illinois.

focus on the household as a social unit. A successful home becomes a social partnership as soon as it is inaugurated. Therefore it should contain seating furniture as soon as possible. The davenport, or whatever might be the most important seating arrangement, should be purchased first. Practical quality and design quality are equally important considerations here.

For the additional seats one of several plans may be adopted. It is expensive in the long run to buy either shoddily constructed or uncomfortable chairs. One purchaser may consider the buying of simple straight line chairs such as could fit later into bedrooms. Another purchaser may buy several of the plastic or laminated wood chairs which are wonderfully comfortable and reasonable. These will make additional pull-up seats when the ménage increases in size. Folding chairs are frequently well designed and well made and are not to be spurned as initial purchases. Extra couch beds can make temporary living room furniture. Wicker furniture which later can be used on the porch has much to recommend it. A bit of ingenuity can be used to cut down old chairs which have good spring seats to make low stools for the young crowd. Strong low bookcases take the place of the old-fashioned window seat for extra guests who come to tea. Cushion hassocks may be the solution if friends are nimble of limb. On the other hand the initial budget may provide for a couple of comfortable good chairs.

Good illumination is both a health necessity and a social requisite. If it is not provided in the architecture of the building (and it probably isn't in many typical first living quarters) then provision for it should be purchased early. Simple and adequate luminaries can now be secured at a reasonable price. Frequently added expenditure merely means additional ornateness without additional practical efficiency or design value. If more money is to be spent for lighting fixtures, be certain that they are worth the cost.

Dining equipment must be purchased at the commencement of any home. Table and chairs may be a temporary purchase if they are a type which can be moved to breakfast room, porch, or yard. Some may prefer to buy a folding or collapsible table which can be placed in the

Residence of: William C. Grauer, "Grassmere," East Claridon, Ohio. **Painting:** William C. Grauer, Associate Professor of Art, Western Reserve University, Cleveland, Ohio. **Textile:** Dorothy Turobinski, Instructor in Weaving and Related Arts, Western Reserve University, Cleveland, Ohio. **Ceramic Sculpture:** "Dryad," Thelma Frazier Winter, artist and ceramic sculptor, Cleveland, Ohio. **Photographer:** G. Colburn Ball, Cleveland, Ohio.

Figure 147. A fine work of art is worth more than stocks and bonds. Its dividends are guaranteed. It improves the quality of experience continually. It demands distinction from its associates but with an enduring sense of noblesse oblige.

living room and do double duty as a living room table or as a game table. A basic set of dishes may be chosen with a focus on practical qualities, price, and appearance. These everyday pieces should be harmonious with whatever better ware is secured for "company" meals. The purchase of the better ware might take place over a period of years.

What about carpets in planned purchasing? They are not as essential as some of the articles previously mentioned. But it is equally important not to skimp on quality standards when they are purchased. If carpeting is wisely purchased with some thought for color and pattern it can be utilized in later houses without loss. Similar rugs, originally planned for a small dining and living room, may be used in a larger living room at a later date. Living room carpeting can be subsequently moved to bedrooms. If the floors are in fairly good condition they might be left bare. This gives a clean look to a room which often is quite suited to crisp modern furnishing. Rubber or composition tiling makes an interesting flooring but it is not without cost.

If taste in the selection of oriental rugs is developed, some good reasonably priced ones may be found. Used as scatter rugs in the living room at first, they will more than pay for themselves by introducing color and pattern interest into dark corners of the house in later years. Scatter rugs or those just large enough to contain a conversational furniture grouping may be purchased and may be used later elsewhere in the house. One good accent rug may be worth its price as a choice art possession.

If the carpets in a house warrant a good quality-or-else type of purchasing, the window treatment may be approached from a different point of view. Spending much money on the window decorations of a temporary abode does not seem wise. No two houses are physically or aesthetically alike and windows in different houses do not present similar problems. It is possible to obtain very good drapery effects with a little expenditure of money. One seamstress bought bolts of sateen and dyed and made the curtains for each room to suit its color scheme. Gauze can be handled in the same effective manner. On the other hand, curtaining can prove

Figure 148. Out of the material of life man can make that which is of the spirit.

Residence of: Richard Davis (Director of the Minneapolis Institute of Art) and Mrs. Davis, Wayzata, Minnesota. **Architect:** Philip Johnson Associates, New York. **Photographer:** Warren Reynolds, Infinity, Inc., Minneapolis, Minnesota.

very expensive. Before untoward money is used for this item it would seem that the home should be relatively permanent, the occupants should have a developed communal taste and a pretty sound basis for judging materials.

Lastly, we come to an important principle to guide our purchasing. Regardless of how much economy has to be practiced elsewhere, when a home is established there may be placed in it something which anticipates the completed scheme in quality and aesthetic excellence. It should represent the very best taste of the owners. It is what will represent the standards of the family. It may not be possible to buy a very large object for this purpose. It may be a small rug, a piece of modern or traditional art, an old ink stand, or similar accessory, but it will set the tone. When making a new purchase it will never again be easy to undervalue it.

If the artistic taste of the household is in the growing stage then this purchase should not be of an expensive work of fine art. Pictures, for instance, are not easily selected. Initial purchases may be of small ones, or of good copies, or of the work of new artists. Any major purchase should be made only after considerable thought.

There is one kind of accessory which should not be denied space in the house. That is the accessory which bespeaks the interests of the occupants. It is to be hoped that these accessories will not need to be purchased. Persons who have arrived at the state of maturity necessary to establish a household should have developed interests which will be explicit in their belongings.

If we bring together the necessary paraphernalia for family living first, for social intercourse second, with a standard of quality which anticipates the future, and with the accoutrements which will make possible the pursuit of what makes life vital and interesting, we will have purchased a stake in that kind of background that is attractive but is not a stage. We will find that the kind of friends whom we like, will like to come to our house.

D. IS A DECORATOR NECESSARY?

Of what service is a decorator [1] in helping to create an artistic interior? In the first place some-

one is necessary to act as mediary between our project and the complicated mercantile world. It is important then to appraise the business reputation of those from whom aid is sought.

Any association is most fruitful if we have developed taste to the point where we know our needs and can make thoughtful decisions. A design, if carried out without cooperation between designer and customer, may be a good design. But rarely is it an adequate art form with complete integration of art factors in terms of the client's needs.

It is important to have the professional capabilities assured of one who is to provide such an intimate article as a background for living. Within the profession a designer should be chosen whose taste, in the sense defined in Chapter XI, is similar to ours.

A good designer should be a good psychologist, a producing artist, a salesman, a banker, and a friend. As a psychologist he may see the type of design which will fit our way of life more clearly than we can. Sometimes we are too close to a situation to analyze it. As a producing artist he should know where to obtain and how to manipulate his media in order to get a beautiful result.

A designer may sometimes tell us and sell us! Salesmanship and persuasion in our interest is often a token of the highest regard. We welcome the doctor who prescribes for us. A decorator, because he is an experienced coordinator, should help us save money. He can provide us with a long range plan. And lastly a good designer is a friend who often must and is willing to expend more than he is paid for in our service. He helps

---

[1] The terms *decorating* and *decoration* and *decorator* are used in this book as synonymous with *designing* and *design* and *designer*. We recognize that the former terms suggest adding decoration to a finished building: perhaps the idea of adding an icing to a bad cake in order to cover its faults may even be suggested. In order to prevent such connotations the name interior designer seems preferable. But the term *interior decorator* is well known and has been given honor by the American Institute of Decorators founded in 1931 which defines a decorator as "one who by training and experience is qualified to plan, design, and execute interiors and their furnishings, and to supervise the various arts and crafts essential to their completion." Some use the term "interior associate," meaning an interior designer who collaborates with the architect and the client in creating a complete art form.

us create a beautiful interior the cost of which is not only reckoned in present effort but in past preparation. His apparent intuition is but a quickly flung bridge connecting the ancient islands of experience. If we have found a good designer for us, then let us, as Polonius advised, "grapple them to thy soul with hoops of steel." With pardon for a mixed reference we may say that his price is beyond rubies.

FINIS

and I know not if, save in this, such gift be allowed to man,
—That out of three sounds he frame, not a fourth sound, but a star.

ROBERT BROWNING *

* From "Abt Vogler" by Robert Browning. Reprinted from the **Complete Poetic and Dramatic Works of Robert Browning** by permission of Houghton Mifflin Company.

The formula W(orld) → S(timulus) → O(rganism) → R(esponse) → W(orld) is now complete. From the world of experience we have found the stimulus from which could be produced the conscious response of beauty. In the process a force has been created which will have its countereffect upon the world. Beauty is a dynamo which can transmit a spiritual power to many who are in its field.

And thus to end these chapters. Good decorating is so simple that it is nothing more than inspired common sense. But it is so difficult that to learn all there is to learn about it would take the interest and love of a lifetime. We may stop anywhere we wish on this path.

Love does not take account of years and effort. From love alone is created beauty. Wherever it is made it stands as eternal witness to the fact that out of the material of life man can make that which is of the spirit.

APPENDIX

READING REFERENCES [1]

Chap. I. The Designer's Problem

Webster's New Collegiate Dictionary. Springfield, Mass.: G. and C. Merriam Co., 1958.[2]

Chandler, Albert R. *Beauty and Human Nature.* New York: Appleton-Century-Crofts, Inc., 1934, pp. 3–23.

Dewey, John. *Art as Experience.* New York: Minton, Balch and Company, 1934, pp. 3–133, 255–271, 300, 309, 320, 324, 326–349.

Gilbert, Katharine E., and Kuhn, Helmut. *A History of Esthetics.* Bloomington: Indiana University Press, 1954, Chaps. XVIII, XIX.

Lynes, Russell. *The Tastemakers.* New York: Harper & Brothers, 1954, Chap. XVIII.

Munro, Thomas. *The Arts and Their Interrelations.* New York: The Liberal Arts Press, 1949, pp. 26–153, 406–411, 433–451.

Perry, Ralph Barton. *Realms of Value.* Cambridge, Mass.: Harvard University Press, 1954, Chap. XVIII.

Santayana, George. *The Sense of Beauty.* New York: Charles Scribner's Sons, 1896, pp. 14–52, 158.

Teague, Walter Dorwin. *Design This Day.* New York: Harcourt, Brace & Co., 1940, p. 15 and Chaps. 4, 15.

[1] This is not intended as a complete bibliography. It indicates the books which have been most influential in shaping the content of this volume. The reader could be introduced to these references and might use them in future studies.

[2] This is the source of all definitions ascribed to a dictionary in this text, unless otherwise noted.

Chap. II. Design Organization

Dewey, John. *Art as Experience.* New York: Minton, Balch and Company, 1934, pp. 95, 106–108, 120–128, 134–213.

Faulkner, Ray. *Inside Today's Home.* New York: Henry Holt & Co., 1954, pp. 83–109.

Goldstein, Harriet and Goldstein, Vetta. *Art in Everyday Life.* 4th ed. New York: The Macmillan Co., 1954, Chaps. 4–7.

Graves, Maitland. *The Art of Color and Design.* New York: McGraw-Hill Book Co., 1941, pp. 3–78.

Kepes, Gyorgy. *Language of Vision.* Chicago: Paul Theobald and Company, 1948, Part I.

Langfeld, Herbert Sidney. *The Aesthetic Attitude.* New York: Harcourt, Brace & Co., 1920, pp. 108–153.

Mather, Frank Jewett, Jr. *Concerning Beauty.* Princeton, N.J.: Princeton University Press, 1935, Chap. V.

Munro, Thomas. *The Arts and Their Interrelations.* New York: The Liberal Arts Press, 1949, Chap. VII, pp. 303–324, 351–378, 398, 409, 411, 419, 464–474.

Rutt, Anna Hong. *Home Furnishing.* 2nd ed. New York: John Wiley & Sons, Inc., 1948, Chap. 2.

Santayana, George. *The Sense of Beauty.* New York: Charles Scribner's Sons, 1896, pp. 91–97, 163.

Teague, Walter Dorwin. *Design This Day.* New York: Harcourt, Brace & Co., 1940, Chaps. 7–9, 12 & 13.

Chap. III. Coordination of Interior Design with Structure

American Public Health Association; Committee on the Hygiene of Housing. *Construction and Equipment of the Home.* Chicago: Public Administration Service, 1951.

Faulkner, Ray. *Inside Today's Home.* New York: Henry Holt & Co., 1954, pp. 275–378, 447–457.

Fitch, James Marston. *American Building, The Forces That Shape It.* Boston: Houghton Mifflin Co., 1948, Chaps. 9–14.

Ford, Katherine Morrow and Creighton, Thomas H. *The American House Today.* New York: Reinhold Publishing Corp., 1951, Chap. 5.

————. *Quality Budget Houses.* New York: Reinhold Publishing Corp., 1954, pp. 90–145.

Hamlin, Talbot. *Architecture, An Art for All Men.* New York: Columbia University Press, 1947, Chaps. 2, 5 & 6.

Nelson, George and Wright, Henry. *Tomorrow's House.* New York: Simon and Schuster, Inc., 1945. Chaps. 8, 10, 13–15.

Pickering, Ernest. *Shelter for Living.* New York: John Wiley & Sons, Inc., 1941, Chaps. 35 & 36.

Ramsey, Charles G., and Sleeper, Harold R. *Architectural Graphic Standards.* 4th ed. New York: John Wiley & Sons, Inc., 1951.

Santayana, George. *The Sense of Beauty.* New York: Charles Scribner's Sons, 1896, pp. 157–163.

Sleeper, C. and Sleeper, R. *The House for You to Build, Buy or Rent.* New York: John Wiley & Sons, Inc., 1948.

Teague, Walter Dorwin. *Design This Day.* New York: Harcourt, Brace & Co., 1940, Chaps. 4–6.

Chap. IV. Functional Planning of Interiors

American Public Health Association, Committee on the Hygiene of Housing. *Planning the Home for Occupancy.* Chicago: Public Administration Service, 1950.

Faulkner, Ray. *Inside Today's Home.* New York: Henry Holt & Co., 1954, pp. 3–82, 513–550.

Fitch, James Marston. *American Building, The Forces That Shape It.* Boston: Houghton Mifflin Co., 1948, Chap. 16.

Ford, Katherine Morrow and Creighton, Thomas

H. *The American House Today.* New York: Reinhold Publishing Corp., 1951, Chaps. 2–4.

————. *Quality Budget Houses.* New York: Reinhold Publishing Corp., 1954, pp. 10–90.

Gutheim, Frederick. *Houses for Family Living.* New York: The Woman's Foundation, Inc., 1948.

Hamlin, Talbot. *Architecture, An Art for All Men.* New York: Columbia University Press, 1947, Chap. 3.

Nelson, George and Wright, Henry. *Tomorrow's House.* New York: Simon and Schuster, Inc., 1945, Chaps. 1–7, 9, 11, 12 & 16.

Peet, Louise J. and Thye, Lenore S. *Household Equipment.* New York: John Wiley & Sons, Inc., 1955, Chaps. 10 & 12.

Pickering, Ernest. *Shelter for Living.* New York: John Wiley & Sons, Inc., 1941, Chaps. 12, 15, 16, 18–25.

Ramsey, Charles G., and Sleeper, Harold R. *Architectural Graphic Standards.* 4th ed. New York: John Wiley & Sons, Inc., 1951.

Schroeder, Francis de Neuville. *Anatomy for Interior Designers.* 2nd ed. New York: Whitney Publications, 1951.

Sleeper, C. and Sleeper, R. *The House for You to Build, Buy or Rent.* New York: John Wiley & Sons, Inc., 1948.

Chap. V. Space and Shape in Interiors

Brinkhoff, George D. *Aesthetic Measure.* Cambridge, Mass.: Harvard University Press, 1933, pp. 6, 14, 27–29, 211, 216, 217.

Chandler, Albert R. *Beauty and Human Nature.* New York: Appleton-Century-Crofts, Inc., 1934, Chaps. 3 & 4.

Dewey, John. *Art as Experience.* New York: Minton, Balch and Company, 1934, pp. 206–214.

Graves, Maitland. *The Art of Color and Design.* New York: McGraw-Hill Book Co., 1941, pp. 81–128.

Hambidge, Jay. *Dynamic Symmetry; The Greek Vase.* New Haven, Conn.: Yale University Press, 1920, Chaps. 1–4, 12.

————. *Practical Applications of Dynamic Symmetry.* New Haven, Conn.: Yale University Press, 1932.

Luckiesh, Mathew. *Visual Illusions, Their Causes, Characteristics and Applications.* New York: D. Van Nostrand Co., Inc., 1922. Chaps. 6, 12 & 13.

Moholy-Nagy, L. *The New Vision.* New York: W. W. Norton & Co., 1938, pp. 160–165.

Mundt, Ernest. *A Primer of Visual Art.* Minneapolis, Minn.: Burgess Publishing Co., 1951, pp. 7–19, 27, 34.

Panofsky, Erwin. *Meaning in the Visual Arts.* Garden City, N.Y.: Doubleday & Co., Inc., 1955, pp. 55–107.

Santayana, George. *The Sense of Beauty.* New York: Charles Scribner's Sons, 1896, pp. 82–95.

Teague, Walter Dorwin. *Design This Day.* New York: Harcourt, Brace & Co., 1940, Chaps. 10 & 11.

Chap. VI. Understanding Color

Chevreul, M. E. *The Principles of Harmony and Contrast of Colors.* Trans. Charles Martel. 3rd ed. London: George Bell and Sons, 1881.

Evans, Ralph M. *An Introduction to Color.* New York: John Wiley & Sons, Inc., 1948.

Gettens, Rutherford J. and Stout, George L. *Painting Materials.* New York: D. Van Nostrand Co., Inc., 1942.

Goldstein, Harriet and Goldstein, Vetta. *Art in Everyday Life.* 4th ed. New York: The Macmillan Co., 1954, Chap. 8.

Graves, Maitland. *The Art of Color and Design.* New York: McGraw-Hill Book Co., 1941, pp. 129–250.

———. *Color Fundamentals.* New York: McGraw-Hill Book Co., 1952, Chaps. 1–15.

Hardy, Arthur C. *Handbook of Colorimetry.* Cambridge, Mass.: Massachusetts Institute of Technology, The Technology Press, 1936.

Helmholtz, Hermann von. *Handbuch der Physiologischenoptik.* 3 vol. Leipsig: Leopold Voss, 1896.

Hering, Ewald, *Zur Lehre vom Lichtsinne.* Wien: Gerold, 1878.

International Printing Ink Corp. *A Series of Monographs on Color.* New York: The Research Laboratories of the International Printing Ink Corp., 1935.

ISCC Comparative List of Color Terms, The.
Washington, D.C.: Inter-Society Color Council, 1949.

Katz, David. *The World of Color.* London: Kegan Paul, Trench, Trubner and Co., Ltd., 1935, pp. 233–247.

Luckiesh, Mathew. *Color and Colors.* New York: D. Van Nostrand Co., Inc., 1938, pp. 92–118.

———. *Color and Its Applications.* New York: D. Van Nostrand Co., Inc., 1921, Chaps. 1–3.

Mayer, Ralph. *The Artist's Handbook of Materials and Techniques.* New York: Viking Press, 1940.

Munsell, Albert H. *A Color Notation.* 10th ed. Baltimore: The Munsell Color Co., 1954.

Optical Society of America, Committee on Colorimetry. *The Science of Color.* New York: Thomas Y. Crowell Co., 1953.

Ostwald, Wilhelm. *Colour Science.* Authorized trans. J. Scott Taylor, 2 vols. London: Winsor and Newton, 1933.

Pratt, Lyde S. *The Chemistry and Physics of Organic Pigments.* New York: John Wiley & Sons, Inc., 1947.

Rood, Ogden N. *Student's Textbook of Color.* New York: Appleton-Century-Crofts, Inc., 1908.

von Fischer, William and Bobalek, Edward G. (eds.). *Organic Protective Coatings.* New York: Reinhold Publishing Corp., 1953, Chaps. 1, 2, 5, 6, 8 & 13.

von Fischer, William: ed. *Paint and Varnish Technology.* New York: Reinhold Publishing Corp., 1948, Chaps. I–VIII, XXI & XXII.

U.S. Department of Commerce, National Bureau of Standards. *The ISCC-NBS Method of Designating Colors* and *A Dictionary of Color Names,* Circular 553. Washington, D.C.: U.S. Dept. of Commerce, 1955.

Chap. VII. Using Color in Interiors

Birren, Faber. *Monument to Color.* New York: McFarlane Warde McFarlane, Part II.

Carpenter, H. Barrett. *Colour.* New York: Charles Scribner's Sons, 1932.

Chandler, Albert R. *Beauty and Human Nature.* New York: Appleton-Century-Crofts, Inc., 1934, Chap. 6.

Goldstein, Harriet and Goldstein, Vetta. *Art in Everyday Life*. 4th ed. New York: The Macmillan Co., 1954, Chap. 9.

Graves, Maitland. *The Art of Color and Design*. New York: McGraw-Hill Book Co., 1941, pp. 129–250.

————. *Color Fundamentals*. New York: McGraw-Hill Book Co., 1952, Chaps. 15–17.

Kepes, Gyorgy. *Language of Vision*. Chicago: Paul Theobald and Company, 1948, pp. 161–167.

Mundt, Ernest. *A Primer of Visual Art*. Minneapolis, Minn.: Burgess Publishing Co., 1951, pp. 20–23.

Chap. VIII. Light as an Aesthetic Factor in Interior Design

Commery, E. W., and Stephenson, E. Eugene. *How to Decorate and Light Your Home*. New York: Coward-McCann, Inc., 1955.

Committee on Art Gallery Lighting of the Illuminating Engineering Society. "Art Gallery Lighting," *Illuminating Engineering*, XL, No. 1 (January, 1945), pp. 11–36.

Evans, Ralph M. *An Introduction to Color*. New York: John Wiley & Sons, Inc., 1948, Chaps. 4 & 16.

Illuminating Engineering Society, *IES Lighting Handbook*. New York: 1959.

Kepes, Gyorgy. *Language of Vision*. Chicago: Paul Theobald and Company, 1948, pp. 143–161.

Nelson, George and Wright, Henry. *Tomorrow's House*. New York: Simon and Schuster, Inc., 1945, pp. 167–175.

Sturrock, Walter and Staley, K. A. *Fundamentals of Light and Lighting*, Bulletin LD-2. Cleveland, Ohio: General Electric Co., 1956.

Teague, Walter Dorwin. *Design This Day*. New York: Harcourt, Brace & Co., 1940, p. 82.

Chap. IX. Texture and the Media of Interior Design

TEXTURE

Mundt, Ernest. *A Primer of Visual Art*. Minneapolis, Minn.: Burgess Publishing Co., 1951, pp. 24–27.

Teague, Walter Dorwin. *Design This Day*. New York: Harcourt, Brace & Co., 1940, Chaps. 5, 6.

WOODS

Sherwood, Malcolm H. *From Forest to Furniture*. New York: W.W. Norton & Co., Inc., 1936.

U.S.D.A., *The Identification of Furniture Woods*, Bulletin 66. Washington, D.C.: Supt. of Documents, 1926.

————. *Wood: Colors and Kinds*, Agricultural Handbook No. 101. Washington, D.C.: Supt. of Documents, 1956.

Whiton, Sherrill. *Elements of Interior Design and Decoration*. New York: J. B. Lippincott Co., 1951, pp. 483–490, 693–723.

TEXTILES

Bendure, Zelma and Pfeiffer, Gladys. *America's Fabrics*. New York: The Macmillan Co., 1947.

Denny, Grace. *Fabrics*. 7th ed. New York: J. B. Lippincott Co., 1953.

Hess, Katharine Paddock. *Textile Fibers and Their Use*. 3rd ed. rev. New York: J. B. Lippincott Co., 1941.

Hooper, Luther. *Hand-loom Weaving*. New York: The Macmillan Co., 1910.

Hunter, George Leland. *The Practical Book of Tapestries*. Philadelphia: J. B. Lippincott Co., 1925.

Lewis, Ethel. *Romance of Textiles*. New York: The Macmillan Co., 1937.

Taylor, Lucy D. *Know Your Fabrics*. New York: John Wiley & Sons, Inc., 1951.

Whiton, Sherrill. *Elements of Interior Design and Decoration*. New York: J. B. Lippincott Co., 1951, pp. 409–419, 442–450.

Wingate, Isabel B. *Textile Fabrics*, 4th ed. Englewood Cliffs, N.J.: Prentice-Hall, Inc., 1955.

FLOOR COVERINGS

Dilley, Arthur Urbane. *Oriental Rugs and Carpets*. New York: Charles Scribner's Sons, 1931.

Hawley, W. A. *Oriental Rugs*. New York: Tudor Publishing Co., 1937.

Hoover Company, The. *Carpets and Rugs*. N. Canton, Ohio: The Hoover Company, 1951.

Lewis, G. Griffin. *The Practical Book of Oriental*

Rugs. 6th ed, rev. New York: J. B. Lippincott Co., 1945.

Mumford, John Kimberly. *Oriental Rugs.* 4th ed. New York: Charles Scribner's Sons, 1915.

Whiton, Sherrill. *Elements of Interior Design and Decoration.* New York: J. B. Lippincott Co., 1951, pp. 491–518.

CERAMICS

Brooklyn Museum. *The Art and Technique of Ceramics.* New York: The Brooklyn Museum, 1937.

Cox, Warren E. *The Book of Pottery and Porcelain.* New York: Crown Publishers, Inc., 1944.

Eberlein, Harold Donaldson and Ramsdell, Roger Wearne. *The Practical Book of Chinaware.* Philadelphia: J. B. Lippincott Co., 1925.

Honey, W. B. *European Ceramic Art.* New York: D. Van Nostrand Co., Inc., 1950.

Whiton, Sherrill. *Elements of Interior Design and Decoration.* New York: J. B. Lippincott Co., 1951, pp. 614–636.

GLASS

Harrington, J. C. *Glassmaking at Jamestown.* Richmond, Va.: The Dietz Press, Inc., 1952.

McKearin, George S. and Helen. *American Glass.* New York: Crown Publishers, Inc., 1944.

Rogers, Frances and Beard, Alice, *5000 Years of Glass.* Philadelphia: J. B. Lippincott Co., 1948.

Skelley, L. *Modern Fine Glass.* New York: Richard R. Smith, Publisher, Inc., 1937.

Whiton, Sherrill. *Elements of Interior Design and Decoration.* New York: J. B. Lippincott Co., 1951, pp. 637–643.

METALS

Bigelow, Francis Hill. *Historic Silver of the Colonies.* New York: The Macmillan Co., 1917.

Kerfoot, J. B. *American Pewter.* New York: Houghton Mifflin Co., 1924.

Wenham, Edward. *Domestic Silver of Great Britain and Ireland.* New York: Oxford University Press, 1935.

Whiton, Sherrill. *Elements of Interior Design and Decoration.* New York: J. B. Lippincott Co., 1951, pp. 644–656.

Chap. X. Total Design and Concrete Design Problems

Kepes, Gyorgy. *Language of Vision.* Chicago: Paul Theobald and Company, 1944, pp. 15–16.

Taylor, Lucy. *Know Your Fabrics.* New York: John Wiley & Sons, Inc., 1951, pp. 235–308.

Whiton, Sherrill. *Elements of Interior Design and Decoration.* New York: J. B. Lippincott Co., 1951, pp. 463–485, 516–518, 525–535, 674–692, 727–735.

Chap. XI. Design and Expression

Bowen, Elizabeth. "How to Be Yourself, But Not Eccentric," *Vogue* (July 1956), pp. 54–55.

Dewey, John. *Art as Experience.* New York: Minton, Balch and Company, 1934, pp. 326–349.

Einstein, Albert. *Ideas and Opinions.* New York: Crown Publishers, Inc., 1954, pp. 66–67—Education for independent thought; 335–337—The common language of science.

Gilbert, Katherine. *Aesthetic Studies.* Durham, N.C.: Duke University Press, 1952, pp. 3–22—Seven senses of a room.

Goldstein, Harriet and Goldstein, Vetta. *Art in Everyday Life.* 4th ed. New York: The Macmillan Co., 1954, Chap. 1.

Perry, Ralph Barton. *Realms of Value.* Cambridge, Mass.: Harvard University Press, 1954, pp. 491–492.

Schoen, Max. *Art and Beauty.* New York: The Macmillan Co., 1932, pp. 89–92.

Schroeder, Francis de Neuville. *A Selection of His Editorials Published in Interiors.* New York: Whitney Publications, 1953, p. 6—Value, or the price of rice; p. 7—A time for contemplation; p. 14—Very hot for May; p. 29—Skilled barbarians.

Stewart, Ross and Gerald, John. *Home Decoration.* New York: Julian Messner, Inc., 1935, Chap. 1.

Chap. XII. Design and Period Styles—Historic Expression

Cescinsky, Herbert and Gribble, Ernest R. *Early English Furniture and Woodwork.* 2 vols. London: G. Routledge and Sons, 1922.

Dutton, Ralph. *The English Interior, 1500–1900.* New York: B. T. Batsford, 1948.

Eberlein, Harold Donaldson, and McClure, Abbot. *The Practical Book of Period Furniture.* Philadelphia: J. B. Lippincott Co., 1914.

Eberlein, Harold Donaldson, McClure, Abbot, and Holloway, Edward Stratton. *The Practical Book of Interior Decoration.* Philadelphia: J. B. Lippincott Co., 1937.

Fletcher, Banister. *A History of Architecture.* New York: Charles Scribner's Sons, 1938.

Hamlin, Talbot. *Greek Revival Architecture in America.* London: Oxford University Press, 1944.

Kimball, Fiske. *Domestic Architecture of the American Colonies and of the Early Republic.* New York: Charles Scribner's Sons, 1922.

Langnon, H., and Huard, F. W. *French Provincial Furniture.* Philadelphia: J. B. Lippincott Co., 1927.

McClelland, Nancy. *Duncan Phyfe and the English Regency.* New York: William R. Scott, Inc., 1939.

Miller, Edgar G. *American Antique Furniture.* 2 vols. New York: M. Barrows & Company, Inc., 1937.

Nystrom, Paul H. *The Economics of Fashion.* New York: The Ronald Press Company, 1928, pp. 3–17.

Rogers, Meyric R. *American Interior Design.* New York: W. W. Norton & Co., Inc., 1947.

Waterman, Thomas Tileston. *The Dwellings of Colonial America.* Chapel Hill, N.C., University of North Carolina Press, 1950.

Yates, Raymond F., and Marguerite W. *A Guide to Victorian Antiques.* New York: Harper & Brothers, 1949.

Chap. XIII. Design and Modern Style—Contemporary Expression

Binyon, Laurence. *The Flight of the Dragon.* London: John Murray, 1927.

Chambers, Frank P. *The History of Taste.* New York: Columbia University Press, 1932, pp 215–240.

Eastlake, C. L. *Hints on Household Taste.* London: Longmans, Green & Co., 1872.

Einstein, Albert. *Ideas and Opinions.* New York: Crown Publishers, Inc., 1954, pp. 360–377—Relativity and the problem of space.

Eliott, Charles W. *The Book of American Interiors.* Boston: James B. Osgood Company, 1876.

Fitch, James Marston. *American Building, The Forces That Shape It.* Boston: Houghton Mifflin Co., 1948.

Ford, James, and Ford, Katherine. *Design of Modern Interiors.* New York: Architectural Book Publishing Co., Inc., 1942.

———. *The Modern House in America.* New York: Architectural Book Publishing Co., Inc., 1946.

Ford, Katherine Morrow, and Creighton, Thomas H. *The American House Today.* New York: Reinhold Publishing Corp., 1951.

Frankl, Paul. *Form and Reform.* New York: Harper & Brothers, 1930.

———. *New Dimensions.* New York: Payson and Clarke, 1928.

Giedion, Sigfried. *Space, Time, and Architecture.* Cambridge, Mass.: Harvard University Press, 1946.

Gilbert, Katharine. *Aesthetic Studies.* Durham, N.C.: Duke University Press, 1952, pp. 25–47.

Gropius, Walter. *The New Architecture and the Bauhaus.* London: Faber and Faber, 1935.

Hiort, Eslojorn. *Modern Danish Furniture.* New York: Architectural Book Publishing Company, 1956.

Hitchcock, Henry Russell. *The Architecture of H. H. Richardson and His Times.* New York: The Museum of Modern Art, 1936.

———. *Painting Toward Architecture.* New York: Duell, Sloan and Pearce, Inc., 1948.

Hitchcock, Henry Russell, and Johnson, Philip C. *The International Style, Architecture Since 1922.* New York: W. W. Norton & Co., Inc., 1932.

Jeanneret-Gris, Charles Édouard (pseud. Le Corbusier). *New World of Space.* New York: Reynal and Hitchcock, 1948.

———. *Towards a New Architecture.* London: John Rodker, 1931.

Johnson, Philip C. *Mies Van Der Rohe.* New York: The Museum of Modern Art, 1947.

Kates, George N. *Chinese Household Furniture.* New York: Harper & Brothers, 1948.

Kishida, H. *Japanese Architecture.* Tokyo: Maruzen Company, 1936.

Lynes, Russell. *The Tastemakers.* New York: Harper & Brothers, 1954.

Mock, Elizabeth B. *If You Want to Build a House.* New York: The Museum of Modern Art, 1946.

Morris, William. *Hopes and Fears for Art.* London: Longmans, Green & Co., 1903.

Morse, Edward S. *Japanese Homes and Their Surroundings.* New York: Harper & Brothers, 1895.

Mumford, Lewis. *The Brown Decades.* New York: Harcourt, Brace & Co., 1931.

————. *The Culture of Cities.* New York: Harcourt, Brace & Co., 1938.

————. *Sticks and Stones.* New York: W. W. Norton & Co., Inc., 1924.

————. *Technics and Civilization.* New York: Harcourt, Brace & Co., 1934.

Nelson, George. *Living Spaces.* New York: Whitney Publications, Inc., 1952.

————. *Chairs.* New York: Whitney Publications, Inc., 1953.

Nelson, George, and Wright, Henry. *Tomorrow's House.* New York: Simon and Schuster, Inc., 1945.

Noyes, Eliot F. *Organic Design in Home Furnishings.* New York: The Museum of Modern Art, 1941.

Pevsner, Nikolaus. *Pioneers of the Modern Movement.* London: Faber and Faber, 1936.

Platz, G. A. *Die Baukunst der Neuesten Zeit.* Berlin: Im Propyläen-Verlag. Suppl. v. 2. 1930.

Reilly, C. *McKim, Mead and White.* New York: Charles Scribner's Sons, 1924.

Robsjohn-Gibbings, T. H. *Goodbye Mr. Chippendale.* New York: Alfred A. Knopf, Inc., 1944.

Rogers, Meyric R. *Italy at Work.* Italy: The Compagnia Nazionale Artigiana, 1950.

Rosenthal, Rudolph, and Ratzka, Helena L. *The Story of Modern Applied Art.* New York: Harper & Brothers, 1948.

Ruskin, John. *Seven Lamps of Architecture.* New York: John Wiley & Sons, Inc., 1866.

Sennett-Willson, R. *The Beauty of Modern Glass.* London: The Studio Limited, 1958.

Sironen, M. K. *A History of American Furniture.* New York: The Towse Publishing Company, 1936.

Sullivan, Louis H. *The Autobiography of an Idea.* New York: American Institute of Architects, Inc., 1926.

Wright, Frank Lloyd. *An Autobiography.* New York: Duell, Sloan and Pearce, 1943.

Yoshida, Tetsuro. *The Japanese House and Garden.* New York: Frederick A. Praiger, 1958.

Chap. XIV. The Total Art Form— A Plan for Accomplishment

Einstein, Albert. *Ideas and Opinions.* New York, Crown Publishers, Inc., 1954, pp. 292–295—In physics and reality (illustrating the diverse means of science and art as they seek the same end).

Emerson, Ralph Waldo. *Essays.* New York: Thomas Y. Crowell Co., Essay XII "Art"—description of the final end of created art.

OUTSTANDING HISTORIC HOUSES
IN EASTERN U. S. BEFORE 1850 WHICH MAY BE VISITED.[1]

Salem, Mass.	The Pioneer Village	*Westmoreland*	Stratford
	"House of Seven Gables"	*Co., Va.*	
Topsfield, Mass.	Parson Capen house	*Fairfax Co., Va.*	Mt. Vernon
Duxbury, Mass.	John Alden house	*Fredericksburg,*	Kenmore
Guilford, Conn.	Henry Whitfield house	*Va.*	
Princess Anne	Adam Thoroughgood house	*Williamsburg,*	John D. Rockefeller, Jr.
Co., Va.		*Va.*	historic restoration
Surry Co., Va.	Bacon's Castle	*Charles City*	Westover
Deerfield, Mass.	Old Deerfield village	*Co., Va.*	Berkeley
Portsmouth,	Pierce house		Shirley
N.H.	Wentworth-Gardner house	*Prince George*	Brandon
Marblehead,	Jeremiah Lee house	*Co., Va.*	
Mass.		*Richmond, Va.*	Wilton
Medford, Mass.	Royall house	*Albemarle Co.,*	Monticello
New York, N.Y.	Van Cortlandt house	*Va.*	
	Dykman house	*Charleston, S.C.*	Miles Brewton house
New Paltz, N.Y.	Jean Hasbrouck house		Colonel William Rhett house
Milbach, Pa.	Müller house (interiors in the		William Gibbes house
	Philadelphia [Pa.]	*New Orleans,*	Vieux Carré (old French
	Museum)	*La.*	quarter)
Cambridge,	John Vassall (Longfellow)	*St. Francisville,*	Greenwood
Mass.	house	*La.*	
Philadelphia, Pa.	Mt. Pleasant	*Natchez, Miss.*	Rosalie (and many others)
	Powel house	*Nashville, Tenn.*	The Hermitage
Annapolis, Md.	Brice house	*Salem, Mass.*	Peirce-Nichols house
	Hammond-Harwood house		Pickering house
		Waltham, Mass.	Gore Mansion
		New York, N.Y.	The Roger Morris or
			Jumel Mansion

[1] The list is by no means complete. An attempt was made to indicate at least one house from each period in various localities. The arrangement is loosely chronological.

MUSEUMS NOTED FOR OUTSTANDING COLLECTIONS
OF DECORATIVE ARTS.[1]

Arles, France	Musée Arlaten (French	*Cambridge,*	William Hayes Fogg Art
	Provincial)	*Mass.*	Museum
Amsterdam, the	Rijksmuseum	*Chicago, Ill.*	Art Institute of Chicago
Netherlands		*Cincinnati, O.*	Cincinnati Art Museum
Baltimore, Md.	Baltimore Museum of Art		Taft Museum
Boston, Mass.	Museum of Fine Arts	*Cleveland, O.*	Cleveland Museum of Art
		Detroit, Mich.	Detroit Institute of Arts
		Dearborn, Mich.	Henry Ford Museum
		Holland, Mich.	Baker Museum

[1] Museums specializing in particular media or in the work of specific localities have been omitted.

Kansas City, Mo.	William Rockhill Nelson Gallery of Art	*Paris, contd.*	Musée des Arts Décoratifs
London, England	British Museum	*Philadelphia, Pa.*	Philadelphia Museum of Art
	London Museum, Kensington Palace	*Salem, Mass.*	Essex Institute
	Victoria and Albert Museum	*San Francisco, Cal.*	San Francisco Museum of Art
New York, N.Y.	Brooklyn Institute of Arts and Sciences	*San Marino, Cal.*	Henry E. Huntington Library and Art Gallery
	Cooper Museum for the Arts of Decoration	*Toledo, O.*	Toledo Museum of Art
	Frick Collection	*Washington, D.C.*	Corcoran Gallery of Art
Paris, France	Musée de Cluny		Freer Gallery of Art
	Musée du Louvre		National Gallery of Art
		Winterthur, Del.	Henry Francis duPont Winterthur Museum

CURRENT DIRECTORY OF FIRMS MENTIONED IN CHAPTER XIII AND A FEW OTHER REPRESENTATIVE ONES

Adler-Schnee Associates, 7403 Puritan Ave., Detroit, Mich. (textiles)

Altamira, 125 East 55 St., New York, N.Y. (furniture, accessories)

Arbuck, Inc., 116 Troutman Street, Brooklyn, N.Y. (furniture)

Baker Furniture, Inc., 10 Milling Road, Holland, Mich. *

Belgian Linen Association, 280 Madison Ave., New York, N.Y.

Bonniers, 605 Madison Ave., New York, N.Y. (accessories)

Charak Furniture Co., 425 East 53 Street, New York, N.Y.

Dan Cooper Design Corp., 10 East 54 Street, New York, N.Y. (interior design)

Inez Croom, Inc., 56 East 55 St., New York, N.Y. (wallpaper)

Denst and Soderlund, Inc., 7355 S. Exchange Ave., Chicago, Ill. (wallpaper)

Directional Furniture Showrooms, Inc., 41 East 57 St., New York, N.Y. (furniture)

Marion V. Dorn, 8 East 54 St., New York, N.Y. (fabrics, wallpapers)

Dunbar Furniture Corp., Berne, Indiana *

Dux, Inc., 1633 Adrian Rd., Burlingame, Cal. (furniture)

Elenhank, Designers, Inc., 347 East Burlington St., Riverside, Ill. (fabrics, wallpaper)

Far Eastern Fabrics, Inc., 171 Madison Ave., New York, N.Y.

Ficks Reed Co., 4900 Charlemar Drive, Cincinnati, Ohio * (furniture)

Edward Fields, Inc., 509 Madison Ave., New York, N.Y. (floor coverings)

Finland House, 41 East 56 St., New York, N.Y. (lighting)

Fortuny Inc., 509 Madison Ave., New York, N.Y. (fabrics)

Gallo Furniture Co., Inc., 1 Park Ave., New York, N.Y.

Robsjohn-Gibbings Ltd., 145 East 72 St., New York, N.Y. (furniture, interior design)

Glenn of California, 130 North First Ave., Arcadia, Cal. (furniture)

Gotham Lighting Corporation, 3701 Thirty-first St., Long Island City, L.I., N.Y.

Gunn and Latchford, Inc., 323 Fifth Ave., New York, N.Y. (oriental wares)

Hansen Lamps, 260 East 53 St., New York, N.Y.

Yasha Heifetz, 16 East 53 St., New York, N.Y. (lighting)

* New York office: 305 East 63 St., New York, N.Y.

Holophane Company, Inc., 342 Madison Ave., New York, N.Y. (lighting)

House of Italian Handicrafts, Inc., 225 Fifth Ave., New York, N.Y.

Irish Export Promotion Board, 33 East 50 St., New York, N.Y.

Italian Marble Mart, 802 Third Ave., New York, N.Y.

J. G. Furniture Inc., 160 E. 56 St., New York, N.Y.

Georg Jensen, Inc., 667 Fifth Ave., New York, N.Y. (accessories); Frederick Lunning Company, distributor for furniture

Johnson Furniture Company, 1101 Godfrey Ave., Grand Rapids, Mich. or Fourth Ave. & 32 St., New York, N.Y.

Katzenbach and Warren, Inc., 575 Madison Ave., New York, N.Y. (wallpapers)

Kent-Costikyan, Inc.,* (custom and imported floor coverings)

Kliegl Bros. Lighting Co. Inc., 321 West 50 St., New York, N.Y.

Kneedler-Fauchere, 451 Jackson Square, San Francisco, Cal. (furnishings)

Knoll Associates, Inc., 575 Madison Ave., New York, N.Y.

Kolb Lighting Company, 394 East 18 St., Paterson, N.J.

Boris Kroll Fabrics, Inc., 220 East 51 St., New York, N.Y.

Jack Lenor Larsen, Inc., 16 East 55 St., New York, N.Y. (fabrics)

Laverne, Inc., 160 East 57 St., New York, N.Y.

Dorothy Liebes Textiles, Inc., 767 Lexington Ave., New York, N.Y.

Lightolier, 11 East 36 St., New York, N.Y.

Mauretania Fabrics, Inc., 50 East 64 St., New York, N.Y.

McDonald, Gene, 509 Madison Ave., New York, N.Y. (wallcoverings)

Menlo Textiles, Menlo Park, California

Herman Miller Furniture Company, Inc., Zeeland, Mich. *

Mills-Denmark, 227 East 56 St., New York, N.Y. (furniture)

Molla, Inc., 425 East 53 St., New York, N.Y.

* New York office: 305 East 63 St., New York, N.Y.

Mueller Metals Corporation, 600 Monroe Ave., Grand Rapids, Mich. (metal furniture)

Nessen Studio, Inc., 317 East 34 St., New York, N.Y. (lighting)

Parzinger Originals, Inc., 32 East 57 St., New York, N.Y. (furniture)

Harvey Probber Showrooms, Inc., 41 East 57 St., New York, N.Y. (furniture)

Jens Risom Design, Inc., 49 East 53 St., New York, N.Y.

Ben Rose, 1129 West Sheridan Road, Chicago, Ill. or 17 East 53 St., New York, N.Y. (textiles, wallcoverings)

John B. Salterini Co., Inc., Covington, Va. or 41 East 57 St., New York, N.Y. (furniture)

Bertha Schaefer Gallery, 32 East 57 St., New York, N.Y. (accessories)

M. Singer and Sons, 36 East 19 St., New York, N.Y. (furniture)

Steuben Glass Company, Corning, N.Y. or Fifth Ave. & 56 St., New York, N.Y.

John Stuart, Inc., Fourth Ave. & 32 St., New York, N.Y. (furniture)

George Tanier, Inc., 521 Madison Ave., New York, N.Y. (lamps, furniture)

Angelo Testa, 49 East Ontario Street, Chicago, Ill. (fabrics)

Thaibok Fabrics, Ltd., 3 East 52 St., New York, N.Y.

Thonet Industries, Inc., 1 Park Ave., New York, N.Y. (furniture)

Kurt Versen Co., 4 Slocum Ave., Englewood, N.J. (lighting)

Hendrik Van Keppel and Taylor Green, 116 S. Lasky Dr., Beverley Hills, Cal. (furniture)

Albert Van Luit & Co., 4000 Chevy Chase Drive, Los Angeles, Cal. or 515 Madison Ave., New York, N.Y. (wallpapers)

V'Soske Inc., 310 Scribner Ave., Grand Rapids, Mich. or 4 East 53 St., New York, N.Y. (rugs)

Widdicomb-Mueller Furniture Corp., Grand Rapids, Mich. *

John Widdicomb Co., 1 Park Ave., New York, N.Y. (furniture)

Willow and Reed, Inc., 1 Park Ave., New York, N.Y. (furniture)

Lee L. Woodard Sons, Owosso, Mich. *

INDEX

Aalto, Alvar, 299
Afghanistan, 204
Africa, 306, 308
After-image, 110–111
Aggregates, 29
Air conditioning, 33–37
Akari, 310
Albers, Anni, 304
Albini, Franco, 302
Aluminum, 217
American Association of Textile Chemists and Colorists, 172n
American Institute of Decorators, 295, 320n
American Museum mat, 244
American Optical Society, test for color vision, 108
American Public Health Association, 37, 40, 55, 56
American styles of furnishing
  Colonial, 260
  Early American or Provincial, 260, 290
  Federal, 265
  Greek Revival, 265
  John Belter, 268
  Mission, 294
  Victorian, 268, 291
Amounts of color in relation to order, 133–134
Amplitude of radiant energy waves, 95
Analogous hue harmony, 133
Anatolian carpet, 205
Angle of incidence and of reflection, 100
Angora goat, 185
Angstrom, A. J., 96n
Angstrom unit, 96n
Animal organic colorants, list of, 102
Anne, Queen, 260
Anode, 215
Anomalous color vision, 108
Antique finish for wood, 182
Antique Oriental rug, 205
Aperture mode of color appearance, 100
Apparent color, 99
Appraisal of modern furniture, 295, 299
Aquatint, 237
Aqueous humor, 106
Architectural terms used in interiors, 182–183
Area, as type of shape, 84
Ariel glass, 308
Armory Show, 292
Art
  comprehensive definition of, 4
  materials of, 11–12
  Munro, definition of, 7n

Art, cont.
  purposes for creating, 7–8
  restricted definition of, 7
  sense in which Dewey defines, 7n
  time-space, 44
Art form
  as related to structure, 32
  complete, 8
  design as a factor in, 8
  expression as a factor in, 8
  functional, 8
Art museums
  list of for decorative arts, 330–331
  Newark, 294
  Metropolitan, 295
  of Contemporary Crafts, 295
  of Modern Art, 295, 301, 308
Art Nouveau, 273
Art objects, lighting of, 159–160
Art qualifying program for a factory, 314–315
Arte Luce, 310
Artek and Pascoe, 299
Artext Prints, 242
Artificial light, 161–164
Artist's proof, 237, 243
Asphalt flooring, 205
Assimilation color effect, 111–112
Asymmetry, 21, 22
Atmosphere of space, 13
Attribute
  of component, 13, 22
  of color, 94–95, 124
  of shape, 84
  of texture, 170, 171–172
Aubusson carpet, 201
Austria, 273, 294
Axis of abscissas and of ordinates, 120
Axminster carpet, 202

Baccarat glass, 213
Bach, Richard F., 295
Bakhtiari carpet, 204
Balance
  appraisal of in living area, 92
  asymmetrical, informal, occult, 21, 22
  bisymmetrical, formal, obvious, 20, 22
  color, 133–134
  in physical science, 20
  inward versus outward, 21–22
Ballet, Russian, 295
Baluchistan (Pakistan), 204
Balustrade, 30
"Barcelona chair," 300
Baroque, 258–263, 290–291
Basalt ware, 208
Basement, cost of, 25n
Basic elements of color education, subcommittee 20 of ISCC, 94n

Bates, Kenneth, 308
Baths, 56–57
Batik process, 194
Bauhaus, 273–274, 295, 304
Bavaria, 209
Beauty
  nature of, 1–4
  Somerset Maugham quotation, 1
Beauvais carpet, 201
Bedrooms
  functions of, 55
  lighting for, 156–157
  planning for, 55–56
  sizes, 55
Behrens, Peter, 273, 294
Belangie, Michael D., 304
Beleek china, 209–210
Belgium, 213, 307
Belter, John, 268
Bending of wood, 181
Bendure, Z. and Pfeiffer, G., America's Fabrics, 194n
Bergamo carpet, 205
Bernadotte, Count Sigvard, 302
Bertha Schaefer Gallery, 307
Bertoia, Harry 310
Bezold-Brücke effect, 109n
Binder for paint, 102–103
Binyon, Laurence
  quotation from Sei-ichi Taki, 93
  quotation, 255
Bird's-eye figure, 178
Birren, F., suggestions for painters, 100
Biscuit firing, 206, 208
Bisque ware, 206
Bisymmetry, 20–21, 22
Blackbody, 162
Black Mountain College Weavers, 304
Black Sea, 203
Blanc fixe, 101
Blister figure, 178
Bloomfield Hills, Michigan, 295
Blow, Richard, 310
Blown-molded glass, 211
Bobbin lace, 188
Bohemian glass, 211, 213
Bokhara carpet, 204
Bonaparte, Louis-Napoleon, 268
Bonaparte, Napoleon, 265
Bone china, 208
Boundary reflection of light, 100
Bracque, 289
Braided rug, 201
Braiding, 188
Brancusi, 240
Brass, 217
Breakfast room, 54
Breuer, Marcel, 299
Brick as facing veneer, 27
Bright clear series, 117

Brightness, 97, 124
British Colour Council, *Dictionary of Colours for Interior Decoration,* 119
Broadloom, 190
Brocading, 194
Bronze, 217
Browning, Robert, quotations, 219, 321
Brussels carpet, 201n
Building as time-space art, 44
Burl grain, 178

Cabriole, 233, 260
Café curtains, 231
Calder, Alexander, 309, 310
Calendering, 195
Cameo glass, 213
Candle per square foot, 150
Candlepower, 150
Cane, 180
Carat, 215
Carolean, 260
Carpenter, H. B., *Colour,* 132n
Carpets, 200–203, 308
    Axminster, 202
    braided rugs, 201
    Brussels, 201n
    Chenille, 202–203
    construction of, 201–203
    finishes, 205
    hooked or tufted, 201, 202
    ingrain, 201
    materials in, 200–201
    Oriental, 203–205
    pads, 205
    power loomed, 201–203
    tapestry, 201
    tapestry velvet, 202
    velvet, 202
    Wilton, 201–202
Carved pile, 193, 203, 204
Carving of wood, 181
Cascella, Pietro, 308
Cashmere fiber, 185–186
Caspian Sea, 203
Cast iron, 216
Castleton china, 308
Cathode, 215
Caucasian Oriental carpets, 203, 205
Ceiling, 29
Cells, wood, 176
Cellulose fibers, list of, 185
Centers of interest, 21, 22
    in living area, 92
Ceramics, 205–211, 308–309
    composition types, 205–208
    consideration of choice, 210–211
    contemporary firms, 209–210
    embellishment, 209
    forming, 208–209
    modern, 308–309
Chagall, 209
Chain warp, 201
Chandler, A. R., *Beauty and Human Nature,* 79n
Change, as quality of design, 18–19
Changing level of illumination, effect on color vision, 109–110
Charles I, II of England, 258–260
Charles VIII, IX of France, 257

Charles X of France, 265
Chenille carpet, 202–203
Chenille yarn, 108
Chevreul, M. E., 110
    concerning color intervals, 133n
Chicago Institute of Design, 295
Chicago Merchandise Mart, 295
Chimneys, 30–31
Chimney pots, 30
China, 208–209
    bone, 208
    Ch'ing, 210
    Coalport, 209
    description of, 208
    Dresden and Meissen, 209
    hard paste, 208
    ironstone, 208
    Ming, 205
    Royal Copenhagen, 209
    Royal Crown Derby, 209
    Royal Doulton, 209
    Royal Worcester, 209
    semivitreous, 208
    soft paste, 208
Chinese Oriental carpets, 203, 204
Ch'ing porcelain, 210
Chippendale chair, 233
Chippendale, Thomas, 260
Chiseleur, 238
Choice of color traits, 127–129
Choice of dominant
    color, 137
    shape, 84–88
    texture, 172
Chroma, 118
Chromatic color, 95–96
Chromatic light circle, 98
Chromaticity, 124
Chromaticness, 97, 124
C.I.E., 122–125
    diagram, 125
    color mixture curves, 123
    Commission Internationale de l'Eclairage, 122n
    imaginary primaries, 123
    standard light sources, A,B,C, 122
    standard chromatic lights, 122–123
    Standard Observer and Coordinate System of Colorimetry, 122
    symbols, 123
    system of color measurement, 122–123, 125
C.I.E.T.A., 190
Circle diagram of light combinations, 98
Circulation areas, 44–46
Clapboards, 27
Classic civilizations, 257
Cleansing air, 35
Clerestory lighting, 160
Climate control, 33–37
Climaxes, 21, 22
Cloth beam, 188
Cloud band, 204
Coalport china, 209
Coinage standard of silver, 214
Colonial style of furnishing, 260
Color, 93–148, 284–289
    achromatic and chromatic, 95

Color, *cont.*
    amounts in relation to order, 133–134
    analogous hue harmony, 133
    apparent, 99
    as a perceptual experience, 109–113
    assimilation effect, 111–112
    as visual force, 129
    balance, 133–134
    blindness, 108
    choice of traits for expressive effect, 127–128
    circles, 98, 105, 111
    complementary hue harmony, 133
    consideration of lightness-darkness in room colors, 139–141
    contrast, law of, 110–111
    curves of the eye, 122–123, 125
    design for specific rooms, 143–148
    dictionaries, 119
    dominant, 137
    effects due to interrelations, 129–134
    final check of order, 141
    genuine, 99
    harmony, 129
    hues to accompany dominant, 137
    illusions through, 134–135
    importance of study, 93–94
    in the contemporary interior, 284–289
    kinds of intervals, 132–133
    locations in a room, 137
    measurement and specification, 120–123, 125
    mixture, additive, 97–98
    mixture, subtractive, 104–106
    modes of appearance, 99–100
    monochromatic or one hue harmony, 133
    natural order of, 132
    order through positioning, 133–134
    orderly arrangement of intervals, 131
    organization of, 113–119
    perception, 109–113
    placement of, 133–134
    planning in interior design, 135–148
    potential today, 284
    psychological attributes of, 94–95
    purity (excitation purity), 124, 125
    quadratic hue harmony, 133
    relation to spatial design, 134
    repetition of traits, 130–131
    saturations to be used in room colors, 141
    spreading effect, 111–112
    stimulus, 95–106
    suggestions from modern painters, 289
    suggested order to be used in planning, 141–142
    tables of reflectance values, 152n
    terms, 124
    triadic hue harmony, 133
    understanding, 93–125
    unity of schemes in a building, 142–143
    usual hue placement, 137–139
    wavelengths, 96
    ways of relating, 130–134

Color and lighting, 152, 157, 162
  combining incandescent and fluorescent, 162
  color effect under fluorescent tubes, 162
  preference for color in lights, 162
Color Association of the United States, Inc., 119
Color design, specific room illustrations, 143–148
Color system, 114–119
  color mixture system, 114–117
  colorant mixture system, 117–118
  nature and importance of, 113
  tests of a good, 114
  visual order system, 118–119
Color vision, 108–112
  anomalous, 108
  effect of illumination on, 109–111
  effect of the response mechanism on, 112
  tests for, 108
  theories of, 108–109
Colorants, 100–106
  definition, 100
  inorganic and organic, 101–102
  in paints, lacquer, varnish, dye, ink, 100, 102–104
  natural and synthetic, 101
  primary, 104
  subtractive, 104–106
Colorimeter, 121, 124
Color Harmony Manual, 115n
  accompanying *Color Names Dictionary*, 117n
  accompanying chart of reflectance values, 152n
Color organization, suggestions for in contemporary design, 289
Color solid, paths through, 131–132
Commery, E. W. and Leighton, K., *Fluorescent Lighting in the Home*, 162n
Commery, E. W. and Stephenson, E. E., *How to Decorate and Light your Home*, 164n
Commonwealth, the, 258
Communication areas, 44–46
Communication, synonym for expression, 7
Community, 41
Comparative list of color terms, 124
Complementary
  colors, 110, 118
  colorants, 105
  hue harmony, 133
  lights, 97, 115
  wavelength, 125
Complex single weave, 191–192
Components, visual, 12, 22
Compound weave, 193
Compression strength, 25
Concrete problems, 222–247
  decorative accessories, 233–247
  floor treatment, 222
  pictures and sculpture, 235–247
  tableware, 234–235
  upholstery, 231–233
  wall treatment, 222–228
  window treatment, 228–231

Condensor lens light, 164
Cones in eye, 107
Constancy, sensation of, 16, 17
Construction
  drywall, 29
  modern, 23
  post and beam, 25–26
  textiles, 188–193
Container Corporation of America, 117
Contemporary
  building, balance in, 21
  expression, 271–310
  firms, 331–332
  furnishing, 291–310
  history, 272–279, 291–299
  reasons for, 271–272
  the present market, 299–310
  use with the traditional, 290–291
Contrast
  color, 110–111
  importance of, 113
  in design, 22
  meaning of, 15–16
Control
  artificial light, 163–164
  general methods of, for light, 151
  natural light, 160
Controlled experiment, 110
Conversation
  light for, 155
  planning areas for, 62
Cooling, as task of climate control, 35
Copper, 217
Cork flooring, 205
Cornea, 106
Cornice board, 231
Cosmic rays, 96
Cottage curtains, 231
Cotton fiber, 185
Cox, W. E., *The Book of Pottery and Porcelain*, 206n
Craft revival styles, 268, 272
Cranbrook Academy of Arts, 295, 304, 309
Crayon
  in cave paintings, 102
  painting, 237
Crimping, 188
Crocheting, 188
Cromwellian (see also Commonwealth), 258
Cross-role figure, 178
Crossed warp weave, 193
Crotch figure, 178
Crystalline lens, 106
Curly figure, 178
Curtain walls, 26
Curtains (see also draperies), 228–231
  café or cottage, 231
  draw or traverse, 228–231
  floor hooks, 231
  glass, 230
  hanging, 230–231
  tie-backs, 231
Cut glass, 211, 213

Dacron, valuable qualities, 187–188
Daghestan carpet, 205
Dali, 239

Dana, John Cotton, 294
Dark clear series, 117
Daylight, definition of, 99
de Carli, Carlo, 302
Decoration as related to structure, 88
Decorator, 320–321
Decorating textiles, glossary of, 196–200
Decorative accessories, 233–247
Definiteness in design, 21
De Gaulle, C., quotation, 127
Delft pottery, 209
Deluxe fluorescent tubes, 162
Denmark, 209, 213, 216
Depth in pattern, 225
Design
  and expression, 249–254
  and modern style, 271–310
  and period styles, 255–268
  beginning of a, 13–14
  definition of, 8, 22, 320
  difficulty of attaining a good, 21–22
  further organization of, 14–15
  integrating a detail in, 19
  of lighting fixtures, 158–159
  outline of organization, 22
  tests of, 13
  through light, 157–158
  types of organization in, 21, 22
  use of old with new, 290–291
Designer, 320
Dessau, 273
Determinants of the modern style, 272
Deuteranopia, 108
DeVore, J. R., *Luminescent Coatings*, 104n
Dewey, J., *Freedom and Culture*, 252n
Dewey, John
  definition of art, 7n
  ordered variation in change, 18n
  quotation, 11
Dichromatism, 108
Diffraction, 97
Diffuse light, 100
Diluents, 101, 102, 103
Dining areas, 58, 155–156
  lighting, 155–156
  planning, 58
  sizes, 58
Dinnerware, as name for pottery and stoneware, 208
Direction, as an attribute of shape, 84
Directional light, 110, 151
Directory of firms dealing in modern furnishings, 331–332
Dirilyte, 215
Discharge printing, 194
Disk mixture of light, 114
Dispersion
  definition, 97
  of pigment in medium, 103
  of resin in medium, 103
Dominance, 16, 21, 22
Dominant
  color, 137
  shape, 84–88
  texture, 172
  wavelength, 124, 125
Domus, 295
Dorn, Marion, 305, 310

Dot, as type of shape, 84
Double weave, 192
Doup harness, 193
Douppioni silk, 186
Dovetail joints, 181
Dowel joints, 32, 181
Dragon, as motive, 204
Draperies (see also curtains), 230–231
Draw or traverse curtains, 228, 231
Dresden china, 209
Driers for paints, 103
Drying oils, 102–103
    linseed, 103
    tung, 103
Drypoint, 237
Drywall construction, 29
Dufy, 239, 307
Dutch process lead, 101
Dwt. (pennyweight), 214
Dyeing, 194–195
Dyes
    definition, 100
    vat, 194

Eames, Charles, 301
Early American
    style of furnishing, 260
    use with contemporary, 290
    wallpaper pattern, 226
Early Georgian style of furnishing, 260
Earth
    as source of heat, 34
    pigments, 101
Earthenware, 206
East Aurora, N.Y., 294
Eckhardt, Edris, 308
Eclectic, 268
Edward VI, 257
Egypt, 263
Ekselius, Carl, 302
Electricity, as radiant energy, 96
Electroplating, 128
Elevation, drawing of, 72, 92
Elizabeth I, 257
Elizabethan, 257
Ellipse, 79
Embellishment added to the basic fabric
    color, 194–195
    finishes, 195
    yarns, 193–194
Embroidered rug, 201
Embroidery, 194
Emphasis, principle of, 16
Empire
    First Empire style of furnishing, 265
    Second Empire style of furnishing, 268
    use with contemporary, 291
Enamels, 103, 206
Enamel undercoater, 103
Encaustic painting, 102, 236
England
    ceramics from, 209
    glass from, 213–214
    historic periods, 257–268
English Restoration, 290
Engraved glass, 213
Engraving, 237

Entertainment, lighting for, 152–156
Escuder, Joseph, 308
Etched glass, 213
Etching, 237
Eurasia, 203
Examples of art forms in interior design, 311–314
Excitation purity of color, 125
Experience
    aesthetic, 2, 3
    materials of, 12, 13
    psychological formula for, 2
    sensations basic to, 4
Explanation, synonym for expression, 7
Exposition, synonym for expression, 7
Expression
    design and, 249–254
    consideration in color planning, 127–129, 135
    consideration in shape planning, 85–88
    consideration in texture planning, 170, 173
    contemporary, 271–310
    historic, 255–268
    meaning of, 7–8
    synonyms for, 7
Extreme-mean proportion, 79, 81, 82
Eye
    color curves of, 121
    description of, 106–108
    functioning in vision, 121–122
    luminosity curve of, 121
    of the normal or standard observer, 121

Fabric, 184
    glossary of decorating, 196–200
Faenza, 206
Faience, 206
Family, definition of, 40n
Family entrance, 46
Farnsworth-Munsell 100 Hue Test for color vision, 108
Fashion, 257
Feather figure, 178
Federal style of furnishing, 265
Feininger, 240
Felt, construction of, 188
Feraghan carpet, 204
Ferro-concrete, 25, 29
Ferro-Enamel Company, 308
Fibers, 184–188
    wood, 176
Fiddleback figure, 178
Figures in wood, 178
Filament
    incandescent, 98
    textile, 186, 188
Fillers for paint, 103
Film mode of color appearance, 100, 124
Finger roll figure, 178
Finish coat in paint, 103
Finishes in wood, 182
Finland, 209, 213, 309
Finzi, Argenteria, 310
Fireplaces, 30–31
Fitness to purpose, 39

Flat pattern, 225
Flax fiber, character of, 185
Flexibility in use of space, 43
Flicker, color term, 124
Flocking, 195
Floor
    coverings, 29, 200–205, 308
    interior, 29
    paint, 103
    plan, making and reading, 64–72
    treatment, 222
Flue, chimney, 30
Fluorescent light, 98–99, 161–164
    advantages of, 161–162
    four colors advised for home lighting, 162
    nature of, 98–99
Focal points, 21
Folk styles, 257
Folke-Ohlsson, 302
Fontana, Lucio, 308
Fontane Arte, 310
Food preparation center, 53–54
Footing, 25, 31
Foot-candle, 150
Footlambert, 150
Ford, Katherine Morrow, and Creighton, Thomas H., quotation, 39
Form, art
    design as factor in, 8
    expression as factor in, 8
    functional, 8
Formal balance, 20–21
Formal design, 21
Fovea centralis, 107
Framing pictures, 242–243
France
    exhibition of 1925, 294, 295
    historic periods, 257–268
    silver from, 216
    State Looms, 307
Francis I, II of France, 257
Frankl, Paul, 302
French-lined mat, 245
French finish of wood, 182
French pleats, 230
Frequency of radiant energy waves, 95
Fresco painting, 102, 236
Fuel for heating, 34
Fuller, Buckminster, 25n
Functional
    art form, 7
    consideration in color planning, 135
    consideration in shape planning, 85
    consideration in texture planning, 172
    consideration in furnishings, 75
Functions
    of the eye, 106
    planning for, 42–43
Furnaces, 34
Furnishings, contemporary, 291–310
Furniture, modern, 299–302
Furniture templates, 72
Furniture, wood, construction of, 183–184

Gabled roof, 26
Gabo, Naum, 309
Gaillard Press, 310

Gambone, Guido, 308
Garage, sizes of, 54
Gate, Simon, 308
Gauguin, 240
General Aniline automatic tristimulus
    integrator, 122
Genuine color, 99
George I, II, 260
George III, IV, 265
Georgian building, balance in, 21
Gerard, Alexander, 305
Germany, 273
Ghiordes carpet, 205
Ghiordes knot, 203, 205
Glare
    cause of, 152
    definition of, 152
    windows in relation to, 160
Glass, 151, 211–214, 308–309
    composition types, 211
    consideration of choice, 214
    contemporary firms, 213–214
    diffusing, 151
    embellishment, 211
    forming, 211
    lighting fixtures, 310
    modern, 308–309
    plate, 214n
Glass curtains, 230
Glass fiber, 187, 188
Glaze
    ceramic, 206
    "peach bloom," 210
Glazing cloth, 195
Glazing medium, recipe for, 101n
Glossiness, 100, 124
Gobelin tapestry works, 110
Good Design Award, 295
Good quality material, 169, 171
Gorevan carpet, 204
Gouache or tempera, 102
Grain, of gold, 215
Graphic processes, 237
Graphs, for color designation, 120
Grasten, Viola, 306
Graves, M., Color Fundamentals, 131n
Greek Revival style of furnishing,
    265
Green, Taylor, 302
Greenough, Horatio, 272
Grid for drawing a room in perspec-
    tive, 72–74
Gromaire, 307
Gropius, Walter, 273
Grotell, Maija, 308
Growth of a tree, 176–177
Guls, 204

Hald, Edward, 308
Hallway
    lighting for, 156
    planning for, 46
    sizes for, 46
Hamadan carpet, 204
Hambidge, J., 79n
Hand
    of material, 170
    of textile, 228
Handcraft movements, English, 292
Hand-painted wallpapers, 310

Hanging
    curtains, 230–231
    pictures, 246–247
Hardoy, 300
Harmony, color, 129
Harness
    definition of, 188–189
    doup, 193
    figure, 191
Harrington, J. C., Glassmaking at
    Jamestown, 211n
Hatchings, 202
Haviland china, 209, 210
Hearth, 31
Heat
    fuel for producing, 34
    insulation to prevent flow of, 33
    systems for transmitting, 34–35
Heddle, 188
Heirloom, 235
Heirloom silver, 216
Helmholtz, Hermann von, 108
Helson-Judd effect, in color, 110n, 158
Henry II, III, IV of France, 257
Henry VII, VIII of England, 257
Hepplewhite, George, 265
Herat carpet, 204
Herez carpet, 204
Hering, Ewald, 109
Hering theory of color vision, 109
Heterogeneous light, 97n, 98
Himalaya Mountains, 203
Historic expression, 255–268
History, our use of, 255–256
Hitchcock, H. R., and Johnson, P. C.,
    The International Style, 275
Hitchcock, H. R., Painting Toward
    Architecture, 284
Hoffmann, Joseph, 273
Holland
    glass from, 213
    pewter from, 217
Home Builder's Association, 41
Home lighting, planning for, 164–165
Home line fluorescent tubes, 162n
Homogeneous light, 97n
Hooked rug, 201
House
    cost of, 41
    Dymaxion, 25n
    New England provincial, 27
    planning for, 41
    site for, 41
    Tudor, 30
House of Hanover, 260
Household
    activities, 43
    changing character of, 40
    definition of, 40
Housekeeping, 40
Housework, 51–55
Hubbard, Elbert, 292
Hue
    caused by reflected and transmitted
        light, 100
    definition of, 94–95
    in list of color terms, 124
    invariant, 109
    less usual hue placements, 138–
        139

Hue, cont.
    psychological attribute of color, 94–
        95
    through mixture of colorants, 104
    usual hue placements, 137–138
Hues to accompany dominant hue, 137
Human organism, 2, 4
Hurvich-Jameson theory of color vi-
    sion, 109n
Hyperbola, 80

IES Lighting Handbook for recom-
    mended levels of lighting, 152n
Illuminance, 150
Illuminant mode of color appearance,
    99–100
Illumination mode of color appearance,
    99–100
Illusions
    general principles, 90–91
    through color, 134
    through shapes, 90–91
    through textures, 174–175
Imaginary primaries, 122–123
Impregnation of wood, 180
Impressionists' use of color, 289
Incandescence (see filament lighting),
    98
Incandescent light, 98, 161
Indefiniteness in design, 21
Index of refraction
    change during drying of paints, 106
    definition, 100n
India, 203, 204
Indian Oriental carpets, 203, 204
Informal balance, 21
Informal design, 21
Infrared heat rays, 96
Ingrain carpet, 201
Inorganic colorants, 101–102
Insulation, 33
Intaglio, 209
Integration
    between groups in living area, 92
    of change and rest, 21, 22
    of details in a design, 19
Intensity
    of aesthetic effect, 13, 17, 22
    of sound, 37
Interference films, 97n
Interior decorator, 320
Interlocked grain, 178
International Commission on Illumina-
    tion, 122
International style, 275
Interpretation, synonym for expression,
    7
Inter-Society Color Council, 94
    Color Aptitude Test, 108
    comparative list of color terms, 95n,
        124
    sub-committee, 20; Basic Elements
        of Color Education, 94
Intervals, color, 131–132
Invariant hues, 109
Iran, 203
Ireland
    ceramics from, 209–210
    modern fabrics from, 307, 308
Iron, 216

Ironstone china, 208
Irrational numbers, 80
ISCC-NBS method of designating
    colors, 119
Islam, 205
Isotints, 117
Isotones, 117
Isotropic, 25
Ispahan, 204
Italy
    furniture designers from, 302
    glass from (see Venetian), 213
    historic periods, 257–260
    "Italy at Work" exhibition, 299
    modern fabrics from, 306–307
    modern movement, 295–299

Jacobean, 258
Jacobson, E., Granville, W., and Foss,
    C. E., *Color Harmony Manual*,
    115n
Jacquard loom, 191, 192, 201, 304
Jalousie window, 29
James I, 258
James II, 260
Japanese ceramics, 210
Jaspé fabrics, 195
Jasper ware, 208
Jeanneret-Gris, C. É., 273
Jensen, Georg, 310
Johnson, Philip, 284n
    H. R. Hitchcock, and P. C. Johnson,
    The International Style, Archi-
    tecture Since 1922, 275n
Jointing, 31–32
Joints, 181
Joists, 25
Juhl, Finn, 302

Kandinsky, 239
Kaolin, 208
Kara Dagh mountains, 205
Karabagh carpet, 205
Karasz, Ilonka, 310
Karasz, Mariska, 307
Kashan carpet, 204
Kashmir goat, 186
Katz, David
    genuine color, 99n
    law of color constancy, 17n
    quotation, 149
Kazak carpet, 205
Kelvin unit, 162
Kepes, Gyorgy, quotation, 167
Kerman carpet, 204
Kermanshah carpet, 204
Khilim, 201, 203n
Khuba carpet, 205
Kitchen, 52–55
Klee, 240, 281
Knitting, 188
Knoll, Florence, 300
Knots, in wood, 178
Knots, in carpet, 203
Knotted pile weave, 193
Knotting, 188
Kofod-Larsen, Ib., 302
Kroll, Boris, 304–305
Kurdish carpets, 204

Lac, 102

Lace, 188, 194
Lacquer
    definition of, 103
    wood finish, 182
Laertes, 171
Lakes, as pigments, 100
Lalique, René, 308
Lambrequin, 231
Lamination of wood, 180
Lampas weave, 191–192
Lappet attachment, 194
Larsen, Jack Lenor, 304
Latchhook, 205
Late Georgian, as style of furnishing,
    265
Lateral geniculates, 107
Latex paint, 103
Lath, 27, 29
Laundry, 52–54
Laverne, Estelle and Erwine, 300
Law of color contrast, 110–111
Lazlo, Paul, 301
Leash, in weaving, 188
Le Corbusier (Charles Édouard Jean-
    neret-Gris), 243, 273, 299
    quotation, 77
Leno
    attachment, 193
    weave, 193n
Lens of the eye, 106–107
Lens, in lighting, 151, 164
Leoncillo, Leonardi, 308
Liebes, Dorothy, 303
Light
    absorbed, 99
    as an aesthetic factor in design, 149–
      165
    as the color stimulus, 95–100
    and mood, 152–157
    artificial, 161–164
    attributes of, 150
    boundary reflection, 100
    character and measurement of, 150–
      151
    design through, 157–158
    directional, 100, 151
    diffuse, 100
    energy, measurement of, 120–125
    fluorescent, 99, 161–164
    for special areas, 153–157
    general methods of controlling, 151
    good quality attained, 152
    incandescent or filament, 98, 161
    modification by matter, 99–100
    natural light in interiors, 160–161
    reflected, 99–100
    refracted, 96
    transmitted, 99–100
    ultraviolet, 96
Light sources, 98–99
    standard C.I.E., 122
Lighting
    adequate, 151–152
    art objects, 159–160
    as refinement on basic structure, 32
    bedroom, 156–157
    clerestory, 160
    conversation, 153–155
    dining, 155–156
    entertainment, 153–156
    hallway, 156

Lighting, *cont.*
    music, 156
    television, 156
Lightmeter, 150
Lightness-darkness
    definition of, 95
    in list of color terms, 124
    in room colors, 139–141
    obtaining through colorants, 106
Lilihan carpet, 204
Limited edition of prints, 237
Line
    as type of shape, 84
    expressive character of, 86–88
    rhythmic, 88
Linen (see also flax), 185
Linoleum, 205
Lithograph, 237
Living areas
    lighting, 153–156, 164–165
    planning for, 60–64
    sizes, 60
Locations of color in a room, 137
Locus, of the color measurement, 120
Loom, 188–194
Lorestan carpet, 204
Louis XII, XIII of France, 257
Louis XIV of France, 260
Louis XV of France, 260, 268, 290
Louis XVI, XVIII of France, 265
Louis Philippe of France, 265
Lumen, 150
Lumia, as art of light, 157
Luminaire
    definition, 158
    for reading, 164
Luminance
    definition, 125
    in list of color terms, 124
    in relation to candlepower, 150
Luminescence, 99
Luminescent paint, 104
Luminosity curve of the eye, 121
Luminous energy, in list of color terms,
    124
Luminous flux, in list of color terms,
    124
Lurçat, Jean, 307
    Designing Tapestry, 307n
Luster, in list of color terms, 124

MacKintosh, Charles, R., 273
Macquoid, P., *A History of English
    Furniture*, 178n
Macula lutea, 107
Maerz, A. and Paul, M. R., *Diction-
    ary of Color*, 119, 147n
Mahogany, The Age of, 178n
Majolica, 206, 208
Major activity areas, planning for, 55–
    64
Majorca, 206, 208
Man-made fibers
    classification of, 186–187
    valuable qualities of, 187–188
Marin, 240
Marquetry, 181
Marsh, Reginald, 240
Mary, Queen of England, 257
Mass
    as related to volume, 84

Mass, *cont.*
    rhythmic relations of, 88
Material, quality of, 169, 171
Mathsson, Bruno, 302
Matisse
    colors suggested from, 289
    design for Dominican Chapel, 157–158
    framing for, 243
Matte surface, 100, 151
Matting a picture, 244–246
Mattson, 240
Maugham, W. Somerset, quotation, 1
Maxwell, J. C., 125
McCobb, Paul, 302
McKearin, G. C., and H., *American Glass,* 211n
Measurement and character of light, 150–151
Measurement and specification of color, 120–125
Mecca, 205
Medieval period, 257
Meissen china, 209
Mercerized yarn, 188
Metallics, valuable qualities of, 187
Metals, 214–217, 309–310
Metamers, 121
Meter, 96n
Metropolitan Museum of Art, 242, 295
Mezzotint, 237
Mexican art, 275, 278
Mexican hand weaves, 306
Micros, 96
Mihrab, 205
Milan, 299
Mille, 96
Miller, Frederick, 309–310
Miller, John Paul, 310
Millimicron, 96
Milk glass, 211
Mineral fibers, 187
Ming china, 205
Minton china, 209
Mirror reflection of light, 100
Mission style, 292
Modern
    accessories, 303–310
    ceramics, glass, enamels, plastics, 308–309
    fabrics, 303–308
    floor coverings, 307–308
    furniture, 299–302
    lighting fixtures, 310
    metals and stone, 309–310
    screens, 310
    wallpapers, 310
    works of fine art, 303
Modern interior, the visual design of, 279–291
Modern painters, colors suggested from, 289
Modern style, 271
    history, 272–279, 291–299
    determinants of, 271–272
    traditional used with, 290–291
Modes of color appearance, 99–100, 124
Module, 25
Mohair fiber, 185
Moiréing, 195

Moisture control, 35
Mollino, Carlo, 302
Mondrian, Piet, 239, 273
Monochromatic hue harmony, 133
Monochromatic plus white light, 115
Monochromatism, 108
Morris, William, 272
Mortise and tenon, 32, 181
Mother style, 256
Mottle figure, 178
Mu, definition of, 96
Munro, Thomas
    definition of art, 7n
    definition of attribute, 13n
    definition of component, 12n
    The Arts and Their Interrelations, 3n
Munsell, Albert, 118, 133
Munsell
    color system, 118–119
    paths through the color solid, 131–132
    student charts, 131n
    value scales for judging reflectances, 152n
Munsell Color Company, Inc., 118
Museum Pieces, Inc., 242
Music, lighting for, 156
Musical instruments, their placement, 62–63

Nakashima, George, 300
Names, importance of to artist, 14
Napoleon Bonaparte, 265
Napping of cloth, 195
Natural colorants, 101
Natural light in interiors, 160–161
Natural order of colors, 132
Natural resins, 103
Nelson, George, 301
Neo-classic design in furnishing, 263–265
    use with contemporary, 291
Nervous system of the eye, 107–108
Nets, as textiles, 188
Newhall, Sidney M., and Brennan, Josephine, G., *The ISCC Comparative List of Color Terms,* 95n, 124
Newton, Sir Isaac, 98
Nickerson, Dorothy, 118n
Noguchi, Isamu, 301
Nongrain-raising stain, 104
Nordiska-Kompaniet, 306
Northern America, 257n
Norway
    glass from, 213
    silver from, 216
No-sag®, 183
Nu-Hue Color Coordinator System, 117–118
Nu-Hue Custom Color Directory, 118
Nylon, valuable qualities of, 187

Oak, The Age of, 178n
Object mode of color appearance, 100
Occipital lobe, 107
Off-hand glass, 211
Öhrström, Edvin, 308
Oil
    as in wood finish, 182

Oil, *cont.*
    in paints, 103
Olbrich, Joseph, 292
Old or semi-antique Oriental rug, 205
On center, 25
O'Neill, Eugene, quotation, 249
Openings in buildings, 29
Opposition, its purpose in design, 16
Optic chiasma, 107
Optic nerve, 107
Optical Society of America, *The Science of Color,* 96n
Orderly arrangement of color intervals, 131–133
Organic colorants
    definition of, 101
    list of and their characteristics, 102
"Organic Design" chair, 301
Organic shape, 88
Organism, human, 2, 4
Organization
    color, 113–119, 289
    for creation, 13
    meaning of, 4
    outline of design, 22
    purpose of, 14
Oriental art
    certain aspects of, 275
    colors suggested from, 289
    in glass, 308
Oriental carpets, 203–205
    antique and semi-antique, 205
    care of, 186
    construction of, 203–204
    descriptions of, 204–205
Oriental countries producing for the modern market, 299
Orozco, 240
Orrefors glass lighting fixtures, 310
Ostwald, William, 115, 130
Ostwald color system, 115–117
Oushak carpet, 205
Outdoor living areas, 60
Outline of design organization, 22
Oyster burl, 178

Painters
    colors suggested from, 289
    suggestions about reproducing color modes, 100n
Painter's color circle, 10
Painting a color scheme, 136–137
Painting, types, 102–103
Paints and protective coatings
    binders, 102–103
    definition of, 102
    driers, 103
    drying oils, 102–103
    film forming properties of, 102–103
    luminescent, 104
    resins in, 103
    vehicle for, 103
Panel heating system, 35
Panneing, 195
Parabola, 79
Paris
    exhibition of 1900, 273
    exhibition of 1925, 292–293
Parisi, Ico, 302
Parzinger, Tommi, 302
Pastel painting, 237

Paths through the color solid, 131–132
Pattern
    abstract, 226
    Early American wallpaper, 226
    flatness and depth in, 225
    in floorcovering, 222
    in relation to a culture, 226–227
    in wallcovering, 222–227
    in windowcovering, 228
    modeled, 225
    non-objective, 226
    non-representational, 226
    realistic, 225
    stylization in, 225–226
Patterned basic weaves, 191
Paul, Bruno, 301
"Peach bloom" glaze, 210
Pen and ink drawing, 237
Pencil drawing, 237
Penetrating stain, 104
Pennyweight, 214
Peony, 204
Perceptual experience of color, 109–113
Perimeter, an instrument, 107
Period, historic, 257
Period styles (see specific styles of furnishing), 255–268
    use with contemporary, 290–291
Persian Oriental carpets, 203, 204–205
Personality, planning for, 42
Perspective
    aerial, 289
    drawing of, 72–75
Petuntse, 208
Pewter, 217
Phosphorescent materials, 99
Photoengraving on fabrics, 195
Photograph, 237
Photometer, 124, 150
Phyfe, Duncan, 265
Physical requirements of adequate lighting, 151–152
Phyllotaxis, law of, 81
Picasso, 209, 289
Pictures and sculpture, 235–247
    choosing, 238–241
    framing, 242–246
    general character, 236
    hanging, 246–247
    media, 236–238
    sources, 242
    where needed, 236
Pietra dura, 310
Pigments
    definition of, 100
    dispersed, 194
Pile weaves, 192–193
Pillow lace, 188
Pintar, Margit, 306
Pirandello, Luigi, quotation, 271
Pitch of sound, 37
Placement of color, 134
Plain background, importance in design, 90
Plain sawed lumber, 177–178
Plain weave, 190
Plaiting, 188
Plan in relation to landscape, 44
Plane, as type of shape, 84

Planning of interiors
    for coordination, 43–44
    for design, 44
    for particular households, 64
    final detail, 44–64
    functional, 39
Planning for home lighting, 164–165
Plans of specific house, 72
Plastic glass, 211
Plastic organization, 239
Plastic wood, 104
Plastics, 217
Plate glass, 214n
Plate mark on prints, 245
Plated silver, 215
Plochere color system, 117
Plumbing, 28–29
Plume figure, 178
Ply, 188
Plywood, 26
    bent, 299
Point lace, 194
Polarization of light, 97n
Polonius, 171, 321
Polyethylene monafilament, valuable qualities of, 188
Pompeii, 261
Ponti, Gio, 293, 302
Poor, Henry Varnum, 308
Porcelain (see also china), 208, 308
Porcellana, 208
Pores, wood, 176, 177
Post and beam construction, 25–26
Pottery, 206–209, 308–309
    definition of, 206
    Delft, 209
    faience, 206
    majolica, 206–208
Power loomed carpets, 201–203
Practical plans for accomplishment in interior design, 315–320
Prayer rug, 205
Preference for colors in lighting, 162
Pressed glass, 211
Primary colorants, 104–105
Primary lights
    definition of, 98
    imaginary C. I. E., 122–123
Primary sensations of color, 109
Primer and sealer, 103
Printing on textiles
    direct, 194–195
    discharge, 194
    roller, 195
    wood block, 194–195
Prints, 237
Prism, 96
Private recreation areas, planning for, 57–58
Probber, Harvey, 302
Production line, technique of, 54
Projector flood light, 164
Proportion
    as quantitative basis for art, 16, 22
    dynamic, 80–83
    extreme-mean, 79, 81
    meaning and importance of, 77
    problem of standards, 79–83
    root rectangles, 82
    static, 79, 80
Proportional triangle, 82

Proposed Terms For Fabric Hands, American Association of Textile Chemists and Colorists, 172n
Propulsion, cumulative, 16
Protanopia, 108
Protective coating (see also paints)
    definition of, 102
    functional listing of, 103–104
Protein derived polymers, valuable qualities of, 187
Protein fibers, listing of, 185
Provincial American, as style of furnishing, 260
Provincial styles, 257
Psychological
    attributes of color, 94–95
    complements in color, 110n
    primary sensations in color, 109
Psychology, definition for experience, 2, 321
Psychophysics, 120–122
Psychophysical measurement, the C. I. E. system, 122–126
Purdy effect, 109
Purity of color, 124, 125
Purkinje effect, 110
Purposes involved in creating art, 7–8

Quadratic hue harmony, 133
Quality of material, 169, 171
Quarter sawed lumber, 177–178
Queen Anne chair, 233
Queen Anne style of furnishing, 260
Queen Elizabeth, 257
Queen Mary, 257
Queen Victoria, style of furnishing, 268
Quilting, 192

Radar, 96
Radiance, 124
Radiant energy
    character of, 95–96
    in list of color terms, 124
    measurement of, 96–97, 120
Radiant flux, 124
Radiant purity, 124
Radio, as radiant energy, 96
Radiometer, 124
Raindrop figure, 178
Ramps, 30
Ratio, 77
Rationalization, 4
Rattan, 180
Ray
    light, 96
    wood, 176–178
Rayleigh, law of scattering, 99n
Raymond and Raymond, Inc., 242
Rayon, valuable qualities of, 187
Reading, luminaires for, 164
Realistic pattern, 225
Receptors of the eye, 106–107
Reed, 180
Reed, as part of loom, 190
Reeves, Ruth, 305
Reflectance, spectral, 120
Reflectances recommended for surfaces, 152

Reflection
    changes in apparent color due to, 106, 111
    mirror or specular, 100
Reflector
    flood light, 164
    spot light, 164
Reflectors, as means of controlling light, 151
Refraction of light, 96
Refractive media of the eye, 106
Régence, French, style of furnishing, 260
Regency, English, style of furnishing, 265
Relation between color and spatial design, 134–135
Renaissance design, 257–258, 290
Repetition for enhancement, 15
Repetitive meter in the visual arts, 18
Reproductions, 237
Republic, French, 268
Requirements of adequate lighting, 151–152
Requirements of expressive lighting, 152–157
Resins
    added to paint, 102–103
    definition of, 103
    natural and synthetic, 103
Resist dyeing, 194
Rest, in design and life, 19–21
Restoration, the English, style of furnishing, 260
    use with the contemporary, 290
Retina, 106–107
Reverberation, time of, 37–38
Review of total design, 219–221
Revolution and Directoire, French style of furnishing, 265
Rhodopsin, 107
Rhythm
    between groups in living area, 92
    general consideration of, 18–19
    progressive, 16, 19
    repetitive, 18
Ribbon stripe figure, 178
Risers, 30
Risom, Jens, 302
Robsjohn-Gibbons, T. H., 302
Rococo (see also Louis XV), 260
Rods in eye, 106–107
Rohde, Johan, 310
Roller printing, 195
Roller shades, 231
Rome, 308
Rood, Ogden N., 111
    color circle as displaced by contrast, 111
Roof
    built-up, 28
    gabled, 26
    structure, 27–28
Roofing materials, 27
Root rectangles, 81, 82
Rosenthal, R. and Ratzka, H., *The Story of Modern Applied Art,* 291n
Royal Copenhagen china, 209
Royal Crown Derby china, 209
Royal Doulton china, 209

Royal Worcester china, 209
Roycrofters, the, 292
Roysher, Hudson, 310
Rubber flooring, 205
Rug types (see also carpets), 200–205
Ruskin, John, 272
Russian ballet, 295
Ryder, 240

Saarinen, Eero, 301
    shell chair, 301
Safety control, 75
Salt glaze, 208
Sampe, Astrid, 306
Sand blasted glass, 213
Sanitation, 33
Saraband carpet, 204
Saruk carpet, 204
Satin weave, 191
Satinwood, The Age of, 178n
Saturation of color
    definition of, 94
    in list of color terms, 124
    in room color schemes, 141
    lowering, 105
Saturation of illumination, effect on color vision, 110
Savonnerie carpet, 201
Sawing wood, 177–178, 180
Scalamandre Silk Company, 168n
Scale, meaning of, 64
Scandinavian
    furniture designers, 302
    textiles, 306
Scandinavians, 295
Scattering of light, 99
Sceap, Anglo-Saxon word, 84
Science
    method of, 7
    relation between art and, 7
    use of by the artist, 7
Sclera, 107
Scratch board drawing, 237
Screen print process, 194, 237
Screen walls, 26
Sculpture, 237–238
Sculptured pile, 193, 203, 204
Seagram building, 284
Sealing of wood, 181–182
Second Empire, of France, as a style of furnishing, 268
Sehna carpet, 205
Sehna knot, 203
Sei-ichi Taki, as quoted by Laurence Binyon, 93
Semivitreous china, 208
Sensation
    basic to experience, 4
    in list of color terms, 124
    importance of the visual, 12
    materials of the visual, 12–13
Senses significant to the interior designer, 12
Serapi carpet, 204
Serigraph (see also silk screen), 194, 237
Service areas, planning for, 44–55
Service entrance, 46
Sgraffito, 209
Shading, 106
Shadow series, 117

Shape
    as a visual force, 88–90
    attributes of, 84
    geometric, mathematical or regular, 88
    in the contemporary interior, 280–284
    organic, freeform and irregular, 88
    origin of word, 84
    planning of in a living area, 91–92
    structural, 88
    traits, choice of dominant, 84–88
    types of, 13, 84
Shape organization, practical suggestions for in the modern interior, 281, 284
Shapes and space, meaning and importance of, 84
Sheathing of framed buildings, 27
Shed, as a loom operation, 190
Sheeler, 240
Shellac, 103
Sheraton, Thomas, 265, 291
Sherwood, M. H., *From Forest to Furniture,* 175n
Shiraz carpet, 204
Shirvan carpet, 205
Shoji screens, 310
Shutters, 231
Shuttle, 190
Siimes, Anne, 308
Silk filament, 188
Silk screen, 194, 237
Sills, 25
Silver and other metals, 214–217
    choice of silverware, 216
    composition of silver, 214–215
    contemporary silver, 215–216
    forming of silver, 215
    other metals, 216–217
Silverpoint, 237
Simplicity, 9
Size
    as an attribute of shape, 84
    effect on color vision, 111–112
Sizing, 195
Skill
    in Munro's definition of art, 7n
    nature of, 8
Skylight, 99
Sleeping and dressing (see also bedrooms)
    planning for, 55–56
    lighting, 156–157
    sizes of areas, 55
Slip, definition of, 209
Smoke chamber, in chimneys, 30
Smyrna rugs, machine, 203
Social areas
    lighting, 153–156
    planning for, 60–64
    sizes, 60
Social entrance, 46
Solar heating, 33–34
Solvents, 103
Sophistication, 9
Soumak, 201, 203
Soumak weave, 193
Sound, character of, 37
Sound conditioning, 32, 37–38
Sources for procuring fine art, 242

Sources of color knowledge, 94
Space
  amount for various households, 40
  and shape in interiors, 77–93
  as related to volume, 84
  complete picture of, 41
  considerations in color planning, 135–136
  created through color, 134–135
  effect of limitations on planning, 41–92
  emphasis on in modern design, 280–284
  illusion of through handling of shapes, 90–91
  through lighting, 157
  uses of, 40
Spar varnish, 103
Sparkle, in list of color terms, 124
Spatial effects from shape interactions, 90–91
Specific illustrations of color design, 144–148
Spectral
  hues, 97
  reflectance, 120
  transmittance, 120
Spectrophotometer, 120, 124
Specular reflection, 100
Spinning, 188
Spode, 209
Spreading, color effect, 111–112
Staffordshire potteries, 209
Stain, 103–104
Stairs, 30
Standard C. I. E. Color Mixture Curves of the Eye, 122–123
Standard fluorescent tubes, 162
Static proportions or static symmetry
  meaning, 79–80
  use in art, 79
St. Louis Exhibition, 292
Steel, 216–217
Steinman, D. B., *The Builders of the Bridge,* 80n
Stencil process, 194
Sterling silver, 214–215
Stone, 217, 310
  mosaics, 217
Stoneware, 208
Storage
  conditions, 49–50
  planning for, 46–51
  types, 46, 49
  sizes, 51
Strengell, Marianne, 304
Strié fabrics, 195
Stringer, stair, 30
Structural design, relation to decorative, 88
Structure
  importance, 23
  modern, 23
  refinements upon basic, 32–38
  type, concrete, ferro-concrete, and steel, 25
  type, wood framing, 25–26
Stuart, period in furnishing
  early, 258
  late, 260
Stucco, 27

Studs, 25
Stuffer yarns, 202
Stump wood, 178
Sturrock, W. and Staley, K. A., *Fundamentals of Light and Lighting,* 152n
Stuttgart housing development, 301
Style
  cycles, 257
  folk, 257
  meaning, 256–257
  mother, 256
  of furnishing, 257–268
  provincial, 257
Stylized pattern, 225–227
Subtractive or colorant mixture, 104–106
Suggestion, synonym for expression, 7
Suitability to purpose, 39
Sullivan, Louis, 278
Surface, as type of shape, 84
Surface mode of color appearance, 100, 124
Surfacer, 103
Surfacing materials, 27, 29
Swag, 231
Swastika, 204, 205
Sweden
  glass from, 213
  silver from, 216
Swivel bobbins, 194n
Symbols, X, Y, Z, etc., 123
Symmetry
  dynamic, 16, 80–83
  Hambidge, Jay, *Dynamic Symmetry, The Greek Vase,* 79n
  static, 79–80
Synthetic colorants
  definition of, 101
  list of lakes, 102
Synthetic flooring, 205
Synthetic resins, 103
Systems, color, 113–119

Tabby weave (see plain weave), 190
Table linen, 235
Tablet weave, 193
Tableware, 234–235
Tabriz carpet, 204
Taipale, Martta, 307
Tapestry
  handwoven, 190, 193, 201
  velvet carpet, 202
Taproots of the modern style, 272–279
Taste
  how a house can teach, 253–254
  nature of, 8–9, 252
  texture and, 172
  training for, 9, 254
  value of, 252
Teheran, 204
Television
  lighting for, 156
  placement of, 63–64
Tempera or gouache, 102
  painting, 236
Templates, furniture, 72
Tensile strength, 25
Tests for color vision, 108
Tetartanopia, 108

Textiles, 184–200
  construction differences, 188–193
  embellishment differences, 193–195
  fiber differences, 184–188
  finish differences, 195
  glossary of, 196–200
  yarn differences, 188
Textile Color Card Association, 119n
Texture, and the media of interior design, 165–217
  as the basic component, 168–169
  attributes of, 170, 171–172
  design, 172
  groupings with woods, 174
  illusions through, 174–175
  intersensory character of, 168
  meaning of, 167–168
  quality in, 169–171
Textures
  as related to the building, 290
  in the contemporary interior, 290
  progression from exterior to interior space, 290
  used in decoration, 175–217
  wood, 174, 178–181
Thailand (Siam), 306
Themes, 19, 21
Theories of color vision, 108–109
Thompson, James, 306
Thonet, Michael, 299
Three mold glass, 211
Throwing, of silk and synthetics, 188
Tie beams, 26
Tiles, as interior surfacing materials, 29
Timbre, of sound, 37
Time-space art, 44
Tint tone and tinting strength, 101
Tinting, definition, 106
Toners, 100
Tongue and groove, 181
Tongue in cheek decorating, 315
Tool room, size and location of, 52, 54
Tooley, F. V. (ed.), *Handbook of Glass Manufacture,* 211n
Total art form, 311–321
Total design and concrete design problems, 219–247
Tracheids, 176
Trait
  as visual force, 17
  in list of color terms, 124
  meaning of, 13
  relation to words, 13–14
  repetition of color, 130–131
Translucent light, 100
Transmittance, spectral, 120
Transparency, 100
Traverse or draw curtains, 231
Treads, stair, 30
Tree growth, 176
Triadic hue harmony, 133
Triangle
  proportional, 82
  shapes, 20
Triennale exhibition, 299
Tristimulus
  coefficients, x, y, z, 123, 125
  measures or values, 123–125
  specification of the equal energy spectrum, 121

Tritanopia, 108
Trompe l'oeil, 168
Troy weight, 214
Trusses, 26
Types of design organization, 21, 22
Tudor, style of furnishing, 257
Tufted rug (see also hooked), 201
Tugendhat chair, 299
Turkey, 203
Turkish Oriental carpets, 203, 205
Turkoman Oriental carpets, 203, 204
Turning, of wood, 181
Tussah silk, 186
Twill weave, 190–191
Two examples of design organization, 221–222
Tynell, Paavo and Helena, 310

Ultraviolet light, 99
Underglaze decoration, 208
Unesco, 242
Unity
  of color within a building, 142–143
  of effect, 13, 19, 22
  of grouping in living area, 92
Upholstery, 231–233
Using color in interiors, 127–148
Usual and unusual
  hue placement, 137–139
  lightness placement, 139–141
  saturation placement, 141
Utrillo, colors suggested from, 289

Valance, 231
Valance lighting, 165
Vallauris, 209, 308
Value, Munsell, 118
van der Post, Laurens, quotation, 249
van der Rohe, Mies, 273, 284n
  Barcelona chair, 299
  Tugendhat chair, 299
Van de Velde, Henri, 273
van Doesburg, Theo, 273
van Gogh, 239
  color scheme, 130
  framing a, 243
Van Keppel, Hendrick, 302
Van Loon, Victoria and William, 310
Variation, for enhancement, 15–16
Variations, weaves using more than one set of warp or weft, 191–193
Varnish
  definition of, 103
  oil, 103, 182
  spirit, 103
Vat dyes, 194
Vegetable colorants, list of, 102
Vehicle, paint, 103
Velvet
  carpet, 202
  weave, 192–193
Vence, France, Dominican Chapel of the Rosary, 157–158
Veneering, 181
Venetian blinds
  control of light through, 160
  placement of, 231
Venetian glass, 213
Venice, 306
Venini, Paolo, 310

Ventilation, 35
Versen, Kurt, 310
Victorian style of furnishing, 268
  use with the contemporary, 291
Vienna Werkstätte, 273, 294
Vietta, designer, 300
Villalobos, D. and J., Colour Atlas, 119
Vinyls, valuable qualities of, 187–188
Visible spectrum, definition of, 96–97
Vision, color
  effect of level of illumination on, 109–110
  defects in, 108
  theories of, 108–109
Vision, nature of, 106–109
Visual
  adaptation, 109–112
  axis, 21, 22
  components, attributes, traits, 12–13, 22
  force, 17
  process, 106–109
  purple, in the eye, 107
  qualities and their spatial alignment, 17–18, 22
Vitality
  of effect, 13, 17–18
  exemplifying qualities of life, 17–18
Vitreous humor, 106
Vodder, Niels, 302
Volume
  as type of shape, 84
  mode of color appearance, 99–100, 124
von Allesch, Marianne, 308
Von Nessen, Walter, 310
V'Soske, Stanislav, J., 308

Wagner, Otto, 273
Walls
  curtain or screen, 26
  interior, 29
  load bearing, 26, 64
Walnut, The Age of, 178n
Warp
  beam, 188
  chain, 201
  definition, 188
  stuffer, 202
Watercolor painting, 236
Water stain, 104
Waugh, Frederick J., 240
Waugh, Sidney, 308
Wavelength
  complementary, 125
  dominant, 125
  of light, 95–97
  of radiant energy, definition of, 95–96
  symbol for, 95
Wax, as a wood finish, 182
Waxes, 102
Ways of relating colors, 130
Ways of securing light in interiors, 160–164
Weaves
  basic, 190–191
  classification of, 191
  variations and extensions of basic weaves, 191–193
Weber-Fechner law, 115n

Wedge joints, 181
Wedgwood, 208, 209
Weft, 188
Wegner, Hans, 302
Weimar, 273
Wells, George, 308
Werkbund, 273
Werkstätte, Vienna, 273, 292
West, James, 304
"Whiplash" line, 273n
Whitman, W., quotation, 127
Wicker, 108
Wilfred, Thomas, 157
William IV, 265
William and Mary, style of furnishing, 260
Williamsburg Prints, 242
Wilton carpet, 201–202
Windows
  double-glazed, 33
  in contemporary buildings, 160
  types, 29
Window treatments, 228–231
Winter, Edward, 309
Wiping stain, 103
Wirkkala, Tappio, 301, 308
Wisdom, 252
White light, definition of, 99
Wood
  block printing, 194–195
  character, 176–178
  clapboards, 27
  filler, 104
  finishes, 181–182
  furniture, construction of, 183–184
  impregnated, 26
  joinery, 181
  lamination, 180
  manufacturing processes, 180–181
  pattern in, 177–178
  siding, 27
Wood, Grant, 240
Woods, list of furniture, 178–180
Woodwork (see architectural terms), 182–183
Wool fiber, 185–186
Work areas, 51–55
Work conditioning, 42
Wormley, Edward, 301
Worsted yarn, 186, 201
Wright, Frank Lloyd, An Autobiography, 278n
Wright, Russel, 308
Wrought iron, 216

xm proportion, 79, 81–82
xm rectangle, 81
X-ray, as radiant energy, 96
X, Y, Z, etc., pertaining to tristimulus values, 123

Yarn differences, 188
Yarns, 188
Yellow spot in the eye, 107
Young, Thomas, 108
Young-Helmholtz, theory of color vision, 108–109

Zeisel, Eva, 308
Zevi, Bruno, quotation, 23